The Baha'i Faith:

Its History and Teachings

William McElwee Miller

The Baha'i Faith

Bahá'í House of Worship
Wilmette, Illinois U.S.A.

The Baha'i Faith:

Its History and Teachings

William McElwee Miller

William Carey Library

533 HERMOSA STREET • SOUTH PASADENA, CALIF. 91030 • TEL. 213-682-2047

LIBRARY
The University of Texas
At San Antonio

In accord with some of the most recent thinking in the academic press, the William Carey Library is pleased to present
this scholarly book which has been prepared from an author-
edited and author-prepared camera-ready manuscript.

Library of Congress Cataloging in Publication Data

Miller, William McElwee.
    The Baha'i faith.

    Includes bibliographical references.
    1. Bahaism. I. Title.
BP365.M49   297'.89   74-8745
ISBN 0-87808-137-2

Published by the William Carey Library
533 Hermosa Street
South Pasadena, Calif. 91030
Telephone 213-799-4559

Contents

Illustrations

To All Who Practice

Independent Investigation of Truth

Introduction

When in the year 1844 A.D. a young man in the city of
Shiraz in Persia announced that he had a divine mission, who would have dreamed that his golden-domed
Shrine in Haifa would one day be visited by thousands
of pilgrims from many lands? And who would have been
so bold as to predict that Ali Muhammad was destined
to be the initiator of a movement which would spread
to all parts of the earth, and would claim the allegiance of millions of people? Perhaps the young
prophet himself had a vision of a glorious future for
his cause, but not many of his countrymen, and no one
outside of Persia, shared his dreams. Yet Ali Muhammad,
better known as the Bab,(1) is now revered round the
world by all those who profess allegiance to the
"Baha'i World Faith."

This remarkable movement, which began when Ali
Muhammad announced that he was the Bab (Gate), was
continued and developed by another man from Persia
known as Baha,(2) and later as Baha'u'llah. The
followers of this Faith, known as Baha'is,(2) maintain that it is the true religion for all the people
of the world for this age, and will unite all races
and religions in one happy family.

Baha'is have produced much attractive literature, in which they tell the story of the founding and growth of their Faith and expound its teachings. In this Introduction I wish to explain why I have undertaken to write a history of the Babi-Baha'i Movement, and I will describe some of the sources on which I have depended for my information. If the reader is not interested in this discussion, he may omit the rest of the Introduction, and begin to read Chapter I.

It was a fortunate day for oriental scholarship when young Edward Browne accidentally stumbled on a copy of a French book by the Comte de Gobineau. "One day some seven years ago," he wrote in 1890, "I was searching amongst the books in the University Library of Cambridge for fresh materials for an essay on the Sufi philosophy.....when my eye was caught by the title of Count Gobineau's *Religions et Philosophies dans l'Asie Centrale*.(3)   I took down the book, glanced through it to discover whether or not it contained any account of the Sufis." It did, and Browne took the book home to read, and was much disappointed in what he learned from it of the Sufis. But when he began to read the account of the Babi(1) movement which constituted the major part of the volume, the effect was very different. He was at once captivated by Gobineau's story of the Bab(1) and his followers. "To anyone," Browne continues, "who has already read this masterpiece of historical composition, this most perfect presentation of accurate and critical research in the form of a narrative of thrilling and sustained interest, such as one may, indeed, hope to find in the drama or the romance, but can scarcely expect from the historian, it is needless to describe the effect which it produced on me .....Count Gobineau's book, then, effected in a certain sense a complete revolution in my ideas and projects."(4)

As a result of reading this book, Edward Browne determined to go to Persia and meet some of the Babis (followers of the Bab) about whom Gobineau had written so brilliantly, in order to learn more about this fascinating movement. He finally succeeded in 1887

in finding a way to travel to this land, which today
is known by its true name Iran,(5) the land in which
the Bab had lived and died, associating intimately
with people who were able to give him the information
and the books which he so eagerly sought. After a
year he returned to Cambridge University where he
became Lecturer in Persian, and there he wrote and
published in the Journal of the Royal Asiatic Society
two lengthy articles on *The Babis of Persia*.(6) He
also wrote the book, *A Year Amongst the Persians*,(7)
which is a mine of most interesting and valuable information. Thus began Browne's deep and sympathetic
interest in the Babi movement, which continued to the
end of his life, and which made him the outstanding
authority on the movement among English scholars, if
not among all western orientalists. Much of the
history of this movement would have been irretriev-
ably lost except for the painstaking and scholarly
researches of Edward G. Browne.

However, Professor Browne did not undertake to
write a formal history of the movement, though no
one could have done this better than he.. Instead,
the results of his researches were recorded chiefly
in his introductions to the books which he translated
from Arabic and Persian into English, and in the
copious footnotes and lengthy appendices full of most
valuable information which he added to the translations, and in articles in the *J.R.A.S.* of which he
contributed a number.(8) Most of these writings are
now out of print, or are unavailable to many readers.
Hence, it is for the purpose of presenting in a con-
cise and orderly fashion the facts which have been
established by Browne and other trustworthy scholars
that this book is being written.

When the Cambridge scholar arrived in Iran in 1887
he soon discovered that the situation was quite different from what he had thought it to be. As he says,
(9) "My researches among the Babis....revealed to me
the fact that since Count Gobineau composed his work
great changes had taken place in their organization
and attitude. I had expected to find Mirza(10) Yahya
Subh-i-Azal....universally acknowledged by them as the

Bab's successor and the sole head to whom they confessed allegiance. My surprise was great when I discovered that so far from this being the case, the
majority of the Babis spoke only of Baha(2) as their
chief and prophet; asserted that the Bab was merely
his herald and forerunner...; and either entirely
ignored or strangely disparaged Mirza Yahya. It took
me some time fully to grasp this new and unexpected
position of affairs..." These followers of Baha
called themselves not Babis but Baha'is.(2)

Browne's admiration for Gobineau's book rightly
remained unabated, for the Comte de Gobineau had a
unique opportunity to give a correct account of the
beginnings of the Babi movement. He was in the
French diplomatic service in Teheran(11) from 1855
to 1858, and again from 1861 to 1863, first as a
secretary and later as minister. He came to Iran
only five years after the Bab had been put to death
in Tabriz, and he was therefore able to secure much
first-hand information regarding him and his followers. Added to a thorough knowledge of Persian and
Arabic, the Comte de Gobineau possessed a remarkable
understanding of the character and beliefs of the
Iranians in general and of the Babis in particular.
His sympathetic interest in the Bab led him to view
the whole movement in the most favorable light possible. Gobineau's book, as Browne says,(12) "though
largely based on the Lisanu'l-Mulk's account of the
Babi movement,(13) embodies also many statements
derived from Babi sources....The work in question must
ever remain a classic and indeed unapproached in the
subject whereof it treats."

When Browne returned to England in 1888 he took
with him a Babi book in manuscript entitled *Tarikh-i-
Jadid* (The New History). This book, as he later discovered, was written in 1880 by Mirza Husayn of
Hamadan with the assistance of several other Baha'i
scholars. In the *New History* there were numerous
references to an earlier work by Mirza Jani from
which Mirza Husayn had derived much of his material.
But when Browne made inquiries in Iran as to Mirza
Jani's history he was unable to find a copy, or to

obtain any information whatever regarding this book.
It seemed that it had entirely disappeared and been
forgotten. So he set to work to translate the *New
History* in preparation for publication. He was surprised and puzzled, however, by the failure of the
book to give any account of Subh-i-Azal, who, according to Gobineau, was the universally recognized
successor to the Bab, and on the other hand by the
importance accorded to Baha, the half-brother of
Subh-i-Azal. When he made inquiries of the Baha'is
they either professed total ignorance of Subh-i-Azal,
or made derogatory remarks about him.

Then a most fortunate discovery made by Professor
Browne in 1892 threw light on the problem. In the
Bibliotheque Nationale in Paris he found a copy of
the lost history written by Mirza Jani, entitled the
Nuqtatu'l-Kaf! This manuscript was one of the Babi
books brought back from Iran by the Comte de Gobineau
and sold at auction after his death. Browne eagerly
compared this book with the *New History*, and discovered
that while the *New History* embodied a great deal of
what Mirza Jani had written in his history, a considerable amount of the material in the older history had
been either changed or omitted by the authors of the
New History. For example, while Mirza Jani gave a full
account of the appointment of Subh-i-Azal by the Bab as
his successor, and a detailed explanation of the exalted position which he occupied, one of equality with the
Bab, the author of the *New History* omitted all this,
and portrayed Baha as the greater person.(14)

Hence, when Browne published his translation of the
New History in 1893,(15) he included in it as an
Appendix the most important passages of the *Nuqtatu'l-
Kaf* which had been omitted or altered in the New
History.(16) Why was this done? "The earliest, fullest
and most interesting history of the Bab and his immediate disciples....was almost completely suppressed,"(17)
wrote Browne,(18) "because it reflected the opinion
which prevailed immediately after the Bab's martyrdom
that his successor was Mirza Yahya Subh-i-Azal, and
thus came into conflict with the Baha'i contention
which arose ten or fifteen years later, and a recension

of it was prepared (known as 'the *New History*!..) in
which all references to Subh-i-Azal were eliminated or
altered, and other features regarded as undesirable
were suppressed or modified." For an explanation of
the events which occasioned the suppression of Mirza
Jani's history the reader is referred to Chapters V
and VI.

Mirza Jani was uniquely fitted to be the historian
of the Babi movement. He was a merchant in the town
of Kashan, and once entertained the Bab for two days
in his home. He travelled extensively with Mirza
Yahya Subh-i-Azal and his brother Mirza Husayn Ali
Baha. He knew intimately all the early Babi leaders.
He was respected as a man of integrity, and he proved
his devotion to the Babi Cause by dying for his faith
in Teheran in 1852 (see Chapter V). In 1910 Browne
published in full the Persian text of Mirza Jani's
history, with most valuable introductions in both
Persian and English.(19) No student of the Babi-
Baha'i movement can ignore the *Nuqtatu'l-Kaf*, which
is the one extant history of the Bab and his early
followers written by a capable Babi historian soon
after the death of the Bab.

The *New History* which was translated and published
by Browne was never published by the Baha'is. It was
soon suppressed, and very few Persian copies are now
in existence. In its place yet another history was
prepared in 1886 by the Baha'i leaders, entitled *A
Traveller's Narrative*. The name of the author was not
attached to the book, but it was later established that
he was no other than Abbas Efendi, the eldest son of
Baha.(21) Hence this may be considered an official
Baha'i history of the movement. A copy was given to
Browne by the author when he visited Baha in Acre
(Akka) in 1890, after having visited Subh-i-Azal in
Cyprus. Of this book Browne writes:(22) "The *Traveller's
Narrative*....represents a further development of the
tendency, to which I have already alluded, to glorify
Baha'u'llah and his Neo-Babi doctrine at the expense
of the Bab and the primitive Babi theology. In the
New History it is still the Bab and his apostles, and
the early martyrs of the cause, whose words and deeds

form the subject matter of the work. In the *Traveller's Narrative* this is no longer the case; it is
Baha'u'llah who is the hero....while the Bab has been
reduced from his high station of 'Point'....to that
of a mere precursor and harbinger of a more perfect
dispensation."

The Persian text of this book, as well as the
English translation with some 320 pages of Introduction and Notes, was published by Browne in 1891,(23)
and these volumes are indeed a mine of information.
In his Introduction Browne calls attention to the
following peculiarities of the *Traveller's Narrative*:
(24) (1) The secondary importance accorded to the
Bab and his early followers. The sufferings of the
first disciples are passed over lightly, and the
deaths of the Seven Martyrs and the massacre of 1852
are largely unnoticed. (2) The belittling of Subh-i-
Azal, who is depicted as a person of no consequence.
"No opportunity is lost of disparaging both his courage and his judgement." (3) Extraordinary temperate-
ness toward the Shah of Iran, and deprecation of the
opposition of the early Babis to the government of
Iran.

Unfortunately, it is the *Traveller's Narrative*, in
which the history and doctrines as recorded by the Bab
in his extant writings and also by Mirza Jani and
Gobineau have been radically revised to conform to the
later Baha'i pronouncements, that has been followed as
authentic history by the authors of many of the more
recent books and articles which have professed to tell
the true story of the rise of the Baha'i Faith. Thus,
by neglecting intentionally or through ignorance the
primary sources, they have to a considerable extent
misrepresented the true history of the movement. As
Browne wrote in 1910:(25) "....the more the Baha'i
doctrine spreads, especially outside of Persia, and
most of all in Europe and America, the more the true
history of the original Babi Movement is obscured
and distorted."(26)

The reader will note that in the early chapters of
this book the author has based his statements largely

on the writings of the Bab and Gobineau and Mirza
Jani, as interpreted by Professor Browne, and has
refrained from quoting the less-reliable versions of
later writers.

The valuable work done by other eminent Western
scholars should not be overlooked, and mention should
be made of M.A.L.M. Nicolas who translated the *Arabic*
and *Persian Bayans* of the Bab into French (1905), and
M. Alexander Toumansky of St. Petersburg who translated the *Kitab-i-Aqdas* of Baha'u'llah into Russian
and published it with a lengthy introduction (1899),
and Baron Victor Rosen who translated and published
other writing of Baha'u'llah. The author has not made
use of these writings, except as they have been quoted
by Browne in his articles and books. Nor has he been
able to benefit from the researches of the German
scholars.

While engaged in the task of rewriting a book
which was published many years ago,(27) the author
was most fortunate in becoming acquainted through
correspondence with another scholar who was uniquely
qualified to supply new historical material and to
throw fresh light on many of the doctrines and the
events of the Babi-Baha'i movement. Mr. Jelal Azal,
a relative of many of the persons whose stories are
related in this book, occupied a government position
in Palestine for a number of years, and was thus in
close touch with happenings in Haifa and Akka. He
also had a very good knowledge of the Persian, Arabic,
Turkish and English languages, and so was able to read
and translate the original writings of the Bab and
Subh-i-Azal and Baha'u'llah and their followers with
greater ease and accuracy than was possible for any
of the European scholars. Mr. Azal most generously
made available to the author the results of his
scholarly research, having supplied more than 1100
pages of most valuable Notes in English, with facsim-
iles of documents in the handwriting of some of the
founders of the movement. These pages have been
numbered, and xeroxed copies have been deposited in
the Library of Princeton University. It is hoped that
this material may be published and made available in

full for the use of scholars. Mr. Azal also kindly
agreed to read and correct the manuscript of this
book. This he did with the greatest care, and many
of his suggestions have been incorporated in the text
and the footnotes. It was a cause of deep sorrow to
the author to learn that only a few weeks after he
sent his comments on the final chapter of the book,
this gracious and gifted scholar died of a heart
attack in Famagusta, Cyprus, where he resided, on
April 5, 1971. My debt to him is great indeed.

In writing the history of the Baha'i movement in
the West, the author has had the very able assistance
of Mr. J. Anthony Sistrom, who has supplied a great
deal of most valuable material which he has discovered
in libraries, or else has received from his Baha'i
friends. He is also indebted to Mr. Will Orick for
permitting him to use material from his personal files,
and for supplying him with much information derived
from his long and intimate acquaintance with the Baha'i
Cause, and to Dr. T. Cuyler Young of Princeton University and the Rev. Cady H. Allen for reading and correcting the manuscript, and to Dr. William N. Wysham for
correcting the proofs. To these friends, and to all
others who have assisted in answering questions and
providing data for this book, the author would express
his sincere thanks.

And he wishes to express sincere appreciation also
to Fleming H. Revell Company for permission to make
use of much material from his early book *Baha'ism:
Its Origin, History, and Teachings* (Revell 1932), and
to the Cambridge University Press for the use of invaluable material in the books written by Professor Edward
G. Browne, and to the Royal Asiatic Society for the use
of Professor Browne's lengthy articles in the Journal
of the Society, and also for permission to incorporate
as Appendix I of this book the translation of *Al-Kitab
Al-Aqdas* by Dr. E. E. Elder. He is also indebted to
the Baha'i Publishing Trust, to Harper and Row,
Publishers, Inc., to George Allen and Unwin, and to
Award Books for material from their publications. In
every case the source is indicated in a footnote.

William McElwee Miller

Philadelphia, 1974

NOTES

1. The *a* in *Bab* and *Babi* is pronounced as in *barn*, and the *i* in *Babi* is like *ee* in *see*.

2. The first *a* in *Baha* has the sound of *a* in *bat*, and the second that of *a* in *barn*. The *i* in *Baha'i*, which is a three-syllable word, is pronounced like *ee* in *see*, and the stress is on the last syllable.

3. First published in 1865 in Paris.

4. *A Traveller's Narrative*, E. G. Browne, Cambridge 1891, Int. pp. X, XI.

5. Iran, meaning the "Land of the Aryans," is pronounced *ee-rahn*, with a light stress on the last syllable.

6. *J.R.A.S.*, 1889, pp. 485-526 and 881-1009.

7. *A Year Amongst the Persians*, Edward G. Browne, London 1893.

8. *J.R.A.S.*, 1892, pp. 259-322 and 433-499 and 637-710; 1897, pp. 761-826.

9. *A Traveller's Narrative*, Int. pp. XV, XVI.

10. *Mirza* is a title formerly used in Iran equivalent to *Mr*.

11. *Encyclopedia Britannica* (1944), Vol. 10, p. 459.

12. *A Traveller's Narrative*, pp. 174, 203.

13. In *A Traveller's Narrative*, pp. 174-188, Browne has given a summary of the contents of this Persian history, the *Nasikhu't-Tawarikh* (Superseder of Histories), written by a gifted Muslim historian about 1852 A.D., which records rather fully the story of the Babi movement from 1844 to 1852.

14. *The New History of the Bab*, pp. 374-382, *Nuqtatu'l-Kaf*, Int. in English, pp. XXXVI, XXXVII.

15. *The New History of the Bab*, translated by E. G. Browne, Cambridge, 1893.

16. Ibid., pp. 327-396.

17. Only two complete copies of the *Nuqtatu'l-Kaf* in manuscript are known to be in existence today, one being that discovered by Browne in the Bibliotheque Nationale (Suppl. Pers. 1071), from which he printed the Persian text, and the other in the Library of Princeton University. See English Int. to *Nuqtatu'l-Kaf*, p. XIII, *New History* Int., pp. XXIX, XXX, and *Notes of Dr. Sa'eed*, pp. 5, 6 (also in the Princeton Library).

18. *Materials for the Study of the Babi Religion*, by E. G. Browne, Cambridge 1918, Int. p. XXIII, *Nuqtatu'l-Kaf*, English Int., p. XXXIV.

19. *Nuqtatu'l-Kaf*, by Hajji Mirza Jani of Kashan, edited by E. G. Browne, E. J. W. Gibb Memorial XV, London 1910.

20. *Efendi* was a Turkish title equivalent to *Mr.*

21. *New History*, Int. p. XIV, *Azal's Notes*, p. 258.

22. *New History*, Int. p. XXXI.

23. *A Traveller's Narrative, Written to Illustrate the Episode of the Bab*, edited and translated with notes by E. G. Browne, Vol. II, Cambridge 1891. For date of this book see p. 67 of T.N., Note 1.

24. *A Traveller's Narrative*, Int. pp. XLV-XLVI.

25. *Nuqtatu'l-Kaf*, English Int., p. XXXV.

26. The last book written by Professor Browne on the Babi movement was his *Materials for the Study of the Babi Religion*, Cambridge 1918, which, like his earlier books, contains most valuable historical documents.

27. *Baha'ism, Its Origin, History and Teachings*, by William McElwee Miller, Fleming H. Revell, New York MCMXXXI.

1
The Islamic Background

It is as impossible for one to understand the Baha'i
Faith without a knowledge of Islam as it would be to
understand Christianity without a knowledge of the
Old Testament. The Baha'i religion is an offshoot of
Shi'ite Islam, and though modern Baha'is may emphasize
the universal aspects of their faith and strive to
disassociate themselves from the past, nevertheless
the foundations of their system rest on the soil of
Iran, which is saturated with Islamic conceptions. It
is of course impossible for us here to give a full
account of the rise of Islam and the development of
the doctrines and practices and civilization of the
Muslims, and the reader is referred to the excellent
books on Islam which are now available. However, to
assist those who may not have the time or inclination
for such a study to understand better the ideas and
attitudes which will be met in the teachings and
actions of the Bab and those who followed him, a very
brief account of the interesting historical background
of the Babi movement will be supplied.

In the year 570 A.D. there was born in the city of
Mecca in Arabia a baby who was named Muhammad, who
was destined to change the religious and political

and cultural aspects of a large part of the world.
Living among people who worshipped idols, but who
knew of a Supreme Deity whom they called Allah (The
God), Muhammad became acquainted with some Jews and
Christians who did not worship images. It was probably, in part at least, as a result of his contacts
with them that a strong conviction came to Muhammad
when he was forty years of age that he had been
appointed by Allah as a prophet, and thereafter till
his death in 632 A.D. he was sure that revelations
from Allah were brought down to him from heaven by
the angel Gabriel. These divine messages were spoken
by Muhammad, were written down by those who heard
them (it is generally supposed that Muhammad was
illiterate), and were later collected in a book called
the Qur'an (Koran).

After receiving his commission Muhammad began to
tell the people of Mecca that Allah alone is God, and
that he who created all things will one day raise the
dead to life, and will reward with the pleasures of
Paradise those who worship him and do good deeds, and
will punish with the fires of Hell those who do not.
A few relatives and friends believed on the new prophet, but most of the Meccans ignored or rejected him.
When Muhammad was asked to show a sign or to perform
a miracle to prove that he was indeed a prophet, his
reply was that the verses of the Koran were his signs,
and he challenged others to produce the like of them.
When he later fiercely denounced the idols and the
idolaters, the Meccans began to persecute him and his
followers. Finally, after thirteen years of persis-
tent but rather fruitless effort, Muhammad resolved to
go north to the city of Madina, where there were
people who had promised to help him. Accordingly, in
the year 622 A.D., he and the little band of faithful
believers came to Madina and henceforth made this
their home. This migration, which is called the
Hegira (*hijra*), marks the beginning of the Muslim
era, and from it all events are dated.

On reaching Madina, Muhammad found himself much
better situated than he had been in Mecca. When his
party, which was growing rapidly, gained supremacy

over the other factions in the city, Muhammad the prophet and preacher became also the ruler of Madina,
with a body of armed men at his back. Having failed
to win the allegiance of the idolaters of Mecca by his
verses and preaching, he now undertook to convince
them by the sword. Seven months after his arrival at
Madina he began to attack the caravans of the people
of Mecca in which most of their wealth was invested.
At first he met with little success, but in 624 A.D.
he succeeded in capturing a large caravan, killing
many of its guards, and dividing the booty among his
followers. This led to other battles, and finally not
only the people of Mecca but also most of the tribes
of Arabia, both Jewish and pagan, were defeated and
submitted to Muhammad. Those who submitted to him as
their political and religious ruler, and to Allah who
had sent him, were known as Muslims (*Muslim* in the
Arabic language means "one who submits"). Those who
refused to become Muslims were in some instances
forced to pay taxes, and in others were put to the
sword. Thus the system established by Muhammad which
was called Islam ("submission") was not so much a
church as a church-state, or theocracy. Muhammad was
both Prophet and King. From the beginning religion
and politics have in Islam been one, at least in
theory.

This remarkable ruler of Arabia had heard that God
had given divinely inspired books to some of the
great prophets of old, in which he had made known to
men the laws, both civil and religious, which he had
ordained for their life on earth, and by the keeping
of which they would merit divine favor and win for
themselves entrance to Paradise. Therefore, in the
Koran, in accordance with the supposed pattern of the
books of previous prophets, along with some inspiring
ascriptions of praise to Allah, we find regulations
for marriage and divorce, the conduct of war with the
infidels, the division of booty, and other civil
matters interwoven with instructions as to worship,
fasting, clean and unclean foods, the care of orphans
and the poor, and various other moral matters.
Muhammad believed that Allah had authorized him to
regulate all phases of the life of believers.

The Prophet of Arabia probably took Moses as his
model of what a prophet should be and say and do, for
he knew more of him than he did of Jesus. He told the
Arabs that as Abraham and Moses and Jesus and other
prophets had been sent to various peoples, so he had
been sent to them. However, his mission was not for
the Arabs alone, it was for all mankind. So he called
upon all men, Jews, Christians and heathen, to acknowledge and obey him. He thought that Jesus had predicted his coming,(1) just as previous prophets had
predicted the coming of Jesus. He made no claims of
divinity for himself, saying that he was only a man
like other men,(2) and he warmly rejected the claims
of the Christians that Jesus is Son of God. He spoke
of himself as the Seal of the Prophets,(3) thus imply-
ing that he was the last and the greatest in the
prophetic line.

Muhammad made no definite provision as to his
successor, one to which all of his followers agreed.
On his death ten years after moving to Madina the
majority of the believers united in choosing Abu Bakr
as Caliph (meaning "vicar" or "successor"), and he
ruled the church-state of Islam in Muhammad's place.
Abu Bakr was succeeded in turn by 'Umar, 'Uthman and
Ali, these four being known as the Rightly-Guided
Caliphs, who were all chosen in the same manner. The
last three were assassinated by other Muslims. To the
democratic Arabs it seemed altogether proper that
their chief should be thus appointed by the people.
They held that the voice of the people was the voice
of God. It was during the reigns of these first four
Caliphs that the armies of the Arabs poured forth from
their barren deserts, overthrew the forces of Persia
and Byzantium, and conquered Mesopotamia, Syria, the
Iranian Plateau and Egypt for Islam. It was their
belief that Muslims must rule the whole world.

However, there soon developed in Islam a party the
members of which held a theory of the succession
totally different from that held by the ruling party.
To them it seemed as impossible for the successor of
the Prophet to be elected by the people as it would
have been for the Prophet himself to be thus chosen.

They contended that as a prophet must be chosen by God, not by the people, so must the prophet's successor be appointed by God and named specifically by the prophet. This party was called *Shi'ite* (meaning "separatist"). Though there came to be many divisions among Shi'ites, they all held firmly to the principle that the successor of Muhammad, whom they called not Caliph but *Imam* (meaning "leader"), "must be a descendant of the Prophet, and must be nominated explicitly by his predecessor, i.e., by the Prophet in the case of the first Imam, and in other cases by the preceding Imam.....the Imam was none the less Imam though recognized only by a small minority, and to recognize and yield allegiance to the rightful Imam was the supreme duty of the believer."(4)

The Shi'ites held that the first Imam, or vice-gerent of their Prophet, was Ali, the cousin and son-in-law of Muhammad (Muhammad left no son to be his heir). They asserted that Muhammad on his return journey from his last pilgrimage to Mecca publicly appointed Ali to succeed him, saying to all the people, "Let whoever owns me as his master own also Ali as his master."(5) They therefore looked upon Abu Bakr, 'Umar and 'Uthman as usurpers, and as enemies of God and his chosen Imam. Thus the Muslim world was from early times divided between the Shi'ites and their opponents the Sunnites. This division has remained till the present day, but the bitterness between the two parties is in many places less than it once was. Though the Shi'ites have always been in the minority in the Muslim world, and were often divided among themselves as to who was the rightful Imam of the age, they have often shown the most passionate devotion to their beliefs and to their leaders. Much Muslim blood has been shed over the question of the succession.

The people of Iran were especially susceptible to Shi'ite influences. They generally despised the Arabs by whom they had been conquered, and in espousing the cause of Ali and his descendants they found an opportunity for expressing their national spirit and maintaining something of their independence. The

Iranians, unlike the democratic Arabs, were imbued
with the doctrine of the divine right of kings, and
had even considered their rulers to be divine beings.
They were therefore quite ready, after their defeat
by the Arabs, to give the Imams the place in their
affection which their own kings had previously
occupied, and to look upon them as supernatural
beings, free from all sin and imperfection, and
endowed with miraculous powers, who ought by divine
right to rule over them in both temporal and spiritual affairs. The Shi'ites never succeeded in gaining
temporal authority for any of their Imams (with the
exception of Ali, who became the fourth Caliph), but
they always longed to do so, chafing under what they
considered the unrighteous rule of worldly Caliphs
chosen by men.

It is estimated that 98% of the people of Iran are
Muslims, the great majority of whom belong to that
sect of the Shi'ites which acknowledges twelve Imams.
This sect became the official religion of Iran after
the Safavid conquest early in the 16th century, and
is so today. The followers of this form of Islam
affirm that Ali and ten of his descendants who one
after another succeeded him suffered violent deaths
at the hands of the Sunnites, and are counted as holy
martyrs. They believe, however, that the twelfth
Imam, Muhammad son of Hasan al-Askari, called by them
the "Imam Mahdi," the "Lord of the Age," the "Proof
of God," "He Who Shall Arise of the Family of
Muhammad (*Qaim-i-Al-i-Muhammad*)," and the "Remnant of
God (*Baqiyyatullah*)," who as a child, immediately
after the death of his father disappeared from the
view of men in Iraq in the year 873 A.D. (260 A.H.),
(6) is still alive, and will again appear on earth.
"For in every age," they say, "there must be an Imam
immune to sin." For a period of seventy years after
his disappearance, the Twelfth Imam communicated his
will to men through four *Babs* (meaning "gates"), whose
title, strictly speaking, is Special Vicegerent
(*Naib-i-Khas*), and who in succession acted as the
channels of grace to mankind. When the fourth Bab
died no one succeeded him, and thereafter Shi'ites
were cut off from direct communication with "The Lord

of the Age," now absent or hidden, but living, and
could only long and pray for his return as Mahdi or
Qaim. This they have done for more than a thousand
years. "O Allah, hasten his joy, and cause us to
behold his victory, and make us his helpers and his
followers!" prays a Shi'ite divine of the fourteenth
century A.D.,(7) and pious Shi'ites make the same
prayer today. They look for the appearance of the
Hidden Imam as earnestly as ever the Jews did for
their promised Messiah.

Books of popular Shi'ite theology(8) contain the
most minute descriptions of the coming of the *Mahdi*
(The Guided One), as the Hidden Imam is often called.
Only God knows the time of his appearing, but some of
the Shi'ites seem to know everything else about it!
His coming will be preceded by wars, confusion,
eclipses of sun and moon, a terrible increase of
infidelity and corruption of morals. Men will cease
saying the prayers, and will lie, take interest and
bribes, build for themselves strong houses, and take
counsel with women. Women will enter business, will
sing in public, and will ride astride. Muslims will
become the most abject of peoples. *Dajjal* will appear
riding on an ass, and will entice many people after
him and destroy them. Then will appear the Mahdi! At
once his 313 faithful followers, who like him have
been hidden for more than a thousand years, will
hasten from the ends of the earth to his side. All
true believers will join him with drawn swords, and
win for him the sovereignty of which he has been
wrongfully deprived these many centuries. His armies
will sweep over the whole earth, killing all who
refuse to submit to their Lord. All former prophets
and Imams will return to earth to aid the Mahdi. He
will bring to an end all oppression, and will fill the
earth with justice. Only Shi'ites will then be found
on the earth, and at last the religion and government
of all mankind will become one. Following a long
reign of these true believers, all will die, and then
will come the Resurrection and the Last Judgment.

For many people of education these predictions would
be interpreted allegorically, or might be rejected as

nonsense. But most Shi'ites in Iran a century ago
took all these details very literally. The swords
which till recent times were hanging in numerous shops
and homes in readiness for the coming of "The Lord of
the Age" proved how real these hopes were to many
people, and how central a place in their expectations
was occupied by the dream of the conquest of unbelievers and the establishment of a universal Shi'ite
theocracy in all lands.

The Shi'ite doctrine of the Imamate is closely
related to their beliefs about the Prophets. They
hold that among and above the 124,000 sinless prophets
whom God sent to guide men, there were certain Great
Prophets, generally thought to be Adam, Noah, Abraham,
Moses, Jesus and Muhammad, who in succession were
God's representatives on earth. Each one of these was
the Prophet for the whole world for a long period of
time, bringing a book of laws from God for all mankind,
and foretelling the Prophet who was to follow. Though
Muhammad was the last of the Prophets, he was followed
by the Imams, who were equal to him in rank, and
differed only in that they did not bring new laws to
replace those of the Koran. There is a popular belief
that the first thing created by God was the "Light of
Muhammad," which abode in Adam and the Great Prophets
who followed him, and which was seen in its perfection
in Muhammad and in the Imams who are one with him.

Among the Shi'ites there have been various sects
the members of which have not contented themselves with
considering the Prophets and Imams as supernatural and
sinless beings with miraculous powers, but have
exalted them yet more highly, saying that they were
emanations of Deity and manifestations of God. These
sects (known as *ghulat*), which were rejected by the
Twelvers as heretical, were usually characterized by
certain cardinal doctrines, chiefly Metempsychosis
(*tanasukh*), Incarnation (*hulul*), and Return (*rij'at*)
of individuals or types in successive cycles. From
time to time in the history of Iran we find individuals putting forward the claim that they were the
"return" of some previous prophet or imam, and were
divine manifestations.(9)

One of these individuals who claimed to be God was al-Muqanna', "The Veiled Prophet of Khorasan," known to English readers through Moore's *Lalla Rookh*. He taught that the Deity had been manifested in all the prophets from Adam down, and had finally come to him. He was successful in gathering about him a great number of people who worshipped him and fought for him, till he and his followers miserably perished in 779 A.D. A half-century later Babak made the same claim, and kept Iran in turmoil for twenty years, during which time he is said to have killed nearly a half-million people. At last he was captured and executed in 838 A.D. As Professor Browne remarks, "these doctrines (of Incarnation, Return, etc.) appear to be endemic in Persia, and always ready to become epidemic under suitable stimulus."(10)

One of the more recent of these heretical sects to appear in Iran, one that was rejected and hated by the Twelvers, was that of the Shaykhis,(11) the followers of Shaykh(12) Ahmad al-Ahsa'i, who died in 1826 A.D. The chief doctrines of this sect were the following: (1) Ali and the eleven Imams who followed him were divine beings; (2) there must always exist among men on earth some person who is in direct supernatural communication with the Hidden Imam, and acts as the channel of grace between him and the Shi'ites; and (3) there is no bodily Resurrection. Shaykh Ahmad was during his lifetime considered by his disciples to be the channel of grace between believers and the Hidden Imam, as was also his successor Sayyid(13) Kazim of Resht. Both of these men were sometimes given the title *Bab* (Gate), by which the first four intermediaries had been known. These Shaykhi teachers led their disciples to expect in the near future the appearance of the Hidden Imam himself. Some tradi-tions said that he would return after a thousand years, and, according to the Muslim calendar, the time was at hand. Thus Shi'ites of all sects were impatiently awaiting his manifestation.

When Sayyid Kazim died in 1843, his disciples were in doubt for some time as to whom they should turn for guidance. Soon two rival claimants for the leadership

appeared, and the Shaykhi brotherhood was torn in two.
One faction followed Hajji(14) Karim Khan of Kirman,
and continued to go by the name "Shaykhi." The other
faction, which was the stronger, followed Sayyid Ali
Muhammad of Shiraz, who adopted the title *Bab*. Hence
his followers became known as Babis.(15)

Having described briefly the beliefs and hopes of
many of the people of Iran in the first half of the
19th century, we are now prepared to proceed with the
story of Sayyid Ali Muhammad the Bab, and the remarkable movement of which he was the central figure.

BIBLIOGRAPHY

Aqa'idu'sh-Shia, Doctrines of the Shi'ites (in Persian).

Brown, David, *The Way of the Prophet*, London, 1962.

Browne, E. G., *A Literary History of Persia*, London.

_____, *Nuqtatu'l-Kaf* (Persian, with English Intro-
    duction) London, 1910.

Cragg, Kenneth, *The Call of the Minaret*, Oxford Univ-
    sity Press, 1956.

Donaldson, Dwight M., *The Shi'ite Religion*, London, 1933.

Gardet, Louis, *Mohammedanism*, New York, 1961.

Gibb, H. A. B., *Mohammedanism*, Oxford University Press,
    1968.

Guillaume, Alfred, *Islam*, Pelican Books, 1954.

The Koran, translated by Rodwell, Everyman's Library.

The Koran, translated by N. J. Dawood, Penguin Books.

Margoliouth, *Mohammed*, Heroes of the Nations Series.

Miller, William M., *Al-Babu'l-Hadi Ashar* (translation
    in English of a Shi'ite Creed), Royal Asiatic Society,
    London, 1928.

Sell, Edward, *The Life of Muhammad*, London, 1913.

Vos, Howard V., *Religions in a Changing World*, Chapter on Islam by William M. Miller, Chicago, 1959.

Watt, W. Montgomery, *Muhammad, Prophet and Statesman*, Oxford University Press, 1961.

Wilson, J. Christy, *Introducing Islam*, New York, 1958.

NOTES

1. From ancient times Muslims have pointed to the promise of the Paraclete, the Comforter (John 14: 16), as a prediction of Muhammad.

2. Koran XVIII:110.

3. Ibid., XXXIII:40.

4. *Nuqtatu'l-Kaf*, E. G. Browne, English Int., p. XX.

5. *Al-Babu'l-Hadi Ashar*, William M. Miller, London, 1928, p. 75.

6. "A. H." indicates year after the Hegira (622 A.D.).

7. *Al-Babu'l-Hadi Ashar*, p. 81.

8. *Aqa'idu'sh-Shi'a*, pp. 73-88.

9. Alfred Guillaume writes in *Islam* (p. 123): The philosophy of the Isma'ilis "is fundamentally neo-Platonistic, and on an emanation basis they build a theory of a chain of manifestations of the world intellect beginning with Adam, each adding to the instruction and achievements of his predecessor." This Isma'ili doctrine was taken over by the Bab and his followers.

10. *A Literary History of Persia*, E. G. Browne, p. 311.

11. *Nuqtatu'l-Kaf*, English Int., p. XXI.

12. *Shaykh* (meaning elder) is a title used in Iran for one learned in Islamic studies.

13. *Sayyid* (meaning lord) is a title used in Iran for a descendant of the Prophet Muhammad.

14. *Hajji* is a title given to one who makes the pilgrimage (*hajj*) to Mecca.

15. The followers of the Bab usually referred to themselves as "The People of the *Bayan*," the *Bayan* being the book of the Bab, as the Koran was the book of Muhammad.

2

The Manifestation of the Bab

Sayyid Ali Muhammad, better known to the world as the Bab, was born in Shiraz in the province of Pars in the southern part of Iran on October 9, 1820 (or possibly on October 20, 1819).(1) He was a descendant of the family of Muhammad the Prophet of Islam. His father, who was a cloth merchant in Shiraz, died when his son was quite young, and the child was left to the care of his maternal uncle, Hajji Mirza Sayyid Ali, who raised him. It is said that he was quiet and modest, and that as he grew older he became studious and pious. When he was about seventeen years of age he was sent to Bushire, the port on the Persian Gulf, to help with his uncle's business. There he earned his living by trade, and spent his spare time in his studies.

After several years the young man, disinclined to continue his commercial pursuits, and becoming increasingly interested in matters of religion, left Bushire for Shiraz. After a short stay there he made a pilgrimage to the shrines of the Shi'ite Imams near Baghdad in Iraq, and remained for perhaps a year. While in Karbala, the site of the tomb of the Imam Husayn, grandson of Muhammad, who was martyred there in 680 A.D., Sayyid Ali Muhammad became acquainted with

Hajji Sayyid Kazim of Resht, the head of the Shaykhi
movement, and was profoundly influenced by Kazim's
lectures which he eagerly attended. He, in turn, by
his gentleness and devotion, won the esteem and
affection of his teacher and his fellow students.
From Karbala Sayyid Ali Muhammad returned to Shiraz,
and there he was married in 1842 A.D.

It is not possible to trace in detail the changes
that took place in the mind and heart of Sayyid Ali
Muhammad during these years. He had probably become
disgusted by what he had seen and experienced of
Islam as it was then practiced in Iran and Iraq. The
lectures of Hajji Sayyid Kazim had centered his attention on the Imams, probably on the Hidden Imam in
particular, who would surely come soon as the long-
expected Mahdi to right the wrongs of the world. Long
meditation and much prayer brought to him the conviction that he himself had been chosen by God for a
special mission to men. Accordingly, on May 23, 1844,
when he was twenty-four years of age, in his native
city of Shiraz, he made the historic declaration
which marked the beginning of the Babi-Baha'i movement.

For what mission did this young man think he had
been divinely appointed, and what rank among the
servants of God did he at this time claim for himself?
Without having a correct answer to these questions it
is not possible to understand aright the significance
of the events of the years that followed. The doctrine
of the person and rank and mission of the Bab will be
discussed more fully in Chapter IV. Here it will
suffice to say that there have been at least three
contradictory theories regarding the initial claims
of the Bab.

The first theory is that Sayyid Ali Muhammad
thought of himself as a Bab, or Gate, not in the
Shi'ite sense of being a vicegerent of the Hidden
Imam, and the intermediary between him and believers,
but rather in being the forerunner of a much greater
person for whom he would prepare the way, as John the
Baptist did for Jesus Christ. Many Baha'is have said
that the Bab thought his mission to be that of

preparing people for the coming of Baha'u'llah, a
major Manifestation of God, who would soon appear. As
we will see later, this interpretation is not in
harmony with the Bab's own statements, or with the
facts of history.

The second theory is that Sayyid Ali Muhammad at
the time of his declaration considered himself to be
the successor to Hajji Sayyid Kazim, the deceased head
of the Shaykhis, and to be like him a Bab, or Gate, to
the knowledge of the Hidden Imam. It was therefore in
the traditional Shi'ite understanding of the term that
he gave himself the title "Bab." However, according
to this theory, the Bab soon became convinced that he
was himself the Hidden Imam who had appeared, and his
followers quickly accepted him as such, and were prepared to fight for the "Lord of the Age," as loyal
Shi'ites were expected to do whenever the Mahdi should
appear. Then, several years later, when the Bab was
in prison, he began (so it is said) to make the claim
that he was not merely the Hidden Imam come to fill
the world with justice, but was a major Manifestation
of God, bringing in a new epoch in God's dealing with
men, and taking the place of Muhammad the Prophet of
Islam, as Muhammad was thought by Muslims to have
taken the place of Jesus as the revealer of God to
the world.

Differing from these two interpretations, the
third theory is that Sayyid Ali Muhammad from the
time of his declaration in 1844 believed himself to
be a major Manifestation of Deity, and in his earliest
writings made this claim for himself. Those who hold
this theory believe that though he took for himself
the Shi'ite terms and titles, such as Bab, Reminder,
Proof of God, etc., he used these terms with a different connotation. It was because of this that he was
usually misunderstood by his contemporaries, and also
by many who later became students of his movement. It
is of course possible that the Bab was not always
consistent in his thinking and in his pronouncements.
However, it is the opinion of this author that the
third theory is closest to the truth, and that while
Sayyid Ali Muhammad may at times have given the

impression that he was a Bab in the traditional sense,
or was the Hidden Imam who had returned after 1000
years, his real intent from the first was that he was
the Gate of God, a Manifestation of God to men,
greater than any which had preceded him. With this
interpretation as the key to the understanding of the
Babi movement, we will proceed with the story of
Sayyid Ali Muhammad, leaving the consideration of the
evidence for the validity of this interpretation to
Chapter IV.

The first person to hear and attest the claim of
the Bab was Mulla(2) Muhammad Husayn of Bushruieh,(3)
a small town in eastern Iran. Mulla Husayn was a man
of learning and influence and great force of character. He had been one of the followers of Hajji
Sayyid Kazim, and in Karbala had become acquainted
with the young student from Shiraz. About five
months after the death of his master he came to
Shiraz and called on his fellow student. To his
great surprise, Sayyid Ali Muhammad quietly informed
him of his mission, and by reading to him portions of
his writings, and answering questions about difficult
points of theology, convinced his guest that he was
the possessor of supernatural knowledge.

The book from which the young claimant read was
Kitab-i-Awwal (First Book), also called the *Commentary
on Suratu'l-Yusuf*, the *Best of Stories*, and other
names. This book had been previously written by the
Bab in Shiraz in the Arabic language. In it the
author refers to himself as the "Bab," the "Reminder
of God," the "Solace of the Eyes" (*Qurratu'l-Ayn*),
the "Letter BA" and the "Point." He calls upon the
monarchs of the world to convey his message to the
peoples of the East and of the West. He informs the
people of the earth that "whoever has obeyed the
Reminder of God has in truth obeyed God." The author
maintains the Koranic prescriptions, and appears to
use the term "Bab" in the traditional Shi'ite sense.
However, between the lines can be read higher claims,
namely those of divine authority and an independent
and universal mission.(4)

SEYYÈD–ALI–MOHAMMED
dit le BÂB

by A.L.M. Nicolas, Paris, 1911

After several days of doubt and indecision, Mulla
Husayn enthusiastically professed faith in the Bab,
and became the first to believe in him, and the Bab
conferred on him the title "Babu'l-Bab" (Gate of the
Gate). Gradually others believed, till there were
eighteen disciples. The last of these was Mulla
Muhammad Ali of Barfurush, a city near the Caspian
Sea, to whom the Bab gave the title "Quddus" (Holy).
(5) These eighteen were called by the Bab "Letters
of the Living." The meaning of this and other terms
will be explained in Chapter IV.

The new disciples, who became known as "Babis,"
went forth to other cities and began to proclaim with
the greatest boldness and zeal the advent of the Bab.
Although Sayyid Ali Muhammad had not yet proclaimed
in full the nature of his mission, it seems that the
Letters of the Living understood clearly that he
claimed to be the bringer of a new revelation, to be
a new Manifestation of God. They read to the people
the writings which the Bab had composed, and pointed
to them as a proof of his divine mission, as the
Muslims have always pointed to the verses of the
Koran as the all-sufficient proof of the mission of
Muhammad. Thus a great stir began to be made all
over Iran, some people showing great eagerness to
believe the good news, and others treating the Bab's
apostles with disrespect and even blows.

While his followers were thus engaged, the Bab with
one of the Letters set out near the end of the year
1844 for Mecca, where, according to one tradition, the
Mahdi would make his appearance, and there he proclaimed himself to a few of the pilgrims. It is said
that he also addressed an Epistle, in which he
declared his mission, to the Sharif of Mecca, who
ignored it. Then he started back toward Shiraz, and
early in the year 1845 reached Bushire. While he
tarried there, one of his zealous disciples, Mulla
Sadiq by name, in giving the call to prayer in a
mosque in Shiraz, openly added the formula, "I testify
that Ali Muhammad is the Gate of God."(6) This innovation incensed many people, and several of the Babis
who were held responsible for it were, at the order of

the governor, seized, severely beaten, and expelled
from the city. Also horsemen were sent to Bushire to
arrest the Bab and bring him to Shiraz. After his
arrival in September, 1845, he was examined by the
governor, who, fearing further trouble, kept him
under observation.

To understand the attitude of the government
officials toward Sayyid Ali Muhammad and the movement
which his claim had inspired, it is necessary to
remember that the putting forward of a claim to be
the Mahdi has always in the history of Islam been
connected with a political uprising. In arresting
the Bab the authorities were only doing their duty in
trying to forestall a probable upheaval. But in this
attempt they were unsuccessful. The fire had already
been kindled, and was spreading rapidly throughout
the land. The people had long been in expectation
of the coming of a deliverer. The government of the
country under the Qajar Dynasty was corrupt and
inefficient. The popular religion was full of super-
stition, and had failed to bring moral and spiritual
renewal to the people of Iran. The Muslim clergy were
often both ignorant and evil men. The rich oppressed
the poor, whose lot was pitiable. The time was indeed
ripe for a revolution. And now, just 1000 years after
the disappearance of the Twelfth Imam, the rightful
ruler who at his return would bring in the new order,
the cry was raised far and near that the Lord of the
Age had come!(7) Bold and eloquent apostles were
going all over Iran proclaiming his advent, and multitudes were eager to believe on him. It is not surprising that the government became alarmed, and took
drastic measures to nip the movement in the bud.

Sometime after the arrival of the Bab in Shiraz,
the religious authorities also became greatly disturbed at the course of events. It is said that they
brought pressure on the maternal uncle of the Bab to
force his nephew to make a formal denial of his
claims. The Bab, accordingly, went to one of the
mosques in Shiraz, and to the great joy of the clergy
read a statement, which they took to be a complete
denial. However, at a later time the Bab explained

in writing that what he meant in his denial of Babhood
was that he was *not* a Bab in the traditional Shi'ite
sense of the term, and he did not claim to be a Gate
to the knowledge of the Hidden Imam.(8)   Later he made
it clear that his claim was to be a Gate of God, that
is, a major Manifestation.

In the early summer of the year 1846 cholera broke
out in Shiraz, and in the confusion caused by this
calamity the Bab managed to escape, and near the end
of the summer of 1846 made his way to Isfahan.   There
he was received by Manuchehr Khan(9) the governor of
the city, who showed him great kindness and afforded
him hospitality and protection.   In Isfahan he married
a second wife, who lived sixty-six years after the
death of her husband.   The governor was a Christian
and a native of Georgia in the Caucasus, whose native
land had been conquered by the Qajars, and who had no
love for the rulers of Iran.   His motive for befriend-
ing the Bab may have been to embarrass the Qajar
government as well as the Muslim mullas.   It is said
that he offered the Bab a strong army with which to
march against the Shah, should he desire to do so.(10)
This offer was declined, for the Bab apparently had no
desire to fight.   However, when his followers later
began to use their swords, according to their account
in self defense, he did not forbid them to do so.(11)
While in Isfahan the Bab met and talked with some of
the leading Muslim clergy of the city.   When asked by
what sign or miracle he could establish the truth of
his claim, he replied, "By verses, for without pause
of pen I can in the space of three hours write a
thousand sentences on any subject that I please."   He
was asked to write a commentary on a portion of the
Koran, and when he did so it is said that his hearers
admitted that such power must be of God, being beyond
the capacity of man.(12)

About this time Mulla Husayn of Bushruieh, the
Bab's First Letter and most zealous apostle, was in
Teheran busily engaged in preaching the good news of
the appearing of the Mahdi and inviting people to
believe on him.   He made a considerable stir in the
capital, and it is said that he even tried to

influence the King, Muhammad Shah Qajar, and his Prime
Minister, Hajji Mirza Aqasi, but without success.(13)
Finally Mulla Husayn was ordered to leave Teheran.

In the early part of 1847 Manuchehr Khan died, and
the governor who succeeded him, wishing to demonstrate
his loyalty to the Shah, sent the Bab in the care of
an escort of armed horsemen to Teheran. When the
party reached Kashan a respectable merchant by the
name of Mirza Jani bribed the guards to allow the Bab
to stop in his house for two days. Mirza Jani later
wrote the earliest and best history of the Babi movement, and in 1852 died as a martyr to the Babi cause.
It is said that at a village near Teheran a number of
believers came to meet the Bab, but the Shah did not
permit the prisoner to enter the capital. Instead, he
was sent off to Maku, a strong fortress on the northwest frontier of Iran, some 500 miles distant from
Teheran. It was hoped that if the Bab were kept out
of sight, the excitement which was being stirred up
in his name would die down of itself.

On the long horseback journey across Iran, and
later while he was in prison, the Bab conducted himself with such mildness and patience that he won the
hearts of more than one of his guards. The Babi
historian is careful to explain that the Bab of his
own free will suffered himself to be thus treated,
for he was "fully able to effect his escape had he so
pleased." "Such a one is able to do what he wills,
for his will is identical with God's will."(14) The
Bab remained at Maku for nine months (from the summer
of 1847 to the spring of 1848). There he was treated
kindly, and was allowed to communicate to a certain
extent with his friends, many of whom came from distant places to visit him. As is evident from the
Bayan, it was in Maku that the Bab declared he was
the "Qa'im."(15) He was then transferred to the
Castle of Chihriq near Lake Rezaieh (Urumia), where
he remained for two years and several months till his
execution in 1850. Here his imprisonment was much
more rigorous than it had been at Maku.

During the previous four years since his declaration in Shiraz, Sayyid Ali Muhammad had continued to

speak of himself as "Bab," but he had been preparing
his followers to accept the higher station which he
now openly claimed for himself in declaring that he was
the Qa'im.(16) As we will see in Chapter IV, in doing
so he intended something different from and greater
than what was meant in the Shi'ite usage of that term.
The Bab spent much time while he was in prison in Maku
and Chihriq in writing the books which were to guide
his followers after he was taken away from them. He
was a most prolific writer. Professor Browne published a list of some twenty-five volumes composed by the
Bab,(17) but it is known that he wrote scores of
other books, most of which have been lost.(18)

During the early part of his Chihriq imprisonment
(summer of 1848) the Bab was summoned to Tabriz by
Nasiru'd-Din Mirza, who was Crown Prince and Governor
of the province of Azarbaijan, and was soon to become
Shah of Iran. There he was examined by the Prince
and the mullas as to his claims. The accounts that
have been given of this trial are contradictory, the
Babi historians representing the Bab in the most
favorable light, and the Shi'ite historians in the
most unfavorable.(19) The account given by Browne,
which has been generally accepted as correct, is
based largely on the *Rawzatu's-Safa*, *Qisasu'l-Ulema*
and *Nasikhu't-Tawarikh*,(20) all written by Shi'ites.

According to these accounts, the Bab admitted that
the writings which were being circulated in his name
were his. When asked what he meant by the title "Bab"
which he had assumed, he replied that it meant the
same as in the tradition attributed to Muhammad, who
said, "I am the City of Knowledge, and Ali is its
Gate." The Bab also said, "I am that person for
whose appearance you have waited a thousand years,
namely, the Mahdi." When he was asked to give his
name and age, the names of his parents, and his birth-
place he did so, only to be reminded that this information did not agree with the names of the Mahdi and
his parents, or with his age, which was one thousand
years. The mullas then asked him questions about
jurisprudence and other sciences which he was unable
to answer, in addition to many foolish questions, to

make him look ridiculous. The assembly then broke up,
and the Shaykhu'l-Islam Hajji Mirza Ali Asghar took
the Bab to his own house, where he had the bastinado
inflicted on him.

Of this trial Browne writes:(21) "That the whole
examination was a farce throughout, that the sentence
was a foregone conclusion, that no serious attempt to
apprehend the nature and evidence of the Bab's claim
and doctrine was made, and that from first to last a
systematic course of brow-beating, irony and mockery
was pursued appear to me to be facts proved no less by
the Muhammadan than by the Babi accounts of these
inquisitorial proceedings."

In his book *Materials for the Study of the Babi
Religion*, Browne published facsimilies and translations of several documents which have an important
bearing on the significance of the trial of the Bab
in Tabriz.(22) The first of these is a letter written
by the Crown Prince to his father Muhammad Shah in
Teheran, informing him of what had happened. His
account of the trial is similar to that given above,
and ends as follows: "When the discussion was concluded, His Reverence the Shaykhu'l-Islam was summoned,
who had the Bab beaten and inflicted on him an exem-
plary chastisement, so that he apologized, recanted,
and repented of and asked pardon for his errors, giving a sealed undertaking that henceforth he would not
commit such faults. Now he is in prison and bonds
awaiting the decision of His Most Sacred, Royal and
Imperial Majesty." It was not long after this that
Muhammad Shah died.

A second document, unsigned and undated, is, to
quote Browne, "apparently in the Bab's handwriting
and consists of a complete recantation of any super-
human claim which he may have advanced or have
appeared to advance. There is nothing to show to
whom it is addressed, or whether it is the recantation
referred to in the last paragraph of the preceding
document or another." However, Dr. Sa'eed Khan of
Teheran wrote concerning this statement: "The original document is kept safely in the Majlis [Parliment

in Teheran]. It was addressed, as the contents well
proves, to the Crown Prince Nasserad-Din Mirza,
afterwards Shah." Dr. Sa'eed here refers to the
original of this document, which bears no seal, and
not to the "sealed undertaking" referred in the report
of the Crown Prince.

The authenticity of the writing, signature or seal
attached to a document may be verified only by sub-
mitting the document to examination by experts.
Specimens of the Bab's writing are extant with which
the writing in this document might be compared, but
as yet, so far as is known, this has never been done.
However, presuming that the document is in the handwriting of the Bab, we will quote the last part of it
as translated by Browne,(23) and attempt to understand
its meaning and purpose:

"Never have I desired aught contrary to the Will of
God, and, if words contrary to His good pleasure have
flowed from my pen, my object was not disobedience,
and in any case I repent and ask forgiveness of Him.
This servant has absolutely no knowledge connected
with any [superhuman] claim. I ask forgiveness of God
my Lord and I repent unto Him of [the idea] that there
should be ascribed to me any [Divine] Mission. As for
certain prayers and words which have flowed from my
tongue, these do not imply any such Mission (*amr*), and
any [apparent] claim to any special vicegerency for
His Holiness the Proof of God (on whom be Peace!) is a
purely baseless claim, such as this servant has never
put forward, nay, nor any claim like unto it. Therefore it is thus hoped from the clemency of His Imperial
Majesty and Your Excellency, that they will exalt the
head of him who continually prays for them by the
favours and graces of their clement and compassionate
court. Farewell."

Since the terms "His Imperial Majesty" and "Your
Excellency" appear in the document, it is clear that
it was addressed, as Dr. Sa'eed Khan said, to the Shah
and the Crown Prince.

The word *amr* which Browne translated "mission"
means "a command, a matter, a thing." It is therefore

possible to change Browne's translation "any [Divine]
Mission" to "any matter." Also, "any such Mission"
may be translated "any matter at all." According to
Mr. Azal,(24) the alternative translation is the
correct one in this context.

"The Proof of God" is a title from the Hidden Imam.
As translated by Browne the Bab says, "any [apparent]
claim to any specific vicegerency title for His Holiness
the Proof of God.....is a purely baseless claim such
as this servant has never put forward, nay, nor any
claim like unto it." Mr. Azal states(25) that the
correct translation is, "any pretension to special
vicegerency for His Holiness the Proof of God is a
purely baseless pretension, and this servant has not
set up any such pretension, nor any other pretension."

Assuming that this document was written by the Bab,
the question is, what was it that he denied? If the
claim of the Bab was, as has been generally thought,
to be a Gate to, or the vicegerent of, the Hidden Imam,
or to be the Imam come again, it is evident that the
Bab does in this statement deny such a claim, and
apparently makes a complete recantation. But if it is
true, as was maintained in the early part of this
chapter, that the Bab did not claim to be a Bab or an
Imam in the traditional Shi'ite sense, but intentionally used the Shi'ite terms with a different meaning,
then this apparent "recantation" is only a rejection
of a position which he had never claimed for himself.
His claim, as we have seen, was higher, He claimed to
be the Gate of God, a major Manifestation.

However, if the Bab thought himself to be in truth
the Gate of God, why did he say, "this servant has not
set up any such pretension, *or any other pretension*"?
And if he claimed to be a new Manifestation, the
founder of a new world religion which would take the
place of Islam, why did he not follow the example of
his ancestor Muhammad, who from the beginning of his
mission declared himself to be the Apostle of God, and
state with unmistakable clarity who he was? Of course,
if he had done so he would have been quickly condemned
to death as a false prophet, because Muslims believe

that no true prophet will ever come to take the place
of Muhammad, the "Seal of the Prophets." So perhaps
the Bab hoped that by using the popular terms which
were acceptable to the Shi'ites, he might win their
allegiance, and prepare them for the later acceptance
of his higher claims. If this was his purpose, it
seems that among the people it met with some success.
But the political and religious authorities were as
unwilling to welcome an Imam as they were to accept a
new Prophet or Manifestation in place of Muhammad.
And so the Bab, whatever his claim might have been,
was rejected.

During the trial proceedings the question arose as
to whether or not the Bab was of sound mind. He,
therefore, "requested that a physician might be
allowed to feel his pulse, and certify to his perfect
sanity."(26) This was done, as we will recount later.

A third document which was translated and published
by Browne is addressed to the Bab, and contains the
fatwa, or sentence of the Muslim doctors of the law.
It is formally sealed by two of them. The second seal
is that of the Shaykhu'l-Islam who had the Bab beaten
in his house. It reads as follows:

"Sayyid Ali Muhammad-i-Shirazi:

"In the Imperial Banquet-hall and August Assembly
of His Highness the Crown Prince of the undeclining
Empire [of Persia] (may God aid, support and strengthen
him!) and of a number of learned doctors, thou didst
admit certain matters each one of which separately
implied thy apostacy and justified thy death. The(27)
repentance of an incorrigible apostate is not accepted,
and the only thing which has caused the postponement
of thy execution is a doubt as to thy sanity of mind.
Should this doubt be removed, the sentence of an
incorrigible apostate would without hesitation be
executed upon thee."

Sealed by: Abu'l-Qasim al-Hasani al-Husayni
              Ali Asghar al-Hasani al-Husayni

Professor Browne also published(28) a letter written by Dr. Cormick, "an English physician long resident in Tabriz, where he was highly respected," to the Rev. Benjamin Labaree of the Presbyterian Mission in Rezaieh, Iran. As far as is known, this is the only extant record of the impression made by the Bab "on a cultivated and impartial Western mind."

"You ask me for some particulars of my interview with the founder of the sect known as Babis. Nothing of any importance transpired in this interview, as the Bab was aware of my having been sent with two other Persian doctors to see whether or not he was of sane mind or merely a madman, to decide the question whether to put him to death or not. With this knowledge he was loth to answer any questions put to him. To all inquiries he merely regarded us with a mild look, chanting in a low melodious voice some hymns, I suppose.....He only once deigned to answer me, on my saying that I was not a Musulman and was willing to know something about his religion, as I might perhaps be inclined to adopt it. He regarded me very intently on my saying this, and replied that he had no doubt of all Europeans coming over to his religion. Our report to the Shah at that time was of a nature to spare his life..... On our report he merely got the bastinado, in which operation a *farrash*, whether intentionally or not, struck him across the face with the stick destined for his feet, which produced a great wound and swelling of the face. On being asked whether a Persian surgeon should be brought to treat him, he expressed a desire that I should be sent for, and I accordingly treated him for a few days, but in the interviews consequent on this I could never get him to have a confidential chat with me, as some Government people were always present, he being a prisoner.

"He was very thankful for my attentions to him. He was a very mild and delicate-looking man, rather small in stature and very fair for a Persian, with a melo-dious soft voice, which struck me much. Being a Sayyid, he was dressed in the habits of that sect..... In fact his whole look and deportment went far to dispose one

in his favour. Of his doctrine I heard nothing from
his own lips, although the idea was that there existed
in his religion a certain approach to Christianity.
He was seen by some Armenian carpenters who were sent
to make some repairs in his prison, reading the Bible,
and he took no pains to conceal it, but on the contrary told them of it. Most assuredly the Musalman
fanaticism does not exist in his religion, as applied
to Christians, nor is there that restraint of females
that now exists."

And so the Bab, after this humiliating and painful
experience in Tabriz, having received the *fatwa* of
the religious authorities, was sent back to his prison
in Chihriq to await the decision of the government in
Teheran. There he remained for about two more years,
engaged in writing his books and epistles, setting
forth his claims, and making laws for his Theocratic
Society.

NOTES

1. For important dates in the life of the Bab, refer
   to *A Traveller's Narrative*, pp. 221, 249-253,
   Azal's Notes, pp. 613, 854.

2. A *mulla* is a cleric of the religion of Islam.

3. Mirza Jani in *New History*, pp. 33-39.

4. *Azal's Notes*, pp. 530, 531, 831, 832, 835.

5. *New History*, pp. 39, 40, 399, 401, *Azal's Notes*,
   p. 839.

6. A Muslim historian in *J.R.A.S.*, July, 1927, p. 451.

7. There is a Shi'ite tradition that the Twelfth Imam
   disappeared immediately after he succeeded his
   father in 260 A.H. It was in 1260 A.H. that Sayyid
   Ali Muhammad put forth his claim to be the Bab.

8. *Azal's Notes*, pp. 729, 733, 747, 832, 841. See
   Appendix II, #34.

9. *Khan* was formerly used in Iran as a title equiva-
    lent to *Sir*.

10. *New History*, p. 211.

11. In the *Bayan* slaying is forbidden - *J.R.A.S.*,
    October 1889, pp. 927, 928.

12. *New History*, p. 209, *Bayan* quoted in *A Traveller's
    Narrative*, pp. 218, 219.

13. *Nasikhu't-Tawarikh*, quoted in *A Traveller's
    Narrative*, p. 176.

14. *New History*, pp. 226, 227.

15. Mr. Azal is of the opinion that the *Bayan* and the
    Seven Proofs written by the Bab indicate that his
    declaration to be the Qa'im was made before he
    left Maku for Chihriq.

16. *New History*, p. 241, *A Traveller's Narrative*,
    pp. 290-295.

17. *A Traveller's Narrative*, pp. 335-347.

18. Browne in *J.R.A.S.*, July 1892, p. 452, *Materials*,
    pp. 198-208.

19. *A Traveller's Narrative*, pp. 277-290, *New History*,
    pp. 285-290.

20. *A Traveller's Narrative*, p. 277.

21. Ibid., 290.

22. *Materials*, pp. 247-260.

23. Ibid., pp. 256-258.

24. *Azal's Notes*, pp. 847-850.

25. Ibid., p. 848.

26. Mirza Jani, in *New History*, pp. 285, 354.

27. *Koran* (Rodwell's translation) III:84: "As for
    those who become infidels, after having believed,
    and then increase their infidelity - their
    repentance shall never be accepted."

28. *Materials*, pp. 260-262.

3
Babi Uprisings
and the Execution of the Bab

While the Bab was in prison in Maku and later in
Chihriq his fiery missionaries were busy travelling
about Iran calling upon the Shi'ites to accept him as
their long-expected Mahdi. Toward the end of the year
1847 Mulla Husayn of Bushruieh, the First Letter of
the Living, went eastward to the province of Khurasan,
meeting everywhere with great success. In Nishapur,
the city of Umar Khayyam, several members of the Muslim
clergy believed, and it seemed for a time that the
whole city might follow their example. But when he
reached Meshed, the shrine city of the Imam Reza, the
eighth in succession after Muhammad, whose tomb is
visited annually by hundreds of thousands of Shi'ite
pilgrims, the mullas rose against him and had him
arrested. However, he managed to escape, and seeing
that he was in peril he gathered a number of his converts about him, and proceeded westward in the direction of Teheran. Others joined him along the way, and
his band became quite formidable. Before long a fight
occurred with the Muslims in which the Babis were
worsted, and they fell back on Shahrud and later proceeded toward the northern province of Mazanderan.(1)

In the meantime a number of Babi leaders had
gathered in a place called Badasht near Shahrud.

Among them were Mulla Muhammad Ali of Barfurush,
Qurratu'l-Ayn and Mirza Husayn Ali of Nur, the first
two being among the Letters of the Living.(2)
Qurratu'l-Ayn was the only woman included among the
Letters.(3) She was learned and eloquent, and on
becoming a disciple of the Bab (whom she had never
seen) she gave herself unreservedly to the advancement of his cause. She travelled widely about the
country, proclaiming boldly the advent of the Bab. By
so doing she incurred the anger of her husband and her
uncle (who was the father of her husband) in Qazvin,
both of whom were influential mullas. Her uncle
publicly denounced the Bab, and in consequence of this
act was shortly afterward murdered in the mosque in
the winter of 1847 by a Babi.(4)

Qurratu'l-Ayn was then divorced by her husband,(5)
after which it became advisable for her to flee from
Qazvin to Teheran. From there she went to Khurasan,
where she joined some of the Babi leaders. At that
time it was contrary to Iranian custom for women to
appear in public in company with men. Hence her freedom of travelling about the country with the Babi
chiefs scandalized many people, and there was probably
some ground for criticism of her disregard of convention. It appears that some of the Babis considered
this period a time of freedom, for they thought they
had been released from the restrictions of Islam, and
the new laws to be given by the Bab had not yet been
revealed or made known to them. The Babi historian
Mirza Jani, stating his own opinion and probably that
of other Babis also, says that the Bab is master of
all men and women, and has the authority to interchange
husbands and wives at will, "and hath given his servant and his handmaid to one another," probably
indicating that he thought the Bab himself had united
Qurratu'l-Ayn with Mulla Muhammad Ali of Barfurush
with whom she was on intimate terms. Since she was a
divorcee such a union would have been permitted by
Muslim law. "And this is assuredly sanctioned by the
Holy Law," continues Mirza Jani, "for our Master hath
certainly as much authority as every other master hath
over his slaves and handmaidens."(6)

At Badasht in the spring of 1848, while the Bab
was still in Maku, there was held a conference of the
Babi chiefs. In this gathering, according to Mirza
Jani,(7) the abrogation of the laws of the previous
Islamic dispensation was announced, thus indicating
that these Babis considered the Bab to be not the
Twelfth Imam who had returned but a new Prophet in
place of Muhammad. Also it was stated that laws
would be necessary only till the time when men have
understood the true nature of the new dispensation.
It is said(8) that Qurratu'l-Ayn at Badasht delivered
a wonderfully eloquent and impressive address which
moved her hearers to tears, in which she stressed the
universal character of the Bab's Manifestation, which
had abrogated the previous dispensation, and the need
for the emancipation of Iranian women. Many other
people beside the Babis had crowded about to listen,
and on hearing her appeal joined the Babi company.
However, things were said and done at Badasht which
caused even some of the Babis to stumble, and they
took their departure. Those who remained seemed to
have been intoxicated by the new teachings, and their
conduct brought down on them the wrath of the people
of the village. On being attacked by them the Babis
dispersed peaceably, to meet again in Mazanderan.(9)

It was at Badasht that Mirza Husayn Ali received
the title "Baha" (Splendor), given him according to
Avareh the historian by Qurratu'l-Ayn,(10) or possibly
by the other Babi leaders. It was not bestowed by the
Bab, the sole grantor of titles. After the conference
Qurratu'l-Ayn met the young Mirza Yahya (Subh-i-Azal),
brother of Baha, who had not been at Badasht, and took
him with her to Nur.(11)

It seems that Mirza Jani felt it necessary to
defend the good name of the Babi cause against the
criticism evoked by the Badasht conference, so he
wrote:(12) "When people say a company [of Babis] went
to Badasht and conducted themselves in an unseemly
fashion, you may know that they were persons of no
mean quality, but the elect of the world, that they
did a great work, and that when men heap curses and

censures on them it is because of their own benighted condition."

The Babis moved into Mazanderan with the full intention of getting control of that province. The time was propitious, for on September 4, 1848 Muhammad Shah had died,(13) and the new king Nasiru'd-Din Shah had not yet ascended the throne, so there was no one prepared to oppose their designs. More than three hundred strong, they entered Barfurush armed. Thus provoking strife, they were soon attacked by the Muslims, and several of them were killed. Then the Babis began to fight. Mulla Husayn, the first to believe on the Bab, "notwithstanding his slender and fragile frame and trembling hand," attacked the man who had killed the first Babi and "sliced him in two like a fresh cucumber." Then six other Muslims were killed. "One child was killed accidentally with its father, a dervish, whom they [the Babis] slew because he purposely gave them a misleading answer to a question which they had put to him as to their road."(14) One of the Babis who was taken by the townfolk was buried alive by them in a well. After a pitched battle of several days duration in Barfurush, the Babis were allowed to retire.

Later in another skirmish the Babis came off victorious, after which they moved to a shrine in the forest called Shaykh Tabarsi. Here they strongly entrenched themselves, hoping to make this position their base for the conquest of Mazanderan. Many people had now joined them, and their numbers reached two thousand.(15) They carried on an active campaign of preaching from their fort, telling the people that the Bab was shortly to become master of the whole world, and bidding them accept him at once. Crowds assembled about the fort, some of whom entered and united with the Babis. Gobineau, relying probably too much on information given him by the Muslim historian Lisanu'l-Mulk, says(16) that within the fort the Babis divided the world among themselves, apportioning to various ones the wealth of India, China and Europe. He says also that the Babis looked upon Mulla Husayn as God, and prostrated themselves in his presence;

that he, in turn, told his principal officers that
they were the "return" of various Imams, and assured
them that if they were killed they would after forty
days come back to the earth again; also that the Bab
from his prison sent them frequent letters of encouragement; and that the fighters reached such a pitch of
frenzy that they asserted that the Bab had predicted
that after their conquest of Mazanderan they would
march on Teheran, capture it, and slay ten thousand
Muslims. We will consider in Chapter IV the extent
to which these dreams which were attributed to the
Babis conformed to the teaching and purposes of their
Master.

Whether or not these reports from within the
Shaykh Tabarsi fort were accurate, it is evident that
to these zelots the hope of the establishment of the
Babi world rule was very real. Moreover, since in
their beseiged fortress they generously shared their
possessions with one another, it was rumored outside
that the Babis practiced community of goods and also
of women.(17) It is, therefore, not surprising that
this strange and aggressive movement was feared both
by the rulers and also by the Muslim populace.

A small government force sent against the Babis,
which had occupied one of the surrounding villages,
was defeated by them in a night attack, the village
was sacked, and one hundred and thirty soldiers and
villagers were massacred.(18) Then a large force
under the command of Prince Mahdi-Quli Mirza was sent
from Teheran by the new Prime Minister with strict
orders to destroy the Babis. The Prince wrote a
letter to Mulla Muhammad Ali (Quddus) asking what he
was fighting for. Quddus replied:(19) "As for thee,
O Prince, let not the world and the presumption of
youth lure thee. Know that Nasiru'd-Din Shah is a
false king, and his helpers shall be chastised in
God's fire. We are the king of truth, who seek after
the good pleasure of God."

The royal forces under the command of the Prince
drew near the fort. But before they were able to
attack it, the Babi leaders, choosing a time when the

enemy were off their guard because of a severe snow-
storm, fell upon them with a picked force of three
hundred men. The Babis fought with such fury that
they dispersed the whole army, and several of the
princes and many of the soldiers were killed. The
Babis lost but three men. Later the Babis made a
night attack on their enemies. The plan of battle in
such attacks was this:(20) "Mulla Husayn, followed
by several other mounted men, would ride in advance
while the rest of his companions followed on foot -
they would put on felt caps, gird their swords to
their belts, and, with bare feet and arms uncovered
to the elbow, rush upon the very center of the hostile
army with cries of 'Ya Sahibu'z-Zaman!' [O Lord of the
Age - another title for the Mahdi]. Then, with swords
not worth more than five krans which they had wrought
for themselves within the castle, they would cut down
men whose gear had cost a thousand tumans [10,000
krans]."

This time also their attack met with complete
success, and the royal army was again routed. But
the Babis suffered an irreparable loss, for their
commander was killed. Mulla Husayn, entitled
Babu'l-Bab, the first to believe on the Bab, and the
strongest of the Babi leaders, was mortally wounded
just in the hour of victory. He died in his saddle
as his horse entered the gate of the fort (January 2,
1849).(21) It is said(22) that he before his death
commanded his officers to be firm in their faith, and
promised them that he would return to earth again in
fourteen days. He bade his intimate friends to bury
him secretly, fearing that the Muslims might find and
mutilate his body, and it is said that he was buried
near the shrine in the fort. After his death his
brother Mirza Muhammad Hasan, a youth of eighteen, by
the appointment of Quddus succeeded to his title and
command.(23)

The death of Mulla Husayn was the beginning of the
end for the defenders of Shaykh Tabarsi. Not only
was their leader gone, but provisions began to run
low, and the Babis were reduced to eating horse
flesh and grass. Some of them deserted to the enemy,

who, on hearing of the famine within the fort, began
to attack more vigorously. The royal army had two
cannons with which they battered down the Babi defenses
and set fire to all the sheds and wooden structures
within the walls, forcing the beseiged to dig tunnels
in which to hide. But in spite of their reduced
strength the Babis fought furiously to the last, realizing that they had little hope for mercy from enemies
whom they had defied for nearly nine months. Finally,
a new commander was sent by the Shah with fresh orders
to destroy the Babis immediately. The survivors in
the fort had nothing whatever to eat, and the royal
troops were trying to scale the walls. But "the
defenders of the castle, hungry and barefoot as they
were, hurled themselves upon the enemy, sword in hand,
and displayed that day a courage and heroism which the
world had never seen before..... So fiercely did they
drive back that mightly host that many, even of the
bravest and boldest, were unable to escape from their
hands."(24)

The commander of the Shah's troops then sent a
message to the Babis, asking on what terms they would
surrender. Mulla Muhammad Ali replied that they
would stop fighting if guaranteed their lives and
permission to leave Mazanderan. Thereupon the
officers of the royal army swore on the Koran that
they would allow them to pass safely out of the province. Then two hundred and thirty men, the sole
survivors of the two thousand people who had at first
gathered in the fort, dragged themselves out, and
walked to the royal camp. There they were given food
to eat. When Mulla Muhammad Ali was questioned as to
why he had raised this insurrection, he laid the blame
on Mulla Husayn, and it is said that he even cursed
Mulla Husayn.(25) The next day the Babis were ordered
to lay down their arms, which they did with great
reluctance, fearing treachery. Their fears were well
grounded, for no sooner had they disarmed than their
enemies massacred them with great cruelty, and their
bodies were left to the wild beasts.(26) Then the
royal troops, overjoyed by their victory, moved off
to Barfurush, taking with them Mulla Muhammad Ali and
several other Babi leaders. There in his native town

Quddus was executed by the hand of one of the Muslim
clergy, and it was said that his body was cut in small
pieces and cast to the winds (May 22, 1849).(27)   The
other chiefs also were killed there. In this tragic
conflict most of the eighteen Letters of the Living
perished. Thus after nine months of fighting the
first and most brilliant attempt of the Babis to establish their rule came to an end. According to the
Muslim historian Lisanu'l-Mulk, 500 of the Shah's
soldiers and 1500 Babis lost their lives in this
fratricidal conflict.(28)

   Some time before the fall of Shaykh Tabarsi, Mulla
Muhammad Ali called for assistance. Among those who
tried to join him in the fort were Mirza Yahya
(Subh-i-Azal) and his older brother Mirza Husayn Ali
(Baha) and Mirza Jani of Kashan,(29) but before they
reached the Babi headquarters they were all arrested
by the local authorities. After being reviled and
shamefully treated by the populace, they were brought
before the mullas, who inflicted the legal castigation
on the others, but Mirza Yahya and Mirza Jani were not
beaten. Later "God delivered them."(30)   But soon,
according to Mirza Jani,(31) Mirza Husayn Ali (Baha)
"fell under suspicion, and it was said that he not
improbably harboured designs of setting up a standard
[on his own account], and so creating further distur-
bances in those regions. Therefore, the notables of
the district [the local officials].....considered it
expedient to send him to the capital." How different
the later history of the Babi movement would have been
had these three men been able to reach Shaykh Tabarsi,
as they wished to do, and perished with Mulla Husayn
and Mulla Muhammad Ali and the rest of the garrison!

   One year after this defeat another serious Babi
uprising took place in the city of Zanjan, which is
situated between Teheran and Tabriz in northwest Iran.
(32)   The moving spirit in this conflict was Mulla
Muhammad Ali of Zanjan entitled the "Proof," who, on
examining a writing of the Bab which was brought to
his notice while the latter was still in Shiraz, had
immediately recognized him as the promised Mahdi, and
had proclaimed him so effectively in the mosque in

Zanjan that three thousand people believed. The Babi
community there then became so strong and bold that
the government authorities began to fear for the consequences. For some time nothing happened to produce
a riot, but at last one of the Babis drew a knife on
a Muslim. This led to blows, and soon the whole city
was in turmoil. The Babis, drawing their swords and
shouting "O Lord of the Age!", assembled in the center
of the city. There they built strong defences, and
prepared to stand a seige. On May 13, 1850 the Muslims
attacked them, but were unable to dislodge them.

Then the Shah sent regiment after regiment of royal
troops till at last thirty thousand were said to have
camped around Zanjan. The Babis defended themselves
with the same frenzied courage which had characterized
the garrison of Shaykh Tabarsi. One man would sometimes put to flight a whole mob of the enemy. The
women also armed themselves, and fought as furiously
as the men. Both the Babis and the Muslims vied with
one another in the savagery of their warfare, giving
no quarter to prisoners, and mutilating the bodies of
the slain. The fighting dragged on for months, and
did not end till late in the year 1850, six months
after the execution of the Bab. When their leader
Mulla Muhammad Ali died of a bullet wound on December
30, 1850, the Babis who remained alive sued for peace.
As at Shaykh Tabarsi, the commander of the royal
armies promised the Babis their lives if they would
surrender. However, when they did so they were all
put to the sword.

Sometime during the year 1850, before the execution
of the Bab,(33) the Babis meditated an uprising in
Teheran itself. One of them revealed the plot, and
the government officials, terrified by the thought of
what might occur if the Babis should actually take up
arms in the capital, frantically arrested all members
of the movement who could be found. Thirty-eight men
were captured, and all were offered their release
provided they would renounce the Bab. Thirty-one of
them agreed to do so, but seven refused, affirming
that they rejoiced to offer their lives as a sacrifice
in the way of their beloved Master. One of the seven

was the Bab's own maternal uncle, Mirza Sayyid Ali.
When led out to be killed in the public square in
Teheran, they were again urged to deny their faith in
the Bab, and so save their lives, but all remained
firm. "This drop of blood - this poor life - is
naught," cried one of them; "were I possessed of the
lordship of the world, and had a thousand lives, I
would freely cast them before the feet of his friends!"
All met their death with fearless courage and joy.(34)

After recounting the details of this event, the
Babi historian proceeds to point out the special value
of the testimony given by the Seven Martyrs. He says
(35) they were men who had enjoyed the respect and
consideration of all; they represented all the more
important classes in Iran - divines, dervishes, mer-
chants, shop-keepers, and government officials; they
died fearlessly, willingly, almost eagerly, declining
to purchase life by that mere lip-denial which, under
the name of *taqia* (concealment) is recognized by the
Shi'ites as a perfectly justifiable subterfuge in case
of peril; they were not driven to despair of mercy as
were those who died at Shaykh Tabarsi; and they sealed
their faith with their blood in the public square of
the capital of Iran. Whatever one may think of the
Babi movement, he cannot but feel sympathy and admiration for men so courageous and so devoted to their
Master.(36)

During the same year (1850) serious Babi uprisings,
which we need not describe in detail, occurred at
Yazd and Niriz in central Iran,(37) the moving spirit
of which was Sayyid Yahya of Darab, who with 150 other
Babis lost his life.(38) Suffice it to say that the
Shah, who was young and had recently come to the
throne, and his Prime Minister Mirza Taqi Khan, were
deeply concerned over the condition of the kingdom,
for it seemed probable that the fire which had raged
in Mazanderan and three other places, and had been
extinguished with such difficulty and with so much
bloodshed, might burst forth in Teheran and destroy
the state.

Hence, while the fighting was going on in Zanjan,
it was decided that the Bab himself must be gotten rid

of, in the hope that when he was gone his followers
would cease to fight. Gobineau makes it clear(39)
that it was not because of his religious views that
the Bab was put to death, for the Iranian government
has seldom taken any interest in suppressing heretics
and free-thinkers, of whom there have been many in
that land. Rather, the Bab was sentenced to death
because it seemed to the authorities that his execution was necessary for the good of the state. Nasiru'd-
Din Shah when he was Crown Prince had presided at
the trial of the Bab in Tabriz, and knew that the
Muslim clergy had pronounced him an apostate worthy
of death. But, though two years had passed since that
trial, the Shah had not ordered his execution, and
probably would never have done so, had not the Babi
uprisings occurred. It seems that the Bab had not
incited his fiery followers to fight, and hence should
not be held personally responsible for what they did.
Nevertheless, it had been his claims to be the Bab and
the Mahdi which had caused these bloody wars, and had
resulted in the deaths of thousands of the Shah's
subjects, both Babi and Muslim. It is understandable,
therefore, that the authorities responsible for the
peace of the country should want to remove from the
scene the one who in their opinion had occasioned all
this strife. Banishment had not proved effective, so
the Bab must die.

Accordingly, orders were issued from Teheran by
the Prime Minister for the Bab to be brought from his
prison at Chihriq to Tabriz and there publicly executed.(40) On reaching Tabriz he was given a form of
trial by a civil tribunal, so that it could be stated
officially that he was being put to death for apostasy.
The members of this court accused him of claiming
divinity for himself, and of writing a Koran of his
own and promulgating it among the people, and they
challenged the Bab to call upon God to send down a
revelation to him in support of his claims. It is
said that the Bab thereupon uttered many verses so
similar to the Koran that his enemies were confounded.
(41) His fate, however, had already been decided, and
the authorities only wished to humiliate him as much
as possible, so as to dispel the halo which, in the
eyes of many people, had gathered about his head. The

poor prisoner was therefore dragged about the city and
treated most shamefully by the mob, after which he was
locked in prison with several of his disciples for
three days.

On the night before his execution the Bab sat talk-
ing with his friends. "Tomorrow they will slay me
shamefully," he said. "Let one of you now arise and
kill me - for it is far pleasanter to die by the hands
of friends than of foes." His disciples all hesitated,
except one, Mirza Muhammad Ali, who arose to obey his
Master. The others stopped him, rebuking him for such
presumption. "This act of mine," he replied, "is not
prompted by presumption, but by unstinted obedience."
The Bab smiled and approved his devotion, and then said
to all, "Tomorrow when you are questioned, repudiate me
and renounce my doctrines, for this is the command of
God."(42) The repudiation coupled with renunciation
was especially impressed upon the Bab's amanuensis
Sayyid Husayn.(43) All agreed to do so, except Mirza
Muhammad Ali (also referred to as Mirza Aqa),(44) who
begged to be allowed to die with his Master, and at
last the Bab acquiesced. Next day the family and wife
and little children of this devoted disciple came to
him and besought him to recant, but he refused to do
so. The other prisoners in obedience to the Bab
recanted, and were released. Thus it became possible
for Sayyid Husayn to carry documents and relics of the
Bab to Subh-i-Azal, as the Bab had directed.(45)

On July 8, 1850, the Bab and Mirza Muhammad Ali,
bare-footed and clothed only in their underwear, were
led out to execution.(46) They were first taken to
the houses of three Muslim clerics from whom a sentence of execution for apostasy according to Islamic
law was procured. The two condemned prisoners were
then dragged through the streets, subjected to every
sort of humiliation, and treated most shamefully. They
were then led to the barracks in the Citadel for their
execution. The execution was carried out by firing
squads of soldiers, who fired three volleys. The
first firing party was composed of Christian soldiers,
and the second of Muslims.

In the presence of a great crowd Mirza Muhammad
Ali was suspended by ropes from the parapet, and his
body was riddled by the first volley of bullets. Then
a second volley was fired by the same firing squad at
the Bab, who was similarly suspended. When the smoke
rolled away, "a cry of mingled exultation and terror
arose from the spectators - for the Bab had disappeared
from sight! It seemed, indeed, that his life had been
preserved by a miracle, for, of the storm of bullets
which had been aimed at him, not one had touched him;
nay, instead of death they had brought him deliverance
by cutting the ropes which bound him, so that he fell
to the ground unhurt."

Had the Bab been able to maintain his presence of
mind and rush out alive and unhurt among the crowd,
the spectators would without doubt have hailed his
escape from death as a miracle of God, and would have
eagerly espoused his cause. No soldier would have
dared shoot at him again, and uprisings would have
occurred in Tabriz which might have resulted in the
overthrow of the Qajar dynasty. However, dazed by
the terrible experiences he had passed through, the
Bab took refuge in one of the rooms of the barracks.
There he was soon found, "was seized, dragged forth,
and again suspended; a new firing party was ordered to
advance (for the men who had composed the first
refused to act again); and before the spectators had
recovered from their first astonishment, or the Babis
had time to attempt a rescue, the body of the young
prophet of Shiraz was riddled with bullets."

What became of the bodies of the two martyrs?
According to some accounts, they were dragged through
the streets, and then thrown outside the city walls
to be devoured by the dogs and wild beasts.(47) But
the Babi historian Mirza Jani writes:(48) "The bodies
of the two victims were exposed for two days, after
which they were buried. Some of the Babis exumed them,
wrapped them in white silk, and, according to the Bab's
own instructions, brought them to Subh-i-Azal, who,
with his own hands, buried them in a certain spot.....
This matter is at present kept secret, and it is

unlawful for any one who has knowledge of it to divulge it till such time as the Lord may see fit to make it known." These words were written not long after the death of the Bab. The later Babi account states(49) that the bodies were secured by a loyal disciple by the name of Sulayman Khan, who was afterward killed in the 1852 massacre of Babis in Teheran;(50) were sent to Teheran in the keeping of Mulla Husayn of Khurasan, who also was killed in the Teheran massacre of 1852; (50) and were buried in one coffin secretly.

It would seem most improbable at a time of turmoil like this that the Babis of Tabriz, even by the payment of a large sum of money to the authorities, should have been able to get possession of the earthly remains of their beloved Master and his loyal disciple. However, Mr. Azal, who has carefully studied the evidence,(51) is convinced that the bodies were secured by the payment of money, were later sent to Subh-i-Azal, who interred them together in the shrine of Shah Abdu'l-Azim near Teheran, where many dead were buried, and later took them to the shrine of Imamzadeh Ma'sum. Afterward they were taken away by the followers of Baha'u'llah.

Professor Browne wrote to Subh-i-Azal to get his testimony as to what became of the Bab's body, and his reply in Persian has been translated as follows: (52) "When the Bab was imprisoned in Chihriq he wrote to say that 'the place of Shah Abdu'l-Azim is a good land, by reason of the proximity of *Wahíd* [which has the same numerical equivalent as Yahya, the name of Subh-i-Azal] for keeping'..... After the martyrdom of the Bab his body was kept in the house of Sulayman Khan and had that Trust [the body] conveyed to Teheran with the assistance of two believers.....I was unwilling to keep that Trust in the precincts of Shah Abdu'l-Azim, as graves of the dead were daily ripped up and others were interred in them. Therefore I deposited it in a spot in the shrine of Imamzadeh Ma'sum. Two persons had knowledge of that spot..... After the 'pretender' [Baha] had set up his pretentions he assigned certain persons to steal the Trust, and the Trust was stolen."

According to this account, the body of the Bab was transferred from one resting place to another, and found little rest. According to the later Baha'i accounts, Abdu'l-Baha had the body brought to Akka in 1899, and arranged for its final interment in a beautiful mausoleum on Mt. Carmel near Haifa in 1910. It is said that the body was laid facing Mecca, as is the Muslim custom of burial. But who can prove that the remains conveyed to Akka and buried on Mt. Carmel were those of Sayyid Ali Muhammad the Bab?

NOTES

1. *New History*, pp. 42-44, Mirza Jani in *New History*, pp. 360-361.

2. For explanation of the "Letters" see Chapter IV.

3. The story of Qurratu'l-Ayn is related in *New History*, pp. 270-284. See also Browne in *A Traveller's Narrative*, pp. 309-314.

4. *Qisasu'l-Ulama*, quoted in *A Traveller's Narrative*, p. 198, Subh-i-Azal in *New History*, pp. 403-404.

5. *Azal's Notes*, p. 859.

6. *New History*, pp. 357-358.

7. Mirza Jani in *New History*, pp. 357-359, Browne in *New History*, pp. 359-360, *Gobineau, I*, pp. 208-211.

8. *Gobineau I*, pp. 208-211, Mirza Jani in *New History*, p. 357, *Azal's Notes*, p. 862.

9. Mirza Jani in *New History*, p. 359.

10. Avareh in *Kashfu'l-Hiyal*, p. 28. The bestowal of the title "Baha" by Qurratu'l-Ayn is confirmed by Abdu'l-Baha's aunt in her reply to him inviting, her to become a Baha'i - *Tanbihu'n-Na'imin*, p. 5. See *Azal's Notes*, p. 865 and *Materials*, pp. 226-227.

11. Mirza Jani in *New History*, pp. 360, 378.

12. Ibid., pp. 358-359.

13. Browne in *A Traveller's Narrative*, p. 32, note 2.

14. Mirza Jani in *New History*, pp. 50, 361.

15. *Gobineau I*, pp. 217-219.

16. Ibid., pp. 219-222.

17. Browne in *New History*, p. 361, note 1, *Azal's Notes*, pp. 863-864.

18. Mirza Jani in *New History*, p. 362, *New History*, p. 59.

19. Ibid., p. 362, Persian Introduction to *Noqtatu'l-Kaf*, p. Sim Ha.

20. *New History*, p. 69.

21. Mirza Jani in *New History*, p. 363.

22. *Gobineau I*, pp. 244-245.

23. *New History*, pp. 95, 363.

24. Ibid., p. 84.

25. Mirza Jani in *New History*, p. 365.

26. *New History*, pp. 86-87, *Gobineau I*, pp. 261-262, Subh-i-Azal in *New History*, 409-410.

27. *New History*, pp. 88, 89, 366, *Gobineau I*, pp. 263-264.

28. *A Traveller's Narrative*, p. 179.

29. Mirza Jani in *New History*, pp. 378-380, *Azal's Notes*, p. 490.

30. Mirza Jani in *New History*, p. 379, *New History*, p. 65.

31. Mirza Jani in *New History*, p. 380.

32. *New History*, pp. 144 ff., Mirza Jani in *New History*, p. 371, Browne in *J.R.A.S. 1897*, pp. 761-827, *Gobineau I*, pp. 272-290.

33. *A Traveller's Narrative*, p. 217, *New History*, p. 261, Mirza Jani in *New History*, p. 370.

34. *New History*, pp. 250-267, Mirza Jani in *New History*, pp. 369-370, Browne in *A Traveller's Narrative*, pp. 211-217.

35. Summary by Browne from *New History*, p. 266, in *A Traveller's Narrative*, p. 216.

36. Since in many of the more recent Baha'i publications reference has been made to "the 20,000 Baha'i martyrs" in Iran, it is necessary to remind the reader that none of those who gave their lives in the struggles described in this chapter were Baha'is. They were all Babis, and owed no allegiance to Baha. And the number of the Babis who lost their lives was probably less than 5,000.

37. *New History*, pp. 116-131, 370.

38. Browne in *New History*, p. 280, note 2, *Nasikhu't-Tawarikh* quoted in *A Traveller's Narrative*, pp. 183-184.

39. *Gobineau I*, pp. 300-303.

40. *New History*, pp. 292-293, *Gobineau I*, pp. 292-307.

41. *New History*, pp. 294-296, *Nasikhu't-Tawarikh*, quoted in *A Traveller's Narrative*, p. 182.

42. *New History*, p. 298.

43. Subh-i-Azal, *New History*, p. 412.

44. Aqa is a title used in Iran equivalent to Sir or Mr.

45. *New History*, p. 299, Mirza Jani in *New History*, p. 381, *Testamentary Dispositions of the Bab* addressed to Subh-i-Azal, in *Azal's Notes*, pp. 550-880, Letter of Dr. Sa'eed Khan to the author. Sayyid Husayn was killed in the Teheran massacre of 1852 (note #50).

46. Browne in *A Year Amongst the Persians*, p. 64, *New History*, pp. 299-308, Mirza Jani in *New History*, pp. 382-383, Browne in *New History*, p. 301, note 1, Haji Sulayman Khan to Mirza Jani in *New History*, pp. 309-310.

47. *Gobineau I*, p. 310, Avareh in *Kashfu'l-Hiyal*, p. 142.

48. Mirza Jani in *New History*, p. 383.

49. *New History*, pp. 311-312, *A Traveller's Narrative*, p. 46, note 1.

50. Browne in *A Traveller's Narrative*, pp. 329 (4) and 332 (26) and 330 (13).

51. *Azal's Notes*, pp. 884-889, *Epistle of the Bab to Sulayman Khan* in *J.R.A.S. July 1892*, p. 481, Browne in *A Traveller's Narrative*, p. 110, note 4.

52. *Azal's Notes*, p. 889, which contain an appendix with the Persian text of Subh-i-Azal's statement, in the handwriting of his son Mirza Ridwan Ali. See *A Traveller's Narrative*, p. 46, note 1. See also Appendix II, #37.

4

The Doctrines and Decrees of the Bab

Before continuing the history of the Babi movement after the death of its founder, we must pause to give an account of the Bab's teachings and precepts. This is no easy task, for the writings of the Bab in which his doctrines are expounded were very numerous, and the style is sometimes most difficult. The Bab wrote in both Persian, which was his mother tongue, and in Arabic the language of the Koran, which to most of the people in Iran was a foreign and largely unknown tongue. Many of the Bab's books were not preserved by his followers, but there are a number of volumes which are still in existance today. These are rare, and with a few exceptions, are in manuscript and have never been translated or printed.(1) Had it not been for the labors of several western scholars, notably the Comte de Gobineau, Professor Edward G. Browne and M. A.L.M. Nicholas, little would have been known in the west of the beliefs and ideas which the Bab left as a heritage to his followers. To Browne, the Comte de Gobineau, and particularly to Mr. Jelal Azal, I am indebted for most of the material in this chapter.

To his earlier books the Bab gave distinctive names, such as "Commentary on the Suratu'l-Yusuf." However, most of the later writings were included under the term *"Bayan"* (Utterance, Exposition). The Bab himself classified all his writings under five categories:(2) 1) Verses in the style of the Koran, 2) Prayers and supplications, 3) Commentaries, 4) Scientific treatises, and 5) Persian treatises. According to Browne,(3) the book known as the *"Persian Bayan"* is "the most systematic, the most coherent, and the most intelligible of the Bab's works." Professor Browne has published in English a very extensive analytical Index of its contents which fills forty large pages, from reading which it is possible for one who does not know Persian to gain some conception of the nature and extent of the Bab's amazing cogitations. (4) The Bayan is, says Browne, a conglomeration of doxologies, mystical rhapsodies, expositions, admonitions, precepts, doctrine and prophecy, much of which was to him "of almost inconceivable incomprehensibility."

In the opinion of the Bab, however, the Bayan has no equal, for it is incomparable and inimitable.(5) He says that if all creatures on earth should unite, they could not produce the like of it. It is identical in essence with the Gospel and the Koran. Whoever believes in it is in Paradise. It includes all things. It must be written in the best handwriting (or may be printed), and carefully preserved. It is to be bound in nineteen volumes. The believer is to read 700 verses of the Bayan night and morning, and if he cannot do this he is to mention God 700 times by saying *"Allahu Azhar"* (God is Most Manifest).

For the historian, one of the most important matters to be considered in a study of the Bab's teachings is his claim for himself. In Chapter I it was explained that the Shi'ite Muslims of Iran and Iraq believe in five or six Great Prophets, who in succession brought God's laws to men and established God's rule on earth, the last and greatest of whom was Muhammad. They also believe that the Imams, a line of twelve (or seven) descendants of Muhammad, have the same rank as Muhammad, and differ from him only in that they did not bring new laws to replace the Koran,

which are to be in effect till the Day of Resurrection.
Shi'ites eagerly await the return of the last Imam,
whom they call the Mahdi and the Qa'im, who is said
to be alive and in hiding somewhere. The beliefs of
the Shaykhis also were mentioned, who attributed divinity to the Imams, and held that there must always
be on earth one who is a channel of grace between the
Hidden Imam and believers, and who understood the
Resurrection predicted by Muhammad not as physical but
spiritual. How did Sayyid Ali Muhammad of Shiraz
relate himself to these various conceptions?

As was explained in Chapter II, convinced that he
had a divine mission, Sayyid Ali Muhammad appropriated
to himself all the names and titles which Shi'ites had
used in connection with their beliefs regarding the
Absent Imam, such as Bab, Mahdi, Proof of God, Remnant
of God, etc. As a result, some of those who believed
on him as well as most unbelievers assumed that he was
using these terms in the sense in which the Shi'ites
used them, and that he was claiming to be either a
Gate to the knowledge of the Absent Imam, or else the
Imam himself whose coming had been so long awaited.

There are indications, however, that from the beginning of his mission the young man from Shiraz in making
use of Shi'ite terminology intended something different,
and did not limit his mission to Shi'ite conceptions
and expectations. In his *First Book* written in Arabic
before his declaration in Shiraz on May 23, 1844,
Sayyid Ali Muhammad while calling himself the Bab
suggested that he had a universal mission, claimed to
be the "Point"(6) (the significance of which term will
be explained later), and commanded the entire company
of monarchs to convey his message to the peoples of
the East and the West.

Moreover, there was no expectation among the
Shi'ites that the Hidden Imam would on his appearing
give new laws to men, for it was assumed that the
Koranic laws were God's final revelations and would
never be replaced by others. But when Sayyid Ali
Muhammad wanted to convince men that he had a divine
mission, what did he do? He did just what the Prophet

Muhammad had done, he pointed to his verses and writings, saying that no one else could produce the like of them. He also began to issue laws and regulations for all aspects of the life of men, both religious and social and civil, as Muhammad had done. And his verses in Arabic were in imitation of the Koran, with which he said his Bayan was identical. In his book the *Seven Proofs* he argued that if it was a miracle, as Muslims agree it was, that Muhammad produced a small book (the Koran) in his native tongue, it is surely a greater miracle that a young man from Iran should be able in a few hours to write thousands of verses in Arabic, which to him was a foreign language, and produce a huge book like the Bayan, which surpasses the Koran in spiritual knowledge and eloquence. The Bab definitely considered himself to be not an Imam, but a Prophet superior to Muhammad.(7)

It seems clear that the Bab's chief disciples early came to understand that their Master was greater than an Imam. When Mulla Sadiq inserted his name in the call to prayer (Chapter II), he proclaimed "Ali Muhammad is the Gate of God (*Babu'llah*)," that is, the Manifestation of God. It is said that at the Badasht Conference Qurratu'l-Ayn explained to the other Babis that the Bab had come to inaugurate a new prophetic dispensation, which had taken the place of the Koranic dispensation inaugurated by Muhammad, and that some of those present therefore considered themselves free from the Islamic regulations.

From his declaration in 1844 till 1848 Sayyid Ali Muhammad made himself known as the Bab. Then, while still in Maku, he proclaimed that he was the Qa'im and Mahdi.(8) It has been generally supposed that he was using these terms with their Shi'ite meaning, and that he who had till now claimed to be the Gate (Bab) to the Hidden Imam at this time put forth a higher claim, namely, that he was himself the Imam, who was commonly called the Mahdi or Qa'im. However, in making this declaration the Bab adopted the title Qa'im (He Who Ariseth) with a new meaning, for in the Bayan he stated that it meant "He who prevails over all men, whose arising is the Resurrection."(9) The Bayan

makes it quite clear that the Bab claimed to be a
Major Prophet.(10)

What then of the orthodox Shi'ite belief that
Muhammad is the last of the Great Prophets? Here the
Bab followed the Shaykhis who maintained that the
Shi'ites were mistaken. They held that when Muhammad
predicted the Day of Resurrection, he was really foretelling the coming of another Prophet who would give
new life to the spiritually dead people of the world.
The Bab claimed to be such a Prophet, and not merely
a Great Prophet, but the Manifestation of the Divine
Will. For an understanding of this doctrine an explanation is necessary.

It is known to students of religion in the Middle
East that much of the teachings of the early Gnostics
and Neo-Platonists was carried over into Islam, and
even today occupies a central place in the philosophy
of the Sufis and Hukama of Iran. The Bab based his
system of doctrine upon these ancient Gnostic conceptions, so that there was little that was new in the
Babi theology.(11) According to the Bab's doctrine,
God while comprehending all things is himself incom-
prehensible. Since the Divine Essence cannot be known
by man, "knowledge of God" means only "knowledge of
the Manifestation of God." From time to time in history, God's Primal Volition (*Mashiyya*), which is an
emanation from the Divine Essence, and by which all
things were created, manifests itself in Prophets who
appear among men, and to know these Manifestations is
to know God. The Divine Volition when manifested in
the Prophet is called the *Nuqta* (Point) of each
prophetic cycle.

For an understanding of this basic Babi belief we
can do no better than to quote several portions of
Azal's Notes:(12) "The Divine Will (*Irada*) can in no
wise be revealed except through the will of the Volition (*Mashiyya*)..... There is One Volition which
manifests itself through One Author (the Manifestation)
in each theophanic cycle. There can be no two Suns of
Truth and no two Authors in one theophanic cycle.....
All that is in the macrocosm is in the Bayan; all that

is in the Bayan is summed up in a prescribed verse;
all that is in the verse is synthesized in the formula
Bismillah ['In the Name of God', a phrase frequently
found in the Koran and often repeated by Muslims]; and
all the Letters in *Bismillah* are created from the Point
of the [Arabic] Letter BA in *Bismillah*, and returns
unto it. The Letter BA is composed of a single straight
line with a diacritical point directly beneath it (ـٮ).
The Point differentiates the Letter BA from its fellows
[other letters], and is in reality its essence. This
Point (*Nuqta*) is the Station of the Volition of the
Divine Manifestation. The Author of the Age is the
Point. The Point is like the Sun, and the other Letters
of *Bismillah* are like Mirrors placed before it. The
whole Bayan is but the evolution of this Point.(13)
That is why the Bab calls himself the Point, the Primal
Point, the Letter BA, the Point of the Bayan..... The
Author of the Age, who is the Bab in the Bayanic dis-
pensation, is the Living (*Hayy*)."

   Thus, according to this doctrine, Adam, who was
supposed by the Bab to have lived 12,210 years before
him, was the Point of the first cycle of which we have
knowledge (there were other worlds before Adam). Later,
Abraham, Moses, Jesus and Muhammad appeared, each one
being the Point of his particular Manifestation. These
Major Manifestations are all one, as the sun of yesterday is one with the sun of today. The mortal form of
the Manifestation changes, but the Volition is the same.
The earlier Manifestations all exist for the later ones,
each is more perfect than its predecessor, and each
attests the preceding Manifestation and predicts the
one to follow. The Bab compares the Major Manifestations to a boy, who as Adam was a mere embryo, as Jesus
was ten years of age, as Muhammad was eleven, and as
the Bab was twelve years of age. From this we see that
the Bab thought the Manifestations appeared about every
one thousand years (a thousand years representing one
year in the life of the boy), and he considered himself
to be the greatest Manifestation which had till then
appeared. As Browne says:(14) "The theory now advanced
by the Baha'is that the Bab considered himself as a
mere herald or forerunner of the Dispensation which
Baha'u'llah was shortly to establish, and was to him

god wears his sunglasses at night.

what John the Baptist was to Jesus Christ, is.....
devoid of historic foundation. In his own eyes, as
in the eyes of his followers, Mirza Ali Muhammad
inaugurated a new Prophetic Cycle, and brought a new
Revelation, the Bayan, which abrogated the Koran, as
the Koran had abrogated the Gospels."

The Bab did not imagine, however, that his would
be the final Manifestation. As the Sun of Truth had
risen again and again in ages past, each Manifestation
more perfect than the one which preceded it, so it
would continue to arise in ages to come. Hence the
Bab spoke of the Prophet in the next Resurrection as
"He-Whom-God-Will-Manifest." One of the striking
features of the Bab's writings is the frequent reference which is made to this greater Manifestation which
is to follow him. In the *Persian Bayan* alone the term
He-Whom-God-Will-Manifest is found some seventy times.
(15) The People of the Bayan, as the followers of the
Bab are called, must all accept Him, and not be like
the Jews who rejected Jesus, and the Christians who
rejected Muhammad, and the Muslims who have rejected
him the Bab. He-Whom-God-Will-Manifest is divine, and
is one with the Point of the Bayan and all other Manifestations. All previous Manifestations were created
for Him, and one verse revealed by Him is better than
a thousand Bayans. If one should hear a single verse
from Him, and recite it, it is better than that he
should recite the Bayan a thousand times. He only can
abrogate the Bayan.(16) He will arise suddenly, and
no one can claim falsely to be He. Only God knows the
time of His coming, but the Bab refers to the time by
the number of the words *Ghiyath* and *Mustaghath*. Each
letter of the Arabic alphabet has a numerical value,
and the letters of these words have the value of 1511
and 2001 respectively. It is clear, therefore, that
the Bab expected the next Manifestation after 1511 and
before 2001 years.

In the *Persian Bayan* we read:(17) "If He shall
appear in the number of *Ghiyath* and all shall enter
in, not one shall remain in the Fire [unbelief]. If
He tarry until [the number of] *Mustaghath*, all shall
enter in, not one shall remain in the Fire, but all

shall be transformed into His Light [belief]." When
He comes the Tree of the Bayan will bear its fruit.
It is clear that the Bab assumed that his dispensation
would last as long as those of the previous Major
Manifestations. He expected that Iran would adopt
his religion and laws, and he wrote detailed regulations for the conduct of the Babi Theocratic Society.

In every Manifestation of Deity, the person or
"Point" has two stations: 1) the station of divinity
in the realm of names and attributes, where he is the
Mouthpiece of God, and says, as the Bab did: "Verily,
I am God; there is no other God but me; all beside me
is my creation;"(18) and 2) the station of humanity
in which he as a creature worships God. The Bab as
the Point embodied in himself the whole Manifestation.
He was dependent on God only, and all others were
created by him and were dependent on him. His
followers usually referred to him as "His Holiness
the Point." He was also called "The Reminder," "The
Most High" and "The Tree of Truth."(19) One of the
many titles for the Twelfth Imam was "The Remnant of
God," and this title also the Bab used for himself.(20)

One of the interesting and unique aspects of the
Bab's system was the order of "The Letters of the Living," who were the first eighteen persons to believe
on him. He, the Sun of Truth, the Living (*Hayy*),
shone on them and gave them life,(21) and they became
Mirrors reflecting his light. There were 18 Letters,
because the numerical value of the Arabic letters in
Hayy is 18. The Letters were not a part of the Major
Manifestation, as has been sometimes erroneously
supposed, but were Minor Manifestations. The Bab was
not dependent on them, but they depended on him. The
18 Letters with the Bab make up the number 19, which
is the numerical value of the Arabic letters in *Wahid*
(One, Unique, i.e., God). The names of all the Letters
are not known. Mirza Yahya (Subh-i-Azal) and his older
brother Mirza Husayn Ali (Baha) were not among the
Letters,(22) and only later became followers of the
Bab. Most of the Letters died in the fighting in
Mazanderan.(23) When they died the Bab did not appoint
others in their places.

The Eighteen Letters of the Living, according to
the Bab, were the "return" of Muhammad, his daughter
Fatima, the twelve Imams, and the four Babs who had
been the intermediaries between the Hidden Imam and
the Shi'ites.(24)   Mulla Husayn, the First Letter,
entitled Babu'l-Bab, claimed to be the return of the
Imam Husayn, grandson of Muhammad.   Mulla Muhammad
Ali, the Last Letter, called Quddus, was thought to
be the return of Muhammad.   Since, according to this
doctrine, Muhammad and all the Imams "returned" as
Letters of the Living, it is evident that the Bab did
not consider himself the return either of the Twelfth
Imam or of the Prophet Muhammad.   He claimed to be
the same Sun which had risen as Muhammad, but was not
his "return."   What the distinction was is not clear
to the author.   Likewise, Qurratu'l-Ayn, the only
woman to become a Letter, was the return of Fatima,
the daughter of Muhammad and the mother of the Imams
Hasan and Husayn.   Other believers beside the Letters
were thought to be the return of saints of the past,
while notorious unbelievers were thought by some
Babis to be the return of Pharoah and other enemies
of the truth.

It is difficult to determine exactly what was
meant by "return" when the word was used by the Babis.
In some instances it seems that it approximates the
doctrine of transmigration of souls, but in other
cases it implies an identy of situation and disposition rather than of soul.   Thus when Quddus (Holy)
was killed at Shaykh Tabarsi the signs of holiness
according to Mirza Jani, passed at once to Subh-i-Azal,
who became his "return."   Professor Browne interprets
this to mean that the virtues and gifts of the martyred
saint were transferred to Subh-i-Azal, who was hundreds
of miles away.(25)   "Return," says Mr. Azal,(26) "is
the appearance of another person, born of other parents, but inspired by God with the same spirit and
power.   This coming again of these persons was fulfilled in the appearance of the Letters of the Living."

As for the Babi doctrine of the Resurrection, which
was thought to be the coming of a new Manifestation,
the Bab held that the length of each Resurrection Day

was the period of time from the appearance of a Manifestation till his death. Thus the Resurrection foretold by Muhammad began with the declaration of the Bab
on May 23, 1844, and it ended with his death on July 8,
1850. As the fruit of Islam is gathered in the Bayanic
Resurrection, so the fruit of the Bayan will be gathered
in the next Resurrection, namely, the appearance of Him-
Whom-God-Will-Manifest. The Bab predicted that this
coming Resurrection would last 19 years. "Meeting with
God" in the Resurrection means meeting the new Manifestation. Between the bright Days of Resurrection are
long dark periods of night.(27)

Likewise, the Islamic doctrines of the Last Judgment, the Trumpet, the Bridge across which men must
pass to Paradise, the Scales in which God weighs men's
actions, the pleasures of Heaven and the pains of Hell,
are understood in an allegorical manner. The Bab says
that the Day of Judgment is not different from any
other day - it passes, and most men are unaware of its
coming. According to the Bab, it was because people
were looking for a literal fulfilment of prophecy that
they always failed to recognize the new Manifestation
when he appeared. Had they interpreted these predictions properly, the Jews would not have rejected Jesus,
nor the Christians Muhammad, nor the Muslims Sayyid
Ali Muhammad. Because they were looking for outward
signs instead of inward reality they failed to believe
and be saved.

Though doctrinal discussions, mystical meditations
and countless prayers for use when visiting sacred
shrines and on other occasions occupy a large place in
the Bab's writings, he gave also many specific directions for the life of his followers here on earth. He
proposed, as Muhammad had done, to set up a universal
Theocratic Society, and issued laws for the regulation
of both civil and religious affairs of the people of
Bayan. We can mention only the principal provisions
of the new system.

Since the numerical value of the word *Wahid* (Unity)
is 19, the Bab decreed that all activities of the
People of the Bayan should be governed by groups of
19 persons. For instance, each city and village was

to have one or more temples for worship, each of which
was to be in charge of 19 attendants. Shrines were to
be erected only over the graves of the Bab and the 18
Letters, and these 19 Holy Places would embrace under
their shadow the graves of other martyrs and holy men.
The holy places of previous dispensations were to be
no longer preserved. All believers living within 250
miles of the Bab's tomb must visit it every year, provided they are in good circumstances, and remain for
at least ten days.(28) Also, they must visit the tombs
of the 18 Letters, travelling if possible on foot.
Pilgrims to these Holy Places must give gifts to each
of the 19 guardians in each shrine.

Moreover, believers who are in good circumstances
must once in their lifetime visit the "Place of the
House," or "God's House," which is the Bab's birth-
place. The place changes in each Manifestation. In
that of Muhammad it was in Mecca, and in that of the
Bab it is in Shiraz. Those believers whose country
is separated by sea from Shiraz are excused from making this pilgrimage, and all women are discouraged
from going to the House. Residents of Shiraz are to
visit the House every year, and give gifts to each of
the 19 guardians. The House is the *qibleh*, or prayer
direction, and Babis must face it in worship and be
buried facing it when they die.

In addition to the pilgrimages to the 19 shrines and
the House in Shiraz, yet another was required, namely,
that to the "Place of the Blow" in Tabriz. This was
the house in which the Bab got the bastinado after his
first trial. Every believer residing in Tabriz and
within a radius of 412 miles of Tabriz, who has reached
the age of 29 and is in good circumstances, was required
to visit this Place every year and remain there 19 days
and perform the prescribed rites. Those who are too
poor to do this must perform the rites at home.

Non-Babis were not to be permitted to reside in the
dominions of a Babi monarch, the inhabitants of which
profess the Babi faith. And no unbeliever was to
reside in Fars, Central Iran, Khurasan, Mazanderan and
Azarbaijan, the provinces of Iran where the Babi faith

had first been propagated. However, non-Babis who carry on business which benefits Babis are exempted from these prohibitions.

The Bab placed great importance upon talismans. Since numbers and names were thought to represent the realities of things, all believers were commanded to wear certain amulets and charms and seals designed by the Bab himself. Charms were to be tied about the necks of infants. It seemed to Gobineau(29) that the Bab wished to revive the ancient paganism of Chaldea which had long been lying dormant, for in his opinion the Babi system was full of animistic practices, and even polytheistic features were not wanting.

A Babi monarch was authorized to seize the properties of non-Babis in his dominions, but if they embraced the Babi faith their properties were to be restored. In the event of the conquest of a country by Babi armies, the most priceless property was to be reserved for the Bab, if he is alive. If he is dead, it is to be held for Him-Whom-God-Will-Manifest. Subject to this reservation, one-fifth of the value of all property so taken was to be applied 1) to the marriages of the People of the Bayan, 2) to grants to the author of the victory, and to his men, and 3) the residue was to be kept for the erection of shrines not yet erected, or for distribution to all the People of the Bayan.

It is not clear how these regulations about conquest of countries and division of booty were to be reconciled with other commands in the Bayan, such as: "No one is to be slain for unbelief, for the slaying of a soul is outside the religion of God.....and if anyone commits it he is not, and has not been, of the Bayan." Coercion for the purpose of conversion to the Babi faith was forbidden. Also, the carrying of instruments of war was forbidden, except in time of necessity and fighting. As far as is known, the Bab did not either encourage his followers who fought so furiously for his cause in Mazanderan and Zanjan, nor did he forbid them to use the sword. Perhaps the prohibition of slaying written by the Bab at the time when the fighting was

going on indicated his disapproval of what his followers were doing. However, if he had clearly forbidden
them to use the sword there would probably have been
far fewer Babi "martyrs."

Whatever severity might be used toward unbelievers,
the Bab enjoined the greatest kindness and gentleness
toward brothers in the faith. He did not authorize
corporal punishment or imprisonment or the use of force,
and capital punishment had no place in his sytem of
government. If taxes were not paid they were not to
be forcibly collected. The only punishments appointed
for the People of the Bayan were fines, and prohibition for men to approach their wives, who presumably
did not share their guilt. It is not clear how these
punishments were to be administered.

It seems that the Bab may have wished to abolish
the outward forms of religion which have played so
important a part in the lives of many Muslims. This,
however, would have been unacceptable to most of his
followers, and so he contented himself with lightening
somewhat the burden of ceremonialism. For Shi'ites
the problem of ceremonial purity is an important one,
since swine, dogs, blood, dead bodies, excrement and
many other things are considered unclean. If anyone
becomes defiled by contact with an unclean object or
person he must make ablution in a prescribed manner in
order to become clean again. The Bab abolished these
regulations, and pronounced all things clean for the
People of the Bayan, thereby making ceremonial ablutions unnecessary. He decreed that an unclean object
may be made clean by saying over it sixty-six times
the name of God, or by exposing it to the action of
the sun, or the earth, air, fire or water, all of which
are clean. Minute directions are given regarding certain very personal matters.

The People of the Bayan were permitted to deal in
business with unbelievers, though they are unclean, and
their property is unclean. For any property transferred by them to believers becomes clean "because of
the honor accorded to it by reason of the association
with the Babi faith."

While regulations regarding ceremonial purity were abolished, the Bayan laid great stress on cleanliness, which was said to be the nearest access to God, and the best of acts of devotion. Every village was to have a hot bath house. Every believer was required to wash himself frequently, remove hair and apply henna to his body, and cut his nails.

The Muslim worship which the Shi'ites are required to perform at least three times each day in the Arabic language facing Mecca was abolished by the Bab. There was to be no congregational worship, like that in the mosques on Friday, except for the dead. Whether in the place of worship or at home, worship was to be performed individually, and so there was no need for an order of clergy to lead the worshippers. The one time of required worship is noon, when the "Unity Prayer" was to be recited. This act of worship is based on the number of *Wahid* (One), which is 19, and consists of 19 prostrations made as the worshipper presumably faces the House of the Bab in Shiraz. The words to be spoken in Arabic 19 times in this daily act of worship were as follows: "God witnesseth that there is no god but He: to Him belongeth creation and command. He quickeneth and causeth to die: then He causeth to die and quickeneth, and verily He is the Living, who dieth not. In His grasp is the dominion of all things: He createth what He pleaseth by His command: verily He has power over all things." (*Persian Bayan*, VII, 19 and other writings of the Bab).

The Bab changed also the Muslim salutation "*Salam Alaykum*" (Peace be to you). In the *Persian Bayan* VI, 5 he directed that the salutation spoken by men should be "*Allahu Akbar*" (God is Most Great), and the reply should be "*Allahu A'zam*" (God is Most Mighty). Women should say "*Allahu Abha*" (God is Most Splendid), with the reply "*Allahu Ajmal*" (God is Most Beautiful).

The Muslim month of fasting, Ramazan (Arabic *Ramadan*) lasts a full lunar month, and when it falls in summer the faithful must refrain from taking food and drink for almost eighteen hours each day for 28 days. The Bab reduced the Fast to one Bayanic month of 19 days,

making it last from sunrise to sunset. And since the
Babi Fast always comes in the spring of the year, and
is the last month of the Babi year, which immediately
precedes No Ruz, the New Year Festival (March 21), it
does not last in Iran longer than twelve hours. As
in the Muslim Fast, eating and drinking is permitted
at night.

The Bab placed great importance upon marriage, which
he made obligatory upon all believers. At the age of
eleven, or at latest when they reach the age of puberty,
they must marry. In the cities the man at marriage
must give to the woman a minimum of 19 and a maximum
of ninety-five *mithqals* of gold, and in the rural areas
the same amount of silver.(30) A man was permitted to
have two wives, but polygamy was discouraged, and the
form of concubinage permitted by Shi'ite law was
strictly forbidden. The Bab himself had at least two
wives. Divorce was permitted only when the parties
had waited a full year. If one of the parties in marriage should die, the widower must remarry within
ninety days, and the widow within ninety-five days.

Though the Bab had no children of his own except an
infant who died, he showed great concern for the training of children. He forbade the beating of boys by
their masters, and all other cruel punishments. It is
probable that his emphasis on kindness and love, as
well as his attitude toward women and children, had
been influenced by his reading of the New Testament,
which was translated into Persian in Shiraz by Henry
Martyn nine years before the Bab was born there, and was
published four years later. The use of the veil by
women, according to the Muslim custom, was forbidden
by the Bab, and men and women were permitted to associate with one another freely, but to avoid all over-
familiarity. The Bab had seen Christians in Isfahan
and Azarbaijan, and in the Bayan he spoke favorably of
their cleanliness and dignity, and was no doubt impressed by their customs. But he stated that in spite of all
their good qualities they are still in the Fire (unbelief), because they did not accept Muhammad, who is
superior to Jesus.

Since the numerical value of the Arabic word *Wahid* (One, i.e., God the One) is nineteen, the Bab thought that everything should be arranged on the basis of the number 19. He accordingly proposed a new calendar with 19 months of 19 days each (19 x 19 = 361) "..... that all may advance through the 19 degrees of the Letters of the Unity from the point of entrance [into the sign of] the Ram to the limit of its course.....in the sign of the Fish." By rejecting the Muslim lunar calendar, and making the ancient Iranian New Year (No Ruz), which usually falls on March 21, the vernal equinox, the beginning of the Babi year, it seems that the Bab wished to demonstrate his patriotic feelings. (31) The first Babi month is called Baha (Splendor), and is the special month of the Point of the Manifestation, who is the Bab in the Bayanic dispensation. The first day of the first month, which is No Ruz, is called the Day of God, and is the day of the Point (the Bab).

The declaration of the Bab in Shiraz on May 23, 1844 A.D. was on Jamad-i-Awwal 5, 1260 A.H., and it has been generally supposed that the Babi Era began on that date, or on the No Ruz which preceded it (March 20, 1844).(31) However, from the Bab's personal Diary, which is in existence, we see that he intended that the Bayanic Era should begin just six years after his declaration. That is, according to the Bab, Jamad-i-Awwal 5, 1266 A.H. (March 19, 1850 A.D.), which was No Ruz in that year, was the first day of the month Baha in year one of the Babi Era (or Farvardin 1, 1229 of the Iranian solar year). This is confirmed in the Bab's *Book of Names of All Things*, and also in the *Tablet of the Temple of the Religion*. Thus Sayyid Ali Muhammad celebrated the beginning of the new Era only four months before his execution.(32)

The Bab made no provision for the intercalary days, omitted between 361 and 365 (or 366 in Leap Year). This lack was later remedied by Subh-i-Azal, his successor. It is of interest that the Bab stated that his mission began "1270 years after the mission of Muhammad." For some reason he preferred to date his mission not from the *Hijra* (622 A.D.), but from the beginning of Muhammad's mission, which the Bab dated ten years prior to the Sojourn to Madina.

Not only did the Bab rearrange the calendar on the basis of the numerical value of the letters in *Wahid* (19), he wished everything to be so arranged. The monetary system, weights, measures, taxes, fines, etc. were to be based on the same principle. The Bayan, the Scripture of the new faith, was to have consisted of 19 grand divisions (*wahids*), each containing 19 subdivisions (*babs*). The Bab predicted the coming of the time when "even the pens on the pencase shall be according to the number of the *Wahid* (19)."

The Bab issued many other regulations for his followers, a few of which we will mention. According to his decree, all books revealed by God in previous prophetic dispensations, presumably the Bible and the Koran, have been abrogated by the appearing of the new Manifestation, that is, their validity has been annulled.(33) When God gives a new revelation, namely, the Bayan (which embraces the great mass of writings of the Bab), believers must refer to it alone for guidance. And as the divinely-revealed books of previous dispensations are abrogated by the Bayan, so are the many books written by men who were followers of previous Manifestations. The Bab, therefore, forbade the reading of all non-Babi books, and commanded that they be burned. He no doubt had in mind the countless volumes composed by Shi'ite theologians and philosophers, which presented many conflicting views of religion, and produced not enlightenment but confusion and unbelief. Therefore, believers must read only the Bayan, and books written by eminent Babi scholars under the shadow of the Bayan. No one is permitted to own more than 19 books, the first of which is to be the Bayan, the precepts of which will be binding on believers till the coming of Him-Whom-God-Will-Manifest. For the Bayan is the Straight Path of Truth. It is obligatory for the People of the Bayan to acquire knowledge and impart it to others. Every monarch to emerge in the Bayanic dispensation must choose twenty-five learned men to assist him in the furtherance of

the Babi faith, and in going to the relief of the weak
and needy.

A detailed arrangement for the division of inheritance is prescribed. Contrary to Muslim law, the Bab
made it permissible to take interest on loans. Everyone is required to follow an occupation to earn his
living. Begging is strictly forbidden, but giving of
charity to the poor is enjoined. Believers are to
wear as fine clothing as they can afford, and to use
gold and jewels if they have them. Men must shave
their faces clean, contrary to Muslim custom. Believers
must not sit on the floor like the Muslims, but sit on
chairs. All personal effects must be changed every 19
years. Foreign travel is forbidden, except for business, or for assisting some person. Arms are not to be
carried within the Bayanic state. Every believer must
take a bath every four days, and teeth must be cleaned
after meals.

It was obligatory that every male believer serve
the Point in person for 19 days, but the Point may
grant exemption. The Point must be treated with
great respect, and his family must be honored by all.
Special prayers are to be said for him and his parents. Every believer who has property worth 100
mithqals of gold must set aside the sum of 20 *mithqals*
as the "Right of God." Of this sum, one *mithqal* is to
go to the Point, and one to each of the 18 Letters,
and one is "for God" (perhaps for charity). After the
deaths of the 19, the tax goes to their heirs, or if
they have none, for the marriage of believers, and the
one *mithqal* for God is to be kept for Him-Whom-God-Will-
Manifest, or spent in the work of the Bayan.

Every family must entertain 19 guests every 19 days,
even though they may be able to serve them nothing but
water. The dead are to be washed once, or may be
washed three to five times, and buried in stone coffins, with engraved rings on their fingers. After
burial their graves must be visited by their friends
once every month (of 19 days). The use of opium,
alcohol and tobacco was forbidden. Pack animals were
not to be over-loaded, and cows must not be used for

riding, or for carrying loads. The milk of asses must
not be drunk, and eggs must not be kept where they
will spoil.

Near the end of the *Arabic Bayan* (X,4) the Bab
wrote: "The essence of religion in your beginning and
return consists in your belief in God beside whom
there is no god; then in Him-Whom-God-Will-Manifest
on the Day of Resurrection in your return; then in the
Book God will send down to him; then in Him-Whom-God-
Has-Manifested under the name of.....Sayyid Ali
Muhammad the Bab; and then in that which God has sent
down to him in the Bayan."(34)

This, in brief, is the system of doctrine and of
society and government which Sayyid Ali Muhammad
believed God wished to establish through him in Iran
and throughout the world. It seems that he realized
the need for a spiritual and social reformation in his
country where at that time religion consisted largely
of empty forms of worship, and where there was little
knowledge of the true God, and little love for men.
The reader may judge for himself the adequacy of the
Bab's theology, and of his laws and precepts for
establishing a just and effective social order for
the world.

Whether the Bayanic system was given by revelation
to the Bab from God, or whether it was the utopian
dream of a man long in prison facing death, it never
became a reality. No king ever adopted the Babi
faith and used his authority to propagate it, and no
nation ever attempted to order the life of its people
in accordance with the laws of the Bayan. If the Bab
was indeed, as he thought himself to be, a Major
Manifestation of God, come to establish a new Theocratic Society which would take the place of Islam and
all previous religious systems, and last for at least
1511 years, why were his high hopes for the future not
realized? Whatever one may think of his claims and
his regulations, one cannot but admire the Bab for his
devotion to the cause for which he gave his life.

NOTES

1. For lists and descriptions of books written by the Bab the reader is referred to *A Traveller's Narrative*, pp. 335-347, *J.R.A.S.* 1892, pp. 445-499 and 637-659, *Materials*, pp. 198-208. The books which were printed are the following (*Azal's Notes*, p. 893): *Arabic Bayan, Persian Bayan, Lawh-i-Haykal al-Din* (Tablet of the Temple of the Religion), *Commentary on the First Verse of Lawh-i-Haykal, Panj Sha'n* (Five Grades), *Dala'il-i-Sab'a* (Seven Proofs) in both Persian and Arabic, *Personal Diary of the Bab, Lawh-i-Hurufat* (Tablet of Letters), *Collection of Autograph Epistles of the Primal Point,* and *Sahifa-i-Adliyya.* Both the *Arabic* and the *Persian Bayans* and the *Persian Seven Proofs* were translated in full into French by A. L. M. Nicholas and published (*Materials,* pp. 182, 204). The writing of the *Arabic* and *Persian Bayans* was probably begun when the Bab was in Maku, and continued after his transfer to Chihriq (*Azal's Notes,* p. 894, and Browne in *A Traveller's Narrative,* p. 274). Neither book was completed, for the former ended with XI, 19, and the latter with IX, 10. Each was to have had 19 Divisions (*Wahids*).

2. *Materials*, p. 201, *J.R.A.S.* 1889, p. 893 and 1892, pp. 452, 462 ff.

3. *Materials*, p. 205.

4. Browne in English Introduction to *Nuqtatu'l-Kaf,* pp. LIV-XCV.

5. Ibid., pp. LVIII-LX.

6. *Azal's Notes*, p. 530.

7. *J.R.A.S.* 1889, pp. 916-917.

8. Mirza Jani in *New History*, p. 369, states that the Bab first called himself "Qa'im" in a letter to Mulla Shaykh Ali.

9. *Azal's Notes*, p. 932.

10. Ibid., p. 835. Refer to the *Persian Bayan* in which the Bab states that he is the Gate of God (I,1 and

II,1), the Sun of Truth (IV,6), and the Point of
the Letter BA (II,17, IV,1, VI,13).

11. *Materials*, p. XIV.

12. *Azal's Notes*, pp. 732-736.

13. *Persian Bayan*, III,8.

14. *Nuqtatu'l-Kaf*, English Int., p. XXIV.

15. Ibid., pp. LXIX-LXXII, *A Traveller's Narrative*,
    pp. 347-349.

16. Bab quoted in *Nuqtatu'l-Kaf*, English Int., p.
    LIV.

17. Ibid., pp. XXV-XXVI (*Persian Bayan*, II, 16, 17),
    Azal's Notes, p. 898.

18. *Nuqtatu'l-Kaf*, English Int., p. LXVII.

19. *A Traveller's Narrative*, pp. 229-230, *New History*,
    p. 374.

20. See Appendix II, #55.

21. *Azal's Notes*, pp. 720-721.

22. Browne in Persian Int. to *Nuqtatu'l-Kaf*, p. 35,
    note 5.

23. Subh-i-Azal in *New History*, p. 417.

24. *Azal's Notes*, pp. 744, 856-857.

25. *New History*, p. 380, note 1.

26. *Azal's Notes*, p. 934.

27. Ibid., pp. 753-760. See Appendix II, #47
    for "19 Years."

28. According to the Babis, the tomb of the Bab is
    at Imamzadeh Ma'sum near Teheran, but according
    to the Baha'is it is on Mt. Carmel near Haifa in
    Israel. The graves of most of the Letters are
    unknown. It is evident that the Bab, by these
    provisions, wished to put an end to the Shi'ite
    practice of visiting the numerous shrines of the
    Imams and their descendants in Iran and Iraq.
    Also he wished the pilgrimage to his birthplace
    in Shiraz to take the place of the Muslim pilgrim-
    age to Mecca.

29. *Gobineau*, II, p. 77.

30. One *mithqal* is equivalent to five grams.

31. Browne in *A Traveller's Narrative*, pp. 424-425.

32. *Azal's Notes*, p. 613. See Appendix II, p. 3, #29 and 30.

33. See Appendix II, #64 and #65.

34. The principal sources for the doctrines and regulations contained in this chapter are: 1) Browne's exhaustive Index to the *Persian Bayan* in *Nuqtatu'l-Kaf*, English Introduction, pp. LIV-XCV, 2) *Gobineau's* Chapter XII on the Books and Doctrines of the Babis (II, pp. 43-101), and 3) *Gobineau's* translation of the Babi book which he calls *Kitab-i-Hukkam* (II, p. 219-337). Browne states that the author of this Book of Commandments is the Bab, and he terms the book "the shorter Arabic Bayan" (*J.R.A.S.* 1889, p. 1001). It seems, however, that the book is the *Lawh-i-Haykal al-Din* (Tablet of the Temple of the Religion), which is a summary of his laws, composed by the Bab while he was in Chihriq (*Azal's Notes*, p. 937). And 4) the scholarly and copious Notes supplied to the author by Mr. Jelal Azal, without whose understanding of the Babi history and doctrines the early chapters of this book could not have been thus written. Material related to the Bab is found in many sections of *Azal's Notes*, especially in pp. 125-130, 530-531, 623-624, 687-782, and 829-937.

5
The Vicegerency
of Subh-i-Azal

It is the belief of the Shi'ite Muslims that the
Prophet Muhammad shortly before his death publicly
appointed his son-in-law Ali as his successor, or vicegerent, to become the first Imam, and that Ali and each
of the succeeding Imams in like manner appointed the
men who were to succeed them as the leaders of the believers. Did Sayyid Ali Muhammad, the Point of the new
Manifestation, follow the example of his ancestor
Muhammad, the Point of the preceding Manifestation, in
naming his vicegerent? Yes, he did. Realizing the
certainty of his early death, the Point of the Bayan
did what his followers expected him to do, and appointed
his successor. Accordingly, after the execution of the
Bab in Tabriz on July 8, 1850, Mirza Yahya Subh-i-Azal
became the recognized head of the People of the Bayan,
was accepted by the Babi community as their divinely
ordained ruler, and continued in this position for some
sixteen years. Since the history of this period has
unfortunately been inaccurately related in some of the
books purporting to give a true account of the Babi and
Baha'i movement, it is necessary for us to present in
some detail the established facts.

Mirza Yahya the successor of the Bab was the son of
Mirza Buzurg of the district of Nur in the

province of Mazanderan. He was born in Teheran in
1831 A.D.(1) His father, according to the Babi historian, was "accomplished, wealthy, and much respected,"
but was not a prince,(2) as some have alleged. Mirza
Yahya's mother and father died when he was a child,
and he was committed to the care of his father's second
wife,(3) who, it is said, was warned in a dream of his
future destiny, and showed him the greatest love and
consideration.(4) His education was supervised by his
half-brother Mirza Husayn Ali, the son of Mirza Buzurg
and this second wife, who was thirteen years older than
Mirza Yahya. This half-brother later became known as
Baha, and long after in Akka as Baha'u'llah.(5) In
his history of the Babi movement written about 1851
A.D., Mirza Jani quotes the following statement which
Mirza Husayn Ali had made regarding his younger brother:(6) "I busied myself with the instruction of
Janab-i-Azal.(7) The signs of his natural excellence
and goodness of disposition were apparent in the mirror
of his being. He ever loved gravity of demeanour,
silence, courtesy, and modesty, avoiding the society
of other children, and their behaviour. I did not,
however, know that he would become the possessor of
[so high] a station." This statement shows how amicable were the relations of the two brothers shortly
after the death of the Bab when Mirza Jani penned
these words, and in what high esteem the elder held
the younger.

When Mirza Yahya was still young, his brother used
to bring followers of the Bab to his house in Teheran,
and it was from their conversations that he first
learned of the appearing of the Lord of the Age. He
read some of the Bab's writings, and about 1847 A.D.
became a believer.(8) So great was his attachment to
his Master, whom he had never seen, that when the Bab
commanded his followers to go to Khurasan, the eastern
province of Iran, the seventeen year old youth tried
to obey, but was forbidden by his brother.(9) Later,
however, he went to Mazanderan, and on the way he met
and became acquainted with Hazrat-i-Quddus,(10) and
accompanied him to Barfurush. There he met Qurratu'l-
Ayn. Both these leaders showed him great kindness and
attention, and at the command of Quddus, Qurratu'l-Ayn

conducted Mirza Yahya to the Nur district in Mazanderan.(11)   We have already described in Chapter III
the attempt that he and his brother at a later time
made to reach Shaykh Tabarsi, and their capture and
release.(12)   Of this period Mirza Jani writes:(13)
"I was in attendance on Janab-i-Azal in Mazanderan,
night and day, for four months or more.....He was
filled with ardour and ecstacy, and I found him ever
disposed by nature to devotion and emancipation such
that he utterly disregarded the world and its circumstances.....He showed a wonderful attachment to
Hazrat-i-Quddus, and used often to read aloud with
sweet utterance the homilies and prayers of that
Master of the world."

When the news of the death of Hazrat-i-Quddus in
Mazanderan on May 22, 1849, reached Mirza Yahya he fell
ill for three days.   Then, says Mirza Jani,(14) "the
signs of holiness (*qudsi*) appeared in his blessed form
.....and this event took place in the fifth year of
the Manifestation of the Truth, so that Janab-i-Azal
became the blessed domain of the Will (*Irada*)....."(15)
Sometime after this Mirza Yahya sent a communication
to the Bab in his prison in Chihriq by the hand of
Mirza Ali Sayyah, on reading which the Bab was overcome with joy, for, said he, "the Bayan has now borne
fruit!"   From this saying Mirza Yahya received the
title, "His Highness the Fruit" (*Hazrat-i-Thamara*).
At once the Bab appointed Mirza Yahya as his successor,
(16) giving him high titles, such as "Morning of
Eternity" (*Subh-i-Azal*), "Splendor of God" (*Baha'u'
llah*), "Second Point" (*Nuqta-i-Thani*) and "The One"
(*Wahid*).(17)   It seems that the title *Subh-i-Azal* by
which the Bab's successor is best known was given him
because he rose to prominence in the fifth year of the
Bab's Manifestation (1849 A.D.), which, according to a
well-known tradition, was characterized by the words,
"A Light which shone from the Dawn of Eternity."(18)

The Bab gave written notice of the appointment of
Subh-i-Azal to the Letters of the Living who had survived the fighting in Mazanderan and to other Babi
leaders, as is recorded in old manuscripts.(19)   Also
to his successor-to-be he sent some of his own personal

effects, such as pencases, paper, writings, clothing
and rings, that, as Mirza Jani observes,(20) "the
outward form might correspond with the inward reality,"
intending that "after him Subh-i-Azal should bear the
divine influences." "He also wrote a testamentary
deposition," says Mirza Jani, "explicitly nominating
him [Azal] as his successor." In this connection Mirza
Jani expresses his own conviction that Subh-i-Azal was
himself He-Whom-God-Will-Manifest whose coming the Bab
had predicted, and other Babis shared this opinion with
him.(21) However, in this matter he was mistaken, for
as we have seen in Chapter IV, the Bab did not antici-
pate the appearance of the next Manifestation before
at least 1511 years, and moreover Subh-i-Azal never
made the claim that he was He-Whom-God-Will-Manifest,
and later in his writings he dismissed this opinion as
erroneous.(22)

When Professor Browne visited Subh-i-Azal in
Cyprus in 1896 he was shown the original document,
written and sealed by the Bab himself, in which the
Bab appointed Mirza Yahya Subh-i-Azal as his successor.(23) Browne published a facsimile of a transcript
of the Arabic text, and has translated it as follows:
(24)

"God is Most Great with Uttermost Greatness.

"This is a letter on the part of God, the Protector,
the Self-Existent, to God, the Protector, the Self-
Existent.

"Say, 'All originate from God.' Say, 'All return
unto God.'

"This is a letter from Ali before Nabil [*Nabil* is
numerically equivalent to *Muhammad*, and *Ali before
Nabil* is *Ali Muhammad*], God's Reminder unto the worlds,
unto him whose name is equivalent to the Name of the
One [*Wahíd* = 28 = *Yahya*, the name of Subh-i-Azal], God's
Reminder unto the worlds.

"Say, 'Verily all originate from the Point of Revelation.'

"O Name of the One [Yahya], keep what hath been
revealed in the Bayan, and enjoin it,(25) for verily
thou art a Mighty Way of Truth."

To this document the seal of the Bab was attached.
"Verily I am the Proof of God and His Light."

It is noteworthy that in this document the Bab
addresses Subh-i-Azal with the same high titles that
he claimed for himself, indicating that he considered
his successor to be one with him. The Shi'ites thought
of Muhammad as the Sun, and Ali whom they held to be
his true successor and one with him, as the Moon,
reflecting the Sun's Light. Just so in the Bayanic
Cycle the Bab was thought to be the Sun, and his successor Subh-i-Azal, the "Mirror of the Bayan," was the
Moon, from whom the Light of God shone forth.

The "testamentary deposition" to which Mirza Jani
referred is found in old Babi manuscripts, and a
facsimile of a transcript of it, with an English translation, has been supplied by Mr. Azal.(26) Among
other things the Bab in this document says to Subh-i-
Azal:

"O Name of Eternity [Azal]! Bear witness that there
is no God but me, the Mighty, the Beloved.....God rules
the place of the Manifestation.....as He pleases by His
command.....When [the Command] is cut off from the
throne recite the verses of thy Lord.....Recite thou
for myself every night and day.....and bear witness
that in truth I am alive in the most spendid (*abha*)
horizon and hear whoever makes mention of me.....If
God manifests grandeur in thy days make manifest the
Eight Paths(27).....and if God manifests not grandeur
in thy days, cleave steadfastly to what has been
revealed and change not one letter.....that men disagree not touching the religion of God.....Preserve
thyself.....Then preserve what has been revealed in
the Bayan, and then what is revealed in thy part, for
verily this is that will subsist till the Day of
Resurrection.

"If God cause one like unto thee to appear in thy
days, then he it is to whom shall be bequeathed the

Command [of the Babi Cause] on the part of God.....
But if such an one appears not, know for a surety that
God hath not willed to make Himself known, and render
up the authority to God.....and ordain theWitnesses who
fear God....."

According to this document, the Bab's instructions
to Subh-i-Azal for the period after his death were as
follows: 1) to recite the Bab's verses; 2) to complete the Bayan by writing the eight Sections (Wahid)
which the Bab had left unwritten (there were to be 19
Sections), thus indicating Azal's oneness with the Bab;
3) in case the time should not be propitious to complete the Bayan, to preserve carefully what the Bab
had written, and to preserve himself; 4) if a worthy
person like himself should appear, to appoint him as
his successor - otherwise he is to appoint Witnesses,
and leave the Cause in the hands of God. Subh-i-Azal
evidently did not consider the time propitious, for he
did not complete the Bayan. After the death of the
Bab he did appoint several Witnesses to assist him in
the administration of the Babi Cause, one of whom was
his brother Baha.(28) He did not appoint a successor,
nor did he leave a Will, nor did he appoint Witnesses
with authority to lead the People of the Bayan after
his death. The reason for his inability to do these
things will appear later.

On the death of the Bab the Babi community accepted
Subh-i-Azal and accorded him the high honor which the
Bab had bestowed on him. As is clearly seen in Mirza
Jani's history, the Babis in 1851 A.D. considered
Subh-i-Azal and the Bab to be one. The Comte de
Gobineau, who was in intimate contact with the Babis
of Teheran from 1855 to 1858 confirms the statements
of Mirza Jani.(29) He says that some of the Babis
thought Subh-i-Azal to be He-Whom-God-Will-Manifest,
while others thought him to be a return of the Bab,
and he was the undisputed leader of the Babi movement.
There is not the slightest historical evidence dating
from this period that anyone other than Subh-i-Azal
was appointed or acted as successor to the Bab. As
Professor Browne writes,(30) "The evidence that at
this period, and for some considerable time afterwards,

Subh-i-Azal.....held undisputed sway over the Babi
Church is absolutely conclusive."

It was no easy task to which Subh-i-Azal, as yet
only nineteen years of age, fell heir when his Master
was executed. The Babis were still in arms against
the Iranian government in Zanjan and in other parts of
the country, and were feared and bitterly hated by the
majority of the Muslim population. The Babis returned
this hatred with interest, and considered both Nasiru'd-
Din Shah and the mullas to be enemies of God and worthy
of death because of their rejection of the Divine Manifestation. The new leader realized, however, that it
was not expedient for the Babis to continue further
this conflict with the government, and he issued orders
for his followers to lay aside the sword.(31) He was
obeyed, and there were no more large uprisings after
the ending of the Zanjan conflict. Subh-i-Azal made
some journeys to visit scattered Babi communities for
the purpose of encouraging the believers. He spent
the summer months in the vicinity of Teheran, and in
the winter went to the warmer regions of his native
province of Mazanderan. He was busily occupied in
arranging, transcribing, and circulating among believers the books of the Bab, and in teaching the Babi
doctrines.(32) Though the Prime Minister was very
hostile to the Babis, it seems that for a time there
was little open opposition to and persecution of the
movement, which continued to grow after the execution
of the Bab. It is impossible to estimate accurately
the number of Babis in Iran at this time. Gobineau
thought that there were some five thousand in Teheran.
(33) No doubt there were many times this number in
the provinces. It was during this brief period of comparative quiet (1851-1852) that Mirza Jani wrote his
history *Nuqtatu'l-Kaf*, to which frequent reference has
been made.(34)

While temporarily free from attacks from without,
the Babi community was distrubed by confusion within.
Mirza Jani has described at length(35) the curious
phenomenon of the appearance of a number of men from
among the Babis who revealed verses and claimed to be
Manifestations of God. He tells the stories of two

of them, Zabih and Basir, who thought they were the
return of John the Baptist and the Imam Husayn. "We,
in reading these pages of Mirza Jani's history,"
writes Browne,(36)"cannot but marvel at the chaos of
'Theophanies' which he describes; but he.....sees
therein only a fresh proof of the greatness and dignity of the 'Manifestation' [of the Bab]." Some of
the Babis, jealous of the honor of their Master
Subh-i-Azal, wished to silence these claimants, but
Mirza Jani states that Azal would not permit this,
demanding only that they recognize his authority.

Mr. Azal has suggested(37) that the cause of this
confusion was chiefly lack of understanding of the
station of the Bab. The Babis were all Shi'ites who
believed that after the return of the Twelfth Imam,
the Imam Husayn, grandson of Muhammad, would return
also. Mistakingly thinking that the Bab had been the
Twelfth Imam, some of the Babis were expecting the
Imam Husayn to appear, and each of these rival "Manifestations" claimed to be he. Some of them also
identified the return of Husayn with the coming of
Him-Whom-God-Will-Manifest foretold by the Bab.

Mirza Jani says of Basir,(38) "He announced himself
to be a 'return' of [the Imam] Husayn, which claim was
substantiated by the production of verses, homilies,
and prayers; and he wrote letters to Hazrat-i-Azal and
Janab-i-Baha(39) concerning his Manifestation. Hazrat-
i-Azal in reply honored him with an epistle expressing
his regards....." Other Babis warmly opposed these
new claimants, and others who later advanced claims,
and strife and even murder resulted. All this prolif-
eration of "Manifestations" was of course entirely
contrary to the Bab's doctrine, according to which he
was not the Twelfth Imam but a Major Manifestation like
Jesus and Muhammad, the Sun of Truth, and it was impossible for there to be in the heaven of reality more
than one Sun at a time, and the next Major Manifestation
was not to be expected for at least 1511 years after the
Bab. Moreover, it was the belief of the Bab that
Muhammad and all of the twelve Imams, including the
Imam Husayn,(40) had already returned as his Letters
of the Living. Hence, from the point of view of the

Bayan these claimants were all false pretenders, and
it is surprising that Subh-i-Azal did not deal more
severely with them.

Some later claimants based their pretentions on
the passage in the *Arabic Bayan* (VI,15) which reads:
"In the year nine ye will attain unto all good."(41)
Interpreting this vague prediction as the appearing
of Him-Whom-God-Will-Manifest nine years after the
Bab's declaration in Shiraz in 1844 A.D., they sever-
ally at the appointed time set forth their claims to
be "He," ignoring the clear statements in the Bayan
about the lapse of 1511 years. They also misinter-
preted a communication from the Bab to a Babi leader
entitled Azim regarding the "two Wahids," namely,
Mirza Yahya Darrab and Mirza Yahya Subh-i-Azal, appro-
priating the prediction to themselves.(42)

In spite of these internal problems it seems that
all went fairly well with the Babis till the summer of
1852 A.D., when an event took place which entirely
altered the situation. For some time rumors had been
going about the Teheran bazaar that the Shah was going
to be killed. Finally, on August 15, 1852, as Nasiru'd-
Din Shah was riding out on a hunting expedition in the
hills above Teheran, three men approached him as
though they wished to present a petition. When they
had come quite near, one of them drew a pistol and
fired at the Shah, wounding him in the arm. Then they
attempted to drag him from his horse and to cut his
throat, but the Shah's retainers rushed up and saved
him, killing one of the assassins and capturing the
other two. When they were questioned the two captives
confessed they were Babis, and said that their purpose
was to avenge the death of the Bab. The man who was killed
was the servant of Mulla Shaykh Ali surnamed Azim, a devoted disciple of the Bab, who had been plotting against
the government for some time.(43) The Muslim historian
says that Azim had induced twelve Babis to agree to take
part in the assassination, but only three of them
arrived on time. That this attempt on the life of the
Shah was the result of a deliberate plot on the part of
the Babis, and not the act of a single madman as some
have incorrectly stated, is adequately proved by

Gobineau, who wrote a most vivid description of the
attempted murder.(44) The pistol had been charged
with shot in order that the assassins might fell the
Shah, and then kill him by cutting his throat, as
they had been ordered to do. The Shah, however, was
not seriously wounded.

The excitement and confusion which followed may be
imagined. The gates of Teheran were guarded, and a
systematic search was made in Teheran and throughout
Iran for the Babi leaders, about thirty-five of whom
were arrested. As the days went by the Shah became
more and more terrified over the situation in his
kingdom, and believing, probably with some reason,
that there was a volcano hidden from sight which was
about to erupt and destroy him and his empire, he
resolved to make an exhibit of the Babis whom he had
gotten into his power. He accordingly divided them
up among the different classes of his subjects, giving
one to the Muslim clergy, another to the princes,
another to the nobles, another to the artillery, etc.,
informing all that the measure of their devotion to
their sovereign would be revealed by the zeal with
which they executed these offenders. It seems that
several of the prisoners were able to prove their
innocence, probably by denying that they were Babis,
and they were released. It is possible that a number
of those sentenced to die had no direct part in the
attempt on the life of the Shah, but to be known as a
Babi was sufficient to condemn one.

On September 15, 1852 the execution was carried
out, each group trying to outdo the others in the
barbarity with which they killed their unfortunate
victims. An Austrian officer in the employ of the
Iranian government was so horrified by the unbeliev-
able brutality of the scenes which he witnessed that
he resigned from his position.(45) Twenty-eight Babis
were done to death, one of whom was the beautiful and
gifted Qurratu'l-Ayn, who had for some time been under
arrest and could not have been implicated in the
attempted assassination. Another was Mirza Jani the
historian. Still another was Mulla Shaykh Ali Azim.
Most of the victims showed the greatest courage and

devotion as they faced death, and their bold testimony
won many new converts to their Cause.(46) From this
time on the Babis were more careful than ever to conceal their faith, and were usually ready to deny it
when their lives were in danger. This practice of
dissimulation (taqia) was approved by their leaders,
as it had been previously approved by the Shi'ites.(47)

Subh-i-Azal and his brother Baha were not of those
who perished. The Shah attempted to arrest the leader
of the Babi movement, and offered a large reward for
his capture. But Subh-i-Azal managed to escape in the
garb of a dervish, and made his way to Baghdad in
Turkish territory, for he realized that he could no
longer live in his native land.(48) After his flight
two regiments of royal troops raided his ancestral home
in the district of Nur in Mazanderan in order to capture him and his followers, arrested members of his
family and a number of his relatives and friends, and
brought them to Teheran, where many of them died in
prison.(49) Five of the arrested persons, including
Mirza Husayn Ali Baha, were kept in prison pending
further investigation, there not being sufficient
evidence to incriminate them.(50) After four months
Baha was released.(51) It has been said that in order
to save his life Baha denied that he was a Babi, as
the Bab had ordered his disciples to do at the time
of his execution. This is not improbable, for it
seems that those prisoners who were known to be Babis
were put to death, whether or not they were proved
guilty of implication in the plot to kill the Shah.(52)

It appears that the Russian Legation in Teheran
helped to secure Baha's release on condition that he
leave Iran,(51) and Baha later stated that both Russian
and Iranian officers accompanied him and his family
when he departed from Teheran one month after his
release. He arrived in Baghdad in April, 1853,(53)
where he joined his brother Subh-i-Azal. Soon many
other Babis followed them to Baghdad.

From the beginning of 1853 till the spring of 1863
Baghdad was the seat of the Vicegerency of Subh-i-Azal,
and the center from which secret Babi propaganda was

carried on in Iran and Iraq. We do not possess a full
account of the happenings of these ten years, for
there was no historian like Mirza Jani to leave a
reliable record of events, but the main features of
the story are clear. Subh-i-Azal was looked upon by
the Babi community as their supreme head, one in rank
and authority with the Bab himself. Baha, however,
was not satisfied with this situation. He probably
realized that the Babi Cause in order to survive needed
stronger leadership than his brother Azal was able to
give. He was confident that he had the ability to
supply this need. But it was necessary for the leader
to have a divine appointment on which to base his authority. Did Baha have this? He had received no authority from the Bab, yet he had a growing conviction
that he was the new Manifestation whose coming the Bab
had predicted.

It is said(54) that when Baha was in Karbala in
Iraq in 1851 he met one day in the street Shaykh Hasan-
i-Zunuzi who was eagerly searching for the promised
Imam Husayn. Whereupon Baha confided to him the secret that he was himself the Imam Husayn, but forbade
him to tell others. Also it is said(55) that after
Baha's arrival in Baghdad two years later he disclosed
secretly to his friend Mirza Aqa Jan "a glimpse of the
as yet unrevealed glory of his station," and Aqa Jan
became the first believer. It seems, therefore, that
Baha had determined at some suitable time to make a
claim for himself, and take over the leadership of the
Cause. However, his attitude and conduct were displeas-
ing to the other Babi leaders, who accused him of
gathering about him a crowd of disreputable people to
assist him in his purpose.(56) Those who sided with
Baha replied that this opposition to him by his brother
and other Babis was due to envy of Baha's increasing
influence.

Of this difficult time Baha later wrote:(57) "In
these days such odours of jealously were diffused that
.....from the beginning of the foundation of the world
.....until the present day such malice, envy and hate
have in no wise appeared."

When at the end of the first year in Baghdad the
Babi leaders administered a severe rebuke to Baha for
his conduct, he became angry, and left Baghdad in the
night, telling no one, not even his own family, where
he was going. For two years he lived as a dervish in
the Kurdish mountains in northern Iraq.(58) Finally,
Subh-i-Azal discovered his whereabouts, and wrote to
him to return. Baha obeyed, wrote a letter of repentance to his brother, and came back to Baghdad in the
spring of 1856 A.D.(59)

Subh-i-Azal then received and forgave his brother
Baha, and showed his confidence in him by delegating
great authority to him, while he himself retired into
greater seclusion.(60) This arrangement, it seems,
was in accordance with the command of the Bab, who
shortly before his death had written a strong letter
to Mirza Husayn Ali (Baha), charging him to take the
best possible care of Subh-i-Azal lest any harm should
come to him.(61) And since the Muslims of Baghdad were
showing more and more hostility toward the Babis, Baha
was able to convince his brother that it was not safe
for him to appear in public, or to see visitors.(62)
Also, this arrangement was agreeable to Subh-i-Azal's
natural disposition, for he, as Professor Browne says,
(63) being a "peace loving, contemplative, gentle soul
.....caring little for authority, and incapable of
self-assertion," was willing to leave "the direction
of affairs in the hands of his half-brother Baha, a
man of much more resolute and ambitious character, who
thus gradually became the most prominent figure and
moving spirit of the sect."

As we noted above, many of the Babi leaders were
prolific writers, and Subh-i-Azal and his brother Baha
were no exceptions, rather, they exceeded them all.
Baha in later years referred to the many "verses" he
had composed in Baghdad, none of which are in existence.
(64) The only book of importance which he wrote while
in Baghdad was the Persian *Iqan*, which in its English
translation by Shoghi Efendi is entitled "The Book of
Certitude." This book was composed about 1862 A.D. for
one of the maternal uncles of the Bab who was still a
Muslim. It was first called *Khaluiyya* (Uncle's), and

Mirza Husayn Ali Baha'u'llah
said to have been taken when he was
he was in Edirne (1863–1868)

later, after the revision made in Edirne or Akka, it
was renamed *Iqan*.(65)   The chief purpose of the *Iqan*
was to prove that the Bab was a Major Manifestation of
God. Baha writes:(66)   "Behold.....how great and lofty
is His [Qa'im, i.e., Bab] station! His rank excelleth
that of all the Prophets, and His Revelation transcen-
deth the comprehension and understanding of all their
chosen ones." The standpoint of the author is that of
a loyal disciple of the Bab. Little of the material
in the book is original, for Baha merely repeats and
elaborates the doctrines already taught by the Shaykhis
and the Bab. There are more references to the Arabic
New Testament than are found in the Bayan. The book
is full of Shi'ite traditions and doctrines. Baha
refers to the Word of God as a "City," and says:(67)
"Once in about a thousand years shall this City be
renewed and re-adorned," and he proceeds to mention
the books which were revealed by God to Moses and Jesus
and Muhammad, "and in this day the Bayan; and in the
dispensation of Him-Whom-God-Will-Manifest.....the Book
which standeth amongst them all transcendent and supreme." Thus Baha agreed with the Bab that the interval
between the Manifestations, including that between the
Bab and the Manifestation to follow him, is "about 1000
years."

It is noteworthy that in the *Iqan* Baha clearly repre-
sents himself as obedient to his brother Subh-i-Azal.
Regarding his sojourn in Kurdistan he says:(68)   "Our
withdrawal contemplated no return, and Our separation
hoped for no reunion. The one object of Our retirement
was to avoid becoming a subject of discord among the
faithful.....until the hour when, from the Mystic Source,
there came the summons bidding Us return whence We came.
Surrendering Our will to His, We submitted to His injunction." He also says,(69) "We have never gloried in any
thing, nor did We seek preference over any soul." However, from the insistence of his appeal in the *Iqan* to
the Babis to accept Him-Whom-God-Will-Manifest, it seems
that Baha was contemplating putting forth his own claim
to superiority, though he had not yet done so.(70)

In Baghdad Baha acquired some property, and he and
Subh-i-Azal also acquired Ottoman nationality.(71) With

the abundant funds at his disposal which came to Subh-i-Azal from the loyal Babis of Iran, in accordance with the laws of the Bab, Baha was able to set up an impressive establishment with adequate facilities for extending hospitality to guests from Iran. His servants would go forth to meet the Shi'ite pilgrims who had come to Iraq to visit the shrines of the Imams, and would conduct them to Baha's center, and there they would be entertained and instructed in the faith of the Bayan.(72) They would usually not even get a glimpse of the Vicegerent of the Bab, for access to Subh-i-Azal was through his intermediary Baha, who often withheld permission under some pretext. Thus Subh-i-Azal, who lived in seclusion and rarely appeared in public, gradually decreased in importance in the eyes of the public as his aggressive older brother increased. To the Turkish officials, and no doubt to many of the Babis also, Baha now appeared to be the actual leader of the movement, although he still acted merely on behalf of Subh-i-Azal.

But Baha was not the only one who at this time was prepared to make a claim for himself. For a man named Mirza Asadullah of Khuy surnamed Dayyan, who had been appointed by the Bab as amanuensis to Subh-i-Azal, declared that he was He-Whom-God-Will-Manifest, and demanded that all the Babis obey him, and some of them became his followers.(73) Baha had a long discussion with him, and Subh-i-Azal denounced him in a book he wrote, but as Dayyan remained obstinate he was murdered by Mirza Muhammad of Mazanderan, probably being drowned in the Tigris River.(74) Dayyan was not the only person thus eliminated by the Babis in Baghdad.(75) There were several others who advanced the same claim as Dayyan. In fact, to quote a Babi writer,(76) "the matter came to such a pass that everyone on awakening from his first sleep in the morning adorned his body with this pretension." The pretensions of these claimants naturally encouraged Baha to press his own claims, for to prevent chaos someone must be in control, and he had a better chance of success than anyone else. Hence, urged on by Aqa Jan of Kashan, later known as Khadimu'-llah (Servant of God), Baha continued to put himself forward.(76) However, the opposition from the other

Babi leaders was so fierce that he was forced to wait awhile longer before openly declaring himself.

Meanwhile, the zealous Babis continued their efforts to convert the Shi'ite pilgrims as they went on their way to visit the shrines of the Imams Ali and Husayn in Najaf and Karbala, an effort which was bitterly resented by the Muslim religious leaders. As a result, there was fighting between the Muslims and the Babis. Finally, the Iranian government, incited by the Muslim mullas, intervened and requested the Turkish government to remove the Babi leaders from Iraq. The letter sent from Teheran to the Iranian ambassador in Istanbul instructing him to try to arrange for this transfer reads in part as follows:(77)

"Sometimes, moreover, he [Baha] hath put his hand to sedition and incitements to murder, as in the case of.....Mulla Aqa of Darband, whom they greviously wounded with intent to kill.....besides sundry other assasinations which took place.....In the face of these proceedings, it would be a proof of the most complete negligence.....on the part of the Iranian government to disregard these acts which may produce such deplorable consequences.....It will not do to leave Mirza Husayn Ali [Baha] there [in Baghdad], or to allow fuller scope to their mischievous ideas and probable actions." The Iranian government, therefore, requested either that Baha and his followers be sent back into Iran where they could be properly watched, or else that the Turkish government "arrange as quickly as possible to deport and detain that mis- chief maker and his several intimates from Baghdad to some other place in the interior of the Ottoman King- dom which has no means of communication with our fron- tiers, so that the channel of their mischief making and sedition may be stopped." When we recall Shaykh Tabarsi and Zanjan and the attempt on the life of the Shah, we are able to understand why the Iranian govern- ment did not want the Babis to make Baghdad, so near the Iranian border, the center for their activities. It is noteworthy that it was not the heretical views of the Babis that the Iranian government feared, but their political activities and their lawlessness. Also, it

is Baha who is held responsible, and the name of
Subh-i-Azal is not mentioned in the correspondence.

It seems that the Turkish government was quite
ready to comply with this request from the government
of Iran, for the quarrels and fightings of the Babis
and Muslims in Baghdad had no doubt been the cause of
great trouble to the authorities there. It was probably because Baha had become a Turkish subject that
the decision was to deport him and his family and
followers to another part of the Turkish Empire, and
not to return them to Iran. Accordingly, in May 1863
Baha and his family left Baghdad on their way to
Istanbul, and were joined in Mosul by Subh-i-Azal who
preceded them by two weeks. They reached Istanbul
after a long and difficult journey of four months,
and there they stopped for another four months. Since
there was a large Iranian colony in Istanbul, and the
Turkish authorities feared they might cause disturbance there as they had done in Baghdad, they were
ordered to proceed yet farther west to the extreme
border of Turkey, and to settle in the city of Erdine
(Adrianople). They arrived there in December 1863,
and there they remained for four and one half years,
far away from their native land.(78)

In most of the Baha'i publications it is stated
that before leaving Baghdad Baha spent twelve days
(April 22 - May 3) in the Garden of Rizwan, and that
he there announced to his followers that he was He-
Whom-God-Will-Manifest. Hence Baha'is observe these
dates as the anniversary of this important Declaration.(79) If such a declaration was made at that
time, which is improbable, it must have been very
private, for even Baha's son Abbas Efendi did not
mention this in his book *A Traveller's Narrative*,
which purports to be a true and authorized history
of the Baha'i Cause. Moreover, the public declaration which resulted in the great schism in the Babi
community was not made till several years later in
Edirne,(80) as we shall see in Chapter VI. Till then
the Babis continued to consider Subh-i-Azal as their
divinely appointed head, though Baha had become their
actual leader.

NOTES

1. E. G. Browne in *A Traveller's Narrative*, p. 56, note 2, Subh-i-Azal in *A Traveller's Narrative*, pp. 373-376, Mirza Jani in *New History*, pp. 374-376, Mirza Jani in *Nuqtatu'l-Kaf*, pp. 238 ff., *Azal's Notes*, pp. 551, 946. For Family Chart of Mirza Buzurg see Appendix II, #8.

2. Avareh in *Kashfu'l-Hiyal*, presumably first edition, p. 30.

3. This wife, whose name was Khadijeh, was a widow when she became the wife of Mirza Buzurg (*Azal's Notes*, p. 633).

4. Mirza Jani in *New History*, p. 375.

5. Avareh in *Kashfu'l-Hiyal*, Vol. I, 6th impression, p. 21.

6. Mirza Jani in *New History*, p. 375.

7. *Janab* is a title equivalent to "Excellency."

8. Subh-i-Azal to Mirza Jani in *New History*, p. 376, Subh-i-Azal in *Materials*, pp. 212, 218-219.

9. Mirza Jani in *New History*, p. 376.

10. *Hazrat*is a title higher than *Janab*, often used for prophets and kings, equivalent to "Highness" or "Holiness."

11. Mirza Jani in *New History*, p. 378.

12. Ibid., pp. 377-379.

13. Ibid., p. 379.

14. Ibid., p. 380.

15. According to the *Persian Bayan* (II,16), all the worlds derive their origin from the Divine Will (*Irada*), which was created by the Divine Volition (*Mashiyya*) which is self-subsisting. In the Koranic Cycle according to the Bab, Muhammad had the station of Volition, and his son-in-law Ali that of Will. Similarly in the Cycle of the Bayan the Bab held the station of Volition, and Subh-i-Azal was given that of Will (*Azal's Notes*, p. 948).

16. Mirza Jani in *New History*, pp. 381, 426, *Nuqtatu'l-Kaf*, p. 244, *Azal's Notes*, pp. 514, 515, 551-555, 605-608. It is said that the date of the appointment was Farvardin 25, 1229 A.H. (about April 15, 1850), and the Bab commanded that this day be observed as a feast (*Azal's Notes*, p. 949).

17. Authors of *Hasht Bihisht*, quoted in *A Traveller's Narrative*, p. 353. The numerical value of the Arabic letters in *Wahid* is 28, the same as in *Yahya* (*New History*, p. 426). *Wahíd* (pronounced Waheed) is a different word from *Wahíd* meaning One (i.e., God), which has the value of 19.

18. Mirza Jani in *Nuqtatu'l-Kaf*, English Int., p. XXXI.

19. *Azal's Notes*, pp. 552, 945, 978, and the Bab's *Five Grades*. See Appendix II, #26 and #27.

20. Mirza Jani in *New History*, p. 381..

21. Ibid., p. 381, *Nuqtatu'l-Kaf*, pp. XXXI, 244.

22. *Azal's Notes*, p. 951.

23. *J.R.A.S.* 1897, p. 763.

24. *New History*, pp. 420, 426, 427, Browne in *J.R.A.S.* 1889, pp. 996, 997, October 1892, p. 763.

25. This is a correction of Browne's translation made by Mr. Azal.

26. *Azal's Notes*, pp. 550, 555, 687, 688, Appendix II, p. 3, #28.

27. That is, the eight Wahids of the Bayan which the Bab had not written.

28. *Azal's Notes*, p. 790.

29. *Gobineau*, Vol. II, pp. 72, 73.

30. *New History*, p. XX.

31. *Gobineau*, Vol. II, pp. 7, 41.

32. Ibid., p. 7, Browne in *New History*, p. XIX.

33. *Gobineau*, Vol. II, pp. 9, 38.

34. Browne in *New History*, p. XIX.

35. Ibid., pp. 384 ff., *Nuqtatu'l-Kaf*, 252-255.

36. *New History*, p. 394.

37. *Azal's Notes*, pp. 953, 977.

38. *New History*, p. 390.

39. Mirza Jani here gives the higher title *Hazrat* to Subh-i-Azal, and the lower title *Janab* to his older brother Baha, whom he seldom mentions in this part of the history.

40. In the *Arabic Bayan* (I,6) the Bab states that the Imam Husayn "*has* returned."

41. See Appendix II, #41.

42. *Azal's Notes*, pp. 979-986.

43. *New History*, p. 392, *Gobineau* quoted in *A Traveller's Narrative*, p. 53, note 1, *Nasikhu't-Tawarikh* quoted by Browne in *A Traveller's Narrative*, p. 185.

44. *Gobineau*, Vol. II, pp. 10-36, *A Traveller's Narrative*, pp. 50, 323-325.

45. *Materials*, pp. 267-271.

46. *Gobineau*, Vol. II, pp. 17-36, *A Traveller's Narrative*, pp. 313, 327-334.

47. *Gobineau*, Vol. II, p. 37.

48. *A Traveller's Narrative*, pp. 354, 374, *New History*, p. XX, *Azal's Notes*, p. 561.

49. *A Traveller's Narrative*, pp. 374-376, *New History*, pp. 414-415.

50. *Nasikhu't-Tawarikh* quoted in *A Traveller's Narrative*, pp. 186, 327.

51. *Materials*, p. 6, *Epistle to the Son of the Wolf* by Baha'u'llah, translated by Shoghi Effendi, Baha'i Publishing Trust 1962, pp. 16, 20-22, *Azal's Notes*, pp. 183-187, 520.

52. Browne in *A Traveller's Narrative*, p. 327.

53. Shoghi Effendi, *God Passes By*, Baha'i Publishing Trust 1965, pp. 108, 109.

54. *Dawn Breakers*, translation of Shoghi Effendi, American Edition, pp. 593-594.

55. Shoghi Effendi, *God Passes By*, p. 115.

56. *Hasht Bihisht*, pp. 301-302.

57. *Iqan* by Baha'u'llah, quoted by Shoghi Effendi in *God Passes By*, pp. 118-119.

58. *A Traveller's Narrative*, pp. 64, 356, *Materials*, pp. 7-9. See Appendix II, #38.

59. *Hasht Bihisht*, quoted in *A Traveller's Narrative*, p. 357, *Azal's Notes*, p. 651.

60. *Azal's Notes*, pp. 596-597.

61. Idem., p. 608, which quotes the Bab's letter to Baha. See Appendix II, #31.

62. *Notes of Dr. Sa'eed Khan*, p. 13 of the translation, deposited in the Library of Princeton University.

63. *New History*, p. XXI.

64. *Azal's Notes*, pp. 15-19, 425-426, 447, 458, 581-582, 587.

65. *Nuqtatu'l-Kaf*, Persian Int., pp. 35-36, *Azal's Notes*, pp. 532-537.

66. *The Kitab-i-Iqan - The Book of Certitude*, p. 244.

67. Idem., p. 199.

68. Idem., p. 251.

69. Idem., p. 249. A more accurate translation of the Persian word *bartari* (translated "Preference") in this connection is "superiority."

70. The following editions of the *Iqan* have been consulted by the author:
    Persian edition, published in Egypt in 1900 A.D.
    The Book of Assurance, translation of the *Iqan* by Ali Kuli Khan, Brentano's, New YOrk, without date.
    The Kitab-i-Iqan - The Book of Certitude, translated by Shoghi Effendi, Baha'i Publishing Trust, 1960.

It is instructive to note that the two Baha'i
translators of the *Iqan* have consistently translated the Persian first person singular, which
Baha used, by the plural "We" with a capital, the
"plural of majesty." More serious than this,
Shoghi Effendi in his translation on p. 251 erroneously rendered the Persian *masdar-i-amr* (the
source of command) as "the Mystic Source," thereby
intentionally concealing the obvious meaning of
the passage. The "source of command" was the
Vicegerent of the Bab, Subh-i-Azal, whom Baha at
the time the *Iqan* was written acknowledged as his
commander. Ali Kuli Khan had in his earlier
translation (p. 180) rendered the phrase correctly.

71. *A Traveller's Narrative*, p. 111, note 1, *God
    Passes By*, p. 146, *Azal's Notes*, pp. 47, 64, 189,
    964.

72. *Notes of Dr. Sa'eed Khan*, p. 8 of the translation.

73. *Gobineau*, Vol. II, p. 6, *A Traveller's Narrative*,
    pp. 357, 365, *Materials*, p. 218, *Azal's Notes*,
    pp. 965, 973.

74. *Hasht Bihisht* states that Baha ordered his servant
    Mirza Muhammad to kill Dayyan (*A Traveller's Narra-
    tive*, p. 357). Baha says the decree was issued by
    Subh-i-Azal (*Epistle to the Son of the Wolf*, pp.
    175-176). In any case it seems that he was executed
    for his claims by the order of one of the Babi
    leaders. For a full discussion of the evidence see
    Azal's Notes, pp. 965-973. See also Appendix II,
    #39.

75. *Azal's Notes*, p. 973.

76. Authors of *Hasht Bihisht*, quoted in *A Traveller's
    Narrative*, p. 358.

77. *Materials*, pp. 279-287.

78. Ibid., pp. 16-19, *A Traveller's Narrative*, pp.
    90-92, *New History*, p. XX, Browne in *J.R.A.S.*
    1889, p. 514, *The Chosen Highway*, Lady Bloomfield,
    p. 59.

79. *Materials*, p. 16, *Baha'u'llah and the New Era*, by
    J. E. Esselmont, Brentano's, first edition, pp.

36-37, *God Passes By*, Shoghi Effendi, pp. 151-155, *Azal's Notes*, pp. 974-975.

80. Edirne was often referred to by the Babis as "the Land of the Mystery," because the numerical value of the Arabic letters in *Edirne* is the same as in *Sirr* (mystery). Also, they say, because it was there that the separation of Light and Darkness took place (authors of *Hasht Bihisht*, quoted in *A Traveller's Narrative*, p. 361). In the schism that occurred there, each party claimed to be Light, and condemned their opponents as Darkness.

6

The Schism Between Subh-i-Azal and Baha

In Edirne the task which faced Subh-i-Azal, who for
some sixteen years had been generally considered by
the Babis to be the divinely appointed Head of the
People of the Bayan, one with the Bab in rank and
glory, was by no means easy. As Professor Browne
writes:(1) "A community like that which.....existed
at Adrianople [Edirne] consisting almost entirely of
exiles and potential martyrs, and in large part of
religious enthusiasts, revolutionary visionaries, and
speculative mystics, whose restless activity, debarred
from external action, is pent up within limits too
narrow for its free exercise, requires a firm hand to
control and direct its energies. Such firmness Subh-
i-Azal seems to have altogether lacked." His older
brother Baha, "a man of much more resolute and ambitious character," had come gradually to occupy the
place of actual leadership, though till now he had
done everything in the name of Subh-i-Azal. However,
about three years after reaching Edirne, probably in
1866 A.D.,(2) with no strong Babi leaders nearby to
oppose him, he suddenly threw off all disguise and
made to the Babi community the claim which he had for
several years been contemplating, that he was He-Whom-
God-Will-Manifest, whose coming the Bab had predicted

(Chapter IV). He then called on Subh-i-Azal(3) and
all the Babis scattered over Turkey, Iran, Syria and
Egypt to acknowledge his supreme authority, and to
accept as God's Word the revelations which he forthwith began to promulgate.

To understand the nature of Baha's claims let us
recall what the Bab in the Bayan had written about
Him-Whom-God-Will-Manifest, who would be another Major
Manifestation (Chapter IV):(4) He is divine, and his
command is God's command. He is not to be asked why
he does anything. All previous Manifestations were
for him, and one verse of his writings is better than
a thousand Bayans. He is to be recognized by himself.
Only God knows the time of his advent, but he will come
not prior to 1511 years, and not later than 2001 years,
after the Bab.(5) He will "reveal verses spontaneously
and powerfully, without study and without the means
accessible to the learned. It is impossible that any
other than He.....can lay claim to the command....."
(6) As we saw in Chapter V, a number of men had
claimed to be a return ot the Imam Husayn, a mirror
within the orbit of the Bayan, and had mistakenly identified Husayn with Him-Whom-God-Will-Manifest. They
were rejected by the Babi leaders as pretenders, and
Dayyan was murdered by the Babis in Baghdad. Nabil,
who made the same claim there, later withdrew it, gave
his allegiance to Baha, and became a Baha'i historian.
(7) Baha, however, because of his position of leadership under Subh-i-Azal and his relationship to Subh-i-
Azal, had a better chance of success than did the
previous claimants. Accordingly, he who had considered himself to be the return of the Imam Husayn now
advanced the claim to be a Major Manifestation of
Deity, the same claim which the Bab had made some
twenty-two years earlier.

Before considering the effect of this declaration
on the People of the Bayan, it is appropriate that we
here give a brief account of the life of the man who
claimed to be He-Whom-God-Will-Manifest. His name was
Mirza Husayn Ali. It is said that he was born on
November 12, 1817 A.D.(8) His father, known as Mirza
Buzurg, a man of considerable influence and wealth

who had come from the district of Nur in Iran's northern province of Mazanderan, died when Mirza Husayn
Ali was about twenty years of age.(9) The young man
received the same kind of classical education from
tutors which was customary for the youth of his class
of society in Iran at that time.(10)

Soon after the Bab's declaration in Shiraz in 1844
A.D., Mirza Husayn Ali met some of the Bab's disciples
in Teheran and became a believer. There is no trustworthy evidence to support the story that a special
message was at this time sent to him by the Bab. The
Bab did not then or later appoint him as one of the
eighteen "Letters," or bestow on him a title.(11)
When the Bab ordered his followers to proceed to
Khurasan, the eastern province of Iran, Mirza Husayn
Ali obeyed, and in Sabzevar he met Qurratu'l-Ayn.
There with her, writes Mirza Jani,(12) "he tarried,
doing her much service both there and at Teheran,
and, indeed, providing her and her companions with
the means of continuing their journey, and bearing
all their expenses.....In short, he remained in Sabzevar till Hazrat-i-Quddus came thither, on whom he had
the honor of waiting, and for whom he entertained the
truest devotion. He was one of the most illustrious
of the great believers, he was present at the revolt
at Badasht, stood firm in his love, expended large
sums of money, and helped the believers in every way."
There is no indication in Mirza Jani's history that
Mirza Husayn Ali played a leading role in the Badasht
Conference. However, it is said that it was here
that Qurratu'l-Ayn bestowed on him the title *Baha*
(Splendor), which is the name of the first month of
the Babi year.(13)

In his account of these events Mirza Jani mentions
Baha much less frequently than his younger brother
Mirza Yahya, usually giving to him the inferior desig-
nation *Janab*, and referring to Mirza Yahya as *Hazrat*.
It is quite clear that Mirza Jani at the time when he
wrote his history in 1851 A.D. considered Baha's posi-
tion to be inferior not only to that of his brother
Subh-i-Azal but also to that of Hazrat-i-Quddus and
Qurratu'l-Ayn and the other Letters.(14) As previously

stated (Chapter III), Baha attempted to reach the
Babi fort at Shaykh Tabarsi, but was arrested by the
local authorities, punished,(15) and released. Baha's
son Abbas Efendi states(16) that "after the death of
the late prince Muhammad Shah [September 4, 1848] he
[Baha] returned to Teheran having in mind (the intention of) corresponding and entering into relations
with the Bab." From this statement it seems that up
to this time Baha had neither seen the Bab, nor had
he been in contact with his Master.(17) Some time
later the Bab wrote to Baha,(18) instructing him to
take the best possible care of Subh-i-Azal, whom he
had appointed as his successor.

There is no evidence from the early documents to
support the statements made by Abbas Efendi in *A
Traveller's Narrative* (pp. 62,63), and also in later
books, that Subh-i-Azal was made a screen to protect
Baha, who from the first was the true leader of the
movement.(19) Nor is there authentic evidence that
Baha played a leading part in the Babi movement prior
to his expulsion from Iran.(20) After the execution
of the Bab in 1850 he left Iran and went to Iraq,
where he remained for about a year (1851-1852 A.D.).
It was at this time that Baha is said to have met
Shaykh Zunuzi in Karbala, and informed him that he
(Baha) was the return of Imam Husayn. When, after
the attempt on the life of the Shah in 1852 A.D., a
number of leading Babis were arrested, Baha was one
of them, probably because he was known to be the
brother of Subh-i-Azal the head of the movement. A
large reward was offered for the arrest of Subh-i-Azal,
but he succeeded in escaping. Twenty-eight of the
prisoners were executed. Baha was kept in prison in
Teheran for four months, and then, a month after his
release from confinement, he left Teheran for Baghdad,
and there he joined his brother Subh-i-Azal in April,
1853 A.D.

In the previous chapter we have told how Baha in
Baghdad gradually took over the leadership of the Babi
community, and came to be looked upon by the Turkish
officials as the chief person. Then in Edirne in 1866
he definitely rejected the role of service to the Babi

Cause under the Vicegerent Subh-i-Azal, and demanded
that all recognize him as supreme ruler, a Divine
Manifestation. It is said that he sent a letter to
Subh-i-Azal demanding his submission, but his brother
refused. Thereupon Baha tried to force Subh-i-Azal
to yield by withholding his share of the allowances
which were paid by the Turkish government through Baha
for the Babis in Edirne. As a result, the family of
Subh-i-Azal lacked food, and his little children
became ill. His wife then went to the wife of the
Turkish governor to complain, an act which was deeply
resented by Baha. The blame for the opposition of
Subh-i-Azal to Baha's claims has been laid by the
Baha'is on Sayyid Muhammad of Isfahan, who had been
an intimate friend of the Bab, and had married the
Bab's widow Fatima.(21)

   Of these events Professor Browne writes:(22)
"Amongst the Babis the effect of this announcement
(for which, no doubt, the way had been already prepared) was little short of stupendous. From Constan-
tinople [Istanbul] to Kirman and from Cairo to
Khurasan the communities of the faithful were rent
asunder by a schism which every subsequent year has
rendered wider and more permanent.....At Adrianople
[Edirne] itself the struggle was short and the triumph
of Baha complete. Subh-i-Azal was so completely deserted, that, as he himself informed me, he and his
little boy had to go themselves to the bazaar to buy
their food. Elsewhere, though active and astute
emissaries were at once dispatched in all directions
by Baha, the conflict, though its issue was from the
first hardly doubtful, was longer maintained. For
the question at issue was not merely whether one
leader should be replaced by another, whether certain
doctrines should be understood in this way or in that,
or whether the ethics, practices or forms of worship
of the sect should be reformed or modified.....but
whether the doctrines and writings of the beloved
Master [the Bab], for which his followers had been
ready to suffer death or exile, were to be regarded
as abrogated and cancelled in favor of a new revelation; whether his chosen vicegerent, whom they had so
long regarded as their Supreme Pontiff and as the

incarnation of all purity, virtue, and heavenly wisdom, was to be cast down from this high position, and
branded as 'the First Letter of Denial' of the New
Dispensation; and whether the Bab himself was to be
looked upon, not as the 'Point of Revelation,' a ver-
itable Manifestation of the Divine, but as a mere
harbinger and precursor of a more perfect Theophany."

It is clear, however, that the vital issue was not
that of reforming the laws and customs decreed by the
Bab, for there is no evidence to indicate that Baha
abrogated the Bayan. The problem was how Baha could
take over the supreme control of the Babi Cause. This
he did by by-passing the Vicegerent Subh-i-Azal, and
proclaiming himself a Major Manifestation.(23)

Though most of the People of the Bayan sooner or
later acknowledged Baha as He-Whom-God-Will-Manifest,
his brother Subh-i-Azal steadfastly refused to do so.
He held fast to the teachings of the Bab, believing
that they were the all-sufficient revelation of God
for the present age, and that they must be accepted
and obeyed by multitudes of people for many centuries,
as the Gospel of Jesus and the Koran of Muhammad had
been, before it would be time for another Manifestation to appear. To Subh-i-Azal and the Babis who
clung to him it seemed utterly unreasonable to believe
that the elaborate system revealed by God to the Bab
could have been established for only twenty-two years.
Had not the Bab in the Bayan indicated clearly that
He-Whom-God-Will-Manifest would not come for at least
1511 years and might not come till 2001 more years
had passed?(24) What farmer would plant a vineyard,
and then before any fruit whatever had been gathered
from it would cut down the vines and plant others?
Surely God would wait long enough to reap some fruit
from the tree of the Bayan before He would remove it
and send another Manifestation!(25)

All the Babis were convinced that the Bab had been
sent by God and was infallible. Then, since Subh-i-
Azal had been appointed by the Bab himself as his
successor, was not he also sent by God, as they had
for sixteen years believed? And did he not possess

divine wisdom, and was he not one with the Bab? How
then could it be possible that such an one as Subh-i-
Azal should be unable to recognize Him-Whom-God-Will-
Manifest when he appears? But Subh-i-Azal rejected
the claim of his brother to be "He!" Hence, for those
Babis who accepted Baha, and later became known as
Baha'is, there was no alternative except to say that
the Bab, who was divinely inspired and knew all things,
had deliberately chosen as his vicegerent a man who
was to become the "Point of Darkness," the chief
enemy of Him-Whom-God-Will-Manifest.(26)

In their effort to escape this dilemma, Baha and
his partisans did two things: first, they got rid of
most of the leading Babis who sided with Subh-i-Azal;
and second, they rewrote the history of the Babi movement, largely ignoring Subh-i-Azal, greatly magnifying
the position and person of Baha, and degrading the Bab
from the position of a Major Manifestation to that of
a "forerunner" of Baha, who was the real Manifestation
for the age. Those who have read the later teachings
of Baha and his son Abbas Efendi (Abdu'l-Baha) regarding truth and love and kindness to all mankind may
find it difficult to believe that the authors of such
noble sentiments could have had any part in the falsification of history or the assassination of opponents.
We are dealing, however, not with what we would like
to believe, but with historical facts established
beyond a doubt which we cannot but accept.

Though this sad chapter of the history has been
largely omitted by the Baha'i historians,(27) the
truth is that of those Babis who remained faithful to
Subh-i-Azal, later known as Azalis or Babis, about
twenty were murdered in Baghdad, Edirne and Akka by
the followers of Baha.(28) Two of those who were
killed were brothers of Fatima the widow of the Bab,
(29) and one was her husband Sayyid Muhammad of
Isfahan, and two were Letters appointed by the Bab.
It has been said that these assassinations were the
work of the too-zealous followers of Baha, and that
he was not himself responsible. However this may be,
could not one who possessed the divine knowledge and
power to influence men which Baha claimed to have,

been able to prevent such acts on the part of his
intimate disciples? And could he not have disowned
them, or at least punished them, for their deeds? As
far as is known he did neither. To understand this
attitude, so foreign to that of religious people in
the West, it should be remembered that the men who
committed these crimes were kindred spirits to those
who had plotted the assassination of the Shah of Iran
(Chapter V). Muslim historians relate that the Prophet Muhammad approved of the assassination of certain
individuals who opposed him.(30) Therefore it might be
argued that if one Manifestation puts down opposition
in this way, could not a greater Manifestation do the
same? "Surely," said an Iranian Baha'i to Professor
Browne,(31) "you cannot pretend to deny that a prophet,
who is an incarnation of the Universal Intelligence,
has as much right to remove anyone whom he perceives
to be an enemy to religion and a danger to the welfare
of mankind as a surgeon has to amputate a gangrened
limb?" Accordingly, acts which to some might seem
criminal could to others with a different point of view
appear as the expression of the righteous will of God.

According to the Azalis, Baha not only sanctioned
the murder of these Babis who refused to accept him,
but also attempted to have his brother Subh-i-Azal
poisoned. The Baha'is replied that it was Subh-i-
Azal who tried to poison Baha.(32) Browne confesses
his inability to decide where the guilt lay, but a
careful study of the evidence indicates that the charges against Subh-i-Azal cannot be substantiated.(33)
Whatever the truth of the matter may be, both sides
agree that an attempt was made by one of the brothers
to poison the other. This is indeed a blot on the
history of the Babi movement in which both brothers
had for a number of years been the leaders. A second
attempt on the life of Subh-i-Azal, according to the
Azalis, was later made by the Baha'i barber in the bath,
after escaping which he separated himself entirely from
Baha and his followers.(34)

Finally, the conflict between the two unequal parties became so fierce that the Turkish authorities
decided to separate them, and apparently without making

any effort to determine who was in the right they sent
all the Babi exiles away from Edirne. Subh-i-Azal and
his family and a few followers were sent to the Island
of Cyprus, and Baha and his family and followers were
sent to Akka (Acre) in Palestine, both regions being
at that time under Turkish rule. In order to keep
informed as to their doings, the authorities detailed
four Baha'is to go to Cyprus to spy on Subh-i-Azal,
and four Azalis to do the same for Baha in Akka. One
of the four Azalis was murdered by the Baha'is before
leaving Edirne, and the other three were likewise
murdered soon after their arrival in Akka.(35) Regarding this Browne writes:(36) "As to the assassination
of the three Azalis.....by some of Baha's followers at
Acre, there can, I fear, be but little doubt.....There
is, however, no evidence to prove that the assassins
acted under orders."

In the *Hasht Bihisht*, a book written by two sons-in-
law of Subh-i-Azal, it is stated(37) that while the
Babis were still in Edirne anonymous letters were written at Baha's direction, and left at night at the doors
of numerous Turkish officials in Istanbul. These
letters stated that 30,000 Babis, whose king was Mirza
Yahya Subh-i-Azal, were concealed about Istanbul, and
were ready to overthrow the Sultan of Turkey, unless
he believed in their religion. It would seem most
improbable that Baha in an effort to discredit his
brother should have adopted a strategy which was certain to injure him also.

However, a document has been discovered by an Iranian scholar in the government archives in Istanbul,(38)
sealed with Baha's seal "Husayn Ali," in which Baha
gives information to the authorities in Edirne against
Subh-i-Azal and his followers, whose names are given,
alleging that they have conspired against the Ottoman
government, and urging that an investigation be made.
The investigation was made, and a report was sent to
the Sultan. The report stated that both Subh-i-Azal
and Shaykh Husayn Ali claimed to be prophets, and
therefore "such men of error could not be left at
large to conduct their disruptive activities unchecked."
The report recommended their transportation for life to

some remote penal places, subject to their being kept
under surveillance or open arrest. The report was
dated June 18, 1868, and the imperial warrant for
their exile was issued in Istanbul on July 26, 1868.
Accordingly, both parties to the struggle left Edirne
for their respective places of exile in the early part
of August, 1868.(39) Thus Baha, in attempting to rid
himself of his brother, succeeded in getting himself
sent under a sentence of life imprisonment to Akka.

Not content with getting rid of the influential
Babis who refused to follow Baha, the Baha'i party
undertook to rewrite the whole history of the Babi
movement so as to make Baha's claims more plausible.
In doing this they reduced the Bab from being an independent Major Manifestation, like Jesus and Muhammad,
to the rank of a "forerunner," like John the Baptist.
They totally ignored Subh-i-Azal, or else portrayed
him as the chief enemy of the truth. And they represented Baha as having been from the first the leading
figure in the Babi movement. This tendency is clearly
seen in *A Traveller's Narrative*, an official though
anonymous history of the movement written by Abbas
Efendi the eldest son of Baha, and also in other Baha'i
writings.(40)

In order for this false version of Babi history to
gain universal acceptance it became necessary that
many of the old Babi books and manuscripts be gotten
rid of, for they gave the lie to the Baha'i statements.
The followers of Baha, therefore, began systematically
to conceal or to destroy the writings of the Bab and
of the early Babis.(41) They were so successful that
when Professor Browne visited Iran in 1888 he was able
only with the greatest difficulty to obtain a copy of
the Bayan.(42) And when he visited Akka in 1890 he
had a similar experience. "I can affirm," he wrote
after his visit there,(43) "that, hard as it is to
obtain from the Baha'is in Persia the loan or gift of
Babi books belonging to the earlier period of the
faith, at Acre it is harder still even to get a glimpse
of them. They may be, and probably are, still preserved there, but, for all the good the enquirer is likely
to get from them, they might almost as well have suffered

the fate [destruction] which the Azalis believe to
have overtaken them." We have already related in the
Introduction how the history written by Mirza Jani
(*Nuqtatu'l-Kaf*) in 1851 was completely suppressed in
Iran, so that Browne was unable to get any information
whatever about this valuable book, and how the one
extant copy in Europe was found by him in Paris, and
published by him, to the consternation of the Baha'i
leaders. By some of them Professor Browne was accused
of having become an Azali, and of having been bribed
by them to publish this book.(44)

Regarding the suppression of Mirza Jani's book,
Browne writes:(45) "It is hard for us, accustomed to
a world of printed books and carefully guarded public
libraries, to realize that so important a work as
this could be successfully suppressed; and equally
hard to believe that the adherents of a religion evidently animated by the utmost self-devotion and the
most fervent enthusiasm, and, in ordinary everyday
matters, by obvious honesty of purpose, could connive
at such an act of suppression and falsification of
evidence.....This fact, were it not established by
the clearest evidence, I should have regarded as
incredible." It is to non-Baha'i scholars such as
Gobineau and Browne and Nicholas, and to the Azalis,
and not to Baha and his followers, that the world is
indebted for the knowledge it has of the writings of
the Bab and the early Babis.(46)

Since the great majority of the Babis became
followers of Baha, our principal concern from now on
will be with the Baha'i branch of the Babi movement
which had Akka for its center and Baha for its head.
However, before leaving Subh-i-Azal and his small
minority of disciples, we will relate briefly the
story of his later life. He with his two wives(47)
and his children and a few followers(48) reached
Famagusta on the Island of Cyprus in August, 1868.
Their sentence was life imprisonment, and they were
given a daily allowance by the Turkish government.
In 1878 Cyprus passed from Turkish to British control,
and the Azali prisoners became pensioners of the
British government. Living thus in isolation Subh-i-

Mirza Yahya Subh-i-Azal

from New History of the Bab
by *E.G. Browne*

Azal was almost completely forgotten, for when Browne
made inquiries about him in Iran in 1887 he was
amazed to discover that the Baha'is whom he met knew
nothing, or pretended to know nothing, about him, and
many said they had never even heard of him. However,
Baha'is sometimes threatened him.(49)

After careful investigation Browne learned that
Subh-i-Azal was in Famagusta, and in March 1890 he
went to Cyprus to visit him. He thus describes his
first meeting with Subh-i-Azal: "We ascended to an
upper room, where a venerable and benevolent looking
old man of about sixty years of age, somewhat below
the middle height, with ample forehead on which the
traces of care and anxiety were apparent, clear searching blue eyes, and long grey beard, rose and advanced
to meet us. Before that mild and dignified countenance I involuntarily bowed myself with unfeigned respect; for at length my long-cherished desire was
fulfilled, and I stood face to face with Mirza Yahya
Subh-i-Azal ('The Morning of Eternity'), the appointed
successor of the Bab."(50)

During a period of two weeks Browne daily spent
several hours conversing with Subh-i-Azal, and obtaining from him a vast amount of first-hand information
regarding the Babi movement. "Of the Bab and his
first apostles and followers," writes Browne,(51) "as
of his own life and adventures, Subh-i-Azal would
speak freely, but concerning the origin of the schism
which for him had been attended with such disastrous
results, and all pertaining to Baha and the Baha'is,
he was most reticent, so that, perceiving this subject
to be distasteful, I refrained for the most part from
alluding to it." Subh-i-Azal and his sons always
treated their visitor with the greatest courtesy.

Thereafter Subh-i-Azal and his sons rendered great
assistance to Professor Browne in his researches by
supplying him with numerous books in manuscript written
by the Bab and by Subh-i-Azal and the early Babis, and
by answering many questions about the Babi writings
and history which Browne put to them.

Subh-i-Azal lived to the age of eighty-one, and died in Famagusta on April 29, 1912. An account of his death and burial, written by one of his sons, who, on becoming a Christian, renamed himself "Constantine the Persian," has been published by Professor Browne. (52) Subh-i-Azal left no will, and appointed no one as his successor, (53) and his followers have carried on no propaganda. However, there are in Iran several thousand people (54) who consider themselves Babis, and who believe that in this unfortunate schism the right was with Subh-i-Azal.

NOTES

1. Browne in *New History*, p. XXI.

2. The date of Baha's declaration (1866-1867 A.D.) was fixed by Nabil, a follower of Baha, in his Chronological Poem, in which he states that Baha was fifty years old when he set forth his claim to be a Manifestation (*J.R.A.S.* 1889, pp. 983-990). The famous Baha'i writer, Mirza Abu'l-Fazl stated that the declaration was in 1868 (*J.R.A.S.* October 1892, p. 703, note 1). Abbas Efendi, eldest son of Baha, in his book *A Traveller's Narrative* (pp. 55, note 3, and 66), in the opinion of Browne "deliberately and purposely antedated the Manifestation" (*J.R.A.S.* April 1892, p. 306), in order to make it appear that Baha had from an early time been a leading figure in the movement. The date of the declaration as given by Abbas Efendi was 1852 A.D., about fourteen years too early. Modern Baha'is give the date as April 22, 1863 A.D. (Shoghi Effendi in *God Passes By*, pp. 148-162), which is at least three years too early. *Azal's Notes*, pp. 1021-1023.

3. The date of this order, according to Shoghi Effendi in *God Passes By*, p. 167, was Shawwal 22, 1282 A.H. (March 10, 1866 A.D.).

4. Browne in English Int. to *Nuqtatu'l-Kaf*, pp. LXIX-LXXI.

5. *Persian Bayan*, II, 16, where the date 2001, the numerical equivalent of the Arabic word *mustaghath*, is clearly stated in words. Refer to Chapter IV. Baha at first attempted to explain the words *ghiyath* (1511) and *mustaghath* (2001) in some way that would not conflict with his claims. However, near the end of his life in his Tablet *O Creator of All Creation*, Baha revoked his earlier interpretation and stated that "He who was named in the Bayan 'He-Who-Will-Appear' [that is, He-Whom-God-Will-Manifest] shall in truth come in the *Mustaghath* with manifest power." He did not explain how it happened that he (Baha'u'llah) had come before the *Mustaghath*. *Azal's Notes*, pp. 256, 257, 1021-1023.

6. *Persian Bayan*, VI, 8. See Appendix II, p. 5, #45.

7. Nabil is the author of the *Dawn Breakers*. *Azal's Notes*, pp. 500, 999.

8. The exact date of Baha's birth is not known, since at that time no official records of births were kept in Iran. A fairly accurate statement of the dates in the life of Baha is found in Nabil's Chronological Poem composed in Akka in 1869 A.D. (*J.R.A.S.* October 1889, pp. 983-990). See also *Azal's Notes*, pp. 450-456, 996, and Browne's Chronological Table for Babi History (*J.R.A.S.* July 1889, pp. 521-526).

9. Browne in *A Traveller's Narrative*, p. 56, note, Mirza Jani in *New History*, p. 374, Subh-i-Azal in *A Traveller's Narrative*, p. 373.

10. *Azal's Notes*, pp. 457-459.

11. Persian Introduction to *Nuqtatu'l-Kaf*, p. 35, *Azal's Notes*, pp. 464-470, 607.

12. *New History*, p. 377, *Nuqtatu'l-Kaf*, p. 240, *Azal's Notes*, p. 482.

13. Avareh in *Kashfu'l-Hiyal*, presumably first efition, p. 28, also statement from Bayan in English Int. to *Nuqtatu'l-Kaf*, p. LVIII. Since the numerical

value of the Arabic letters in *Baha'* is 9, Baha'is attach great importance to this number.

14. *New History*, pp. 310, note 1, 375, *Azal's Notes*, p. 483, 498, 515.

15. Mirza Jani in *Nuqtatu'l-Kaf*, p. 242.

16. *A Traveller's Narrative*, p. 62.

17. *Azal's Notes*, pp. 477, 478.

18. *Dr. Sa'eed's Notes*, p. 15 in translation, *Azal's Notes*, p. 608. See Appendix II, #31.

19. *Azal's Notes*, pp. 503 ff.

20. Ibid., pp. 448, 479-485.

21. Ibid., pp. 642 ff., Mirza Jawad in *Materials*, pp. 21-24.

22. *New History*, pp. XXII, XXIII.

23. *Azal's Notes*, pp. 1000, 1009.

24. *Nuqtatu'l-Kaf*, p. XXV, *Persian Bayan*, II, 17, *J.R.A.S.* July 1889, pp. 514, 515.

25. Authors of *Hasht Bihisht* in *J.R.A.S.* October 1892, p. 686.

26. Browne in *Nuqtatu'l-Kaf*, pp. XXXIII, XXXIV.

27. The assassinations of Azalis by Baha'is at this period are entirely overlooked by Baha in his writings, by Abbas Efendi in *A Traveller's Narrative*, by Shoghi Effendi in *God Passes By*, as well as in later Baha'i accounts of the history of the movement. See *Azal's Notes*, pp. 548, 1013.

28. The names of a number of Azalis murdered by the Baha'is are given by Browne in the Persian Int. to *Nuqtatu'l-Kaf*, p. 42, and also in *New History*, pp. XXIII, XXIV, and *J.R.A.S.* July 1889, p. 517, and by the authors of *Hasht Bisht* quoted by Browne in *A Traveller's Narrative*, pp. 359-373.

29. Both of these brothers wrote refutations of the claims of Baha, and it was because of this that they were murdered by Baha's followers (*Azal's Notes*, pp. 543, 566, 567).

30. *Nasikhu't-Tawarikh*, vol. II, part 1, pp. 132, 135 (quoted in *Life of Muhammad* by Sell, pp. 124-130).

31. *A Traveller's Narrative*, p. 372.

32. Ibid., pp. 368, 369, *J.R.A.S.* April 1892, pp. 296, 297, *Materials*, pp. 22, 23. Many years after these events Abbas Efendi (Abdu'l-Baha) in his Will and Testament (Persian text, p. 4, line 9) stated that "Subh-i-Azal shed the pure blood [of Baha] in Edirne," an allegation which Baha himself never made, and for which no adequate evidence exists (*Azal's Notes*, p. 1015).

33. *Azal's Notes*, p. 198.

34. *J.R.A.S.* April 1892, p. 297.

35. *A Traveller's Narrative*, pp. 361, 370, *J.R.A.S.* July 1889, pp. 516, 517.

36. *A Traveller's Narrative*, p. 370. See Appendix II, #72, in which Baha'u'llah admits the assassins acted under orders.

37. Authors of *Hasht Bihisht*, who were Shaykh Ahmad Ruhi and Mirza Aqa Khan, both of Kirman (*Azal's Notes*, p. 1016), quoted in *A Traveller's Narrative*, p. 360.

38. *Journal of the Book Society of Iran* (Rahnama-i-Kitab) April 1963, pp. 102-110. The article is by Dr. Muhammad Ali Muwahhid. The file in the archives in Istanbul is No. 1475, #12 and 13. It is probable that much more information bearing on the Babi history may lie buried in the Istanbul archives. See Appendix II, #7 and #13.

39. *Azal's Notes*, p. 1016.

40. Refer to the Introduction of this book, also to Browne in *New History*, p. XXXI, and to *A Traveller's Narrative*, p. XLV.

41. Subh-i-Azal quoted in *A Traveller's Narrative*, p. 343, *J.R.A.S.* July 1892, p. 452, *Azal's Notes*, pp. 207-213.

42. *J.R.A.S.* July 1889, pp. 505, 506.

43. *New History*, p. XXVIII.

44. It is said that this charge is found in the Persian book *Bada'i'l-Athar*, vol. II, by Abbas Effendi.

Many years passed, and then in 1970 a book was published under the title *Edward Granville Browne and
the Baha'i Faith*, by H. M. Balyuzi, George Ronald,
London. The author, a learned Baha'i, in this
volume which contains much valuable information,
has undertaken to prove that Professor Browne was
prejudiced in favor of the claims of Subh-i-Azal,
and in his later years was in his writings unfair
to Baha'u'llah and his followers.

Mr. Balyuzi devotes 25 pages of his book to a consideration of the *Nuqtatu'l-Kaf*, which Browne had
published in 1910. He maintains that while Hajji
Mirza Jani did write a history of the Babi movement,
the book which Browne published was not the original
work, but was a forgery composed later by some
follower of Subh-i-Azal. It is therefore untrust-
worthy, and does not possess the great importance
attached to it by Browne.

Also, Mr. Balyuzi questions the authorship of the
long Persian Introduction to the *Nuqtatu'l-Kaf*,
and gives reasons why he thinks Professor Browne
was not the author, though it bears his name. It
is evident that the purpose of the questioner is
to discredit the testimony of Browne to the appointment of Subh-i-Azal by the Bab as his successor,
which Mr. Balyuzi strenuously denies.

Mr. Balyuzi describes Subh-i-Azal as a weak and
unworthy person. Yet he concedes that, in the
words of Shoghi Effendi (*God Passes By*, p. 163),
Subh-i-Azal after the execution of the Bab was the
"recognized chief of the Babi Community" (p. 39).
But, we ask, if the Bab failed to appoint a
successor (which is improbable), was there not
among the devoted and able followers of the Bab
some one worthy to be chosen by them as the chief
of their community, and their leader in those
difficult years? How did it happen that a very
young man (19 years of age when the Bab died),

weak and unworthy in the opinion of Mr. Balyuzi,
who was not one of the Letters of the Living, and
had not even seen the Bab, was recognized by the
Babis as their chief? Might it not have been
because the Babis all believed that the Bab himself had appointed him? This is what Subh-i-Azal
and other faithful followers of the Bab have maintained. And Professor Browne agreed with them.

Mr. Balyuzi rightly speaks of Edward Browne as an
"eminent orientalist, matchless among his peers,
for his knowledge of Persia and Persian, a man of
great charm and great learning" (p. 121). Yet he
maintains that Browne was unaware that the *Nuqtatu'*
l-Kaf was a forgery, and that he had been deceived
by it. It should be remembered that the Comte de
Gobineau presumably acquired his manuscript of this
history while he was in Iran (1855-1858, 1861-1863),
and brought it with him to France not later than
1863. It was this manuscript that Browne published.
Hence, the book in its present form must have been
written sometime before 1863, and prior to the
declaration of Baha'u'llah and the division in the
Babi community. Whether, therefore, the book published by Browne was written entirely by Mirza
Jani before his death in 1852, or whether others
wrote the book after the death of Mirza Jani and
gave his name to it, the *Nuqtatu'l-Kaf* is by far
the earliest account in our possession of the early
Babi history, written by Babis. It accordingly
merits the importance attached to it by Edward
Browne.

Another fact which should not be forgotten in considering the authenticity of the *Nuqtatu'l-Kaf* is
that there is another manuscript copy of this book
in the Library of Princeton University, which had
previously belonged to Dr. Sa'eed Khan of Teheran.
In a note on p. 35 of his book, Mr. Balyuzi states
that he had known Dr. Sa'eed, whose "probity was
unquestionable." Dr. Sa'eed has stated that his
copy of the *Nuqtatu'l-Kaf* had been carefully compared with that published by Browne, and had been
found to be in substantial agreement with it. Dr.
Sa'eed did not consider his copy to be a forgery.

But even if it should be proved that the charge
of Mr. Balyuzi is true, and that Browne in 1910
published as authentic a spurious work, why did
not some Baha'i scholar at once call his attention to his mistake by publishing a critical
review of the book? Or why did not Abdu'l-Baha
himself, when he met Professor Browne in 1912 in
London, explain to him his mistake, and give him
the opportunity to retract his erroneous statements?
Browne never admitted that he had been mistaken in
his estimate of the authenticity of the *Nuqtatu'l-
Kaf*, for he was evidently convinced that he had not
erred. There is a well-known Persian verse which
says:

> If I see a pit, and a blind man nearby,
> If I sit in silence, a sinner am I.

Did not the failure of Abdu'l-Baha to warn Edward
Browne of the pit of error into which he saw him
falling, make him also responsible for his friend's
mistake?

However, if Browne had never seen and never published the *Nuqtatu'l-Kaf*, he would probably have
maintained to the end his firm belief that Subh-i-
Azal had indeed been appointed by the Bab to
succeed him. For even before his journey to Iran
in 1887 he had been convinced by the writings of
the Comte de Gobineau and others that Subh-i-Azal
by the appointment of the Bab was the chief of the
Babis. His later studies and the finding of the
Nuqtatu'l-Kaf only confirmed Browne in his belief.

It is indeed regrettable that now after sixty
years, when Edward Browne is no longer able to
defend himself, his competence as a scholar, and
even the integrity of his character, should be
thus called in question.

45. *Nuqtatu'l-Kaf*, p. XXXIV.

46. For lists and descriptions of extant Babi manuscripts see Browne in *J.R.A.S.* 1892, pp. 433-499,
and *Materials*, pp. 198-243.

47. Subh-i-Azal married in all at least six wives and
    had fifteen children, some of whom died in infancy.
    Three of his wives remained in Iran when he fled
    to Iraq in 1852. It has been said that Fatima,
    the Isfahan wife of the Bab, was later married for
    a time to Subh-i-Azal, but this is denied by
    others. She was finally given in marriage to
    Sayyid Muhammad of Isfahan. A complete list of
    the wives and children of Subh-i-Azal is given in
    Azal's Notes, pp. 560-563, 566-572.

48. An official document gave the number of adults as
    sixteen (*A Traveller's Narrative*, p. 381).

49. Ibid., p. XV, *Nuqtatu'l-Kaf*, p. XXXIV. See Appen-
    dix II, p. 3, #32 and 33.

50. *A Traveller's Narrative*, p. XXIV.

51. Ibid., p. XXV.

52. *Materials*, pp. 311 ff.

53. *Azal's Notes*, p. 557.

54. In 1930 A.D. Dr. Sa'eed of Teheran estimated the
    number of Babis (Azalis) in Iran to be about 1500,
    counting women and children. Mr. Azal, during his
    visit to Iran in 1963, estimated the number to be
    from 4000 to 5000. It is said that they have no
    organization.

7

The Manifestation of the Baha'u'llah

When Mirza Husayn Ali Baha was in prison in Teheran
following the Babi attempt on the life of the Shah,
the Russian minister helped to secure his release.(1)
In Baghdad the British Consul General offered the
protection of the British government to Baha, but
this offer was rejected, since he preferred to accept
Turkish nationality.(2) When in Edirne he was in
difficulty with the Turkish government, Baha turned
to France for hlep. He wrote a letter to the Comte
de Gobineau, former French minister in Iran and historian of the Babi movement, imploring him "to lay
the petition of this servant at the foot of the throne
of the Monarch of the Age [Napoloen III]," in order
that he might become a protege of France. Gobineau in
reply informed Baha that he had delivered his message
to Napoleon, but said that His Majesty had not been
pleased to signify his pleasure in the matter. However, he informed Baha that he was at liberty to
address himself to French diplomatic missions in
Turkey to have his grievances redressed.(3) Baha was
delighted, but his hope for assistance from France was
shortlived, for in the war with Prussia in 1870 France
was defeated, and the Emperor lost his throne.

And so Baha, a subject of Turkey and a political prisoner, without assistance from any government, began to play his new role as a Divine Manifestation and ruler of the great majority of the Babis scattered throughout the Near East. As has been pointed out by Sir Cecil Spring-Rice,(4) formerly British Minister at Teheran, the problem which Baha had to solve was not merely one of succession to the leadership of the Babi movement, but whether the religion which he represented was to become a world religion addressed to all mankind, or was to remain only an obscure Persian sect. For while the Bab had confidently predicted the time when his religion would cover the earth, it had already become clear to Baha, as it was clear to unprejudiced observers from the first, that such a system as that outlined by the Bab could never make any headway outside Iran. Many of the laws laid down by the Bab were entirely unsuited to the needs of mankind, either in Iran or out of it, and the hope cherished by the Bab's zealous followers of establishing by force a Babi theocracy had proved impossible of fulfilment. Accordingly, Baha, while not abrogating the Bayan of the Bab, adopted a policy of ignoring some of the impractical aspects of the Babi system, and its connection with Shi'ite Islam, and of emphasizing the universal character of the religion of which he had become the head. As he moved westward, he came near to lands in which many Christians and Jews resided. Hence he undertook to attract them as well as Babis and Muslims to himself. One way in which he did this was by issuing numerous epistles, or Tablets (*Lawh*), as they were called, in which he set forth his claim to be a Manifestation of God, and commanded people to accept and obey him.

In the *Lawh-i-Nasir*,(5) which is one of the earliest writings composed after his declaration, Baha says: "I revealed all the heavenly books by the glorious tongue of (Divine) Might;" that is, he, speaking as the Divine Will, claims to be the author of the Bible, the Koran and the Bayan. He also claims he is the Bab returned to earth again, saying, "In the Bayan I admonished all in the language of power." And he speaks of the execution of the Bab at Tabriz as though he had been the victim, saying, "At length they suspended my

glorious body in the air, and wounded it with the
bullets of malice and hatred, until my spirit returned
to the Supreme Companion." Baha complains bitterly of
the sufferings he is enduring from his enemies, and he
charges Nasir, probably some Babi to whom the epistle
is addressed, not to listen to anyone who tries to
turn his heart from the love of Baha. He addresses
Nasir as "O my slave!" How different is this attitude
from that revealed in the Iqan written a few years
earlier when he declared that he "never sought supremacy over anyone."(6)

It is probable that the *Suratu'l-Muluk* (Chapter of
Kings) like the *Lawh-i-Nasir* was composed before Baha's
departure from Edirne. In this epistle he addressed
the rulers of the earth and bade them acknowledge him.
(7) "O Kings of the earth!" he wrote, "Hearken to the
voice of God from this fruitful, lofty Tree." The Bab
had called himself the Tree of Reality, in reference
to the burning bush from which God addressed Moses,
and Baha here adopts the same title.(8) The tone in
which he addressed the Sultan of Turkey was hardly conciliatory.(9) "Hast thou heard, O King, what hath
befallen us at the hands of thy ministers, and what
they have done unto us, or art thou of the heedless?
.....I will tell Your Majesty of what befell us at the
hands of these oppressors. Know then that we came at
thy command and entered into thy city with conspicuous
honour, but were expelled from it with dishonour,
wherewith no dishonour in the world can be compared."
Baha also commanded the kings to reduce their armies.
"Be at peace one with another, and reduce your armies
that your expenses may be diminished," he writes.(10)
"And [even] if ye should raise up differences between
yourselves, ye will not need great military forces,
but only so much as will suffice for you to guard your
domains and realms." This is perhaps Baha's first
written appeal for world peace.(11) There is no evidence that the *Suratu'l-Muluk* was ever received by or
dispatched to the kings of the earth to whom it was
addressed, but it no doubt deeply impressed the followers of Baha to whom it was read. They probably did
not have the privilege of listening to the reading of
Baha's appeal to the Comte de Gobineau to intercede on

his behalf with the Emperor of France, which was written about the same time as the Epistle to the Kings.

Neither appeals nor protests availed, and in the
first part of August, 1868 the Babi leaders, those who
were loyal to Subh-i-Azal as well as those who had
followed Baha, were deported from Erdine. Baha and
about seventy of his family and adherents made the
long journey by carriage and then by ship to Acre
(Akka), a penal colony on the Mediterranian coast near
Haifa. There they arrived on August 31. The weather
was hot, and for a time the exiles suffered much from
crowded quarters and bad food. Of this period Mirza
Jawad, who was with Baha and was his devoted disciple,
writes thus in his *Historical Epitome*:(12) "So the
[military] barracks had the honor of receiving them,
and they locked the doors and set military sentinels
over them. That night we could obtain no water to
drink, save such stale and stagnant water in the tank
there as was absolutely unfit for drinking. The community also remained without food that night until
morning. After that, however, there were assigned to
each one three loaves of bread, but they were utterly
unfit for food, and used to be exchanged in the market
for two [bettér] loaves so that it might be possible
to eat them. In all ways matters went hard with this
community." The climate was bad, and soon half of the
exiles fell sick, and some died.

"After the lapse of some months," continues Mirza
Jawad,(13) "the hardships which befell them gave rise
to doubt in the minds of those who were of the company of His Holiness our Master [Baha], and they began
to turn aside from the path of truth and steadfastness,
and to forsake loyalty and love.....The schism was
fierce, nor do I care to discuss it in detail." After
two years Baha and his family were removed from the
military barracks and provided with a house in the
town of Akka. "We were given a comfortable house with
three rooms and a court," said the daughter of Baha to
Mr. Phelps.(14) They continued to live in different
houses in the town for nine years.(15)

In Akka Baha had ample leisure to meditate, and to
prepare the proofs for his claim to be a new Manifestation.

The Bab had adduced his "verses" as the proof that he
spoke for God, and Baha in like manner issued numerous
Tablets and other pronouncements which he said were
the Words of God.   But these supposedly inspired utterances did not convince everyone that their author was
truly the "He-Whom-God-Will-Manifest" predicted by the
Bab, and so Baha used all his erudition and ingenuity
in producing other grounds on which to base his claims
to Divinity.   Mr. Jelal Azal has made an exhaustive
study of this subject, the results of which are contained in his *Notes*(16) and to him I am indebted for
the material included in this brief summary.

As has been noted in previous chapters, the only
one in the Bayanic Dispensation who was authorized to
bestow titles was the Point of the Manifestation, and
the Bab was most generous in giving very high and
mighty titles to his Letters and to his Vicegerent
Subh-i-Azal.   But there is no valid evidence whatever
that the Bab gave a title to Mirza Husayn Ali. Avareh
has stated that when others received titles from the
Bab at the Badasht Conference, Mirza Husayn Ali was
hurt because none was given to him.   So to comfort him,
Qurratu'l-Ayn bestowed on him the title *Baha* (Splendor,
or Glory), one which she had herself received from the
Bab.(17)   Others may have called him by this name, but
there is no valid evidence that the Bab ever did so.
On March 27, 1850, only three months before his death,
the Bab, according to the notation in his personal
Diary, wrote an epistle to "238, the brother of the
Fruit."   As we have seen, the Fruit was Subh-i-Azal.
The numerical value of the Arabic letters in Husayn
Ali is 238.   Hence, it seems that when the Bab wrote
his epistle to Mirza Husayn Ali, charging him to take
the utmost care of Subh-i-Azal, he used no title in
addressing him, but referred to his younger brother
as "the Most Glorious *(Abha)* Element."   The epistle
clearly indicates that it was written by a superior
to an inferior.(18)

Thus, whether this title was given by someone not
authorized to bestow titles, or whether it was self-
assumed, Mirza Husayn Ali became Baha, and for his
purpose a better title could not have been found.
Baha was the name given by the Bab to the first of

the 19 months of his calendar. Also, Baha was the
name given by the Bab to the first day of the first
month, which was the great Iranian festival of No Ruz.
(19) Moreover, the word *baha* is found in its various
forms many hundreds of times not only in the writings
of the Bab but also in the Scriptures of the Jews and
Christians. Mirza Husayn Ali no doubt spent many
hours searching for this beautiful word in all the
sacred writings, and claiming it wherever it was found
as a reference to himself. The result was most satisfying to him and his followers, but not always to
others. It was as though a man who became dissatisfied with his surname should decide to change it and
become Mr. Love, and then persuade himself and others
that every reference to *love* in the Bible was a reference to him. If he had previously been embarrassed
by an inferiority complex, the assurance that "the
greatest of these is love" would no doubt give him
much encouragement.

But even better than *Baha* was a phrase found in the
Bayan, namely, *Baha'u'llah* (The Glory of God). This
he took as his full title, and by this name he is
known today. According to the Bayan, this is a title
for each of the Divine Manifestations.(20) The Bab
pronounced it in the Bayan(21) "the best of names,"
and he assumed it for himself, and also bestowed it
on Subh-i-Azal.(22) But like Esau's birthright it was
taken by his brother.

In claiming all occurrences of *Baha* as references
to himself, Mirza Husayn Ali frequently read the passages out of context, and usually failed to state the
chapter and verse from which he was quoting. Thus he
often appropriated to himself words and statements
which were intended for others. For example, in his
testamentary document addressed to Subh-i-Azal, the
Bab wrote: ".....bear witness that in truth I am alive
in the Most Splendid (*Abha*) Horizon." The reference
of *Abha* is here to the Bab and to Subh-i-Azal, but was
taken by Baha as belonging to himself.(23) Similarly,
in his *First Book* the Bab mentioned "red ruby ships
intended for the people of Baha." By *Baha* he meant
himself (the Bab), since he was *Baha'u'llah*. But his

brother appropriated this phrase, and in the *Kitab-i-Aqdas* (p. 47) referred to a red ship for his followers (Baha'is).(24) In the same way Baha appropriated the title "Remnant of God" which the Bab in his *First Book* had used for the Hidden Imam, and in a later writing had taken for himself. In these and in numerous other ways the new Manifestation sought to justify his claims.(25)

As the Bab gave titles to some of his faithful followers, so Baha'u'llah used his prerogative as a new Manifestation to bestow titles on certain believers. (26) To his first wife Asiya whom he married in Teheran in 1835 A.D., and who bore him six children, he gave the title "Nawwaba," because she was the daughter of Nawwab (Highness) of Teheran. To his second wife Bibi Fatima, his cousin whom he married in 1849 A.D., who also bore him six children, he gave the title "Supreme Cradle," a title reserved for the Queen-Mother in Iran. To his third wife Gohar whom he married in Baghdad or Edirne, who bore him a daughter Furughiyya, he gave no title. Since Baha'u'llah was the Tree of Truth his sons were called "Branches." Abbas Efendi, eldest son by his first wife, received the title "Most Mighty (*A'zam*) Branch," and Mirza Muhammad Ali, eldest son by his second wife, became "Most Great (*Akbar*) Branch." The other sons were given the titles "Most Pure Branch" and "Most Luminous Branch." And to his daughter Bahiyya was given the title "Supreme Leaf."(27) One of his faithful followers received the title "Servant of God," another became "Divinely Fragrant," and the barber was entitled "Barber of Reality." Perhaps the possession of these marks of dignity made it somewhat easier for these exiles to endure their lot.

According to Mirza Jawad,(28) the Azalis who had been sent to spy on the Baha'is began after a time to cause them great annoyance by attempting to arouse the natives of the town of Akka against them. The Muslims of Akka were all Sunnites, and were quite intolerant of heretics such as the Baha'is. Therefore, in order to avoid trouble, Baha'u'llah and his followers took great pains to conceal their real beliefs, as they had done previously in Iran, Baghdad and Edirne, and to

profess and practice in public the faith of Islam.
Accordingly, they went regularly to the Muslim mosques
and recited the prayers after the manner of the Sunnites. They also kept the Muslim month of fasting
Ramazan, and tried in every way possible to convince
the Muslims that they were one with them. So successful were they in this effort that when Baha'u'llah and
his son and successor Abbas Efendi died, the Sunnite
clergy conducted their funeral services. This they
would never have done had they realized that Baha'u'
llah claimed to be a Manifestation of God, greater
than Muhammad. The title "Baha'u'llah," the Splendor
of God, was therefore carefully avoided in Akka, and
the leader of the Baha'is was known as Baha Efendi,
or Baha'u'Din, the Splendor of Religion.(29) This
attempt to conceal the nature of their faith, says
Mirza Jawad, was being thwarted by the Azalis, who
began to circulate among the people of Akka some of
the verses of Baha'u'llah, with interpolations of
their own. "Their numerous efforts to stir up mischief," he says, "and their provocative actions caused
bitter sorrows to all the Friends, and grievous trouble befell them."

Finally, the Baha'is determined to get rid of the
trouble-makers. On January 23, 1872, seven of the
Baha'is came upon three of the Azalis in a house in
Akka and murdered them.(30) Though some Baha'i
writers have entirely omitted this part of the history,
there is no doubt whatever that the assassinations
took place.(31) Whether this deed was done in obedience to the command of Baha'u'llah, or was contrary
to his orders, is uncertain.(32)

The Turkish authorities at once arrested Baha'u'
llah and his sons and most of the male members of the
Baha'i community, and kept them in confinement for
several days. Baha'u'llah and his sons were soon
released. The seven murderers were sent to the har-
bour, where they were kept in prison for some years,
and were later freed. Sixteen other Baha'is were
kept in prison for six months, and were then released,
in answer, says Mirza Jawad, to a prayer taught them
by Baha'u'llah.(33) It was not without reason that

the Turkish authorities used some severity in their
treatment of the Baha'is in Akka.

While Subh-i-Azal and Baha'u'llah were enduring
life imprisonment in distant lands, what was happening
to the Babis in Iran? Most of them had become Baha'is,
and were sometimes persecuted by the Muslims. Some
had become Azalis, and were opposed by both Muslims
and Baha'is. Ever since the massacre which had resulted from the Babi attempt on the life of the Shah in
1852, all of them had practiced "concealment" in order
to be able to live their lives in peace among their
unbelieving neighbors. Little is known as to the numbers or the activities of these people who, when recognized, were generally despised as heretics. So
effectively did they conceal their beliefs, that, as
Professor Browne discovered when he visited Iran in
1887, it was almost impossible to make contact with
them. During these years there were occasional out-
bursts of opposition, with a few murders. Some Muslims
who wished to get rid of their personal enemies would
do so by branding them as "Babis," and getting them
killed. Mirza Jawad in his Historical Epitome lists
about thirty-one Baha'is who were killed in Iran and
Iraq between 1866 and 1891.(34) It is not known how
many Azalis were killed by Baha'is and Muslims, but
the number was not very large. The statements often
heard about the many thousands of Baha'i martyrs in
Iran are entirely false.

One of the Baha'i martyrs deserves special notice.
He was a young man who came from Khurasan to Akka in
1869 to visit Baha'u'llah, and from him received the
name *Badi'* (Wonderful).(35) Badi' volunteered to
deliver in person, without speaking to anyone about
his mission as he journeyed from Akka to Iran, an
epistle which Baha u'llah had written to Nasiru'd-Din
Shah.(36) In this epistle Baha'u'llah addressed the
Shah with great humility, saying he has always been a
loyal subject of the Shah, and condemning the attempt
on the Shah's life. He put the blame for all the
evil that had occurred on the Muslim clergy, and begged the Shah to grant freedom to the Babis in Iran to
live and practice their religion in peace and freedom.

The letter was carried by the young messenger on foot
to Teheran, where, in accordance with instructions
given him by Baha'u'llah, he stood by the wayside
till the Shah passed, and succeeded in giving the
message into his hands. When the Shah realized who
the sender of the message was he became greatly disturbed, and remembering the attempt on his life seventeen years before, he commanded that the messenger
be tortured to find out whether he had any accomplices,
and then put to death. Badi' showed the greatest
courage in enduring suffering, and died for his Master.
The date was July, 1869. No doubt this event which
was publicized throughout Iran made it more necessary
than before that the Baha'is conceal their faith.

Muslim historians relate that Muhammad sent letters
from Madina to the kings of Persia and Byzantium and
other countries, bidding them to acknowledge him as a
Prophet of Allah.(37) Following his example Baha'u'
llah, probably in the early part of his residence in
Akka, composed a number of epistles which he addressed
to numerous rulers.(38) To the Czar of Russia he
said, "One of thy ambassadors did assist me when I
was in prison, in chains and fetters [in Teheran in
1852]. Therefore hath God decreed unto thee a station
which the knowledge of no one comprehendeth."(39) He
severely condemned Napoleon III for his failure to
assist him, and predicted his downfall.(40) (The epistle was probably composed *after* he lost his crown in
1870). He praised Queen Victoria for abolishing
slavery and establishing representative government.
(41) He violently denounced the Sultan of Turkey for
the wrongs done to him and his followers in Akka.(42)
The Epistle to the Shah of Iran is very different from
the conciliatory message sent by Badi', for the tone
"is one of fierce recrimination." The Shah is severely
rebuked for killing the Bab, and the attempt of the
Babis to assassinate him is excused if not approved.
(43) To the Pope, Baha'u'llah proclaims himself as
God the Father, as the Comforter promised by Christ,
and as Christ himself come again, and bids him and
all Christians accept him. "Dost thou dwell in palaces," he asks the Pope, "while the King of Manifestations is in the most ruined of abodes [Akka]? Leave

palaces to those who desire them, then advance to the
Kingdom with spirituality and fragrance."(44) Baha'u'
llah also addressed messages at this or at a later
time to America, Austria, and Germany. There is no
evidence that any of these epistles were ever sent,
or were ever received by those to whom they were
addressed. It is inconceivable that a subject of
Turkey, banished to Akka as a political prisoner,
should send a letter like the one referred to above
to his Sultan. The result would have been the same
fate that befell the unfortunate Badi' in Teheran. It
is evident that the purpose of these eloquent epistles,
known as the *Alwah-i-Salatin* (Epistles of the Kings)
was to impress the Baha'is with the boldness of their
Master. This purpose was fully achieved.

After living in various houses in the town of Akka
for nine years, Baha'u'llah in 1877, to quote Mirza
Jawad once more,(45) "rented the palace of Abdu'llah
Pasha which lies to the north of Akka at a distance
of about an hour and a half [by carriage] from the town;
and at times he used to live in the town and at other
times in the Palace, until the year 1880, when he
rented the palace of Udi Khammar [the Mansion of Bahji],
situated in a northerly direction at a distance of half
an hour from Akka. Most of his time he passed in this
Palace in the company of his three sons and his family
and his Honour the Servant of God, while Abbas Efendi
with his sister and children remained at Akka.(46)
Sometimes he used to visit the town, and while he
dwelt outside the town visitors, whether pilgrims or
Companions, used to have the honour of seeing him after
permission had been obtained by them, and used to spend
some days and nights there.....Many spots in the town
were honoured by the approach of our Master Baha'u'llah,
and likewise numerous places and villages outside it
.....So likewise he visited Hayfa four times," once
remaining there three months. From this account by a
devoted follower we learn that while Baha'u'llah was
not free to leave the district he was yet given a
great deal of freedom to move about Akka and its envir-
ons as he pleased. He was by no means "in prison"
during most of his sojourn there. The palaces and
beautiful gardens which Baha'u'llah at first rented

and later bought were made possible for him by the
large sums of money and generous gifts which poured
to him from his faithful followers in Iran and other
lands.(47)

During his years in Akka, contrary to his custom
when he was in Baghdad and Edirne, Baha'u'llah lived
largely in seclusion. No one was allowed to visit him
except by special permission. Each visitor was carefully prepared for his audience with the Manifestation
of God. He was told that what he saw when he came
into the Divine Presence would depend on what he was
himself - if he was a material person he would see
only a man, but if he was a spiritual being he would
see God.(48) When his expectations had been sufficiently aroused, the pilgrim was led into the presence
of Baha'u'llah and was permitted to gaze for a few
moments upon "the Blessed Perfection," care being
taken that the visitation should end before the spell
was broken. The almost magical effect of such visits
is seen in the account which Professor Browne has
given of his experience in Akka in 1890.(49)

After visiting Subh-i-Azal in Cyprus (Chapter VI),
Browne came to Beirut, and there asked permission by
telegraph to visit the Baha'i headquarters in Akka.
When this was granted he travelled on horseback, a
journey of three days, to Akka. Of this journey he
writes:(50) "The last day was perhaps the most
delightful of all, and I was greatly astonished on
entering the Acre plain to behold a wealth of beautiful gardens and fragrant orange groves such as I had
little expected to find in what Baha has stigmatized
as 'the most desolate of countries'." After his
arrival in Akka he was welcomed by Abbas Efendi,
eldest son of Baha'u'llah, "a tall strongly-built man
holding himself straight as an arrow, with white
turban and raiment, long black locks reaching almost
to the shoulder, broad powerful forehead indicating
a strong intellect combined with an unswerving will,
eyes keen as a hawk's, and strongly-marked but pleasing features.....One more eloquent of speech, more
ready of argument, more apt of illustration, more
intimately acquainted with the sacred books of the

Jews, the Christians, and the Muhammadans, could, I
should think, scarcely be found.....About the greatness of this man and his power no one who had seen
him could entertain a doubt."(51)   By Abbas Efendi
Browne was conducted to the palace outside the city
where Baha'u'llah resided.   There he spent five most
interesting days, and was deeply impressed by the
hospitality of the Baha'is, and by the "spiritual
atmosphere" which pervaded the place.

"During the morning of the day after my installa-
tion at Behje [the palace ," continues Browne,(51)
"one of Baha's younger sons entered the room where I
was sitting and beckoned to me to follow him.   I did
so, and was conducted through passages and rooms at
which I scarcely had time to glance to a spacious
hall, paved.....with a mosaic of marble.   Before a
curtain suspended from the wall of this great ante-
chamber my conductor paused for a moment while I
removed by shoes.(53)   Then, with a quick movement
of the hand, he withdrew, and, as I passed, replaced
the curtain; and I found myself in a large apartment
.....Though I dimly suspected whither I was going
and whom I was to behold (for no distinct intimation
had been given to me), a second or two elapsed ere,
with a throb of wonder and awe, I became definitely
conscious that the room was not untenated.   In the
corner where the divan met the wall sat a wondrous
and venerable figure, crowned with a felt head-dress
of the kind called *taj* by dervishes (but of unusual
height and make), round the base of which was wound
a small white turban.   The face of him on whom I
gazed I can never forget, though I cannot describe
it.   Those piercing eyes seemed to read one's very
soul; power and authority sat on that ample brow.....
No need to ask in whose presence I stood, as I bowed
myself before one who is the object of a devotion
and love which kings might envy and emperors sigh
for in vain!   A mild dignified voice bade me be
seated, and then continued: 'Praise be to God that
thou hast attained!'."

The audience lasted about twenty minutes. Baha'u'
llah spoke of the sufferings he had endured, though

he desired only the good of the world. He wanted all
men to become one in faith, and be as brothers. He
wished diversity of religion and race to cease. He
said that these fruitless strifes and ruinous wars
would pass away, and the "Most Great Peace" would come.
"Let not a man glory in this," he said, "that he loves
his country; let him rather glory in this, that he
loves his kind....." He also read aloud to his visitor
one of his Tablets. Before his departure from Akka,
Browne was given by Abbas Efendi a copy of *A Traveller's Narrative* in Persian, which, he was told, was
an authentic history of the movement. Only later did
he learn that the author was no other than he who
presented the book to him. (54)

It is interesting to compare with this enthusiastic
account written by Professor Browne the impression of
an Azali traveller who went to Akka to see Baha'u'llah.
"The misleading of the Black Darkness," he writes, (55)
"brought me into the City of Blood, the town of Akka
.....There I plainly saw the manifestation of plurality, to wit, the combination of thunder, lightning,
darkness, and the thunder-bolt.....For these are they
who have hidden the light of their original potential-
ity with the darkness of the attributes of wicked
souls and the effects of a corrupt nature, and have
been veiled from the Truth by Untruth." The first of
the "unbelieving souls and manifestations of infidelity" whom he met on the seashore was Abbas Efendi,
whom he calls "the Whisperer," a name for the devil.
"After that," he continues, "I saw the rest of the
Wicked One's followers, and heard the words of each.
Their sayings and arguments consist of a farrago of
names, baseless stories, calumnies, falsehoods, and
lies, and not one of them has any knowledge of even
the first principles of the religion of the Bayan or
of any other religion. They are all devoid of knowledge, ignorant, shortsighted.....hypocrites, corrup-
ters of texts, blind imitators." After several days
this follower of Subh-i-Azal was admitted to the
audience-chamber of Baha'u'llah. "When I was come
there," he says, "and looked upon that Arch-idol.....
that rebellious Lucifer, that envious Iblis [the devil],
I saw a form on a throne, and heard the 'lowing of the

calf'."(56) It is quite evident that this Azali was
not converted by his visit to Akka, and neither was
Professor Browne.

The location of Baha'u'llah in Akka, which was much
more accessible to the people of Iran than was Cyprus,
the place of Subh-i-Azal's banishment, no doubt helped
to accelerate the growth of Baha'ism. For from the
time he was taken to Akka, many of his followers began
making the pilgrimage there in the hope of seeing their
Lord. Baha'u'llah, however, did not encourage the
Baha'is in their desire to visit him. First of all,
there was too great risk of their seeing and hearing
things in Akka which might weaken their faith. There
was a saying among the Baha'is of Iran that whoever
went to Akka lost his faith.(57) And then the presence of large numbers of zealous believers in the
city would undoubtedly have led to complications with
the native Muslim population. The Baha'is in other
lands were therefore told that if they gave to Baha'u'
llah the money they would have spent on their journey
they would gain the same merit as if they had come
before his Presence.

However, the intimate relationship between him and
his followers was carefully maintained. The place of
personal visits was taken by personal epistles, or
Tablets, which were sent by the hundreds to the believers in Iran and other lands, answering their
questions, and praising them for their fidelity to
the Cause. These letters were all carried by hand,
as it was dangerous to entrust them to the posts.
Browne describes one of the couriers whom he met in
Iran, an old man who used to go to Akka each year
carrying with him letters from the Baha'is of southern
Iran. Then, when the replies to these communications
had been written by Baha'u'llah's scribe, and signed
by him, they were taken by the courier to their various destinations. His task was not without its
perils. He told Professor Browne how on one occasion,
when he had been arrested in a village in Iran, he
had eaten his whole pack of letters rather than let
them fall into the hands of enemies! The Baha'i who
received an epistle from his Master was indeed a

fortunate man. He would show it to his brothers in
the faith, who would kiss it and ask for copies of
it, and he would then lay it away among his choicest
treasures. The secluded life which he led gave
Baha'u'llah ample opportunity for dictating these
epistles. He composed a vast number of them, in
addition to numerous longer treatises, some of which
will be considered in Chapter VIII. All of these
writings were believed by the Baha'is to be the Word
of God.

Baha'u'llah lived in Akka or in its suburbs for
twenty-four years. During this period the numbers
and influence of the Baha'is in Iran and in other
lands continued to increase. Browne estimated their
number in Iran in the year 1892 to be five hundred
thousand,(58) but since there was no census, and since
the Baha'is concealed their faith, no accurate figures were possible. Usually they were able to live
in peace with their Muslim neighbors, and for as long
as they did not stir up trouble they were rarely mol-
ested.(59) The Iranian government has recognized
four religions, Zoroastrianism, Judaism, Christianity
and Islam, but has never recognized Baha'ism, and so
Baha'is in Iran have been officially classed as Muslims.

Regarding the final period of Baha'u'llah's life,
Mirza Jawad writes as follows:(60) "External conditions were the opposite of those which first prevailed,
for his fame waxed great; power, majesty and triumph
were apparent.....[But] notwithstanding these circumstances and materials of glory, ease, and joy, we used
to discover signs of sadness in His Holiness our Master
Baha'u'llah to an extent which neither writing nor
utterance can express." He then quotes several of the
sayings of his Master which reveal his sorrow.(61) "By
God's life, all things weep for what hath befallen
this oppressed one at the hands of those who deny,
after we had created them for pure truth, and had
taught them the clear straight way of God. Alas, alas
for what hath befallen me from every tyrant, from
every sinner, from every liar!.....There hath descended on this oppressed one that which hath no like-
ness and no similitude.....I desire a dark and narrow
dwelling, that I may lament and weep over my wrongs."

This sadness was not due to any financial difficulties, for Baha'u'llah had been able with funds which his agents collected for him to provide well for himself and his family. He purchased lands for each of his four sons in villages in the vicinity of Akka, as well as in the Galilee and Haifa districts, and had these properties registered in their names.(62) But there were other problems in his family which gave him concern. He foresaw the trouble which Munira Khanum (63) the wife of Abbas Efendi might cause, and he charged his three younger sons to guard his writings carefully lest any of them fall into her hands and be destroyed by her.(64) He no doubt also realized that there would be another power struggle after his death, similar to the one which had caused his banishment to Akka. This, says Mirza Jawad, was the chief cause of his great sadness.(65)

At length Baha'u'llah fell ill, and at the age of seventy-four died on May 29, 1892. His body was buried according to the rites of the Sunnite Muslims in the house of his son-in-law Sayyid Ali Afnan in the Bahji Garden,(66) and his tomb soon became a shrine for the Baha'is who visit Akka. His youngest son Badi'u'llah Efendi wrote thus to Professor Browne about his father's death:(67)

"O friend of my heart, and delight of my soul! In these days the showers of affliction do so descend from the clouds of the firmament of fate, and the thunderbolts of griefs and sorrows do so succeed one another, that neither hath the tongue strength to describe, nor the pen power to utter them. For the horizon of the Phenomenal World is bereft of the effulgences of the Sun of Wisdom and Revelation, and the throne of the Universe is deprived of the radiance of the Most Luminary.....The Sun of Truth has bidden farewell to this earthy sphere, and now shines with a brightness which waneth not in the regions of Might and Glory." And after further expressions of grief, he quotes several passages from his father's book, the *Kitab-i-Aqdas* (Most Holy Book), one of which is: (68) "O people of the earth! When the Sun of my Beauty sets, and the firmament of my form is hidden, be not troubled; arise for the helping of my work and

the advancement of my Word throughout the worlds.
Verily we are with you under all conditions, and will
help you with the Truth." No doubt the son's grief
was shared by many who looked to Baha'u'llah as the
Manifestation of God for this age.(69)

NOTES

1. Mirza Jawad in *Materials*, p. 6.

2. Ibid., pp. 11, 12.

3. Gobineau's correspondence with Baha is preserved
   in La Bibliotheque Nationale in Strasbourg, France,
   the document being marked "3534." See *Azal's Notes*,
   pp. 360, 367, 376-396, 422, in which a full account
   of this correspondence is given, with a translation
   of large portions of Baha's letters, in which he
   begs for help, and never once alludes to his divine
   mission, or to Subh-i-Azal's rejection of him, and
   refers to himself and his fellow-prisoners as
   Babis. See Appendix II, #23 and 24.

4. *Materials*, p. XXI.

5. *A Traveller's Narrative*, p. 96, note 1, *J.R.A.S.*
   October 1889, pp. 949-953.

6. *Kitab-i-Iqan* (Book of Certitude), translated by
   Shoghi Effendi, p. 249. The translation of the
   Persian phrase is by Browne.

7. *J.R.A.S.* April 1892, pp. 268-283.

8. Ibid., p. 276, note 2.

9. Ibid., p. 278.

10. Ibid., p. 275.

11. The occasion for this and other appeals to the
    kings of the earth to reduce their armies and be
    at peace among themselves was probably the strug-
    gle between Russia, France and England for supre-
    macy in the Near East. While Baha was in Baghdad

the Crimean War was fought between Russia on the one side, and Turkey, Great Britain and France on the other. About the time he came to Edirne, France for a short time occupied Syria. When he was being transferred from Edirne to Akka, war almost broke out between Turkey and Greece. In 1870 France was defeated by Prussia and Napoleon III fell. In 1877 war again broke out between Russia and Turkey, and Turkey was defeated. Since the outcome of these struggles would have a direct bearing on his own fate, Baha no doubt watched with deep concern all that the nations were doing. It did not require a prophet then any more than now to predict that the race for supremacy would end in destruction. Baha was not the first to appeal for peace. An International Congress of peace societies was held in London in 1843. In 1848 a second Congress was held at Brussels. The third was held in Paris in 1849 under the presidency of Victor Hugo. Others were held at Frankfurt, London and Manchester. Still another was held at Paris at the International Exposition of 1878. Baha had himself witnessed the horrors of civil war in the Babi uprisings in Iran. While in Akka he read the newspapers (*Baha'i Scriptures*, p. 146), and was informed of these many efforts to secure peace. Therefore, however much we may honor Baha'u'llah for including "the Most Great Peace" in the program of his new dispensation, it is not surprising that he did so.

12. *Materials*, p. 45. This account was written in 1904.

13. Ibid., p. 50.

14. *Abbas Efendi*, by Phelps, Putnam's 1903, p. 66.

15. Mirza Jawad in *Materials*, p. 58.

16. *Azal's Notes*, pp. 607-611, 682-786, 974-1027.

17. Ibid., pp. 684, 712-716.

18. Ibid., pp. 607-611. See Appendix II, #29. 30 and 31.

19. Ibid., p. 691.

20. Ibid., p. 697.

21. Bayan quoted in *Nuqtatu'l-Kaf*, p. LVIII.

22. Authors of *Hasht Bihisht* quoted in *A Traveller's Narrative*, p. 353.

23. *Azal's Notes*, pp. 686-689.

24. Ibid., pp. 698-700.

25. Ibid., pp. 718-721.

26. Authors of *Hasht Bihisht*, quoted in *A Traveller's Narrative*, pp. 361, 362, Avareh in *Al-Kawakib*, Vol. II, pp. 4, 6, 8. For lists of members of the family of Baha'u'llah see Mirza Jawad in *Materials*, pp. 62, 63, and Browne in *Materials*, pp. 320, 321. See also Appendix II, #25. In addition to the three wives named here, it is stated by Avareh that when Baha'u'llah was seventy years of age he married Jamalieh, the fifteen year old niece of "Muhammad Hasan the servant" (*Kashfu'l-Hiyal*, vol. I, 6th impression, p. 104). See also *Azal's Notes*, pp. 626, 1033. Baha did not divorce any of his wives, and all of them, with the possible exception of Nawwaba, survived him.

27. *Azal's Notes*, p. 1029.

28. *Materials*, p. 51, 52.

29. *Azal's Notes*, p. 58.

30. Idem., p. 1031.

31. Authors of *Hasht Bihisht* quoted in *A Traveller's Narrative*, pp. 361-364, 370, 371, *J.R.A.S.* July 1889, p. 517, October 1889, pp. 995, 996.

32. In one of his Tablets written near the end of his life, and published in a book of 295 pages called *Ishraqat, Tarazat (and) Tajalliat*, on pages 12, 14-15, Baha'u'llah repeatedly admonished his followers to avoid sedition, strife, murder and plunder, and to associate with all sects of people with love and friendship. Then he added: "Though in the early days there had been revealed from the Supreme Pen what is obviously repugnant to the new Cause of God, for instance passages such as these, 'the necks have stretched out in discord, where are

the swords of thy Power, O Dominant of the Worlds?'
But the object thereof was not strife and sedition,
.....[but] that the oppression of the Pharoahs of
the earth has reached such a pitch that the like
of this verse had been revealed from the Supreme
Pen. And now we exhort God's servants not to ad-
here henceforth to some of the utterances, and not
to become a cause of hurt to other [fellow] servants." In this rather veiled statement it seems
that Baha'u'llah admits that the "swords" were
literally used at his command by his followers
against his enemies, but that this must not be
interpreted by his followers in later times as
permission to engage in sedition and murder. However, "in the early days" the zealous followers
of Baha'u'llah, acting on the authority of this
and other statements of their Master, were able
to assassinate a number of Azali leaders in various
places, as has been narrated in Chapter VI. See
Azal's Notes, pp. 189-193, and 1111-1113A, and
Appendix II, #72.

33. *Materials*, pp. 55-58.

34. Ibid., pp. 35-43, *Azal's Notes*, p. 502.

35. *J.R.A.S.* October 1889, pp. 954-960, *A Traveller's
Narrative*, pp. XLV, 102-105, *Materials*, pp. 47-49.

36. A part of this epistle is found in *A Traveller's
Narrative*, pp. 108-151, 390-400.

37. *Life of Mohammad*, Muir, London 1861, vol. IV,
p. 54.

38. *J.R.A.S.* October 1889, pp. 953-972, *Azal's Notes*,
pp. 373-424, *Baha'i Scriptures*, pp. 67-188.

39. *J.R.A.S.* October 1889, p. 969.

40. Ibid., p. 968.

41. Ibid., p. 970.

42. Ibid., pp. 960-963.

43. Ibid., pp. 954-960.

44. Ibid., pp. 963-966.

45. *Materials*, pp. 58-60.

46. Baha'u'llah and his second wife lived in the
    Mansion at Bahji, while his first wife lived with
    her son Abbas Efendi and his wife and his sister
    in Akka. Baha's third wife and her daughter lived
    in a house opposite the Mansion (Subhi, *Payam-i-
    Padar*, p. 107).

47. *Azal's Notes*, pp. 48-51.

48. Niku, *Filsifa-i-Niku*, vol. II, p. 127.

49. *A Traveller's Narrative*, pp. XXX, XLIII.

50. Ibid., p. XXX.

51. Ibid., p. XXXVI.

52. Ibid., p. XXXIX.

53. See Exodus 3:5.

54. *A Traveller's Narrative*, p. XLII, *Materials*, p. 4,
    note 1.

55. *J.R.A.S.* October 1889, pp. 694, 695. The traveller
    was Mirza Aqa Khan a son-in-law of Subh-i-Azal
    (*Azal's Notes*, p. 1033).

56. The reference is to the Golden Calf which the
    Children of Israel worshipped at Mt. Sinai (Exodus
    32:1-6, Koran 2:48, 88, etc.).

57. Niku, *Filsifa-i-Niku*, Vol. II, p. 128.

58. This figure is certainly much too large (*Azal's
    Notes*, p. 1024).

59. Browne in *A Traveller's Narrative*, pp. 410, 411.

60. *Materials*, pp. 59-61.

61. Ibid., pp. 61, 62.

62. *Azal's Notes*, p. 49.

63. *Khanum* in Persian usage is the equivalent of Miss
    or Mrs.

64. *Azal's Notes*, p. 89.

65. *Materials*, p. 61. See Appendix II, #21.

66. Ibid., p. 61, 62.

67. *J.R.A.S.*, October 1889, pp. 706, 709.

68. *Al-Kitab Al-Aqdas*, by Baha'u'llah, translated by
    E. E. Elder, Royal Asiatic Society, London 1961,
    p. 34.

69. It is interesting to note that in the year 1889,
    three years before the death of Baha'u'llah, a man
    in India (now Pakistan) put forth the claim that
    he was the recipient of divine revelation. Mirza
    Ghulam Ahmad, born into a Muslim family in Qadian
    in the Panjab, like the Bab in Iran forty-five
    years earlier, became deeply influenced by the
    popular expectation of the coming of the Mahdi.
    Finally he announced that he was the great world
    Teacher whose coming had been predicted by the
    scriptures not only of the Jews, Christians and
    Muslims, but also of the Zoroastrians, Hindus,
    and Buddhists, and that the hopes of all the na-
    tions were to be fulfilled in him. He taught
    that God from time to time sends "renewers" of
    religion, and he claimed that in him as the Mahdi
    the Prophet Muhammad had made his "second advent."
    He rejected, however, the popular conception that
    the Mahdi was to be a man of war, and said that
    his *jihad* (religious war) was to be only a spiri-
    tual warfare. He attacked the mullas for keeping
    the people in ignorance, and so made many enemies.
    Accordingly, he was condemned as an apostate by
    the orthodox Muslims, and some of his followers
    were killed. In spite of this opposition many
    people believed on him, and became known as
    Ahmadis, and carried on aggressive missionary
    work at home and in other lands. Since the claims
    of Mirza Ghulam Ahmad greatly resembled and absol-
    utely contradicted those of Baha'u'llah, it is not
    surprising that there was no love lost between the
    Baha'is and the Ahmadis. One of the Ahmadi mis-
    sionaries by the name of Sadru'd-Din wrote a pam-
    phlet in Persian to prove the fallacy of the Baha'i
    faith.

8

The Doctrines and Decrees of the Baha'u'llah

It is impossible in one chapter to give more than an outline of the teachings of Baha'u'llah. Like the Bab and Subh-i-Azal, he was a very prolific writer, and during a period of some thirty years he is said to have composed more than one hundred volumes and countless epistles.(1) Most of his writings were addressed to individuals or groups of believers who had asked him questions, and were usually not very lengthy. They were called "Tablets." Some were written in Persian, some in Arabic, often in a style which is difficult to understand. No collection of all these writings has been made, or could be made. However, all are considered by Baha'is to be the Word of God. As Professor Browne discovered during his sojourn in Iran, the Baha'is have no definite canon of Scripture, as do Jews, Christians and Muslims. Some of the writings of Baha'u'llah have been trans-lated into other languages, and are being circulated outside the Arabic and Persian areas, so that it is now possible for a larger number of readers to become acquainted with his doctrines and commandments and exhortations. Notably a large and well-edited book of 576 pages entitled *Bahai Scriptures* (2) was published in 1923 with the approval of the Bahai Committee on

Publications in America, more than half of which consists of writings of Baha'u'llah. More recently
another compilation of his writings and those of his
son Abdu'l-Baha has been published by the Baha'i Publishing Trust under the title *Baha'i World Faith*.(3)
This book of 449 pages "has been compiled," according
to the editor, "to replace the work published in 1923
under the title of *Baha'i Scriptures*, and contains
later and more accurate translations."(4) To these
volumes the reader is referred for first-hand acquaintance with Baha'u'llah's teachings.

The theological background of the Baha'i faith is
the same as that of the Bayan of the Bab. Baha'u'llah
like the Bab taught that God is unknowable except
through his Manifestations. He considered the Great
Manifestations to be those referred to by the Bab,
namely, Adam, Noah, Abraham, Moses, Jesus and Muhammad.
Having himself been a Babi, and knowing that he and
all the other early Babis had considered the Bab to
be a Major Manifestation of God who had taken the
place of Muhammad, Baha'u'llah did not deny this belief. However, he sought to lessen the status of the
Bab by frequently referring to him as "my forerunner,"
and he made it to appear that the chief function of
the Bab was to prepare the way for him, a much greater
Manifestation. As was explained in Chapter VI, Baha'u'
llah claimed to be He-Whom-God-Will-Manifest, and took
for himself all the high titles and divine attributes
which the Bab in the Bayan had said the coming Manifestation would possess (Chapter IV). He also said
he was the "return" of the Imam Husayn of the Shi'ites.
(5) Also he claimed to be the "return" of Jesus
Christ, and the Comforter promised by Christ (Gospel
of John 14:16,17), as well as the Manifestation of God
the Father.(6) Though the Bab undertook to establish
a universal religion,(7) he directed his appeal almost
entirely to the Shi'ite Muslims. Baha'u'llah, however,
extended his invitation to Jews, Christians and Zoroastrians as well, and appealed to them from their own
Scriptures. The position which Baha'u'llah claimed
for himself was not merely that of a teacher or prophet,
but was that of God. Hence, his words purported to be
not those of man, but of God Himself.

Baha'u'llah claimed to have knowledge which no one
else possesses, or is able to possess. He says that
nothing can move between heaven and earth without his
permission. He is infallible in everything. "If He
declares water to be wine, or heaven to be earth, or
light to be fire, it is true and there is no doubt
therein; and no one has the right to oppose Him, or to
say 'why' or 'wherefore'.....Verily no account shall
be demanded of Him for what He shall do.....Verily if
He declares the right to be left, or the south to be
north, it is true and there is no doubt therein.
Verily He is to be praised in His deeds and to be
obeyed in His command. He hath no associate in His
behest and no helper in His power; He doeth whatsoever
He willeth, and commandeth whatever He desireth."(8)

According to the doctrine of Manifestations, whenever a new Manifestation appears it is incumbent on
all men of all religions in the world to lay aside
their former beliefs and practices and accept Him-Whom-
God-Has-Manifested and submit to his new laws and
follow his teachings. The Bab claimed to be the new
Manifestation after Muhammad and undertook to establish
a Theocracy and a new state of society, based on the
laws of the Bayan, and governed by Babi rulers. As we
have seen, the opposition was too strong, many lives
were lost, and the Bab's hope was not realized. Baha'u'
llah, by claiming to be the Manifestation predicted by
the Bab, was able to take over the leadership of the
movement. He, like the Bab, proposed to establish a
Theocracy and a new state of society, which would be
governed by Baha'i rulers on the basis of doctrines
and laws given by Baha'u'llah. It should be clearly
understood that Baha'u'llah gave to men not only ethical and spiritual principles which could be taken or
refused, but also civil laws for his proposed society
which would be enforced by the political and police
powers of a Baha'i state. This will become clear when
the laws are considered later in this chapter.

The people who believed on the Bab were all Shi'ite
Muslims, who had followed a religion of law which prescribed in amazing detail what they were to eat and
drink and wear, how they were to bathe, how many wives

a man could take, how and when they could divorce
their wives, what things were ceremonially clean and
what unclean, how the dead were to be buried, how
inheritance was to be divided among the heirs of the
deceased, how and when to pray and to fast, etc.,
etc. The Bab, as we have seen in Chapter IV, changed
many of the Shi'ite laws, and established another
system of law which in some matters was more detailed
and difficult to observe than that of Islam. But
before the Babis had been able to learn and practice
these regulations, Baha'u'llah came forward as a new
Manifestation, and the Babis who followed him at once
began to ask what his laws were. Should they obey
the laws of the Bayan, or had the Bayan been abrogated
by him, as the Koranic laws had been abrogated by the
Bab? And if so, what rules for life and worship did
Baha'u'llah give them?

Since Baha'u'llah had claimed to be He-Whom-God-
Will-Manifest, it was to be expected that he would at
once abrogate the Bayan, and give his followers a new
Book from God. Strange as it may seem, there is no
evidence whatever that Baha'u'llah abrogated the Bayan.
On the contrary, while he was in Baghdad in 1862
Baha'u'llah wrote a letter in which he said:(9) "I
swear by God that if any of the people of the Bayan
[Babis] was to mention that the Book [Bayan] is abrogated, may God break the mouth of the speaker and the
calumniator."

Then, if the Bayan is not abrogated, are its laws
binding on Baha'is as well as on Babis? Such questions
continued to come to Baha'u'llah after he reached Akka,
and he accordingly supplied the answer. As he wrote
in his *Ninth Eshraq* near the end of his life:(10) "His
Holiness the Forerunner [the Bab] revealed laws. But
the world of command was dependent on acceptance.
Therefore, this wronged one [Baha'u'llah] implemented
some of them, and revealed them in *Al-Kitab Al-Aqdas*
couched in other terms.....Some laws of new doctrines
were also revealed."(11) This book, which he named the
Most Holy Book,(12) perhaps because in both Arabic and
Persian the Bible is called the Holy Book, was composed
in 1872, or soon after.(13) It was written in the

Arabic language, like the Koran, though most of the
Baha'is at that time were Iranians to whom Arabic was
a foreign language. The Aqdas, as the book is frequently called, is small, about the size of the Gospel
of Mark, but it is the most important of all the Baha'i
literature. To it alone of all his books did Baha'u'
llah refer in his Will ("The Book of My Covenant") when
he wrote:(14) "Reflect upon that which is revealed in
my book the Aqdas," calling attention to the provision
given in it regarding the succession. Likewise his
son Abbas Efendi (Abdu'l-Baha) in his Last Will and
Testament wrote:(15) "Unto the Most Holy Book everyone must turn, and all that is not expressly recorded
therein must be referred to the Universal House of
Justice." And Shoghi Effendi, the great-grandson of
Baha'u'llah, the first Guardian of the Cause, states
(16) that this little volume "may rank as the most
signal act of His [Baha'u'llah's] ministry." "This
Most Holy Book," he continues, "whose provisions must
remain inviolate for no less than a thousand years,
and whose system will embrace the entire planet, may
well be regarded as the brightest emanation of the
mind of Baha'u'llah, as the Mother Book of His Dispensation, and the Charter of His New World Order."

The Most Holy Book was not printed for a number of
years after it was written, since it was no doubt
impossible to publish such a book in Syria where
Baha'u'llah could not openly make known his claims.
After some years the author authorized his son Mirza
Muhammad Ali and Mirza Aqa Jan of Kashan (called the
"Servant of God")(17) to revise the Aqdas and other
of the sacred writings, and then take them to Bombay
and supervise the publication of them. This was done
in 1890. The *Iqan* and the *Kitab-i-Mubin* (*Sura-yi-Hay-
kal*) and the *Kitab-i-Iqtidar* and other books as well
as the *Kitab-i-Aqdas* were thus published for the first
time. Since all these writings were revised prior to
publication, they in their present form are to be
dated near the end of the Akka period of the life of
Baha'u'llah, and while he no doubt approved changes
made in the text by the revisers, they cannot be
considered the work of Baha'u'llah alone.(18)

Realizing the importance of the *Kitab-i-Aqdas* in the Baha'i system, Professor Browne in 1889 published in English a resume of its contents.(19) In 1899 a Russian scholar, A. M. Tumansky, published the Arabic text of the Aqdas, with a translation into Russian, and a lengthy introduction.(20) Also, several other western scholars have published translations of portions of the book. However, no complete translation into English had been made till 1961, when Dr. E. E. Elder, a competent Arabic scholar, with the assistance of several scholars who had an intimate knowledge of Baha'i terminology and beliefs, published *al-Kitab al-Aqdas*, an accurate and readable translation of the whole book, with introduction and notes.(21)

However, in view of what the founder and leaders of the Baha'i movement have said about the unique importance of the Aqdas, it is surprising, to say the least, that as yet no authorized translation made by Baha'i scholars of the whole Aqdas has been published, either in Persian the language of Iran, or in any other language. In *Bahai Scriptures* among the 262 pages filled with the words of Baha'u'llah, only a few brief paragraphs taken from the Most Holy Book are to be found. Likewise in the later publication entitled *Baha'i World Faith - Selected Writings of Baha'u'llah and Abdu'l-Baha (1956)*, the Aqdas is referred to in the index (p. 457) only six times, and the book contains no quotations of any length from this "brightest emanation of the mind of Baha'u'llah." It is almost impossible to obtain an Arabic copy of the Aqdas, and even the headquarters of the Baha'i Faith in America stated in writing that they had never had a copy of the book.(22) In 1944 Shoghi Efendi, the Guardian of the Cause, stated that "the codification of the Kitab-i-Aqdas, the Mother-Book of the Baha'i Revelation, and the systematic promulgation of its laws and ordinances are as yet unbegun."(23) But more important than a codification is an authorized translation, and certainly a scholarly Baha'i translation of this book is long overdue.

Although, as was stated above, Baha'u'llah did not by a decree abrogate the Bayan of the Bab, he was

successful in eliminating it. Not only did he forbid
his followers to read it,(24) he also caused it to be
removed from circulation so completely that most of
his followers were entirely uninformed as to its contents. He then, according to his own account quoted
above, reproduced some of the laws of the Bayan,
changed others, added numerous exhortations, and
issued the resulting production as his own Most Holy
Book. Mr. Azal has made an exhaustive study of the
relation of the Aqdas to the Bayan,(25) and has demonstrated, as our notes will indicate, that most of the
laws found in the Aqdas are derived from the Bab's
Bayan. He calls the Aqdas "a rehash of the Bayan."

Because of its unique importance in the Baha'i
system, and the fact that it is so little known, Dr.
Elder's translation of the entire Aqdas is included
as Appendix I at the end of this volume, and the
reader is encouraged to study it with care. However,
to assist him in becoming acquainted with this book
of Baha'u'llah's laws, we will now give a rather full
summary of the contents of the Most Holy Book. The
book begins with a statement regarding the necessity
of knowing Baha'u'llah. "The first thing that God
ordained concerning His creatures is the knowledge
of the Sunrise-place of His revelation and the Rising-
place of His Cause, who was the Station of Himself in
the world of command and creation. Whoever attains
unto Him attains unto all good, and whoever is deprived of Him is of the people of error, even though
he perform all [good] works."(26)

He then enjoins obedience to the commands which
follow, saying, "From My stipulations there passes the
sweet smell of my gown, and by them the standards of
victory are erected on hillocks and hills. The tongue
of My power has spoken in the might of My greatness,
addressing My people, [saying], 'Perform My stipulations
out of love for My beauty'." (27)

First there come regulations for worship. "Worship
has been ordained for you - nine prostrations to God
Who sent down the verses; when noon is past, in the
morning and in the late afternoon.....Whenever you

desire to worship, turn your face towards My most holy
direction."(28)   The Muslim worship consists of seventeen prostrations each day, divided among the five
times of prayer, with prescribed words in the Arabic
language, as the worshipper faces Mecca. The Babi
worship consists of nineteen prostrations at noon facing Shiraz. The worship ordained by Baha'u'llah is
briefer, and is to be performed three times each day,
between sunset and two hours after sunset, and between
sunrise and noon, and between noon and late afternoon.
The words to be repeated are not given in the Aqdas.
The worshipper is to face the place where Baha'u'llah
resides, which is Akka.(29)

   As in the Bayan, all congregational worship is
abolished, except in the case of prayers for the dead.
The wearing of garments which contain the hair of
animals, or which are made of their skins, or have
buttons of bone, does not render worship invalid, as
is the case in Islam. All men and women above the age
of fifteen must say the prayers, but the old and sick
are excused. If water for the ablutions before worship is not available, the worshipper must say in Arabic five times, "In the Name of God, the Purest, the
Purest." Women during their menstrual periods are
not to perform the worship but are to make the ablutions, and repeat in praise to God ninety-five(30)
times each day, "Praise be to God, the Possessor of
Countenance and Beauty!" Travellers are to make one
prostration only, or if this is impossible, to say,
"Praise be to God!" After completing the required
prostrations, the worshipper is to sit on the floor
with feet crossed under him and hands on his knees,
and repeat eighteen times, "Praise be to God, the
Possessor of the kingdoms of this world and the next!"
All the prayers are to be in Arabic. God is to be
thanked for "this great Grace," presumably, for this
new Revelation.(31)

   Then follow the regulations for fasting.(32)   "O
multitude of creation, we have ordained the Fast for
you, certain limited days. After the completion of
them we have made al-Nayruz [No Ruz] a feast for you."
In his arrangements for the Fast and also for the Badi'

Calendar, Baha'u'llah adopted what the Bab had prescribed in the Bayan. The arrangement for the Fast
is as follows: The year is to be divided into nineteen months of nineteen days each (19 x 19 = 361).
The nineteenth month is the month of the Fast. Immediately following the Fast comes the ancient Iranian
festival of No Ruz (New Year), which is to be observed with joy and gladness. The four or five intercalary days were placed between the eighteenth and
nineteenth months, and were to be spent in entertaining relations and friends and in feeding the poor.
Thus Baha'u'llah followed the Bab in restoring the
old Iranian solar year in place of the Arabian lunar
year, and in giving religious sanction to the observance of the great festival of No Ruz, which from
ancient times had been celebrated at the vernal equinox (on or about March 21) as the first day of the
new year, a national rather than as a religious feast.
(33) During the nineteen days of the Fast, no food
or drink is to be taken from sunrise till sunset.
The Baha'i Fast is, therefore, less severe than that
of Islam, which lasts for twenty-eight days, and when
Ramazan comes in the summer the day may be sixteen
hours long. "This does not cause difficulty for the
one who is on a journey, or for the ill, for the
pregnant woman, or the one who is nursing," that is,
such persons are exempt from fasting.

Each day every believer should wash his hands, then
his face, and having seated himself facing God [at
Akka] should repeat ninety-five times, "*Allahu Abha!*"
(God is Most Splendid). "In like manner, perform
ablutions before Worship because of a command from
God."(34) Murder, adultery, back-biting and calumniation are unlawful.(35)

Then follows the law of Inheritance as given by
the Bab - "Thus commanded He who gave Good News of
Me."(36) According to the Bayan, the property of the
deceased must be divided into nine unequal parts.
Two parts are to be used for funeral expenses, and
the balance is then to be divided into 42 equal parts,
of which 1) Children will receive 9, 2) Husbands or
Wives 8, 3) Fathers 7, 4) Mothers 6, 5) Brothers 5,

6) Sisters 4, and 7) Teachers 3, making a total of 42.
This division, however, was changed by Baha'u'llah.
He says that when he heard the protests of unborn
children saying that they would not get enough of the
inheritance, he doubled their share, and reduced the
shares of others. How this was to be done is not
stated in the Aqdas, but Baha'u'llah in another of
his books entitled *Question and Answer* made the division as follows: 1) Children 18, 2) Husbands or Wives
6.5, 3) Fathers 5.5, 4) Mothers 4.5, 5) Brothers 3.5,
6) Sisters 2.5, and 7) Teachers 1.5, total 42. Then
follow in the Aqdas directions as to how the division
is to be made in special circumstances. When there
are no heirs to the portions for any of the above
classes, their shares are to go to the House of Justice. It would be interesting to know how many loyal
Baha'is during the past century since this law was
given have been able to divide their possessions in
accordance with this scale.

Next, provision is made for the House of Justice
named above.(37) In every city there shall be a House
of Justice, "and the souls according to *al-Baha* will
assemble in it." The numerical value of the Arabic
letters in *Baha'* is nine, hence the House of Justice
must have nine or more members. They are to be God's
stewards, and must consult about the welfare of men
for the sake of God.

Male believers who are able must "make the pilgrimage to the House",(38) that is, the Bab's house in
Shiraz, and the house occupied by Baha'u'llah in
Baghdad. All Baha'is must be engaged in some useful
occupation, for work is worship.(39) The kissing of
the hands of men, as was done to show respect to
religious leaders, is forbidden. Also it is forbidden
to confess sins to men.(40) Believers are bidden to
arise and serve the Cause, but not in a way that will
cause them to be troubled by the unbelievers. Ascetic
practices are forbidden.(41) "Whoever attains unto
My love has a right to sit on a throne of native gold
in the chief seat.....Whoever is deprived of my Love,
were he to sit on the ground," the very dust would
cry out in horror.

Then comes a warning against any one who may falsely claim to be a Manifestation.(42)   "Whoever claims
Command (*amr*) before the completion of a thousand
years is a false liar.....Whoever explains this verse
or interprets it in any other way than that plainly
sent down, he will be deprived of the Spirit and
Mercy of God.....Fear God and follow not your illusions." Baha'u'llah in this statement made it clear
that his dispensation will last at least till A.D.
2866.

Next, believers are told not to be troubled "when
the sun of My beauty goes down and the heaven of My
temple is hidden,"(43) that is, when Baha'u'llah dies,
but they must rise up and help the Cause. They are
warned against pride of wealth and position.

Religious endowments(44) are to be controlled by
Baha'u'llah as long as he lives, and at his death the
control is to go to the "Branches," that is, his sons.
After them it is to go to the House of Justice.

The shaving of the head, as was done by some Muslim
men, and was permitted in the Bayan, is forbidden. Men
are not to allow their hair to fall below their ears.

Then comes the law for the punishment of a thief.
(45) "Banishment and prison have been commanded [as
punishment] for the thief. For the third offence put
a sign on his forehead [brand him]. Thus he will be
known, so that the cities and the provinces of God do
not receive him. Beware lest pity take hold on you..."

The use of gold and silver vessels is not forbidden
as in Islamic law.(46) Cleanliness and good manners
in eating are prescribed.

It is incumbent on every father to have his sons
and daughters properly educated.(47) If he fails to
do so, the House of Justice must supervise their education, using charity funds for this purpose when
necessary. "Whoever educates his son or anyone's sons,
it is as though he had educated one of My sons."

Next is given the punishment for adultery.(48) "God
has commanded that every adulterer and adulteress pay
a fine to the House of Justice. The sum is nine
mithqals of gold. For the second offence double the
punishment.....Whoever is overcome by sin, let him
repent and turn back to God. He, indeed, forgives
whom He wills....." Since the Babi *mithqal* is intended, the amount of fine for the first offence would
have been, at the time the Aqdas was published, about
$21.00.

Music, forbidden in Islam, is permitted.(48) "We
have made it lawful to you to listen to [singing]
voices and to songs. Beware lest listening take you
beyond the bounds of good breeding and dignity."

While Baha'u'llah lives, disputed points are to be
referred to him for settlement.(49) After his death
they are to be referred to his writings. "O People,"
he says, "do not be troubled when the kingdom of My
Manifestation has disappeared.....In My Manifestation
there is wisdom, and in My Disappearance there is
another wisdom."

"Hospitality has been prescribed [as an obligation],
once every month, even though it be with water only."
(50) In this way believers will be drawn close together. "Be like the fingers of the hand and the limbs
of the body." The people of Iran pride themselves on
their hospitality.

When a hunter kills his prey he must name the name
of God,(51) and the game will become lawful for him to
eat, without cutting its throat, as is required in
Islam. "Take care not to be wasteful in that [hunt-
ing]."

Then comes the punishment for the murderer and the
incendiary. "Whoever burns a house intentionally,
burn him. Whoever kills a person with intent, kill
him. Take the ordinances of God with hands of power
and might.....If you condemn them [the incendiary and
the murderer] to perpetual prison, you have done no
harm according to the Book."(52)

The regulations for Marriage fill several pages of
the Aqdas.(53)   "God has ordained marriage for you.
Beware lest you go beyond two [wives], and whoever is
satisfied with one of the handmaidens, his soul is at
rest and so is hers, and one does no harm in taking a
virgin into his service." All must marry, that there
may be born "those who will make mention of Me among
My creatures." People are warned not to corrupt the
earth with immorality. In the Bayan the Bab had made
the consent of the two parties the condition for
marriage, but Baha'u'llah changed this regulation to
make the consent of the parents of the bride and groom
also a condition, to insure harmony in the family situation. In Muslim marriages it is customary for the
husband to give the bride a dowry (*mahr*). Baha'u'llah
followed this custom in his marriage regulations, just
as the Bab had done. In the Aqdas as in the Bayan,
the maximum amount of the dowry was set at ninety-five
mithqals of gold for city dwellers, and the same
amount of silver for villagers, and the minimum amount
was nineteen *mithqals*. "Relationship by marriage is
not realized except by [payment of] dowries." If a
husband goes on a journey he must inform his wife and
fix the time for his return. If he does not keep his
word, and does not inform his wife, she must wait
nine months for him, after which she is free to remarry. If trouble should arise between husband and
wife, he must not divorce her within a year. If after
a year the wound is not healed "there is no harm in
divorce." As in Islam, no provision is made for the
woman to divorce her husband. After divorce the man
may take his wife back again at the end of every month,
provided she has not married someone else. "God loves
union and agreement and hates division and divorce."

Traffic in slaves is forbidden.(54) Believers must
adorn themselves "with the beautiful garments of [good]
works." "Let no one oppose another; nor one person kill
another.....Do you kill him whom God brought to life
through a Spirit from Him?"(55)

Ceremonial uncleanness is abolished, but cleanliness
is enjoined.(56) "Catch hold of the rope of Purity so
that no traces of filth are seen in your clothes.....

There is no harm, however, in one who has an excuse
[for not being clean].....Cleanse every unseemly
thing with water which has not changed in three respects [that is, in color, smell or taste]. Fear God
and be of the purified. The prayers of the one who
is seen with filth on his clothes do not ascend to
God.....Use rose water, then pure perfume. This is
what God, who had no beginning, loved from the beginning."

The Bab had commanded in the Bayan that all non-
Babi books should be abandoned. Baha'u'llah abrogates
this law.(57) "We have permitted you to read of the
learning [of the Islamic doctors] what is useful to
you, but not that which results in controversy in
speech."

Baha'u'llah then addresses various kings and rulers
of the earth, and exhorts them to accept him. "By
God," he says, "we do not desire to take possession
of your kingdoms, but we have come to possess your
hearts.....Blessed is the king who arises to help My
cause in My kingdom and cuts himself off from all but
Me!" The king of Austria [the Emperor Franz Joseph]
is rebuked because he passed Akka on his way to
Jerusalem [in 1869] without stopping to inquire about
Baha'u'llah.(58) To the king of Berlin [probably
Wilhelm I] he says, "Beware lest conceit keep thee
from the Rising-place of Manifestation and passion
screen thee from the Possessor of the Throne and the
Earth." To the rulers of America he says,(59) "O
kings of America and chiefs of the multitude in it,
hear what the Dove on the branches of Continuing
Eternity warbles, saying, 'There is no god besides
Me, the Continuing, the Forgiving, the Generous.'
Adorn the temple [body] of the Kingdom with the garment of Justice and Piety, and its head with the
crown of the Remembrance of your Lord. The Ottoman
Empire is severely rebuked and threatened,(60) no
doubt because of its treatment of him.

The address to Iran is most conciliatory, though
it was here that the Babis had suffered most. "O land
of *al-Ta* [Teheran], do not be sorrowful for anything.

God has made thee the Rising-place of the Joy of the
worlds. If He Wills, He will bless thy throne through
him who rules with justice and gathers the sheep of
God which have been scattered by wolves.....Rejoice
thou in that God has made thee the Horizon of Light
since the Rising-place of Manifestation [Baha'u'llah]
was born in thee and thou art called by this Name.....
Things shall be overturned in thee and the multitude
of people shall rule thee." The province of Khurasan
also is addressed with words of hope.(61)

Since the Aqdas was not published till 1890 A.D.,
and was not translated from Arabic, it is improbable
that any of the kings and rulers here addressed ever
read or heard of the messages intended for them.

Baha'u'llah then continues giving laws and regulations for his people. First he prescribes the amount
of the capital tax.(62) "If anyone possesses a hundred *mithqals* of gold, nineteen *mithqals* of them are
for God, the Maker of earth and heaven. Beware, O
people, lest you deny yourselves this great favour.
We have commanded you to do this although we can do
without you.....By that command God desired the purification of your wealth.....O people, do not be dishonest in the duties owed to God; do not spend [God's
money] except by His permission." This money was to
be given to Baha'u'llah, and there is evidence that
this was done by many Baha'is.(63)

To the learned men of Islam who criticized the
style of the writings of Baha'u'llah, he replies that
his Book is itself the standard, and "that which the
nations have may be weighed by this Great Balance."
(64) This is the same as the reply of the Muslims to
those who criticized the style of the Koran.

Then follow more regulations.(65) The nails are
to be pared. A weekly bath must be taken in water
sufficient to cover the whole body. It is not permissible to get into water that has already been used,
or to go to the bath-houses of the Iranians, in which
the water in the pools was seldom changed. "It is
like pus and purulent matter".....It is better for one

who washes his body to pour water over him instead of getting into it. Indeed, He desired to make matters easy for you....."

"The wives of your fathers are unlawful unto you." (66) Since this is the only limitation imposed by Baha'u'llah's marriage laws, it has been inferred by some that all other women may be lawfully married. And regarding pederasty he says, "We are ashamed to mention the commandments regarding boys."

The lips are not to be moved in prayer as one walks through the streets,(66) as is sometimes done by those who wish to be seen of men. Worship is to be performed in a place of worship, or in one's own home.

"The writing of a will has been made incumbent on everyone.....One must adorn the top of the page with the Most Great Name and confess his faith in the Unity of God, in the Appearance of His Manifestation."(66) In this way the Baha'i testifies that he died in the faith.

There are to be two great festivals.(67) The first commemorates the declaration of Baha'u'llah. The date for this is not given in the Aqdas, but it is observed by Baha'is in the Feast of Rizwan from April 21 to May 2 (Chapter V). The second festival "is the day on which We sent Him who should tell the people the Good News of this Name by which the dead are raised," that is, the declaration of the Bab, which was on May 23. It is noteworthy that Baha'u'llah here refers to the Bab not as a previous Manifestation, but as one whom he had sent to tell the good news of his coming. Then reference is made to another festival, which comes on the first day of the first month (*Baha*) of the Babi year, namely, the ancient Iranian national Feast of No Ruz (March 21). "It is the source and beginning of the months, and in it moves the breath of life," that is, the coming of spring. "Blessed is the one who apprehends it with joy and sweetness."

When ill, "consult the skilful ones of the physicians. Indeed, We have not set aside the means [of

healing] but have rather established them by this
Pen."(67)

The Bab had commanded that when his followers came
to him they should bring him as a gift their most
precious possession. Regarding this command Baha'u'
llah says, "We have exempted you from this as a favour
from Him. He, indeed, is the Generous Giver."(68)

The "Sunrise-place of Remembrance" (*mashriq al-
adhkar*) is the name given to Baha'i places of worship.
It is good to go to such places "in the early mornings,
mentioning [the Name of God], remembering, and asking
forgiveness." The worshipper should sit in silence,
listening to those who chant the verses given by
Baha'u'llah, for in this way a spiritual state is produced.(68) "He who speaks other than that sent down in
My Tablets is not one of Mine."

"God has permitted those who so desire to learn
different languages that they may propagate the Cause
of God and tell of it in the east and west of the
earth, and make mention of it among the states and
religious groups."(68) The use of alcohol is discouraged. "The rational person does not drink that
which takes away his reason."(69) Then follows this
excellent injunction: "Adorn your heads with the
crown of faithfulness and integrity, your hearts with
the cloak of piety, your tongues with true veracity
and your temples [bodies] with the garment of good
breeding."(69)

Next comes a brief command of great importance for
followers of Baha'u'llah. "When the Sea of Union [with
Me] is dried up and the Book of Beginning is finished
in the End, then turn to the one whom God desires, the
one who is a Branch from the ancient Root."(69) That
is, one of his sons is to succeed him, but he does not
here indicate which son is intended. More definite
directions were given in Baha'u'llah's *Book of My
Covenant* (Chapter IX).

Freedom, says Baha'u'llah, is a dangerous thing.(70)
"We see some people who desired freedom boasting of it.

Page 180, first para., last line: son should be son-in-law

Page 200, first para., after line 17 insert these words:
did not submit but was greatly frightened. A friend seeing his
fear told him he had nothing to be afraid of. Dr. Kheiralla

Page 255, third para., next to last line: Efenti should be Efendi

Page 274, in place of lines 4, 5, and 6, insert these words:
Administration, there were in Iran several former leaders in
the Cause who not only repudiated the Administration, but also
denied the validity of the

Page 323, first para., l. 14: 1960)." should be 1960)." (47)

Page 326, first para., l. 11: omit (47)

Page 347, l. 8: after Promised insert the words:
One of all religions. His coming ushers in the

Page 349: CONCLUSIONS should be CONCLUSION in title

Page 444: In place of lines 6-10 in first para., insert these words:
(Iran) as a missionary of the Presbyterian Church, and he
remained in service in Persia until retirement in 1962.
He was given the D.D. degree by Washington and Lee University
in 1932. He and his wife now reside in Philadelphia.

The Bahá'í Faith: Its History and Teachings

William McElwee Miller

--ERRATA--

Page xiv, third para., l. 8: Efendi, should be Efendi, (20)

Page 25, second para., l. 1: from should be for

Page 69, Note 32: omit p. 3,

Page 72, second para., l. 18: (Wahíd) should be (Wahíd)

Page 78, second para., l. 11: Wahids should be Wahíds

Page 83, title of picture, l. 3: omit he was

Page 89, Note 17, l. 3: Wahíd should be Wahíd

Page 89, Note 17, l. 5: Wahíd should be Wahíd

Page 89, Note 26, l. 2: Omit p. 3,

Page 108, Note 6, l. 1: omit p. 5,

Page 114, Note 49, l. 2: omit p. 3,

Page 115, second line of title: omit the

They are in manifest ignorance. The consequences of
freedom end in sedition, the fire of which is unquenchable.....Man must be under regulations.....Look at
mankind; they are like sheep, they must have a shepherd to keep them.....Freedom is in following My
commands."

"The number of months is nineteen according to the
Book of God."(70)   Thus Baha'u'llah adopts the Babi
calendar.

Also, in the matter of the burial of the dead he
adopts the regulations given by the Bab. The dead
are to be buried, as directed in the Bayan, in coffins
of "crystal or rare stones or beautiful hard woods."
But the inscriptions on the rings which must be placed
on their fingers are to be different from what the Bab
had commanded, and for both men and women the inscription (in Arabic) is to be: "I had my origin in God
and I returned to Him; I am separated from all but Him,
and I hold fast to His Name, the Merciful, the Compassionate."(71)   The Bab had commanded that the body be
wrapped in not more than five garments of silk and
cotton, but Baha'u'llah says, "Whoever is unable to do
this, one of them will be sufficient for him." Moreover, the carrying of dead bodies to shrines at distant places, as the Muslims did, is forbidden. "It
is unlawful for you to carry the dead body farther
than the distance of an hour from the city. Bury him
with joy and sweetness in a nearby place."(71)   This
would be four or five miles, when horse-drawn vehicles
were used.

Then follows a long exhortation to mankind, first
those who have believed on the Manifestation, and then
those who have not.(72)   "O multitude of Creation, hear
the call of the Possessor of Names. He calls you from
the direction of His Most Great Prison [Akka], saying,
'There is no god besides Me, the Powerful, the Proud,
the Scoffer, the Exalted, the Knower, the Wise.'" They
are reminded of what the Bab, "who told the Good News
of Me," had said about Baha'u'llah, and the Babis who
had not accepted him are urged to do so. "Whoever
knows Me, knows the Desired One. Whoever turns his

face to Me, turns his face to Him who is worshipped...
It is better for a person to read one of My verses
than for him to read the books of the ancients and the
moderns.....O Multitudes of *al-Bayan* [Babis], I adjure
you by your Lord, the Merciful, to look with the eye
of equity at what has been sent down in Truth [the
writings of Baha'u'llah], and be not of those who see
the proof of God and deny it." And again Baha'u'llah
insists that the chief purpose of the Bab was to exalt
him, "this Unapproachable, Extraordinary Manifestation."

The Shi'ites of Iran considered peoples of other
religions unclean, and so were forbidden to associate
with them. Baha'u'llah says,(73) "Associate with
those of other religions with joy and sweetness, that
they may find in you the odour of the Merciful. Take
care that the fanaticism of the Days of Ignorance among
mankind does not take hold on you." And he adds, "Take
care not to enter a house when its owner is absent,
unless [you have] his permission.(74) Persist in doing
good on all occasions, and be not of the careless ones."

One of the five "pillars of religion" in Islam is
the paying of the Poor-rate (*zakat*). Baha'u'llah
adopted this, saying, "It has been ordained for you
that you make pure [lawful] your food by paying the
poor-rate."(75) He promises to tell later in detail
on what property the poor-rate is to be paid. Both
begging and giving to beggars is forbidden. "It has
been ordained that everyone earn his living. Whoever
is unable to do so, let the guardians and the rich
appoint for him what is sufficient."(75)

In the Bayan quarreling, disputing, and striking
were forbidden, and anyone who caused sorrow to another
was required to pay a fine of nineteen *mithqals* of gold,
or if poor, of silver. Baha'u'llah says that in this
Manifestation his followers are exempted from this
penalty, and are exhorted to righteousness and piety.
"Do not approve for another what you do not approve
for yourselves."(75)

He then commands that they "recite the verses of
God every morning and evening. Whoever does not recite

does not fulfill the covenant and bond of God."(75)
But it is not good to become proud through reading and
praying a great deal. "Were one to read one of the
verses with joy and sweetness, it were better for him
than if he recite lazily the volumes of God."(76)
Children must be taught to chant the verses of God in
such a way "that the hearts of those who sleep are
attracted."

The Bab commanded that house-furnishings must be
renewed every nineteen years, and both he and Baha'u'
llah "exempt him who is unable to do this."(76)   Also,
the Bab commanded that believers must take a bath
every four days. Baha'u'llah says, "Wash your feet
every day in summer, and in winter once every three
days."(76)   Then follows this exhortation which is an
echo of the Sermon on the Mount, "Whoever becomes
angry with you, meet him with gentleness. Whoever
does evil to you, do not do evil to him. Leave him
to himself and depend on God, the Avenger, the Just,
the Powerful."(76)

The verses of God are not to be recited from high
pulpits, as in the mosques, but from a platform, on
which the reciter is seated.(76)   Gambling and the
use of opium are forbidden. Invitations to feasts
and banquets are to be accepted "with joy and gladness,
and whoever keeps his promise [to come] is secure from
threats."(77)

It is forbidden to carry arms "except in times of
necessity."(78)   The wearing of silk, which was forbidden in Islamic law, is made permissible for Baha'is.
Also the Bab gave certain regulations regarding clothing and the hair and the beard. Baha'u'llah says,(78)
"God has lifted from you the commandment restricting
clothing and beards, as a favour from Him.....Do what
the upright minds do not disapprove of.....Blessed is
the one who is adorned with the garment of good breeding and conduct!" And to justify these changes in the
divine regulations he says, "If God should make lawful
what was forbidden in the eternity of past eternities,
or vice versa, no one should find fault with Him."(78)

Next come several pages of condemnation of the
Shaykhis in Kirman (Chapter I) and the doctors of
Islam for their rejection of Baha'u'llah.(79) They
are urged to recognize the truth of God, and believe,
and are warned against preventing people from coming
to him.

Then follows another important command, briefly
given.(80) "O people of Creation, whenever the dove
flies from the forest of praise and makes for the
furthermost hidden goal, then refer what you did not
understand in the Book to the Bough which branches
from the Self-Subsistent Stock." That is, after the
death of Baha'u'llah, questions about the interpretation of his Book are to be referred to his son. He
does not here state which son is intended.

Once more Baha'u'llah appeals to the people of the
Bayan to recognize and accept him.(81) "Take care,"
he warns, "not to argue with God and [dispute] His
Cause. He was manifested in such a way that He knows
thoroughly all that was and will be.....Take care that
what is in *al-Bayan* does not keep you away from your
Lord, the Merciful. By God, it [the Bayan] was sent
down as a reminder of Me, if you only knew. The sincere find in it only the odour of My love and of My
Name.....O People, face towards what has been sent
down from My Highest Pen. If you find in it an odour
of God, do not turn away from it and do not deprive
yourselves of the Grace and benefits of God."

Then follows a stern appeal to an unnamed opponent,
who was his brother Subh-i-Azal.(82) "O Rising-place
of Deviation, quit concealing [the truth]!.....By God,
my tears have flowed down My cheeks when I saw thee
following thy passion and forsaking the One who created
thee and fashioned thee. Remember the Grace of thy
Master when We educated thee by night and day for the
service of the Cause. Fear God and be of the penitent
to God." The allusion is to Baha'u'llah's tutoring
his brother when he was quite young. Then, referring
to Hajji Sayyid Muhammad Isfahani, Baha'u'llah says,
"God has taken the one who seduced thee." This devoted
Babi, who became the husband of the second widow of the

Bab, was held responsible by Baha'u'llah for the failure of Subh-i-Azal to accept him as a Manifestation,
and was assassinated by the Baha'is in Akka in 1872.
(83) "Therefore," continues Baha'u'llah, "return to
Him [God] submissive, humble, and humiliated. He will
pardon thy evil doings. Thy Lord is, indeed, the
Relenting, the Powerful, and Merciful." But in spite
of this plea Subh-i-Azal never submitted to his brother.

Of the Most Holy Book he says,(82) "This is a Book
that has become a lamp for the feet of all those in the
world and his straightest way for the worlds. Say:
Indeed, it is the Rising-place of the knowledge of God,
if you only knew. It is the Sunrise-place of God's
commands, if you only knew."

Finally on the last page a few more commands are
added.(84) Animals are not to be overloaded. "Whoever
kills a person by mistake must pay blood-money to his
people, and the amount is one hundred *mithqals* of gold.
Peoples of the councils of different countries are to
"choose a language among the languages, to be spoken
by those on earth. Choose likewise the handwriting to
be used.....This is a means for [attaining] union, if
you only knew, and the greatest reason for agreement
and civilization."(85) And again he says, "The smoking
of opium has been prohibited to you.....Whoever smokes
it is not one of us."

Then the Most Holy Book ends with these words:

"Fear God, O people of intelligence,

By My Most Great, Most Holy, High, and Most Spelndid
Name!"

In the above summary all the important laws and precepts (but not all the exhortations) contained in this
book of fifty English pages have been noted in the
order, or rather disorder, in which Baha'u'llah prepared them. It will be remembered that the Bab had
said that He-Whom-God-Will-Manifest would abrogate the
Bayan.(86) Accordingly, Baha'u'llah, claiming to be
He, proceeded to change certain Bayanic regulations,

as we have seen above, though he never stated categor-
ically that the Bayan had been abrogated. It is evident, therefore, that the laws of the Bayan which were
not changed or rescinded by Baha'u'llah in the Aqdas
remain in effect for Baha'is. But how are they to
know these laws if copies of the Bayan are not available to them?

As one studies the Aqdas it becomes clear that
while it contains numerous ethical and religious teachings which might be followed in any society anywhere,
such as kindness to others, abstention from drink and
opium, provision for worship and fasting, etc., there
are also in it numerous laws which presuppose the
existence of a Baha'i State, with an executive, a
judiciary and a police force. How else could taxes
and fines be collected, and crimes be punished by
imprisonment and death. Baha'u'llah definitely anticipated the time when the "People of Baha" like the
People of Islam will establish a regime in which
Religion and State will be one. The Most Holy Book
is supposed to contain the basic laws for this world
Theocratic-State for the coming one thousand or more
years.

As we have seen, mention is made several times in
the Aqdas of the House of Justice (*Baytu'l-Adl*), which
must be established in every town, and to which various civil and religious reponsibilities are assigned.
There is also a suggestion that there is to be a
Supreme House of Justice, one of the duties of which
is to administer the religious endowments after the
death of Baha'u'llah. But no clear directions are
given in the Aqdas for the formation or the responsi-
bilities of such a body.

However, in the Eighth Eshraq of the *Book of
Eshraqat*, Baha'u'llah amended the Aqdas, as follows:
(87) "This passage by the Supreme Pen [Baha] has been
written at this moment and shall be read [together
with and] as forming part of the *Kitab-i-Aqdas*.
Affairs of the people are dependent on godly men of
the House of Justice. They are the agents of God.....
each day calls for an order, and each moment for an

expediency. Consequently matters shall be referable to the House of Justice so that it may put into practice whatever it considers to be the requirements of expediency.....All political matters shall be referable to the House of Justice....." From this statement it is evident that Baha'u'llah anticipated a time when a state, having a parliamentary system of government, shall have adopted Baha'ism as the state religion, with full authority to legislate for the conduct of the state, subject to the provisions of the Aqdas. As Mirza Badi'u'llah, the youngest son of Baha'u'llah says,(88) "The purpose underlying this command is that matters should be dealt with by consultation and not by one man rule."

It is said that the last book written by Baha'u'llah before his death was the *Epistle to the Son of the Wolf*.(89) In this Epistle of 180 pages Baha'u'llah addressed the son of the Muslim leader who had ordered the execution of two notable Baha'is in Isfahan (c. 1880 A.D.),(90) but the message is intended for everyone. Baha'u'llah sternly rebukes this man, whom he calls "Shaykh," for his evil deeds, and bids him repent and believe. He bemoans all the sufferings he (Baha'u' llah) has endured from his enemies, and defends himself from the charges brought against him, which he denounces as false. Toward the Shah of Iran, who had ordered the execution of the Bab and had bitterly opposed the Babis, he shows a most conciliatory attitude, saying that he has ever striven for the peace and good of the people of Iran and of the world. He begs the Shah to treat well the Baha'is in Iran. He quotes long sections from his own previous writings. He also quotes much from the sayings and writings of the Bab, whom he calls his forerunner, but neither he nor his interpreter indicates from what writings of the Bab these quotations are taken. He quotes passages from both the Old and the New Testaments in order to convince Jews and Christians, and the Koran and Islamic traditions for the benefit of Muslims. Here at the end of his life he restates his claims to be a Manifestation, and appeals to the People of the Bayan (followers of Subh-i-Azal) to accept him. And he bitterly complains of the wicked opposition of his brother Subh-i-Azal, whom he calls "Mirza Yahya,"

and those who had followed him. Baha'u'llah forbade
the publication of this Epistle during his lifetime,
and it was not published till later.(91)

Some of the finest of Baha'u'llah's words found in
various writings of his are the following, which are
quoted by Mirza Jawad in his Historical Epitome:

"All of you are the fruit of one Tree and the leaves
of one Branch. It is not for him who loves his country
to be proud, but [rather] for him who loves the whole
world."(92)

"O people of Baha! Ye are the Rising-places of Love
and the Daysprings of Divine Grace. Do not defile the
tongue with the vituperation and cursing of anyone.
Keep the eye from that which is not seemly. Be not
the cause of sorrow, much less of strife and sedition."
(92)

"By the Most Great Name, if one of the Companions
vexeth any one, it is as though he had vexed God Himself. Ye are forbidden strife, quarreling, sedition,
murder and the like thereof with a stringent prohibition in God's Book."(93)

"I swear by the Sun of the Dawning of the Divine
Unity, if the Friends of God be slain it is better in
the eyes of this Oppressed One than that they should
injure anyone."(93)

"O people of God, do not concern yourselves with
yourselves: take thought for the reformation of the
world and the purification of its peoples. The reformation of the world will be [effected] by good and
pure deeds and gracious and well-pleasing virtues."(94)

"O people of earth, make not God's Religion a cause
of difference amongst you! Verily He hath revealed
the Truth for the concord of all who are in the world."
(94)

In *Bahai Scriptures* this saying of Baha'u'llah's is
quoted:(95) "The principle of faith is to lessen words

and to increase deeds. He whose words exceed his acts, know verily that his non-being is better than his being, and death better than his life."

What has attracted many persons in various lands to Baha'u'llah has been not some unique service rendered by him to humanity, and not the laws which he promulgated for his proposed Baha'i Theocracy, but rather these ethical and humaniterian teachings regarding peace and unity among the people of the world. These teachings are, says Professor Browne,(96)"in themselves admirable, though inferior, in my opinion, both in beauty and simplicity to the teachings of Christ." "Moreover," continues Browne, "as it seems to me, ethics is only the application to everyday life of religion and metaphysics, and to be effective must be supported by some spiritual sanction; and in the case of Baha'ism, with its rather vague doctrines as to the nature and destiny of the soul of man, it is a little difficult to see whence the driving-power to enforce the ethical maxims can be derived." This was the mature judgement of a great scholar who had studied Baha'ism with sympathy for more than thirty years.

Shortly before his death Baha'u'llah sent to Professor Browne a little manuscript entitled *Good News* which contained a compendium of his principal teachings composed especially for Browne. These were in brief as follows:(97)

1) Expunction of the commandment for *Jihad* ("Holy War") from the Book of God.

2) All sects and peoples to associate with one another with joy and sweetness.

3) Permission to study foreign languages, with a recommendation that kings and ministers of state choose one existing language and script as a medium for international communication, or else create one.(98)

4) Baha'is must loyally serve and support any king who extends protection to their faith.

5) Baha'is must behave themselves honestly, truthfully and sincerely towards the country in which they dwell.

6) Promise of the Most Great Peace revealed by the Supreme Pen.

7) All are permitted, subject to the dictates of decency and good taste, to follow their own inclinations as to dress and the wearing of the hair.

8) Christian monks and priests must abandon their seclusion and engage in useful service. "We have vouched them permission to marry."

9) Sins are to be confessed not to men but to God.

10) Expunction of the commandment (of the Bab) for the annullment of books from writings and tablets.(99)

11) The study of useful arts and sciences is commanded.

12) All men must learn and practice some craft, trade or profession.

13) Subject to the rules for worship laid down in the Aqdas, the House of Justice is the competent authority to enact legislation for the people.

14) Pilgrimages to the tombs of saints and martyrs (as commanded by the Bab) are no longer obligatory.

15) The best form of government is a combination of a monarchy and a republic.

These are the "Baha'i Principles" as stated by Baha'u'llah himself in 1891. Most of them are taken from the Bayan and the Aqdas. It is instructive to compare this statement with the *Iqan*, written by Baha'u'llah some thirty years earlier, to see how his interests had broadened as a result of his experience and his studies of books and newspapers dealing with world problems while in Akka.(100) It is also instructive to compare this list of teachings with the

"Principles" attributed to Baha'u'llah which were later adopted by Baha'is.

The Will of Baha'u'llah and his provision for the succession and the leadership of the Baha'i Cause after his death will be considered in the following chapter.

NOTES

1. Mirza Jawad in *Materials*, p. 64.

2. *Bahai Scriptures*, edited by Horace Holley, approved by Bahai Committee on Publications, New York, Brentano's, 1923.

3. *Baha'i World Faith*, Baha'i Publishing Trust, Wilmette, Illinois, 2nd edition 1956.

4. Ibid., p. 454.

5. *Azal's Notes*, p. 254, *God Passes By*, by Shoghi Effendi, Baha'i Publishing Trust, 1965, p. 94.

6. *Azal's Notes*, p. 423, *Bahai Scriptures*, pp. 102-104, *God Passes By*, p. 94.

7. *Persian Bayan*, III, 6, 8.

8. *Bahai Scriptures*, pp. 241, 243.

9. *Azal's Notes*, pp. 165, 599, 1055, 1056, 1086, *Letter No. One of Baha*. See Appendix II, #4.

10. *Azal's Notes*, p. 1086.

11. From this statement it is clear that Baha'u'llah had read and studied the Bayan. It is therefore surprising to find in his *Epistle to the Son of the Wolf* (translated by Shoghi Effendi, Baha'i Publishing Trust) on page 165 the following confession: "God testifieth and beareth me witness that this Wronged One [Baha'u'llah] hath not

perused the Bayan nor been acquainted with its contents."   See Appendix II, #66.

12. *al-Kitab al-Aqdas or The Most Holy Book*, translated by E. E. Elder, The Royal Asiatic Society, London, 1961, p. 51.   *Kitab-i-Aqdas* is the Persian name of the book.

13. *God Passes By*, p. 213.

14. *Bahai Scriptures*, p. 261.

15. Ibid., p. 554.

16. *God Passes By*, p. 213.

17. *Materials*, pp. 9, 17.   See Appendix II, #62.

18. Browne in *Materials*, p. 195, *Baha'i World 1926-1928*, p. 200, *Azal's Notes*, pp. 7-13, 83, 89, 114, 249, 365, 366, 1059.

19. *J.R.A.S.*, October 1889, pp. 972-981.

20. *Materials*, p. 187.

21. See Note #12.   The Introduction and Notes of the 1961 edition should be corrected to conform to what the author, after getting fuller and more accurate information, has written in the present volume.

22. Letter to Mr. Will Orick.

23. *God Passes By*, p. 411.

24. *Azal's Notes*, p. 1090.

25. Ibidl, pp. 1054-1087.

26. *Aqdas*, p. 23.

27. Ibid., p. 24.

28. Ibid., pp. 24, 25.   "The worship of nine prostrations is a dead letter.   In actual practice Baha'is hold three services of one prostration each" (*Azal's Notes*, p. 1060).

29. *Aqdas*, pp. 25, 60.

30. The number 95 derives its authority from *al-Bayan*, the name first applied to God.   All the mystery of the Bayan is manifest in this name; because the

numerical value of *al-Bayan* (=94) plus the *Wahid* without number (=1) make 95. Also, the numerical value of the letters in *Wahid* (=19) multiplied by the number of the letters in *Bab* (=5) is 95. Note that the number 19, to which the Bab attached so much importance, is retained in the Baha'i system (*Azal's Notes*, pp. 1062, 1063).

31. *Aqdas*, pp. 26, 27. All these matters regarding worship are fully provided for in the Bayan.

32. *Aqdas*, pp. 27, 28.

33. Browne in *A Traveller's Narrative*, pp. 418-425. *The Baha'i World 1936-1938*, pp. 447, 448, states that the Baha'i Era commences with the year of the Bab's declaration (May 23, 1844 A.D., 1260 A.H.), and quotes Baha'u'llah as saying, "The year of the Declaration of the Bab must be regarded as the beginning of the Badi Calendar." The No Ruz after the declaration (March 21, 1845) is accounted the first No Ruz of the Badi Calendar. However, according to the clear statements by the Bab in his autograph personal *Diary*, in the book *Five Grades* (pp. 12, 16, 19) and in other writings by him, the Babi Era (Badi Calendar) began on No Ruz (March 19) of 1266 A.H. and 1850 A.D., shortly before the Bab's execution. It is noteworthy that Baha'u'llah decreed that his Era begin, not at the time of his declaration, nor at the time decreed by the Bab, but at the time of the declaration of the Bab, whom he called his Forerunner. For a full discussion of the Badi Calendar see *Azal's Notes*, pp. 1065-1068.

34. *Aqdas*, p. 29. These provisions for worship are taken from the *Persian Bayan*, V, 17 and VIII, 10.

35. *Aqdas*, p. 29. Taken from *Persian Bayan*, IV, 5 and *Arabic Bayan*, X, 5.

36. *Aqdas*, pp. 29-31, *Azal's Notes*, p. 1070.

37. *Aqdas*, p. 31. The Bab had provided for a council of 25 members to assist the Babi authority which would be established (*Arabic Bayan*, XI, 2). Baha replaced this by a House of Justice of 9 or more members.

38. *Aqdas*, pp. 32, 33, 59.

39. *Aqdas*, p. 32. Taken from *Arabic Bayan*, VIII, 17.

40. *Aqdas*, p. 32. From *Persian Bayan*, VII, 14, where it is commanded that forgiveness should be sought from the Manifestation as long as he lives, and after his death it must be sought from God.

41. *Aqdas*, p. 33. From *Persian Bayan*, VI, 7 and VIII, 15, *Arabic Bayan*, X, 10, where it is commanded that all must marry.

42. *Aqdas*, p. 34.

43. *Aqdas*, pp. 34, 35.

44. *Aqdas*, p. 36. There is no provision in the Bayan which would enable the Bab or his appointed successor to control religious endowments.

45. *Aqdas*, pp. 36, 37. The *Arabic Bayan*, X, 5 forbids theft, but there is no provision for banishment, imprisonment or branding.

46. *Aqdas*, p. 37. From *Persian Bayan*, VI, 9.

47. *Aqdas*, pp. 37, 38. The Bab in his book *Four Grades* made full provision for the education of one's children.

48. *Aqdas*, p. 38. The *Arabic Bayan*, X, 5 says that adultery is a thing to be eschewed. The imposition of a fine is Baha'u'llah's provision. There is no provision in the Bayan regarding music.

49. *Aqdas*, p. 39.

50. *Aqdas*, pp. 39, 40. From *Arabic Bayan*, XI, 17.

51. *Aqdas*, p. 40. There is no provision in the Bayan for hunting.

52. *Aqdas*, p. 40. The *Arabic Bayan*, X, 5 forbids arson, but it appears that it makes no provision for punishment. Murder also is strictly forbidden in the *Persian Bayan*, IV, 5, and in the *Arabic Bayan*, XI, 16 it is commanded that the murderer must pay 11,000 *mithqals* of pure gold to the heirs of the murdered person.

53. *Aqdas*, pp. 40-43. In the *Persian* and *Arabic Bayans*, VI, 16 the Bab commanded that a husband may not absent himself from his home for more than two years if on land, and more than five years if at sea. Baha'u'llah removed this restriction. Except for this and other minor amendments, all the provisions regarding marriage found in the Aqdas are taken from the *Arabic Bayan*, VI, 12, 17, VIII, 15, X, 10.

54. *Aqdas*, p. 43. It appears there is no provision in the Bayan regarding slavery.

55. *Aqdas*, p. 44. From *Arabic Bayan*, X, 18.

56. *Aqdas*, pp. 44, 45. Full provision is made for this in *Persian* and *Arabic Bayans*, IV, 10.

57. *Aqdas*, p. 45. The Bab taught that when a new Manifestation appears the Book of the previous Manifestation is abrogated, and its validity is "destroyed." Likewise, religious books written by men in the former dispensation no longer have validity. The Bab, accordingly, forbade the Babis to read the books written by the Muslim theologians (*Persian Bayan*, VI, 6). He permitted them to read only the Bayan, or books with the prescribed colophon from the *Arabic Bayan*, X, 11. The Bab forbade the tearing up of books (*Azal's Notes*, p. 1076).

58. *Aqdas*, pp. 47, 48.

59. Ibid., p. 48.

60. Ibid., p. 49.

61. Ibid., pp. 49, 50.

62. Ibid., pp. 50, 51. This law, except for the provision for the disposal of the money, is from the *Arabic* and *Persian Bayans*, VIII, 16.

63. Avareh in *Kashfu'l-Hiyal*, presumably first edition, p. 133, *Azal's Notes*, pp. 48-51.

64. *Aqdas*, p. 51. This also is from the *Persian Bayan*, II, 1.

65. *Aqdas*, pp. 52, 53. The rules for cleanliness are from the *Bayans*, IV.

66. *Aqdas*, p. 53. Pederasty is forbidden in the *Arabic Bayan* X, 5. It appears there is no prohibition in the Bayan against moving lips in prayer in the street. The provision regarding places of worship is taken from the *Arabic Bayan* IX, 9, and that for writing a will is from the *Arabic* and *Persian Bayans*, V, 13.

67. *Aqdas*, p. 54.

68. *Aqdas*, p. 55. The Bab's provision for bringing the most priceless thing to him is found in the *Persian Bayan*, VI, 16. The Bab did not forbid the learning of foreign languages, but the study of the "Science of Obsolete Words" (*Persian Bayan*, IV, 10).

69. *Aqdas*, p. 56. The use of alcohol is forbidden in the *Arabic* and *Persian Bayans*, IX, 8.

70. *Aqdas*, pp. 56, 57. There appears to be no provision in the Bayan regarding freedom.

71. *Aqdas*, p. 58. The provisions for burial are taken from the *Arabic Bayan*, V, 11 and VIII, 11.

72. *Aqdas*, pp. 58-62.

73. Ibid., p. 62.

74. Ibid., p. 62. From the *Arabic Bayan*, VI, 16.

75. *Aqdas*, p. 63. In *Arabic Bayan*, VIII, 17, begging and giving to beggars is forbidden, and earning one's living and giving relief to the destitute is commanded.

76. *Aqdas*, p. 64. The reading of verses is commanded in the *Arabic Bayan*, V, 8. Bathing is enjoined in the *Arabic Bayan*, VIII, 6. High pulpits are forbidden in the *Arabic Bayan*, VII, 11. Gambling and the use of opium are forbidden in the *Arabic Bayan*, IX, 8 and X, 5.

77. *Aqdas*, p. 65.

78. *Aqdas*, p. 66. Carrying arms except in time of necessity was forbidden in the *Arabic Bayan*, VII, 6. The provisions about clothing and hair are taken from the *Persian Bayan*, VI, 9 and VIII, 8.

79. *Aqdas*, pp. 67-69.

80. Ibid., p. 70.

81. Ibid., pp. 71-72.

82. Ibid., pp. 73-74.

83. Browne in *A Traveller's Narrative*, pp. 93, note 1 and 370.

84. *Aqdas*, p. 74. Provisions regarding overloading animals, and killing by mistake, and blood-money are taken from the *Arabic Bayan*, X, 15 and X, 8, 16

85. *Aqdas*, p. 74. An artificial language known as Esperanto was invented for universal use by a Polish physician Dr. L. L. Zamenhof before the Aqdas was revised and printed in 1890.

86. *Persian Bayan*, English Introduction to *Nuqtatu'l-Kaf*, p. LIV.

87. *Azal's Notes*, pp. 334, 335. See Appendix II, #67.

88. Ibid., p. 332.

89. Translated by Shoghi Effendi, Baha'i Publishing Trust.

90. Browne, *J.R.A.S.*, July 1889, pp. 489-491, and Browne, *A Traveller's Narrative*, pp. 400-403.

91. *Azal's Notes*, p. 14.

92. *Materials*, p. 65.

93. Ibid., p. 67.

94. Ibid., pp. 69, 70.

95. *Scriptures*, p. 158.

96. *Materials*, p. XXI.

97. *J.R.A.S.*, October 1892, p. 678, *Azal's Notes*, pp. 1090-1098. See Appendix II, #69.

98. A new script called *Khatt-i-Badi'* was created by
    Baha's son, Mirza Muhammad Ali, and was approved
    by his father. A specimen was printed in Avareh's
    Kashfu'l-Hiyal, vol. III, 3rd printing, pp. 188-
    189. See *J.R.A.S.*, July 1889, p. 498 and October
    1892, p. 709, note 3. See Appendix II, #70.

99. See Note 57.

100. Baha'u'llah had agents posted in Beirut, Cairo,
    Damascus and other cities who furnished him regu-
    larly with daily papers, periodicals and books on
    world problems. For example, he received from
    the famous Sayyid Jalalu'd-Din Afghani a copy of
    the periodical he was publishing in Cairo, and he
    read the article in the Arabic Encyclopedia which
    the Sayyid had written on the Babi movement.
    Evidence of his wide reading is found in his
    Tablets (*Azal's Notes*, pp. 1114-1115). See Appendix
    II, #73.

9

The Rule of Abdu'l-Baha

Just as the Bab, following the Shi'ite principle by
which each Prophet and Imam appointed his successor,
designated Subh-i-Azal to succeed him, so Baha'u'llah
in like manner named his successor. As we have seen,
he indicated in the *Kitab-i-Aqdas* some years before
his death that he was to be succeeded by "him whom
God has meant, who has branched from this ancient
Root."(1) By this he meant that his successor was to
be his son, but he did not specify which of his four
sons was intended. However, before his death Baha'u'
llah clarified this important matter in his Will and
Testament, which he called *Kitab-i-Ahdi* (Book of My
Covenant), in which he says: "The reference in this
blessed verse is to the Most Mighty Branch (*Ghusn-i-
A'zam*, the title for Abbas Efendi)." Then he contin-
ues: "Verily, God hath decreed the station of the
Most Great Branch (*Ghusn-i-Akbar*, the title for Mirza
Muhammad Ali) after the station of the former. Verily,
He is the Commanding One, the Wise. We have surely
chosen the Most Great after the Most Mighty because
of a command from the Knower."(2)

From this passage it is clear that it was Baha'u'
llah's intention that he should be succeeded by his

eldest son Abbas Efendi, a man of about fifty years
of age at the death of his father,(3) and that Abbas
Efendi should be succeeded by another son Mirza
Muhammad Ali (the eldest son of Baha'u'llah's second
wife), then about forty years of age. It is inexcusable that the Baha'i compiler of *Bahai Scriptures*
should have translated *akbar* "Greater" when he translated *a'zam* "Greatest," thus indicating that the rank
of Mirza Muhammad Ali was lower than that of Abbas
Efendi. And although it was claimed that the translation in *Baha'i World Faith* was "more accurate" than
that in *Bahai Scriptures* (Chapter VIII), this same
flagrant mistranslation is repeated in that volume on
pages 209-210 where *Akbar* the title of Muhammad Ali
is translated Great, and *A'zam* the title of Abbas is
rendered Most Great. The two Arabic words used in
the titles given by Baha'u'llah to his two older
sons both mean "great" or "mighty," and both are here
to be translated by the superlative Most Great or
Most Mighty. *Akbar*, the title of Muhammad Ali, is
the same used in the Baha'i term "Most Great Peace,"
and in the Muslim confession "God is Most Great." It
is even more inexcusable that Shoghi Effendi should
have been guilty of the same erroneous translation
when he quotes this passage, saying that Baha'u'llah
"ordains the station of the *'Greater Branch'* (Mirza
Muhammad-Ali) to be beneath that of the *'Most Great
Branch'* (Abdu'l-Baha, [that is, Abbas Efendi])."(4)
The reason for this mistranslation will become evident
as we proceed with the story.

Both of these sons had been loyal to their father,
and were trusted by him. Abbas Efendi was appointed
by Baha'u'llah to be in charge of external affairs of
the Cause, and Mirza Muhammad Ali was given charge of
internal affairs.(5) Baha'u'llah did not think
highly of Munira Khanum, the wife of Abbas Efendi,
and perhaps it was in part for this reason that Abbas
Efendi and his wife and daughters and sister and
mother lived together in the city of Akka,(6) while
Baha'u'llah and his other wives and sons and the
remaining members of his family lived in the Bahji
Palace several miles away. To Abbas Efendi was given
the responsibility of writing the authorized version

of the history of the Babi-Baha'i movement, which he
did in 1886 as an anonymous work under the title *A
Traveller's Narrative*.(7) He procured the property
on Mt. Carmel near Haifa on which, as a result of
his efforts, the mausoleum for the Bab was later
built.(8) To Mirza Muhammad Ali also was given great
responsibility. To him Baha'u'llah dictated his
Epistles, and to him were entrusted all the sacred
writings.(5) And to him was given the authority to
revise, with the help of a trusted believer, and to
publish several of Baha'u'llah's books, including the
Aqdas.(9) This was done in Bombay in 1890, two years
before the death of the father, and there is no evidence that Baha'u'llah expressed any dissatisfaction
with the service rendered by his son.

When the Bab chose Mirza Yahya as his successor
and gave him high titles, he appointed one whom he had
never seen, and later it might have been said by some
that in doing so he made a mistake. However, such a
criticism could not be made of Baha'u'llah, for he
chose as his successors his own sons, men known and
trusted, not only by him but also by all the Baha'is.
And to prevent the kind of schism which had occurred
between him and Subh-i-Azal, he made the appointment
quite definite and clear in his Will. In this docu-
ment(10) the father, no doubt realizing that trouble
was brewing and might erupt after his death, pleads
with all members of his family and all believers to
love and honor the Branches and to love one another
and live in peace. "The creed of God is for love and
union," he says, "make it not the cause of discord
and disunion.....He hath forbidden disputes and strife
with an absolute prohibition in the Book [Aqdas]. This
is the command of God in this Greatest Manifestation
.....O My Branches, My Twigs and My Relations! Make
not the course of order to be the cause of confusion
.....Respect and regard for the Branches is incumbent
upon all."(11)

Unfortunately, these pleas for harmony fell on
deaf ears. The sad story of the events that followed
the death of Baha'u'llah are related thus by Mirza
Jawad, who had come with Baha'u'llah from Edirne, and

had remained a faithful follower all through the years
at Akka:(12)   "Alas, alas for what we see today!   All
these spiritual virtues and humane practices have
undergone a complete change.   Concord has been replaced
by dissension, constancy by cruelty, and affection by
enmity.   Dissent and mutual avoidance have appeared in
this community.....antagonism and separation arose
between father and son, brother and sister, husband
and wife, and so forth; nay, God be our refuge! even
envy and hatred."   The cause of this dissention was,
according to Mirza Jawad, "the love of self and seeking after supremacy" of Abbas Efendi.

Mirza Jawad continues,(13) "The first differences
which happened after the death of His Great Holiness
our Master within this community was that Abbas
Efendi concealed some part of the book of [Baha'u'llah's]
Testament entitled "the Book of my Testament," which
book was given to him by Baha'u'llah in his own holy
writing.   The detail of this is that on the ninth day
after the Ascension [i.e., the death of Baha'u'llah]
Abbas Efendi chose nine persons from amongst the Companions, one of whom was the author (of this book) and
disclosed to them this document, concealing, however,
a portion of it with a blue leaf [of paper], without
any reason or justification, and gave it to them that
they might enjoy the blessing of its perusal.   One of
them...read...to the place concealed by the blue leaf,
whereupon Abbas Efendi said to the persons above mentioned, 'Verily a portion of this book is concealed
for a good reason, because the time doth not admit of
its full disclosure'."   Later on the same day it was
read to a number of other relatives and believers,
down to the concealed portion.

"Let it not be hidden," concludes Mirza Jawad,
"...that the injunctions set forth in the above-mentioned book all refer to this community generally;
how then could it be right for Abbas Efendi to dis-
close what he wished and conceal a portion thereof?
For there is no doubt that if what was concealed had
not been suitable [for general publication] His Holiness Baha'u'llah would not have written it in his
august writing."

There is no question that Baha'u'llah appointed
Abbas Efendi as his successor. But what authority
was he to have? The Bab had indicated that his
successor Subh-i-Azal had the same rank that he had,
and was one with him.(14) But Baha'u'llah made it
very clear that anyone who succeeded him could never
claim to share his rank as a Great Manifestation. For
before his death he had stated in the *Kitab-i-Aqdas*
(15) that anyone who claims "Command," that is, claims
to have the rank of a Manifestation, before a thousand
years is a false liar. Hence, Abbas Efendi was not
authorized to take his father's place, and be a continuation of his Manifestation. But very soon it began
to appear that this was what he wanted to do. He
called himself *Abdu'l-Baha* (the Slave of Baha), and
professed perfect submission to his father's will.
But he also assumed the title, "the Center of the
Convenant," a title which many Baha'is thought belonged only to God.(16) "Abbas Efendi," writes Mirza
Jawad,(17) "after he had attained to supremacy.....
claimed such lofty stations and high degrees as belong
exclusively to Divine Theophanies." And he quotes
several pages of sayings of the new leader which show
how high his aspirations were.

One of Abbas Efendi's claims was that he alone had
the right to interpret the writings of Baha'u'llah.
"This servant is the expositor of the Perspicuous Book,
and whatever of God's writings is not confirmed by
this servant is not worthy of credence."(18) In
another place he says,(19) "You must ask him [Abdu'l-
Baha] regarding the meaning of the texts of the verses.
Whatsoever he says is correct. Without his will not a
word shall anyone utter." Though he never called himself a new Manifestation, by claiming to be the sole
infallible interpreter of the Word of God, and by
asserting that his writings were equally authoritative
with those of his father, he assumed a station of
which Baha'u'llah would most probably have warmly disapproved. Modern Baha'is, however, fully agree to
these claims. For instance, the volume entitled *Bahai
Scriptures*, to which frequent reference has been made,
has two parts. Part I comprises the verses of Baha'u'
llah, and Part II (larger than Part I), the writings

and addresses of Abdu'l-Baha. Both are considered
equally authoritative. "The words of Abdu'l-Baha.....
have equal rank and spiritual validity with those of
the Manifestation."(20)

It seems that most of the Baha'is, both in Akka and
abroad, were quite ready to follow their divinely-
appointed leader, no matter what station he might
claim for himself. However, there were a number who,
like Mirza Jawad, for various reasons deeply resented
the attitude and the acts of Abdu'l-Baha, and the
leader of the opposition soon came to be Mirza Muhammad
Ali, brother of Abbas Efendi, and appointed by Baha'u'
llah as the second in succession. It seems that
Muhammad Ali did not claim to be the rightful successor
to his father, for he had no right to the leadership of
the Cause till Abbas should die. His protest, and that
of those who joined him, was against the claims of the
"Center of the Covenant" to absolute authority. He and
his party called themselves "Unitarians,"(21) while
they were stigmatized by Abdu'l-Baha and his followers
as "Violators of the Covenant."(22)

The strife waxed fierce, and much was said and done
by both sides that was unseemly. The Unitarians
sought a conference with the party of Abdu'l-Baha that
they might refer the matter to the writings of Baha'u'
llah,(23) as had been commanded in the *Kitab-i-Aqdas*.
(24) Abdu'l-Baha did not reply to their frequent
requests, and the conference was never held. It seems
that almost all of the members of the family of Baha'u'
llah sided with Mirza Muhammad Ali and the Unitarians.
Shoghi Efendi says(25) that Baha'u'llah's two surviving wives, his two other sons, his daughter and her
husband, and other relatives, "all united in a determined effort to subvert the foundations of the Covenant," and Abdu'l-Baha "was left alone....." He,
accordingly, took disciplinary action and excommunicated all of his relatives who opposed him.(26) Not
only so, but he later deprived them of their allowances, which Baha'u'llah had previously given them
from the funds that came to him from the believers in
Iran and other lands.(27)

'ABDU'L-BAHĀ

The original photograph was signed and presented to the author by his
grandson, Shoghi Efendi

A Precious souvenir presented to my dear friend M. Miller
Haifa, Palestine, March 23 1923   Shoghi Rabbani

The sons and relatives of Baha'u'llah, being exiles and political prisoners in Akka, had not learned to support themselves and had depended on gifts from others for their living. The fact that the action of Abbas Efendi in cutting off their shares of the income caused them real difficulty is attested by Rosamund Dale Owen, a long-time resident in Haifa. She has stated in her book *My Perilous Life in Palestine*(28) that she was well acquainted with the three sons of Baha'u'llah in Akka.(29) She was much concerned about the financial condition of Mirza Badi'u'llah, the youngest son, and his family of seven people, who were facing starvation because the eldest brother Abbas Efendi had cut off their allowances, and she had given them considerable assistance. So when she was asked to act as arbitrator in their quarrel she was quite ready to do so, and wrote to each of the three brothers, inviting them to meet her at the tomb of their father and there together read his Will. She hoped in this way to clear up any misunderstanding about Baha'u'llah's arrangements for the division of the allowances. Mirza Badi'u'llah and Mirza Muhammad Ali at once replied in writing and agreed to comply to her suggestion. But though she wrote a second time to Abbas Efendi he did not reply. It was therefore impossible for her to help in solving the problem. Mrs. Owen expressed surprise at this lack of love in the family of Baha'u'llah, when his teachings about love were so frequently quoted by his followers in the West. The correctness of Mrs. Owen's account has been attested by the son of Mirza Badi'u'llah.(30)

After five years of strife *Janab-i-Khadimu'llah*, the Servant of God, who had first encouraged Baha'u'llah to put forward his claim to be a Manifestation, and had been his lifelong amanuensis, invited all the Companions to the shrine of Baha'u'llah on the anniversary of his death, and according to Mirza Jawad,(31) addressed them as follows: "This servant hath been silent all this time and hath not uttered a word, for fear of giving rise to dissension. Now, however, I perceive that my silence causeth increase of discord in God's Religion; therefore I say unto you that the deeds and words which have issued from Abbas Efendi

and his company are all contrary to God's commands,
and at variance with his injunctions revealed in the
Holy Scriptures. The Covenant and Promise mentioned
aforetime in the Immaculate writings refer exclusively
to previous and subsequent Theophanies, but Abbas
Efendi hath appropriated them to himself, and ye have
so accepted them, wherein ye have greatly erred."

Then Mirza Jawad related(32) that when Abbas Efendi
was informed of what was going on he immediately
appeared on the scene, seized the old man (the Servant
of God) by the hand, and "expelled him from the house
bareheaded and barefooted, while his followers beat
him on the head and face." Paying no attention to his
protests, they dragged him to the tomb of Baha'u'llah,
"where Abbas Efendi struck him with his hand a painful
blow," after which he was imprisoned in a stable.
Later, after being released, he went to the house of
Abbas Efendi in Akka, hoping to have a conference with
him about the situation, but he was refused admittance,
and finally was handed over to the police. Four years
later he died, and all the relics and writings of
Baha'u'llah which were in his possession were taken
away by night by Abbas Efendi. "These included twelve
Holy portraits (of Baha'u'llah), 217 Holy Tablets...,
and a number of the Holy head-dresses, garments and
hairs, besides many sacred books."(33)

This is the story as told by the Unitarians. And
now let us hear what the followers of Abdu'l-Baha have
to say. It will be sufficient to quote what Shoghi
Effendi, the grandson of Abdu'l-Baha has written in
his history *God Passes By* in the chapter entitled "The
Rebellion of Mirza Muhammad-Ali."(34) Of Abdu'l-Baha
he says: "His (Baha'u'llah's) own beloved Son, the
apple of His eye, His vicegerent on earth, the Executive of His authority, the Pivot of His Covenant, the
Shepherd of His flock, the Exemplar of His faith, the
Image of His perfections, the Mystery of His Revelation, the Interpreter of His mind, the Architect of
His World Order, the ensign of His Most Great Peace,
the Focal Point of His unerring guidance - in a word,
the occupant of an office without peer or equal in the
entire field of religious history....." Such an one,

he concludes, was fully qualified to guard the Cause,
blazon abroad its fame, and consummate its purpose.(35)

But first, says Shoghi Efendi, a crisis arose "at
the very heart and center of His faith, and was provoked by no one less than a member of His own family,
a half-brother of Abdu'l-Baha, specifically named in
the Book of the Covenant, and holding a rank second to
none except Him who had been appointed as the Center
of that Covenant." The result of this crisis was that
"an irreparable breach (was created) within the ranks
of Baha'u'llah's own kindred," sealing "ultimately
the fate of the great majority of the members of His
family, and gravely damaging the prestige.....of the
Faith itself. The true ground of this crisis was the
burning, the uncontrollable, the soul-festering jea-
lousy...of Abdu'l-Baha...in Mirza Muhammad-Ali, the
archbreaker of the Covenant. An envy as blind as that
which had possessed the soul of Mirza Yahya [Subh-i-
Azal].....as deep-seated as that which had blazed in
the bosom of Cain and prompted him to slay his brother
Abel, had...been smouldering in the recesses of Mirza
Muhammad'Ali's heart."(36) Then followed a long list
of charges made by the Unitarians against Abdu'l-Baha:
(37) "To friend and stranger, believer and unbeliever
alike, to officials both high and low, openly and by
insinuation, verbally as well as in writing, they
represented Abdu'l-Baha as an ambitious, a self-willed,
an unprincipled and pitiless usurper, who had deliberately disregarded the testamentary instructions of His
Father; who had, in language intentionally veiled and
ambiguous, assumed a rank co-equal with the Manifestation Himself..... He had, for His private ends,
fomented discord, fostered enmity...that He had actually corrupted the Holy Text, interpolated passages
written by Himself."

The same charges were hurled back at the followers
of Muhammad Ali. They were accused of stealing sacred
writings, of corrupting the texts, and even of con-
spiring to murder Abdu'l-Baha. "The Covenant of
Baha'u'llah had, by acts such as these," says Shoghi
Efendi "been manifestly violated."(38) And years later
near the end of his life Abdu'l-Baha in his Will and

Testament wrote that Muhammad Ali and his partisans
are "ferocious lions, ravening wolves, and blood-
thirsty beasts, in whose talons are held fast this
wronged servant of Thine."(39) These men who brought
such grievous accusations against one another were
brothers, both sons of Baha'u'llah, both Most Great
Branches from the ancient Stock, both chosen by their
father to be in turn his successors, and both enjoined
by him in his Will to honor and love one another.

Writing about a pamphlet which had been composed
by one of the followers of Abdu'l-Baha in 1898, Professor Browne remarks,(40) "One fact which is very
clearly brought out by this pamphlet is that the
detestation in which the followers of Abbas Efendi
hold the rival faction of his half-brother Muhammad
Ali equals, if it does not exceed, that in which the
Baha'is generally hold the Azalis, and far surpasses
the dislike entertained by any of these three parties
for the adherents of other creeds which stand entirely
outside the Babi-Baha'i circle.....This second schism
amongst the Babi community.....was singularly fierce
and bitter." And in another place(41) he writes of
the same quarrel: "This last schism, I confess, and
the bitterness to which it gave rise, created a very
painful impression on my mind, for, as I have repeatedly inquired of my Baha'i friends, where is the com-
pelling and constraining power which they regard as
the essential and incontrovertible sign of the Divine
Word, when, in the face of such texts as 'Associate
with (the followers of all) religions with spirituality and fragrance' and 'Ye are all the fruit of one
Tree and the leaves of one Branch', they can show such
bitter animosity towards those of their own household?"
Excellent advice for persons in such a situation was
given later by Abdu'l-Baha himself. He said,(42) "If
two souls quarrel and contend about a question...dif-
fering and disputing...both are wrong... Should there
appear the least trace of controversy, they must remain
silent....."

Not only did Abdu'l-Baha and his followers not
remain silent, they went beyond angry words. Browne
has published evidence(43) which proves conclusively

that at least in one instance the old Babi method of
assassination was resorted to by Abdu'l-Baha to get
rid of a dangerous enemy. A certain Mirza Yahya, who
had been first an Azali, then had become a Baha'i,
and finally had given his whole-hearted support to
Muhammad Ali and the Unitarians, was carrying on active
propaganda against Abbas Efendi. Finally, Abdu'l-Baha
issued a Tablet in which he sternly rebuked Mirza Yahya
for his disobedience and commanded him to repent and
desist from his opposition, if perchance he might be
forgiven. "For if not," he added, "then expect the
Divine Vengeance, and look for blackness of face
[disgrace] in both worlds.....For abasement, remorse
and disgrace shall be the portion of those who violate
the Covenant of the High, the Mighty." This threaten-
ing message was taken at Abdu'l-Baha's orders to Jedda,
near Mecca, where Mirza Yahya was living in the home of
the Iranian Consul, his father-in-law, who was faithful
to Abdu'l-Baha, and was read to him by the bearer.
Mirza Yahya refused to repent, and said he had no
faith in either the sender or his father (Baha). A
few nights later Mirza Yahya was found in the house in
a serious condition with blood flowing from his throat,
and after several days he died. This occurred in
October, 1898.

The messenger who had carried the Tablet to Mirza
Yahya and had read it to him was Hajji Mulla Husayn.
This man reported what had happended in a letter, in
which he declared(44) that "God, mighty in His glory,
has removed Yahya, that incorrigible Covenant-breaker...
The simoon of Divine Wrath blew, and the gale of Celestial Anger breathed, and his [Yahya's] darkened
spirit, fulfilled with envy and hatred, descended to
the abyss of Hell." In November, 1898 a pamphlet was
published in Egypt(45) describing this event as a
remarkable instance of Abdu'l-Baha's foreknowledge and
power. The author, Hajji Mirza Hasan, a follower of
Abdu'l-Baha, says that never was so clear a threat
followed by so swift and condign a punishment, or so
explicit a prophecy so speedily accomplished; for
though God's patience is almost inexhaustible, there
at last comes an end to it, and the guilty must perish.
The cause of the sudden death of Mirza Yahya, having

occurred in the Iranian Consulate in Jedda, was not investigated, and was no doubt accounted an act of God.

While these unhappy events were taking place in Akka, the first Baha'i missionary to America was busily engaged in preaching and making converts in the West. The interesting story of Dr. Khayru'llah (Kheiralla), called by his Master a "Second Columbus, Conqueror of America," and his successful mission will be told in the following chapter. The glowing reports which came from him must have brought much comfort and hope to the Center of the Covenant and his party in Akka. Meanwhile, Abbas Efendi continued to live and worship as a Muslim, saying the Muslim prayers, and keeping the Fast of Ramazan, just as his father had done. And the marriages and funerals in the family were all conducted according to the Muslim rites by the Muslim religious leaders.(46)

Abdu'l-Baha was without doubt a man of great ability and possessed a commanding personality, as is seen from the impression made by him on Professor Browne (Chapter VII). While he was warmly hated by the "Covenant-breakers" he was literally adored by some of the new converts who began coming from America to visit "The Master" in Akka. One of them, Mr. Horace Holley, who became one of the outstanding Baha'i leaders in America, and edited *Bahai Scriptures*, speaks thus of his feelings on meeting Abdu'l-Baha:(47) "He displayed a beauty of stature, an inevitable harmony of attitude and dress I had never seen or thought of in men. Without ever having visualized the Master, I knew that this was he. My whole body underwent a shock. My heart leaped, and my knees weakened, a thrill of acute, receptive feeling flowed from head to foot.....From sheer happiness I wanted to cry.... While my own personality was flowing away...a new being, not my own, assumed its place. A glory, as it were, from the summits of human nature poured into me....In Abdu'l-Baha I felt the awful presence of Baha'u'llah, and....I realized that I had thus drawn as near as man now may to pure spirit and pure being."

In the same manner some of the American women who came to Akka in December, 1898 saw in Abdu'l-Baha one

to be worshipped. Says Mrs. Phoebe A. Hearst in a
letter from Washington dated November 19, 1899:(48)
"The Master I will not attempt to describe. I will
only state that I believe with all my heart that He
is the Master, and my greatest blessing in this world
is that I have been privileged to be in His Presence
and look upon His sanctified face....Without a doubt
Abbas Effendi is the Messiah of this day and generation, and we need not look for another."

Another member of the same party was quoted in the
Literary Digest as follows:(48) "Dr. Kheiralla went
ahead, and by the violent beating of my heart I knew
that we were soon to see the Blessed face of the
Prince of the House of David, the King of the whole
world. We reached the door and stopped - before us in
the center of the room stood a man clad in a long garment with a white turban on His head, stretching out
one hand toward us....We stood thus for a moment unable
to move - when my heart gave a great throb and, scarcely
knowing what I was doing, I held out my arms, crying,
'My Lord, my Lord!' and rushed to Him, kneeling at His
blessed feet, sobbing like a child. He put His dear
hands upon our beloved heads and said, in a voice that
seemed to our ears like a strain of sweet music, 'Welcome, welcome, my dear children, you are welcome, arise
and be of good cheer.'"

Not long after this, Dr. Henry H. Jessup, who was
for many years a resident in Beirut and head of the
famous American Christian Press in that city, visited
Haifa and called on Abbas Efendi. After a friendly
conversation about religious matters, in which Abbas
Efendi told Dr. Jessup that he believed that Jesus
Christ was the Saviour, and that he himself had faith
in him as his Saviour, and believed that Christ would
come to judge the world, Dr. Jessup told him of this
article in the *Literary Digest* which he had read. He
said that in the article it was stated that a woman
from America had fallen at his feet, weeping, and
saying, "My Lord, my Lord!" "Now," continued Dr.
Jessup, "I could not believe this, and thought it a
newspaper invention. I want to ask you whether this
is true. Can it be right for the creature to accept

the worship due only to the Creator?" Abdu'l-Baha
smiled, and seemed somewhat disturbed, and asked why
Dr. Jessup had changed the subject. Then he said
calmly, "I am only the poorest and humblest of servants." And soon the visit came to an end.(49)

When Baha'u'llah and his followers were sent to
Akka as political prisoners in 1868 they were for
some time confined to the city. After several years
they were given considerable liberty of movement, and
were allowed to travel to other parts of the country.
Then because of the activities of the Baha'is and the
strife which we have described, the Ottoman government
sent a commission to investigate the situation, and as
a result of its report the freedom which they had
enjoyed for more than twenty years was taken from them,
and they were once more confined to the city of Akka.
This occurred in 1901.(50) The entire blame for this
unfortunate occurrence was placed by Abdu'l-Baha on his
brother Mirza Muhammad Ali, whom he charged with giving false information to the Turkish authorities. This
restriction was continued till the Revolution of 1908
in Turkey, when all political prisoners were set free.
Thereafter the Baha'is could go anywhere they wished.

Though confined in Akka, Abdu'l-Baha was not pre-
vented from receiving visitors, and many came to him
both from the West(51) and also from the East. The
Western pilgrims picture the Master as spending his
time in deeds of loving service to the poor and needy
and in visiting the sick and afflicted in their homes.
One who visited Akka at this time writes:(52) "It is
the custom of Abdu'l-Baha each week, on Friday morning,
to distribute alms to the poor. From his own scanty
store he gives a little to each one of the needy who
come to him to ask assistance." The writer then describes the crowd of a hundred beggars whom he had seen
waiting to receive money from Abdu'l-Baha. It seems
that the son had forgotten that giving to beggars had
been forbidden by his father in the Most Holy Book.
However, an Iranian seeker for truth who came to Akka,
having travelled some two thousand miles, much of the
way on foot, told quite a different story.(53) During
the seventy days while he was with the Baha'is in Akka,

having dined with Abbas Efendi himself, he saw nothing
of this attention to the poor. Many guests were entertained, but they were chiefly officials and important
people. It seems that the Westerners heard nothing
while there of the strife that had split the family of
Baha'u'llah into two hostile camps, and they were not
permitted to see the members of the family whom Abdu'l-
Baha had excommunicated. Says Mr. Thornton Chase:(54)
"Five days we remained within those walls, prisoners
with Him who dwells in that 'Greatest Prison.' It is
a prison of peace, of love and service. No wish, no
desire is there save the good of mankind, the peace of
the world....All trouble, tumults, worries, or anxie-
ties for worldly things are barred out there." "These
men are Lovers," writes Mr. Phelps,(55) "lovers of God,
of their Master and Teacher, and of each other, and of
all mankind."

Much of the time of Abdu'l-Baha was spent in writing,
for he, like his father, carried on a large correspondence with believers in Iran and in other lands, and
his Tablets were as highly esteemed as had been those
of Baha'u'llah. By the strength of his personality and
the remarkable influence which he exercised over his
followers he was able to draw the great majority of the
Baha'is of the world after him, and the Unitarians
never became a strong party, and gradually disappeared
from the scene. After the restrictions of travel were
removed, Abdu'l-Baha in 1911 made a journey to Europe
and Egypt. Next year he sailed for America, where he
remained for seven months, and on the return journey
again visited Europe, Great Britain and Egypt. A
fuller account of his work in the West will be given
in the following chapter.

During the eight years that followed these journeys
Abdu'l-Baha remained in Haifa, which is near to Akka.
At the time of the First World War (1914-1918) he is
said to have done much for the relief of the famine-
stricken peoples about him, and to have been most gen-
erous in giving of his own provisions to the poor.(56)
Finally, Haifa fell into the hands of the British, and
Turkish rule came to an end on September 23, 1918.
"From the beginning of the British occupation, large

numbers of soldiers and Government officials of all
ranks, even the highest, sought interviews with Abdu'l-
Baha....So profoundly impressed were the Government
representatives by his noble character and his great
work in the interests of peace, conciliation, and the
true prosperity of the people, that a knighthood of
the British Empire was conferred on Abdu'l-Baha, the
ceremony taking place in the garden of the Military
Governor of Haifa on the 27th day of April, 1920."
Thus the Center of the Covenant became "Sir Abdu'l-
Baha Abbas, K.B.E."(57)

During the winter of 1919-1920 Mr. J. E. Esselmont
spent two and a half months in Haifa as the guest of
Abdu'l-Baha, and writes of his gracious host as
follows:(58) "At that time, although nearly seventy-
six years of age, he was still remarkably vigorous,
and accomplished daily an almost incredible amount of
work. Although often very weary he showed wonderful
powers of recuperation...His unfailing patience,
gentleness, kindliness and tact made his presence like
a benediction.....Both at lunch and supper he used to
entertain a number of pilgrims and friends, and charm
his guests with happy and humorous stories.....'My
house is the home of laughter and mirth,' he declared,
and indeed it was so. He delighted in gathering
together people of various races, colours, nations
and religions in unity and cordial friendship around
his hospitable board."

On Friday, November 25, 1921, Abdu'l-Baha attended
the noonday Muslim prayer at the Mosque in Haifa, and
afterwards distributed alms to the poor with his own
hands, as was his wont. Less than three days later he
died, on November 28.(59) The following day the funeral services were conducted by the Muslim clergy, and
a very large number of people from various religions
attended, along with the British High Commissioner and
other officials of the Government. Nine representatives from the Muslim, Christian and Jewish communities spoke in praise of the deceased, and then the
body was carried to Mt. Carmel and buried in the mausoleum of the Bab,(60) and his grave became a place of
pilgrimage for Baha'is. The provision which Abdu'l-Baha

made for the future of the Baha'i Cause will be considered in Chapter XI.

                              NOTES

1. *Aqdas*, p. 56.

2. *Bahai Scriptures*, p. 261. The Arabic text of the
    original is given in *Azal's Notes*, pp. 78-79. See
    also Avareh's official history *Al-Kawakib - Al-
    Durriyya*, vol. II, pp. 20-22. See Appendix II,
    #59.

3. According to Mirza Jawad (*Materials*, pp. 62, 320),
    Abbas Efendi was born in Iran in 1841. The state-
    ment made by some Baha'is that his birth occurred
    "on May 23, 1844, in the very hour in which the
    Bab declared his mission" (Esselmont, *Baha'u'llah
    and the New Era*, first edition, p. 53) is clearly
    a fiction.

4. *God Passes By*, p. 240.

5. *Azal's Notes*, p. 89.

6. Ibid., p. 88.

7. See Introduction.

8. *God Passes By*, pp. 241, 345.

9. *Azal's Notes*, pp. 89, 1059 (with text). See
    Appendix II, #62.

10. *Scriptures*, pp. 259-262.

11. Ibid., pp. 260-261.

12. *Azal's Notes*, pp. 73-74, 195. *Materials*, pp. 74
    ff., from "*An Epitome of Babi and Baha'i History*,"
    by M. Jawad (1904), translated from Arabic by
    Browne.

13. *Materials*, p. 75.

14. See Chapter V.

15. *Aqdas*, p. 34.

16. *God Passes By*, p. 243, *Azal's Notes*, pp. 97, 153.

17. *Materials*, p. 77.

18. Ibid., p. 78.

19. *Star of the West*, November 23, 1913, p. 238.

20. *Baha'i World*, 1926-1928, vol. II, p. 81, *Azal's Notes*, p. 217.

21. *Materials*, p. 81.

22. *God Passes By*, pp. 246, etc.

23. *Materials*, p. 82.

24. *Aqdas*, p. 39.

25. *God Passes By*, p. 247, *Azal's Notes*, p. 153.

26. *Azal's Notes*, pp. 45, 251.

27. Ibid., pp. 51, 299, *Materials*, p. 85.

28. *My Perilous Life in Palestine*, George Allen and Unwin, London, 1928, pp. 230-234.

29. Ziya'u'llah, the third son of Baha'u'llah, died in 1898 (*Materials*, p. 85).

30. *Azal's Notes*, p. 443.

31. *Materials*, p. 87.

32. Ibid., p. 88.

33. Ibid., pp. 90-91.

34. *God Passes By*, pp. 244 ff.

35. Ibid., p. 245.

36. Ibid., p. 246.

37. Ibid., p. 248.

38. Ibid., p. 249.

39. *Baha'i World*, 1926-1928, vol. II, p. 82.

40. *Materials*, p. 167.

41. Browne, *Nuqtatu'l-Kaf*, p. XLIX.

42. *Scriptures*, p. 544.

43. *Materials*, pp. 155-167.

44. Ibid., pp. 164-165.

45. Ibid., pp. 158 ff.

46. *Azal's Notes*, p. 66.

47. Quoted by Robert P. Richardson in *The Open Court*, October 1916, p. 665.

48. *Materials*, pp. 97, 98, *The Literary Digest*, October 20, 1900, *Azal's Notes*, p. 444. The person referred to was Mrs. Lua Moore Getsinger, whose own detailed report of this visit is found in *Persia* by Asaac Adams, privately published in 1900, probably in Chicago, pp. 478-484.

49. Henry H. Jessup, *The Outlook*, June 22, 1901.

50. *God Passes By*, pp. 263-272, *Materials*, pp. 91, 92.

51. In *Baha'i World 1940-1944* there is a list of about 100 people from the West who visited Akka prior to 1912.

52. Quoted in *Baha'u'llah and the New Era*, Esselmont, first edition, p. 58.

53. *Ten Muslims Meet Christ*, W. M. Miller, Eerdmans 1969, pp. 109, 111.

54. *Baha'u'llah and the New Era*, p. 59.

55. *Abbas Efendi*, Phelps, Putnam's, 1903.

56. *Baha'u'llah and the New Era*, pp. 63, 64.

57. Ibid., p. 64.

58. Ibid., pp. 64, 65.

59. Ibid., pp. 65, 66.

60. *God Passes By*, p. 313.

10

The Baha'i Faith
Goes West and East

Since the time when the followers of Muhammad set
forth from Arabia in the seventh century of the Christian era to make Islam the religion of the world, no
other new religion born in the Near East attempted to
become a universal religion till Baha'i missionaries
less than a century ago undertook to convert to their
faith the peoples not only of the East but also of
the West. In this chapter we will tell the most interesting story of the establishment of the Baha'i Cause
in America, and in other distant lands.

The first Baha'i missionary to America was Dr.
Ibrahim George Kheiralla (Khayru'llah), a native of
Lebanon, and a graduate (1870) of the American College
in Beirut which had been founded by Protestant missionaries.(1) Dr. Kheiralla was born in a Chaldean family
in 1849, the year before the death of the Bab in Iran.
It was said by one who knew him well that he was a man
of "great mental acumen," who at various times was a
teacher, a healer of nervous diseases, a writer, a
trader, and "pretty much everything else."(2) It was
said that because of his irregular conduct he was
rejected by his Christian community in his native land.
(3) He was "a man of strong mind, acute argumentative

faculties, fine conversational powers and altogether
an interesting personality."(4)

   In 1872, four years after the arrival of Baha'u'
llah in Akka, Kheiralla went from Lebanon to Egypt,
where he remained for twenty-one years engaged in
trade.   There in 1890 he was converted to the Baha'i
faith by Hajji Abdu'l-Karim of Teheran.(5)   In reply
to a letter which he wrote to Baha'u'llah, he received
a Tablet from his Master.   Soon after the death of
Baha'u'llah in 1892, Dr. Kheiralla went to Russia on
personal business, and from there travelled to Europe,
and thence to America, where he arrived in December
1892.   A writer in Cairo who knew the facts has stated
that Abdu'l-Karim paid the travel expenses of Dr.
Kheiralla, with the understanding that money received
in America would be divided with him.(6)   The missionary at once began as he had opportunity to tell the
Good News of "the Appearance of the Father and the
establishment of His Kingdom on earth," and it was
through his tireless efforts that the Baha'i Cause was
first established in the New World.   After spending
some time in New York and Michigan, Dr. Kheiralla
went to Chicago in February, 1894, which he made his
center.   In the Congress of Religions which was held
in connection with the Chicago Exposition in 1893,
the Babi-Baha'i Movement had received favorable notice,
and there were numerous people in and about Chicago
who were eager to learn more about this new religion
from the East.

   After having made many converts, Dr. Kheiralla
wrote to Abdu'l-Karim in Cairo and also to Abdu'l-Baha
to report his success.   When his Greek wife who had
remained in Cairo refused to join him he divorced her,
and in 1895 married an English woman.   With her he
made a journey to England, and then returned to Chicago,
"where he applied himself day and night, without weary-
ing, to teaching the people."   In Kenosha, fifty miles
from Chciago, he met with great success.(7)   In 1896
he published a book entitled *Babu'd-Din, The Door of
the True Religion - Revelation from the East*, in which
he refuted the Christian doctrine of the atonement.(8)
The method used by the missionary was that of teaching

inquirers in private lessons, saying that this religion was not for the masses but for truth-seekers only.
One of the first private pupils wrote: "In their
secret lessons they allegorize and explain away; in
public by means of mental reservation and the use of
words in a double sense, they appear as they wish to
appear."(8) And he adds that the Baha'i Cause "has
succeeded because, like a counterfeit coin, it has
passed for what it is not."(9)

Some of the new converts had moved to New York, and
on their invitation Dr. Kheiralla went to Ithaca and
New York City to meet and teach the eager inquirers, of
whom there were many. In New York City he divided the
200 seekers into three groups which met in different
places. At the end of four months in 1898, 141 of
these had become believers, and "he formed them into
a congregation and set over them as a teacher Mr.
Howard MacNutt." He also made visits to Philadelphia
where there was a small group of believers. While in
New York he composed his book *Beha'U'llah* in two volumes,(10) in the Preface of which he states that the
purpose of the book is to "demonstrate that the Everlasting Father, the Prince of Peace, has appeared in
human form and established His kingdom on earth." In
the same year two of his pupils were married in his
house in New York, and received his blessing. They
were Mr. and Mrs. E. C. Getsinger, who taught inquirers in Ithaca, and later in California. It was estimated that in two years Dr. Kheiralla had converted no
less than 2000 Americans, 700 or more in and about
Chicago, 250 in Wisconsin, 400 in New York, and the
rest in Boston and other places.(11)

How did this pioneer missionary from the East proclaim the message of Baha'u'llah and win hundreds of
converts in a country where Christian ideas were prevalent? Fortunately, one of the persons who attended
the New York meetings took careful notes on Dr.
Kheiralla's lectures, and sent them at once to Professor Browne in England. Later Browne published this
correspondence in full.(12) The correspondent was
impressed by and attracted to Dr. Kheiralla, but was
greatly puzzled by many things he said. From her

reports it is evident that the first ten lectures had
little to do with the Baha'i faith, and dealt with
metaphysics, dreams, numbers, allegorical interpretations of the Bible, prayer, etc. But the intense
curiosity of the hearers was aroused by the promise
of the revelation of some mystery in the eleventh
lesson. Accordingly, in that lecture the appearance
of the Bab, Baha'u'llah and Abdu'l-Baha was proclaimed.
The Bab had announced that the Father had come, and
the Father was Baha'u'llah. Abdu'l-Baha was Jesus
Christ, the Son of God. The Millennium, said Dr.
Kheiralla, would come in 1917, when one third of the
people of the world would become Baha'is. He stated
that there were at that time (1898) fifty-five million
Baha'is in the world. He interpreted all the prophecies
in the book of Daniel and the Revelation as applying
to Baha'u'llah, in order to convince Christians that
his coming had been foretold in their Bible. "We have
been taught nothing about the life and character of
Baha," wrote the correspondent, "no ethics, no religious life, does he pretend to teach."

Only persons who were willing to write a letter to
Abdu'l-Baha, professing faith in him, were permitted
to attend more than thirteen lectures. The letter
given to the students to sign and send was in part as
follows:

"To the Greatest Branch,

In God's Name, the Greatest Branch, I humbly confess the oneness and singleness of Almighty God,
my Creator, and I believe in His appearance in
the human form; I believe in His establishing His
holy household; in His departure, and that He has
delivered His kingdom to Thee, O Greatest Branch,
His dearest son and mystery. I beg that I may be
accepted in this glorious kingdom and that my name
may be registered in the 'Book of Believers'.....

                    Most humbly thy servant.."

To those who wrote the letter great spiritual gifts
were promised, and a knowledge of the "Greatest Name"

of God. "I am sorry to say," wrote the correspondent, "that some people have sent the letter for the sake of the rest of the teaching and for a mysterious something which they hope to get.....An air of mystery is over the whole affair."

The converts were not told that any books had been written about the Bab or Baha'u'llah, and all were hopelessly ignorant of the history of the movement. Subh-i-Azal was not mentioned, except to be called Satan. One of the most enthusiastic believers, when asked who Subh-i-Azal was, said "that she had heard him lecture - she thought he was one of the Hindoo Swamis!" Of Dr. Kheiralla the correspondent wrote: "When I met him I saw that at last I had found one who really believes his own teaching and is giving all that he has to spread what he thinks is true; right or wrong, he is faithful." No charge was made for attendance at the lectures. Mr. A. P. Dodge paid all the expenses of the missionary and his wife while they were in New York.(13)

In the summer of 1898 a pilgrimage was arranged to Akka. Mrs. Phoebe Hearst was to pay the expenses, and Dr. and Mrs. Kheiralla were invited to join the party, along with Mr. and Mrs. Getsinger and several others. As they passed through England and France Dr. Kheiralla gave the "Most Great Name" to a number of believers, thus establishing the Baha'i faith in Europe. After visiting Egypt the members of the party, numbering in all sixteen persons, in December arrived in Akka, and were there welcomed by a representative of Abdu'l-Baha. When Dr. Kheiralla entered the house in which Abdu'l-Baha lived, he received a very cordial welcome. Abdu'l-Baha kissed him, and said, "Welcome to thee, O Baha's Peter, O second Columbus, Conqueror of America!" He had a fez put on his head as a mark of special honor, and took him to the tomb of Baha'u'llah, telling him that he was the first pilgrim to whom the door of this chamber had been opened for prayer. He was also given the unique honor of joining Abdu'l-Baha in breaking ground for the Mausoleum which he was about to build on Mt. Carmel, in which was to be placed the body of the Bab soon to be brought from Iran. "This is an

honor which none of the believers except thee has
enjoyed," said Abdu'l-Baha to him. And he gave him
the title of "Shepherd of God's flocks in America."
(14)

However, before long difficulties began to arise.
Dr. Kheiralla was eager to explain his teaching to his
Master, and to discuss questions of theology with him,
but Abdu'l-Baha was not inclined to answer the questions put to him and was displeased when his missionary differed with him. Dr. Kheiralla wanted copies
of books of Baha'u'llah which he did not possess, but
Abdu'l-Baha would not give them to him, even denying
their existence, and he had to acquire them later in
Egypt. Moreover, none of the pilgrims was permitted
to see any of the other members of the family of
Baha'u'llah, except the sister of Abdu'l-Baha, or any
followers of Mirza Muhammad Ali, though they learned
of the serious split in the family. Dr. Kheiralla
stayed six months, long enough to understand fully
what was going on. Then the Getsingers accused Dr.
Kheiralla of immoral conduct, and Abdu'l-Baha repeated
these stories to Mrs. Kheiralla, with the result that
on their return to Egypt she left her husband. And
"certain financial irregularities of the party further
disgusted Mrs. Hearst and chilled her faith."(15) So
the pilgrimage was not an altogether happy experience.
However, one of the prophecies of Abdu'l-Baha made a
profound impression on the Americans. Once when they
were seated at table Mr. Getsinger asked his host for
permission to take his photograph. Abdu'l-Baha
refused, saying that it would be taken only when his
father's crown should be placed on his head and he
should be led forth to martyrdom, when thousands of
rifle bullets should pierce his body. "His words,"
says Mirza Jawad, "had a great effect, so that some
of the auditors wept bitterly."(16) This prophecy was
never fulfilled.

After returning to America Dr. Kheiralla became
increasingly estranged from Abdu'l-Baha. As he studied
the *Kitab-i-Aqdas* and other writings of Baha'u'llah he
became convinced that the claims which Abdu'l-Baha was
making for himself were unjustified, and from his

conduct and correspondence he concluded that he was
double-faced in his dealings, and was promoting discord rather than harmony and love among believers. So
after seven months Dr. Kheiralla definitely broke with
Abbas Efendi and went over to the party of Mirza
Muhammad Ali.(17) At the same time the devotees of
Abbas Efendi in America rejected Dr. Kheiralla. Of
this development Dr. Samuel M. Wilson, who was acquainted with Dr. Kheiralla writes as follows:(18) "Mr.
Getsinger, on his return to America, announced that he
was to be the representative of Abbas Effendi because Dr.
Kheiralla's teachings were erroneous and his conduct
immoral. Dr. Kheiralla responded with counter charges
against his accuser.....The Chicago and Kenosha assemblies were rent asunder. In the correspondence, some
of which I have in my possession, they hurl at each
other such terms as falsehood, lie, malevolence,
injustice....." Some of the leaders were accused of
dishonesty in handling the finances of the Cause.
Several hundred of the believers sided with Dr.
Kheiralla, and became known as "Behaists," but the
majority, who called themselves "Baha'is" remained
faithful to Abdu'l-Baha.

Immediate steps were taken by Abdu'l-Baha to destroy the influence of the "Shepherd of God's flocks
in America," and to prevent the sheep from being led
astray. In 1900 Abdu'l-Karim, the man who had converted Dr. Kheiralla in Egypt, was sent from Akka to
try to win him back and quiet matters, "but he poured
oil on the flames."(18) "He promised me plenty of
money," wrote Dr. Kheiralla later,(19) "and when I
refused he denounced me and prohibited believers from
buying or reading my books." Abdu'l-Karim was not
notably conciliatory in his remarks to the apostate.
(20) "O violator (of the Covenant), thou spotted
snake, thou shalt be seized with a great torture and
punishment," he said, and he declared that he would
call on God for vengeance against Dr. Kheiralla. When
the first messenger failed others were sent from Akka.

The first of the new emissaries was Hajji Mirza
Hasan of **Khurasan**, a leading Baha'i from Cairo, the
author of the pamphlet describing the death of Mirza

Yahya at Jedda (Chapter IX). He came to Chicago, and
according to Dr. Kheiralla made the following statement to him on November 30, 1900:(21) "I came here
especially to bring you back to your allegiance to
Abbas Efendi, and am prepared to stay ten years if
necessary. If you return to Abbas Efendi, I will cause
the American believers to follow you as head in everything even better than before. If you will not listen
to me and become a follower of Abbas, your abode will
be in the bowels of the earth.....If you will not listen your life will be short. If Abbas Efendi should
give me the word to cut you to pieces, or to tear your
eyes out, or to kill you, I will do so at once.....".
"He then repeated to me," continued Dr. Kheiralla,
"the fate of Mirza Yahya of Jedda, and offered me a
copy of the pamphlet published by himself entitled
The Great Miracle of Abbas Efendi.'" Dr. Kheiralla
replied, "I know these Orientals better than you do.
I know what they did to the Azalis." At the next
discussion he had police concealed in his house for
protection.(22)

Next came Mirza Asadu'llah of Isfahan and Mirza
Abu'l-Fazl of Gulpayagan,(23) learned and experienced
Baha'i missionaries and authors. They, too, failed
in the attempt to bring back the lost sheep and their
"Shepherd," but they had some success in making new
converts. Nevertheless, the disgraceful quarrel caused
many believers to desert the Cause. In 1902 Dr. Pease
wrote:(24) "About 1700 have left us because they
would not engage in religious scandal. The whole number in the country is now 600 or 700. Of these 300
are Behaist (Unitarians); the others are Abbasites of
one sect or another, holding belief that Abbas is Lord
and Master." According to the U.S. Census of 1906,
the Behaists had dwindled to 40, and the Baha'is had
increased to 1280. Both sides wrote books and pamphlets stating their own case and denouncing their
rivals. The spirit of love and forgiveness was notice-
ably absent from these polemics.

Some years later Dr. Kheiralla wrote as follows:(25)
"Abbas Effendi is a powerful and shrewd Turkish and
Romish diplomat combined; and his policies are put in

practice with such management and tact as to overwhelm
even his most intelligent followers.....He meets all
his visitors with love and kindness and surrounds them
with some of his adherents at Akka and Haifa, who move
with them wherever they move and humbly serve and obey
them, and never leave them alone until they go to bed.
Then they report to him all the events of the day.
This system of spying is used in all countries where
there are followers. He keeps his followers from
reading the Revelations of Baha'U'llah, that they may
remain ignorant of the true teachings of the Bahai
religion. His talks and writings are pathetic and
full of accusations against his brother..... In this
way he gains their sympathy and estranges them [his
visitors] from his good brother, so that they may not
meet him and learn the truth. He made rules to interfere in all the actions, dealings and correspondence
of his followers with each other, and always tried to
split them into parties against each other in order
that all of them might appeal to him and ask his
assistance. The worst thing he has done is to put
himself between his followers and their God, and to
threaten them with hell fire if they dare to disobey
him."

   In 1914 Dr. Kheiralla formed in Chicago the "National
Association of the Universal Religion," under the head-
ship of Mirza Muhammad Ali, whom he claimed to represent
in the U.S.A. The purpose of the Association was "to
promulgate the amalgamation of all different religions
into one Universal Religion." He composed twenty-six
"Requisitions" for the members, drawing on the Bible
and the *Kitab-i-Aqdas* and the doctrines of Universalism.
A "Branch Association" was established in Newark, New
Jersey.(26) Of this Association no trace can be found
today. Even Dr. Kheiralla, Baha's Peter, seems to have
been completely forgotten. In the New Testament, Judas
Iscariot is named as one of the Twelve Apostles of Jesus,
but in the official lists of Baha'i missionaries to
America the name of Ibrahim George Kheiralla never
appears.

   The arrival of the numerous Baha'i missionaries from
the East, and the progress of the Cause in the West,

were publicized in the American press, and no doubt
many readers were amazed at what they read. The front
page of the *New York Herald* of August 12, 1900 was
adorned with pictures of Akka and of Abbas Efendi, and
had the headlines: "These Believe that Christ has
Returned to Earth" - "Strange Faith has Attracted Many
Followers" - "A New Gospel According to Abbas of Acre."
(27) The article begins as follows: "Is Christ living
in the world today? There are tens of thousands of
persons who believe that He is.....There are hundreds
who claim to have looked upon the face and to have
listened to the voice of the Divinity."

The North American (Philadelphia) of February 16,
1902, with pictures of Abbas Efendi and two of the
missionaries in their oriental robes, has the heading,
"The Astonishing Spread of Babism." The article states
that hundreds have been converted to Abbas Efendi in
Baltimore, and quotes a statement of Mirza Abu'l-Fazl,
who said: "If we make the same percentage of converts
throughout the country as we have made in Baltimore
and Washington, within a year's time the Babi faith
will have two million adherents in the United States."
(28) He added that "thus far about 30,000 followers
of Abbas Efendi are claimed in America." It is evident
that the learned speaker had not consulted the U.S.
Census reports.

On December 18, 1904 the *New York Times* carried a
full page article under the heading, "Babist Propaganda Making Headway Here,"(29) describing "a Sunday
morning gathering of New York believers in this New
Oriental Cult," with a history of the religion and its
"Present High Priest," the "Master at Acre," Abbas
Efendi. Nearly 200 men and women were present.
"Oriental silken garments swished as a group of hand-
somely gowned women entered the Tabernacle. Men of
iron gray hair and steel gray eyes - thinkers and
doers rather than dreamers - accompanied them.....
There were men from Wall Street, and Broadway and
Fifth Avenue men, "whose names figure frequently in
the public prints, and whose fortunes run into many
figures." They had "plenty of financial sinew to
support the movement and Him Who Lives at Acre." At

the close of the meeting it was announced that a few
days previously nine American pilgrims, including Mr.
Howard MacNutt, conducted by Mirza Abu'l-Fazl, had
"started for Acre to acquaint the One Who Lives There
with the amazing progress the Cause is making in America." Without doubt their arrival with gifts was a
great encouragement to the One who was confined in the
city of Akka by the Turkish authorities as a result of
the quarrel in the family of Baha'u'llah.

Mirza Muhammad Ali
Second Son of Baha'u'llah

As the number of Behaists (Unitarians) decreased,
so did the fame of Dr. Kheiralla. He wrote to Professor Browne after some years(30) that after "the
sad dissension reached the West" he had refrained from
missionary work, thinking that calling "the people to
this Great Truth was equivalent to inviting them into
a quarrel." However, after the visit of Abdu'l-Baha
to America in 1912, "his false teachings, his misinter-
pretations of Baha'ism, his dissimulations....aroused
me to rise up for helping the work of God." He seems
to have met with but little success in his efforts to
defeat the party of Abbas Efendi, and in 1929 he died,
the year before his Guide, Mirza Muhammad Ali, died
in Hayfa.(31) With them died the party of the "Unitarians."

The Baha'i Cause, having suffered greatly from
internal strife, made little progress in America till
the visit of Abdu'l-Baha himself in 1912. After the
Turkish Revolution in 1908 the "prisoners" in Akka
were free to travel wherever they wished, and Abdu'l-
Baha soon took advantage of this welcome liberty to
visit the lands in the West where his zealous missionaries had prepared the way for him. It is noteworthy
that he did not go to Iran, the land of his birth,
where the great majority of Baha'is were then to be
found. His first long journey out of Akka, where he
had lived for forty-three years, was to France and
England in 1911. He spent some time in London and
Paris, meeting believers and inquirers, and giving
many addresses. On the return journey he visited
Egypt, then under British rule, where many Iranian
Baha'is had gone seeking freedom and business.

This tour proved so rewarding that in the spring of
1912 Abdu'l-Baha, no doubt at the invitation and the
expense of the believers in America, set forth on a
journey which lasted nearly two years. His coming had
been prepared for long in advance by attractive publicity. The *New York Times* of July 2, 1911 published
a full-page article entitled "Bahaism, Founded in
Martyrdom, Taking Root Here." In large letters it
stated that "Though This Persian Religion Was Established Only Seventy Years Ago, Its Followers Have

Suffered Persecutions Rivaling Those of the Early
Christians - Now Numbers 10,000,000 Adherents." There
were pictures of Abdu'l-Baha, of a group of bearded
and turbaned Baha'i leaders, of "the prison in which
Baha Ullah wrote many of his books," as well as of
his house in Akka, and his tomb. The article played
up the persecutions which the Baha'is have endured,
stating that the number of martyrs in Iran in the
years 1848-1852 was 10,000, and according to some,
30,000. It was not explained that those who died
were not Baha'is but Babis, and the number of the
Babis killed in the several insurrections (Chapter
III) is less than 5,000. The story of the history of
the movement told in the article is that derived from
A Traveller's Narrative, not from the more accurate
history of Mirza Jani. "The sect inculcates," says
the article, "a love of the world rather than of
country, and declares all religions to be equally
true." It is clear that the author of the article
possessed more literary skill than knowledge of the
history of the Babi-Baha'i Movement.

On the arrival of Abdu'l-Baha in New York a woman
reporter was sent to interview him, and her story
appeared as a full-page article in the *New York Times*
of April 21, 1912, under the heading: "A Message
From Abdul Baha, Head of the Bahais." The article
begins thus: "Within the last week there has come to
New York an old man with a worn and beautiful face,
who wears a long brown gown and a white turban, and
speaks the strange-sounding guttural language of
Persia. On the pier he was welcomed by hundreds of
people, for he is Abdul Baha, or "The Servant of God,"
the head of the Bahaist movement, and he is known to
tens of thousands of followers all over the world as
the 'Master'. For forty years he had been in prison,
and his father, the former head of the Bahaists, died
in prison....They preached the love of God and the
brotherhood of man, and for this the Persian Government
exiled and the Turkish Government imprisoned them."

After giving the orthodox Baha'i account of the
history of the Cause, the reporter tells of her interview with the Master. She found the reception room in

his apartment filled with flowers. "A rather small
man with a white beard and the kindest and gentlest
face in the world held out a hand. In his brown
habit he was extraordinarily picturesque, but one did
not think of that, for he smiled a charming smile,
and walking before and holding his visitor's hand, he
led her to a chair." Evidently the Master was as
happy to meet the reporter as she was to meet him. In
fact, he told her so. After praising the women of
America, and speaking about the oneness of humanity,
and dictating a message to the people of America, he
gave his visitor a rose as she was departing, patted
her on the shoulder, and spoke to her in Persian.
His interpreter said, "He says he is pleased with
you." Nor was she the only one whose heart was won
by this picturesque and kind old man. One of the
American Baha'is said to the reporter, "For that man
I'd jump head first from a fifteenth story window."
And the reporter added, "So it is with everybody who
has come in contact with Abdu'l-Baha."

With this auspicious beginning, Abdu'l-Baha's
triumphal tour took him to many parts of America. He
addressed the Persian-American Educational Society
in Washington on April 20. This was an organization
operated by Baha'is, one of whom was Mirza Ahmad
Sohrab, of whom we will hear later.(32) On May 1
in the Rizwan Feast Abdu'l-Baha was present in
Wilmette, Illinois, for the dedication of the grounds
on which the famous *Mashriqu'l-Adhkar* was to be built,
and his picture taken with a group of friends on this
occasion may be seen in the *Baha'i World*.(33) A site
of five acres near the shore of Lake Michigan north of
Chicago had been purchased, and "Abdu'l-Baha, using a
golden trowel, broke ground, and others of the different races who were present used picks and shovels and
prepared a place into which Abdu'l-Baha put a stone.
He said: 'The mystery of this building is great. It
cannot be unveiled yet, but its erection is the most
important undertaking of this day. This temple of
God in Chicago will be to the spiritual body of the
world what the inrush of the spirit is to the physical
body of man....The *Mashriqu'l-Adhkar* will be like a
beautiful Bouquet. The central lofty edifice will

have nine sides, surrounded by nine avenues interlac-
ing nine gardens where nine fountains will play. There
will be nine gateways and columns....Further, its
meetings are to be held on the ninth of each month.'"
(34) It will be remembered that 9 is the numerical
equivalent of the Arabic letters in *Baha*'. The plans
for the temple were elaborate, and the money came in
slowly, but at last it was finished at a cost of two
and a half million dollars, and was dedicated on May
2, 1953. Could the Master have seen the realization
of his dreams he would no doubt have been very happy.

On August 16, 1912 Abdu'l-Baha and his Iranian
followers visited the beautiful Green Acre Baha'i
Center at Eliot, Maine, and remained there a week.
After the Congress of Religions in Chicago in 1893, a
gifted lady named Miss Farmer established at Greenacre
an annual summer conference, the purpose of which was
to bring together people of diverse creeds and opinions for friendly discussion. Many of the outstanding
lecturers of America were brought to these conferences,
which became quite famous. "The general spirit of the
place was that each should look upon a heretic.....not
as a person to be avoided or merely tolerated, but as
one to learn from and sympathize with." One of the
many religions represented in the Greenacre conferences
was Baha'ism, and some of the people in attendance were
converted to this faith. Later Miss Farmer herself,
after a visit to Akka, professed faith in Abdu'l-Baha.
By degrees the Baha'is were able to gain control of
the conference, and to transform it into a Baha'i
gathering. This was contrary to the wishes of Miss
Farmer, who wanted it to remain as a meeting place for
all varieties of opinion, and she was so greatly disturbed that she became insane. Finally, the property
was acquired by the Baha'is, and was for many years
the most important of their centers in America. After
Miss Farmer's conversion, the spelling of the name was
changed from "Greenacre" to Green Acre," with reference
to the city in which the Master resided.(35)

In the *Baha'i World* there is an interesting picture
of Abdu'l-Baha as he walked about the Green Acre
grounds followed by three Iranian disciples.(36) Their

names are not given, but friends recognized two of
them as Mirza Ahmad Sohrab and Dr. Fareed, both of
whom were later rejected. In the conference Abdu'l-
Baha delivered lectures on "The Investigation of
Reality" and "Love." "A divine joy seemed to fill
the heart of Abdu'l-Baha at Green Acre, for here were
found many souls capable of responding to his message.
His time was fully occupied with interviews and
addresses."

Later Abdu'l-Baha went to Canada, and as far west
as California. He gave addresses, always through his
gifted interpreter, in Christian churches and various
other religious gatherings, in women's clubs, colleges,
peace societies, and all sorts of groups and organizations. His principle in his public addresses was "to
talk about things upon which we agree and say nothing
about things upon which we differ."(37) "His own
press agents were active and aggressive, furnishing
many articles for newspapers and magazines. The re-
porters took the exaggerated statements of the Baha'is
without sifting. He performed his part fairly well and
allowed himself to be interviewed and photographed with
the patience of an actress. He posed for the 'movies'
....He sat for an oil painting and approved of his bust
in marble."(38)

After this busy and successful seven months tour in
America, Abdu'l-Baha sailed from New York on December
5, 1912 for Great Britain. There he remained six weeks,
visiting various cities, encouraging believers, giving
addresses as before, and receiving many notables. He
then spent two months in Paris, after which he visited
Germany and Austria. Finally, he resided for six
months in Egypt, and reached Akka on December 5, 1913,
after an absence of twenty months. This long tour was
no doubt both pleasant to the traveller and profitable
to the Cause.

A most enthusiastic and optimistic account of these
travels is found in *God Passes By* (Chapter XIX), written by Shoghi Effendi, the grandson of Abdu'l-Baha, in
which the places visited are listed and many of the
important personages who were received by him are

mentioned by name. He writes:(39) "As soon as He
was released from his forty-year long captivity....
He arose with sublime courage, confidence and resolu-
tion to consecrate what little strength remained to
Him, in the evening of His life, to a service of such
heroic proportions that no parallel to it is to be
found in the annals of the first Baha'i century. Indeed His three years of travel, first to Egypt, then
to Europe and later to America, mark, if we would
correctly appraise their historic importance, a turning point of the utmost significance in the history
of the century." In closing his account of the tour
Shoghi Effendi says:(40) "A most significant scene
in a century-old drama had been enacted. A glorious
chapter in the history of the first Baha'i century
had been written. Seeds of undreamt-of potentialties
had, with the hand of the Center of the Covenant Himself, been sown in some of the fertile fields of the
Western world. Never in the entire range of religious
history had any Figure of comparable stature arisen to
perform a labor of such magnitude and imperishable
worth."

However, not all who met Abdu'l-Baha on these
journeys were able to share the enthusiasm of Shoghi
Effendi. In Washington, D.C., Ellen Slayden in May,
1912 wrote thus in her journal:(41) "Abdul Baha, 'The
Comforter', 'The Beloved One', etc. etc., of the
Bahaists has come and gone, and considering how interested I was in his coming, I am shamefully indifferent
to his departure. I helped at the afternoon meetings
for him in Mrs. Parsons' beautiful home for three
successive days, and Saturday evening at a reception
for five hundred people, and never got a moment of
spiritual exaltation. He was just a *nice old man* who
might sit in an oriental market place and expound
platitudes to his heart's content, like the good Pasha
in the Arabian Nights, but his doctrines and his way
of presenting them are too elementary for this wicked
and perverse generation. He was followed by crowds,
he talked and answered questions from five o'clock
A.M. till midnight, and must have been weary beyond
telling, though his followers assured me he could not
feel fatigue because he was sustained by the spirit.

But none of these things proved his divinity nor even
his special apostleship to me. I think it is the turban, the long white robe and slippers, and patriarchal
wagging of his long gray beard and the mystery of the
Persian tongue that attracts people who reverence anything that is priestlike and unusual. When he sat in
a large chair and said oracularly, his interpreter
repeating, 'I love all humanity. All men are brothers.
There is only one good. Sorrows must come, but every
night has a day, every day has a night, every spring
has an autumn, every autumn has a spring,' his followers listened eagerly and wrote it into their notebooks
....If he had worn a sack suit and spoken English no
one would have listened. He is undoubtedly sincere,
kind and unworldly, but it is absurd for such moral
milk for babes to be administered to justices of the
Supreme Court, scholars and public officials..."

   Another interested observer wrote:(42) "The visit
of Abdul Baha did not leave any great impression. His
personality had no deep influence. He appeared conspicuous neither for intellectuality nor for spirituality...I was in Baltimore when he was there. He caused
scarcely a ripple on the surface. His addresses were
tame and full of platitudes. It was told me that his
visit led to doubt and coldness on the part of some
adherents....One of the distinguished clergymen whose
pulpit he occupied said to me, 'The man has no special
message. He is a fakir.'....Some of the American
disciples, especially the ladies, idolized him." No
doubt the memories of the many kindnesses shown him
by people of all races and religions during these
journeys helped to cheer the weary traveller during
the last years of his pilgrimage in Akka.

   Since the story of the introduction of the Baha'i
Faith to America has been told at some length, no
attempt will be made to give a detailed account of the
spread of the movement in Great Britain and Europe. As
we have already noted, both Abdu'l-Baha and his missionaries visited the various countries, spoke in
churches and in all sorts of gatherings, met inquirers,
and established Baha'i groups, as they had done west
of the Atlantic. Some of the writings of Baha'u'llah

and Abdu'l-Baha were translated and published in English and French and German. After his return to Akka,
Abdu'l-Baha directed to the scattered groups of believers an "unceasing flow of His Tablets."(43)

However, it was not only in the West that converts
to the Baha'i Cause were being made, for in the East
also zealous believers were busily engaged in telling
the Good News of Baha'u'llah. Two "teachers," presumably American Baha'is, went to Japan in 1914 and
established meetings in Tokyo. There some young people who were dissatisfied with other religions found
the Baha'i Message acceptable. "It does not require
of them to give up the past teachings, but rather
explains that the foundation of all religions is one,"
writes Miss Agnes Alexander.(44) A number of Baha'i
books were translated into Japanese and published, as
were many newspaper articles. Abdu'l-Baha during the
last years of his life addressed nineteen Tablets to
people in Japan. And from Japan the Baha'i Message
was taken in 1921 to Korea. The number of converts
in Japan and Korea at that time is not known, but it
was not great.

Many Iranians had gone from their country to India
to trade or to reside, and Baha'is soon found that
India under British rule was a field in which they
could labor with a freedom they did not enjoy anywhere in the Near East. There they published a monthly magazine in English, Persian and Burmese, and there
the *Kitab-i-Aqdas*, the *Iqan*, and other important Baha'i
books had been published in 1890 and brought back to
Akka. But while some converts were made from the natives of India, it is evident from the photograph of
"Representative Baha'is of India" in the *Baha'i World*
(45) that most of the believers were not Indians but
Iranians. However, Mrs. Inez Cook, an American Baha'i,
wrote a most interesting account(46) of her visit to
the village of Kinjangoon in Burma, all the 800 inhabitants of which, according to Mrs. Cook, had been converted by Sayyid Mustafa, an Iranian Baha'i missionary.
One would like to know more of the subsequent history
of this Burmese "mass movement." The Baha'i Message

was taken further east to Australia and New Zealand
by American believers.(47)

In order to enjoy the freedom which Tzarist Russia
offered, some Iranian Baha'is emigrated to the Caucasus and to Russian Turkistan, and there they prospered,
both materially and religiously. The first *Mashriqu'l-
Adhkar* (Baha'i temple) to be built was erected in
Ishqabad in Turkistan, near the northern border of
Iran. While it was under construction it was visited
in 1908 by Mr. Mason Remey, a Baha'i leader from America, who wrote of it as follows:(48) "The *Mashriqu'l-
Adhkar* stands in the center of the city, surrounded by
a large garden, which is bounded by four streets. It
rises high above the surrounding buildings and trees,
its dome being visible for miles.....The building in
plan is a regular polygon of nine sides.....At the
four corners of the garden are four buildings. One
is a school. One is a house where traveling Baha'is
are entertained. One is to be used as a hospital....
Much of the property in the immediate vicinity of the
enclosure belongs to Baha'is, so the *Mashriqu'l-Adhkar*
is the center of the community materially, as well as
spiritually. That which impressed me more than all
else....was the fact that the Baha'is of the East had
all worked with one accord and had given freely toward
its erection..."

When Abdu'l-Baha was in Chicago in 1912 he said:(49)
"In all the cities of Persia there are *Mashriqu'l-
Adhkars*, but the great 'dawning point' was founded in
Ishqabad. It possessed superlative importance because
it was the first *Mashriqu'l-Adhkar* built. All the
Baha'i friends agreed and contributed their utmost
assistance and effort. His holiness, the Afnan, devoted
his wealth, gave all he had to it....The *Mashriqu'l-
Adhkar* in Ishqabad is almost completed.....Now they are
building a hospital, a school for orphans, a home for
cripples, a hospice and a large dispensary. God willing when it is fully completed it will be a paradise. I
hope the *Mashriqu'l-Adhkar* in Chicago will be like this."

Of this undertaking Shoghi Effendi wrote:(50) "This
enterprise must rank not only as the first major

undertaking launched through the consecrated efforts
of His [Abdu'l-Baha's] followers....but as one of the
most brilliant and enduring achievements in the history of the first Baha'i century." This temple was
later taken over by the Soviet government and made an
art gallery, and the Iranian Baha'i community in
Ishqabad, as in other parts of Russia, was dispersed,
many of the Iranians being sent back to Iran.(51)

In parts of the Near East where most of the population were Sunnite Muslims, and where there was little
or no freedom of religion, there were few Baha'is who
were not Iranians. One of the largest groups of
believers outside Iran was found in Egypt, where many
Iranians resided, and where under British rule Baha'is
were able to publish books and carry on other activities which were not possible in lands under the rule
of Turkey.

Naturally the largest number of Baha'is during this
period was in the land of Baha'u'llah's birth. The
Baha'is were located in all the larger cities and
towns as well as in many villages of Iran, but since
no census was ever taken it is impossible to make an
accurate estimate of their numbers. Following the
example of their leaders in Akka, they usually conformed to the religious practices of their Shi'ite
Muslim neighbors and seldom professed openly their
Baha'i faith. However, meetings that were more or
less secret were held in homes, and tactful but effective missionary work was carried on by a number of quite
able apostles, as well as by many of the faithful, both
men and women. Books were prepared and printed outside
Iran, or secretly in Iran, containing detailed instructions for giving the Baha'i Message to Muslims, Jews,
Christians and Zoroastrians whom they would try to convert, and for answering the objections of these unbelievers. Even the Baha'i young people were often clever
and effective propagandists of the Cause. Not only
Muslims but also a number of Jews and a few Zoroastrians
were converted. However, while new converts were being
made, many who once professed faith fell away, and it
is probable that the number of Baha'is in Iran in 1921
was less than that in 1892.

The government of Iran recognized four religions,
Zoroastrianism, Judaism, Christianity and Islam, and
allowed the three minority groups to worship and conduct their affairs according to the laws of their
several religions. Though the Baha'is out-numbered
the Zoroastrians, and claimed to be more numerous
than the Jews and Christians of Iran, they were not
recognized as a separate religious community, but
were counted as Muslims, and were seldom persecuted
by the government. However, when the Baha'is became
too aggressive in propagating their religion they sometimes stirred up fanatical opposition on the part of
the Muslims, which occasionally resulted in riots and
murders. The worst of these occurred in Yazd and
Isfahan in 1903 when a hundred people were said to
have been killed. However, not all of the unfortunate
people counted as "martyrs" were Baha'is, for it sometimes happened that a person who wished to get rid of
an enemy or a creditor would brand him as a Baha'i,
and would then incite the Muslim clergy or the authorities to kill him for being an infidel. The total
number of Baha'i martyrs in Iran during the reign of
Abdu'l-Baha has been given by one authority as 25,
and by another as about 100.(52) Shoghi Efendi has
given the names and an account of the sufferings of
some of these martyrs.(53) The usual tolerant attitude of the Iranian government(54) is indicated by
the fact that many Baha'is were employed in the Post
Office and the Customs and in other government offices.
In the provinces there was usually less freedom than
in the Capital.

During the Revolution in Iran (1906-1909), which
resulted in the granting by the Shah of a Constitution
and the establishment of a Parliament, Baha'is were
forbidden by Abdu'l-Baha to become involved in the
struggle, and usually took no part in freeing their
country from the despotic rule of the Kajar Dynasty.
(55) In fact, there is evidence that both Abdu'l-Baha
and his followers in Iran were sympathetic to the Shah
before his defeat by the Constitutionalists.(56)

The Iranian Baha'is were fairly numerous and some
of them had wealth, but they did very little as a

group to minister to the sick and poor and uneducated portion of the population of their country, though it was commonly reported that they were often ready to find jobs for people whom they were trying to convert. There were several good schools in Teheran and other places which were established by Western Baha'is, and for a time a small medical work was carried on by foreigners, not by the Iranian believers.

Baha'is in Iran differed little from their Muslim neighbors. Outwardly they wore the same clothes, and their women usually appeared in public covered by the same sort of veils used by Muslims. Nor were their characters and morals different. They sometimes practiced polygamy, as did some of the Muslims. They usually practiced *taqiya* (concealment of religious belief), and this often led to lying as to their religion, and to untruthfulness and dishonesty in general. Though there were of course exceptions, Iranian Baha'is on the whole were not at the time of Abdu'l-Baha conspicuous for the virtues of purity, honesty, truthfulness, love and service to others which their leaders in Akka had enjoined on them. Of their devotion to Abdu'l-Baha there was no question, but like some adherents to other religions they often failed to demonstrate their faith in their daily lives.

Before the death of Abdu'l-Baha, his Cause had been carried to many lands, both East and West, but the number of Baha'is in all the world was still comparatively small, probably less than 50,000.(57)

Notes

1. The picture of George Kheiralla is to be seen in the Alumni Magazine of the American University of Beirut, Spring 1970, p. 4, with the graduates of 1870, the first class to graduate from that institution.

2. Dr. H. H. Jessup, *The Outlook*, June 1901, p. 453.

3. Letter of Dr. Sa'eed to the author.

4. Samuel G. Wilson, *Bahaism and its Claims*, Revell 1915, p. 266.

5. Mirza Jawad, *Materials*, pp. 93, 94. This account is confirmed by Dr. Kheiralla's own book *O Christians! Why Do Ye Believe Not On Christ?* Chicago 1917, in which he tells the story of his life.

6. *Materials*, p. 143.

7. Ibid., pp. 95, 96, Wilson, p. 266.

8. *Wilson*, p. 266.

9. Ibid., pp. 267, 268.

10. *Beha'U'llah (The Glory of God)*, by Ibrahim George Kheiralla, Chicago 1900.

11. *Wilson*, p. 267.

12. *Materials*, pp. 115-142.

13. Ibid., p. 125.

14. Ibid., pp. 99, 100, *O Christians!*, pp. 171 ff.

15. *Wilson*, pp. 268, 269.

16. *Materials*, p. 108.

17. Ibid., pp. 109-112. According to Dr. Kheiralla (*O Christians!*, p. 181), it was Mirza Muhammad Ali who bestowed on him the degree of Doctor of Divinity.

18. *Wilson*, p. 269.

19. *The Three Questions*, p. 23.

20. *Wilson*, p. 270.

21. *Materials*, p. 154.

22. *Wilson*, p. 270.

23. Of the four Iranian missionaries to America, Mirza Abdu'l-Karim (1900), Mirza Asadu'llah (1900), Hajji Mirza Hasan (1900), and Mirza Abu'l-Fazl (1901), the first three finally fell away from the Baha'i Cause.

24. *Wilson*, p. 271.

25. *O Christians!*, pp. 176, 177.

26. Ibid., pp. 182-190.

27. *Materials*, p. 150.

28. Ibid., p. 151.

29. Ibid., p. 152.

30. Ibid., p. 171.

31. A relative has stated that Dr. Kheiralla died in Beirut on March 8, 1929, and was to the end a believer in Baha'u'llah.

32. *Materials*, p. 183.

33. *Baha'i World 1926-1928*, Vol. II, pp. 115, 120.

34. *Wilson*, p. 279, *Star of the West*, June 5, 1914.

35. *Baha'i World 1926-1928*, Vol. II, pp. 151 ff., Robert P. Richardson, *The Open Court*, August 1915, pp. 478 ff. and March 1931.

36. *Baha'i World*, Vol. II, p. 150.

37. *Star of the West*, March 1913, p. 18.

38. *Wilson*, p. 275.

39. Shoghi Efendi, *God Passes By*, p. 279.

40. Ibid., p. 294.

41. *Washington Wife*, Journal of Ellen Maury Slayden 1897-1919, Harper and Row 1963, pp. 172, 173.

42. *Wilson*, p. 281.

43. *God Passes By*, p. 303.

44. *Baha'i World*, Vol. II, pp. 42, 43.

45. Ibid., p. 144.

46. Ibid., pp. 141-143.

47. Ibid., p. 40.

48. Ibid., pp. 121, 122.

49. Ibid., p. 119.

50. *God Passes By*, p. 300.

51. Ibid, pp. 360, 361.

52. *Azal's Notes*, p. 502, *Wilson*, p. 137.

53. *God Passes By*, pp. 296-299.

54. *A Year Amongst the Persians*, Edward Browne, London, 1893, p. 101.

55. *Persian Revolution*, Edward Browne, pp. 424-429.

56. *Wilson*, pp. 138-141.

57. Avareh, the Baha'i historian, after his defection stated in his book *Kashfu'l-Hiyal* (first printing, p. 192) that Shoghi Efendi after becoming Guardian in 1922 took a census of the Baha'is of the world, and found that the number of men, women and children was 20,000. According to *Azal's Notes* (P. 722), at the time of the death of Abdu'l-Baha the number of Baha'is in Turkey, Egypt, Lebanon, Syria, Iraq, Saudi Arabia, Palestine and Jordan did not exceed one thousand. There were not more than 200 in India and Burma. There were about thirty in the United Kingdom, France and Germany, and sixty in Ishqabad (Russia). The U.S. Census of 1916 gave the number in America as 2,884. No accurate statistics for the Baha'is of Iran have ever been available.

11

The Teachings and Will of Abdu'l-Baha

At the time when Abbas Efendi was a child his father
Baha was an ardent disciple of the Bab. The Bab was
executed when Abbas was nine years old, and from that
time, till he reached the age of twenty-five, he, like
his father, was obedient to Subh-i-Azal his uncle, the
successor to the Bab. When his father Baha in 1866
claimed to be a new Manifestation, Abbas Efendi became
a Baha'i. His beliefs, therefore, were first those of
the People of the Bayan (Chapter IV), and later those
inculcated by his father Baha'u'llah (Chapter VIII).
As long as his father lived, Abbas Efendi faithfully
followed his teachings. He when a Babi had held the
doctrine, on which the Babi system was built, that God
is unknowable except in his Manifestations, who are
one with his Will. These Manifestations, who appeared
at intervals of about one thousand years, were, according to the doctrine of the Bab and Baha'u'llah, the
same as the Great Prophets of Islam, Adam, Noah,
Abraham, Moses, Jesus and Muhammad. To these the
Babis added Ali Muhammad the Bab, whom they considered
the greatest of the Manifestations who had so far
appeared. This was undoubtedly the belief of Abbas
Efendi before he bacame a Baha'i. He then professed
faith in his father as the greatest of the Manifestations,

and relegated the Bab to the position of Forerunner
for Baha'u'llah, and portrayed Subh-i-Azal as the
arch-enemy of the Cause of God. This change in his
belief is clearly seen in the book which he wrote in
1886, *A Traveller's Narrative*, which set forth the
official Baha'i version of the history of the movement
(see Introduction).

When Baha'u'llah died in 1892 and Abbas Efendi
became, in accordance with his father's Will, the
divinely appointed head of the Baha'i community, the
first problem which faced him was that of his own
position and authority. In his Will, as well as in
the *Kitab-i-Aqdas*, Baha'u'llah had commanded all
believers to honor and obey the Branches, especially
the two eldest who were in turn to succeed him.(1)
Baha'u'llah had been a Manifestation, and he spoke as
God. But how will his successor speak, and how much
authority will he have? Baha'u'llah had made it quite
clear that his son could not follow his example and
claim to be a Manifestation, for in the *Kitab-i-Aqdas*
(2) he had stated, "Whoever claims Command (*amr*) before
the completion of a thousand years is a false liar.....
Whoever explains this verse or interprets it in any
other way than that plainly sent down, he will be deprived of the Spirit and Mercy of God..." However, he
also commanded(3) that after his death all matters
which his followers do not understand in the Aqdas are
to be referred to the Branch. But will the interpretations of the Book by the Branch be infallible? And
will the decisions and pronouncements of the Branch be
absolutely authoritative, as were those of Baha'u'llah?

As we have seen, Abbas Efendi gave to himself the
title *Abdu'l-Baha* (The Slave of Baha) to indicate his
complete submission to his father. But he also claimed
for himself the sole right to interpret the writings of
Baha'u'llah, and called himself the Center of the Covenant. In Chicago he quoted a saying of his father,
from the *Book of His Covenant*, as follows:(4) "Verily,
I have appointed a person who is the Center of My
Covenant. All must obey Him; all must turn to Him; he
is the expounder of My Book and He is informed of My
purposes. All must turn to Him. Whatsoever He says

is true, for verily, He knoweth the texts of My Book.
Other than He, none knoweth the Book." And again he
said,(5) "He [Baha'u'llah] has, therefore, commanded
that whatever emanates from the Center of the Covenant
is right....while everything else is error....whoever
deviated the least from the Center of the Covenant is
of the people of treachery and well deserves the wrath
of God."

As was recorded in Chapter IX, when Abbas Efendi
began to assume these titles and exercise this authority, a number of the old and devoted and prominent
followers of his father, who had access to the Will of
Baha'u'llah and to the Aqdas, became disaffected and
left him. However, as his appointment as the first
successor to Baha'u'llah could not be called in question by anyone, the majority of Baha'is, including a
number of the missionaries of the faith, readily gave
him the same reverence and devotion that they had
given to his father, and received and cherished his
"Tablets" as inspired and infallible pronouncements.
Abdu'l-Baha became to them not so much a new Manifestation as an extension of Baha'ullah. Probably the
death of the father made little difference to the
believers in Iran and other lands, because his son,
the Most Mighty Branch, did for them all that Baha'u'
llah had done. In the *Kitab-i-Aqdas* Baha'u'llah had
said(6) that men are like sheep and must have a shepherd to keep them. Abdu'l-Baha undertook to be that
shepherd, and many, but not all, of the sheep followed
him. Over them he exercised absolute authority.

When Baha'u'llah in 1866 took over the leadership
of the Babi movement and undertook to lead the Babis
forward, he made certain changes in the laws given by
the Bab, claiming that he was himself a new lawgiver
sent by God. When his son Abdu'l-Baha assumed the
leadership of the Baha'i community, he realized that
the changes made by his father were not drastic enough,
and still more reforms in the religion must be made if
it were to survive and expand. Since he was not a
Manifestation he could not abrogate the laws of Baha'u'
llah and give new ones in their place, so it was necessary for him to content himself with being an Interpreter

and change the impractical regulations by his infallible interpretation. This he did as occasion arose.
For example, one of the most impractical and impossible of the laws of the *Kitab-i-Aqdas*, which Baha'u'llah
had taken from the Bayan of the Bab, was the law of
inheritance.(7) What could the Interpreter do with
this? For all practical purposes he abrogated it by
declaring that this law is "to be enforced only when
a man dies intestate, and that every man has the right
to dispose of his property as he thinks fit."(8)
Baha'u'llah had stated(9) that "the writing of a
Will has been made incumbent on everyone," so no obedient Baha'i would ever die intestate.

Likewise, the only limitations which Baha'u'llah
in the *Kitab-i-Aqdas* places on marriage are that a
man may not marry more than two women at the same
time, and that a son may not marry his father's
wives.(10) This second provision seemed to Abdu'l-
Baha to give to a man too much latitude, so he de-
clared(11) "that this does not mean that he is free
to marry any other woman, but that the more distant
the relationship between a man and woman the better
it is." Thus the divine laws were made to conform
to the opinions and customs prevalent in the world
of the Twentieth Century into which Abdu'l-Baha was
introducing the Baha'i Cause.

It seems that Abdu'l-Baha even more than his father
was disinclined to engage in the mystical and metaphy-
sical speculations which had characterized the writings
of the Bab. When Dr. Kheiralla, just back from America,
tried to engage his Master in a discussion about the
Essence of God, he was quietly pushed aside.(12) Abdu'l-
Baha said that he did not want any disagreement with
the learned men of Iran. He was content to maintain
in his contacts with the East the same basic beliefs
about God and man and the world that had come to his
father from the Shaykhis and Sufis.

However, when the Center of the Covenant began to
turn his attention toward the West he found the situation quite different, and it became necessary for him
to adjust his teaching to the beliefs of people who

had been influenced more or less by Christian or
western concepts. Dr. Jessup of Beirut once compared
Abbas Efendi to a tower clock in the military barracks
in Beirut which had two faces. The eastern face gave
the hours from sunset, as was done then in the East,
while the western face gave the hours from noon as was
done in the West. So, said Dr. Jessup, Abbas Efendi
presented one face to the Muslims and the Turkish
Government and the Baha'is of Iran, and quite a different face to the Europeans and Americans who visited
him in Akka, and whom he later visited in their own
lands.(13) Having studied the Bible he might possibly
have said in self-defence that he, like Paul, had to
become all things to all men that he might by all
means win some followers.

Both the Bab and Baha'u'llah had read the Bible,
and the writings of both were somewhat influenced by
Biblical teachings. In the *Iqan* especially Baha'u'-
llah refers to and interprets the meaning of several
passages from the Bible, though most of his references
are to the Koran. Both of these men sowed their seed
chiefly in soil that was Islamic, and they did not
grapple with the problem of presenting their doctrines
to people who called God "Father" and who considered
Jesus to be the Son and perfect revealer of God. We
have in the previous chapter seen how Dr. Kheiralla,
himself from a Christian background, sought to make
Baha'ism intelligible and attractive to Americans. He
largely ignored Muhammad, who was never greatly
admired by Christians either in the West or in the
East. He introduced Baha'u'llah as the Manifestation
of God the Father, and therefore greater than Jesus
Christ the Son of God. And who was Abdu'l-Baha? He
was Christ come again, as he had promised! So the
American converts came to Akka to see Christ, and some
of them worshipped him as "Master."

Did Abdu'l-Baha accept this interpretation? It
seems that at first he did so, for he gave the highest
praise to his clever missionary who had converted so
many people in the West to the Baha'i Cause. A little
later the learned Baha'i writer Mirza Abu'l-Fazl went
to America and spent several years there as a missionary

of Abdu'l-Baha. He published several books in English,
in which he undertook to prove that the coming of
Baha'u'llah and his son had been predicted in the
Bible. For example, he stated that when God said in
Psalm 2, "Kiss the son lest he be angry,"(14) the
reference was to Abdu'l-Baha. Also when it was said
in the book of Isaiah(15) that "the branch of the Lord
will be beautiful and glorious," the Most Mighty Branch
is foretold. Likewise, the same Branch is spoken of in
the book of Zechariah, when the Lord says,(16) "Behold,
the man whose name is the Branch....and he shall build
the temple of the Lord....and he shall bear the glory,
and shall sit and rule upon his throne...." Mirza
Abu'l-Fazl explains the passage as follows:(17) "And
these gracious verses and great tidings are exceedingly
clear. After the occultation of the Blessed Lord
[Baha'u'llah], the Branch of His Excellency shall sit
on the throne of praise. The Branch that springeth
forth from the Ancient Stock shall take his place upon
the throne of glory, and shall build the temple of the
Lord, in other words, he shall build the place around
which the arch-angels circle, and shall make the word
of God powerful and victorious in East and West." The
reference in Zechariah is, of course, to the appointment of Zerubbabel as ruler in Jerusalem (538 B.C.).

In like manner verses from the New Testament are
interpreted by Mirza Abu'l-Fazl as clear references to
Abdu'l-Baha. Thus when Jesus says,(18) "For the Son
of man shall come in the glory of his Father with his
angels," the Father is Baha'u'llah and the Son of man
is Abdu'l-Baha. Again, when in the book of Revelation
it is said,(19) "The kingdom of the world is become
the kingdom of our Lord, and of his Christ: and he
shall reign for ever and ever," we are told that the
Lord is Baha'u'llah, and his Christ is Abdu'l-Baha,
who will reign for ever. Regarding these interpretations of Mirza Abu'l-Fazl, Richards writes:(20) "There
is nothing in the teaching of Baha'u'llah to justify
this method of interpretation, for, though he teaches
that all references to God in Scripture are to be read
as referring to the Manifestation, he definitely claims
to possess a unique station which is shared by none.(21)
Throughout Mirza Abu'l-Fazl's teaching we see the

tendency to associate Abdu'l-Baha with his father as
possessing equal glory. He sits on the throne of
glory, and the kingdom is equally his... It is Abdu'l-
Baha who judges men, and rewards them according to
their deeds. He is no longer the interpreter of Baha'i
teaching and the slave of Baha'u'llah, he is the co-
ruler, showing forth in himself all the glory that
belonged to Baha'u'llah as the perfect Manifestation."

It seems that Abdu'l-Baha accepted these interpretations, as he had approved the preaching of Dr.
Kheiralla, for there is no evidence that he repudiated
either the teaching or Mirza Abu'l-Fazl the teacher.
However, after his visits to the West it appears that
he found these high titles and the worship which some
gave to him a cause of embarrassment, and in 1914 he
expressed himself quite strongly about his position.
(22) He said: "I am Abdul Baha, and no more. I am
not pleased with whoever praises me with any other
title. I am the Servant at the threshold of the
Blessed Perfection....Whoever mentions any other name
save this will not please me at all....After the Departure of the Blessed Perfection and until the Appearance
of the next Manifestation there is no other station
save the *Station of Servitude*, pure and absolute." And
at another time he stated:(23) "I am not Christ, I am
not Eternal God, I am but the servant of Baha." However, by many of the Baha'is he was still thought to
be one with his Father in power and glory, and his
writings were included with those of Baha'u'llah in
their sacred Scriptures.(24) Thus the Editors in the
Foreword to the Excerpts from the Will of Abdu'l-Baha
published in the *Baha'i World* write:(25) "By the
appointment of Abdu'l-Baha as the Center of His Covenant, Baha'u'llah prolonged His own ministry for well-
nigh thirty years.....For the words of Abdu'l-Baha,
according to the text of this appointment, have equal
rank and spiritual validity with those of the Manifestation (i.e., Baha'u'llah)." We may, therefore, con-
clude that in the West as well as in the East Abdu'l-
Baha was widely thought of as a divine being, a continuation of the Manifestation of Baha'u'llah.

Since all that Abdu'l-Baha wrote and spoke is considered by his followers as inspired and infallible

teaching, and since he between 1892 and 1921 spoke and
wrote a very great deal, it is of course impossible to
give in this chapter more than a few samples of his
precepts and pronouncements. The English reader is
referred to *Bahai Scriptures*(24) in which are found
nearly 300 large pages filled with the words of Abdu'l-
Baha, most of which were directed to people in the
West. Also to *Baha'i World Faith*(26), and to other
translations of his teachings.

Abdu'l-Baha taught that Baha'u'llah is God Manifest.
"This is the day in which the Lord of Hosts has come
down from heaven on the clouds of glory,"(27) and he
is the greatest of the Manifestations,(28) and was
foretold in all the previous Scriptures.(29)   "The
Abha Beauty is the Supreme Manifestation of God and
the Dayspring of His Most Divine Essence."(30)   It is
noteworthy that Abdu'l-Baha, even in America and
England, did not often speak of God as "Father." Probably one reason was that he, coming out of a Muslim
tradition in which it was considered blasphemous to
call God "Father" and Jesus "Son of God," found it
difficult to use these terms. Moreover, according to
his belief, God is impersonal and unknowable. "Personality is in the Manifestation of the Divinity, not
in the essence of the Divinity.....By 'seeing God' is
meant beholding the Manifestation of Himself."(31) "No
one hath any access to the Invisible Essence. The way
is barred and the road impassable."(32) If God does
not possess personality, it would of course be impossible to address him as "Father," or to address him at
all. So Abdu'l-Baha usually follows the Islamic custom
of calling him "Lord," and of speaking of believers not
as "children of God,"(33) but as God's "slaves," which
in English has been translated "servants." Even the
eldest son of Baha'u'llah the Lord took as his title
the "Slave of Baha."

Muslims have often accused Christians of corrupting
their Scriptures, and have said that the Bible is no
longer authentic. This charge was pronounced false by
Baha'u'llah, and both he and his son frequently referred to the Bible as a proof of their doctrines. However
when the Bible teaching did not agree with Baha'i ideas

it was often interpreted in a way to change completely the meaning. For instance, all miraculous events like the healing of the sick and the resurrection of Christ were said to have only a spiritual meaning.

Abdu'l-Baha declared that all the holy Manifestations were united and agreed in purpose and teaching, and here he names Zoroaster and Buddha along with the traditional Manifestations.(34) (We wonder what the Bab would have said of this innovation.) "There is no differentiation possible," he continued,(35) "in their mission and teachings; all are reflectors of reality ....and reality is not multiple; it is one....But the followers of these systems have disagreed." Therefore, he says,(36) "When Christians act according to the teachings of Christ they are called Baha'is. For the foundations of Christianity and the religion of Baha are one." As the sun of today is the same as the sun of yesterday, so the Manifestations are all one Sun. (37) Hence, all the great religions are true, and all followers of these faiths can and should unite on one world faith, which is the Baha'i Faith.

This teaching was pleasing to people in the West of Unitarian and Universalist and ultra-liberal tendencies, who resented the exclusive claims of Christianity as well as of Islam. For those members of the Christian community who had only a superficial acquaintance with Christianity and the other religions it was quite easy to assent to the proposition that all religions are one. The question as to whether a Jew could remain a member of the synagogue, and a Christian a member of a church, on becoming a Baha'i was not answered clearly by Abdu'l-Baha. However, since he attended the Muslim mosque and observed the rites of Islam in Akka, and was recognized by Muslims as being one of them, the conclusion could easily be drawn that such dual membership of Baha'is was possible and desirable.

Though Abdu'l-Baha was welcomed in a number of churches during his tours in the West, and was permitted to speak in them, it seems that he did not think highly of the Christian Church. Of course, from

his point of view, Christians had twice failed to
believe on God's Manifestations, once when they rejected Muhammad, and again when they rejected Baha'u'
llah, so their guilt was great, and their Church was
a body without a spirit. In reply to a question from
a member of a church he wrote:(38) "Thou hast questioned how thou canst accept this divine Cause, for
thou art a member of the church. Know thou: in the
day of the Manifestation of Christ, many souls became
portionless and deprived because they were members of
the Holy of Holies in Jerusalem. According to that
membership, they became veiled from his brilliant
Beauty. Therefore, turn thy face to the Church of
God, which consists in divine instructions and merciful exhortations. For what similarity is there between
the church of stone and cement, and the Celestial Holy
of Holies? Endeavor that thou mayest enter this Church
of God.....Although they consider the wine and the
bread in the church as the blood and body of Christ,
yet this is but appearance and not reality.....The per-
formance of the celebration of baptism would cleanse
the body, but the spirit hath no share; but the divine
teachings and the exhortations of the Beauty of Abha
will baptize the soul. I hope that thou wilt receive
this baptism."

From the New Testament Abdu'l-Baha had learned the
primary importance of Love, and love to all men
occupied a large place in his teaching. In his
address on Love at Green Acre in 1912 he said(39) that
"love is the cause of the existense of all phenomena
and that the absence of love is the cause of disinte-
gration or non-existence.....If love were extinguished,
the power of attraction dispelled, the affinity of
human hearts destroyed, the phenomena of human life
would disappear....Real love is the love which exists
between God and His servants - the love which binds
together holy souls.....Were it not for the love of
God hearts would be inanimate, spirits would wither...
Among the signs of His Love which appear in the world
are the Dawning-Points of His Manifestations....For
the sake of guiding the people they have willingly
forfeited their lives...They have accepted the cross
....Therefore consider how much they love. Were it

not for their love for humanity, Spiritual Love would
be a mere name."

And in another connection he says:(40) "Let us
have love, and more love, a love that melts all opposition, that sweeps away all barriers, that conquers
all foes, a love that aboundeth in charity....Each one
must be a sign of love, a center of love, a sun of
love....a universe of love. Hast thou love? Then thy
power is irresistible." And again:(41) "You must
love humanity in order to uplift and beautify humanity.
Even if people slay you, yet you must love them.....
We are creatures of the same God, therefore we must
love all as children of God even though they are doing
us harm. Christ loved his persecutors. It is possible
for us to attain to that love."

After reading these beautiful words it is disappointing to discover in other utterances of Abdu'l-Baha that
he found it impossible to love certain people. It
appears that he to the end of his life cherished great
bitterness toward the "Covenant-breakers," the leader
of whom had been his own brother Mirza Muhammad Ali.
In his Will he speaks of them as "ferocious lions,
ravening wolves, blood-thirsty beasts,"(42) and there
is no evidence that he ever forgave and showed love
to them.

In his addresses and epistles to people in the West,
Abdu'l-Baha said little about the Manifestation who
followed Christ, who according to the Bab and Baha'u'-
llah was superior to Christ, for he knew that people
acquainted with the Bible and the Koran would not readily agree that Muhammad occupied a higher place than
Christ, and that the teachings of the Koran were
superior to those of the Sermon on the Mount. Usually
he by-passed Islam, and spoke of Baha'u'llah as the
Manifestation after Christ, or the return of Christ.

It is evident from his teachings that Abdu'l-Baha
was not so much concerned about man's relation to God
as he was about the problems of man's life on earth.
"In short," he wrote,(43) "by religion we mean those
necessary bonds which unify the world of humanity."

And again,(44) "All the religions are revealed for the
sake of good fellowship. The fundamentals, the foundations, of all are fellowship, unity and love." And so
he spoke much about the unity of all mankind.

It is unfortunate that some of the public pronouncements of Abdu'l-Baha were marred by inaccuracies which
have found their way into the *Bahai Scriptures*. For
example, he said:(45) "The Blessed Perfection Baha'u'-
llah belonged to the royal family of Persia." But it
is well known that he was not a prince. Also he said:
(46) "The Blessed Perfection was a prisoner twenty-
five years. During all this time he was subjected to
the indignities and revilement of the people. He was
persecuted, mocked and put in chains." And again:(47)
"After twenty-four years in the greatest prison, Acca,
His life was ended in great trouble and hardship. In
short, all the time of the sojourn of the Blessed Perfection [Baha'u'llah]....in this mortal world, He was
either restrained with chains or kept under hanging
swords, enduring the most painful afflictions." While
Baha'u'llah had many troubles, he lived during the
later years of his life in comfort in the Bahji Palace
outside Akka, where there were no chains or swords.

In speaking of Nasiru'd-Din the Shah of Iran he
said:(48) He was "a despot who through his decree could
kill a thousand men each day. There was not a day during which he did not kill many people." While the
Shah was not without faults, this statement of his
ferocity is of course a gross exaggeration. In the
same paragraph the Babi heroine Quarratu'l-Ayn is
called a "Baha'i", whereas her rank among the Babis
was higher than that of Baha. And there also appears
the statement,(49) so often quoted by Baha'is, that
"for the establishment of International Peace the
blood of twenty-thousand Baha'is was split." As was
stated previously, it is doubtful whether there have
been in all more than two or three hundred Baha'i
martyrs. And if the Babis, killed in the insurrections, are counted as Baha'is, a fact which was strenuously denied by Baha in his conciliatory epistle to
the Shah,(50) probably less than five thousand of them
lost their lives. And to say that either the Babis or

the Baha'is died for International Peace is hardly
exact. Nor was his remark that Sarah was the sister
of Abraham's mother(51) any more accurate. Finally,
the thousands of Jews whose ancestors have lived in
Iran for 2500 years would certainly be surprised to
learn from Abdu'l-Baha(52) that "before the rise of
Christ....the name of Moses had not been heard in
Persia."

These glaring inaccuracies suggest that the infallibility of the Interpreter did not cover details of
history. It is easier to overlook such minor mistakes,
however, than to excuse Abdu'l-Baha for untrue statements such as the following:(53) "In the Orient the
various peoples and nations were in a state of antagonism and strife, manifesting the utmost enmity and
hatred toward one another. Darkness encompassed the
world of mankind. At such a time as this, Baha'u'llah
appeared. He removed all the imitations and prejudices
which had caused separation and misunderstanding, and
laid the foundation of the one religion of God. When
this was accomplished, Mohammedans, Christians, Jews,
Zoroastrians, Buddhists all were united in actual
fellowship and love." And again:(54) "We have for
our subject the reconciliation of the religious
systems of the world.....Do not question the practi-
cability of this and be not astonished. It has been
effected and accomplished in Persia [Iran].....No
traces of discord or difference remain; the utmost
love, kindness, and unity are apparent. They are
united and live together like a single family in harmony and accord. Discord and strife have passed away.
Love and fellowship now prevail instead." The impression which one would get from hearing these statements
about the influence of Baha'u'llah in his native land
is that Baha'ism is the dominant religion in Iran,
and that because of it religious strife has disappeared. The most charitable thing that can be said is
that Abdu'l-Baha left Iran when a boy and had not seen
it since, and was quite uninformed as to the situation.
The Baha'is have always been a small minority in Iran,
and their presence has unfortunately created discord
more often than it has produced peace.

When Abdu'l-Baha was at Clifton, England, on January 16, 1913, he made a memorable address in which, among other things, he said:(55) "Nearly sixty years ago when the horizon of the Orient was in a state of the utmost gloom, warfare existed and there was enmity between the various creeds.....at such a time His Highness Baha'u'llah arose from the horizon of Persia [Iran] like a shining sun. He boldly proclaimed peace, writing to the kings of the earth and calling on them to arise and assist in the hoisting of this banner. In order to bring peace out of the chaos, he established certain precepts or principles." He then proceeds to enumerate and explain ten of the "principles" of Baha'u'llah. Briefly they are as follows:

1) "The independent investigation of truth."

2) "The oneness of the human race."

3) "International peace."

4) "The conformity of religion to science and reason."

5) "Religious, racial, political, and patriotic prejudice" must be banished.

6) "The equality of men and women."

7) "All classes of society are to work together in love and harmony."

8) "The parliament of man" as a court of last appeal in international questions.

9) "Universal education."

10) "A universal language."

It is instructive to compare this list with that drawn up by Baha'u'llah himself some twenty-three years earlier (Chapter VIII). Since most of these "principles" are not found in the fifteen items listed by Baha'u'llah, it is more accurate to attribute these

ten principles to Abdu'l-Baha himself. Most of them
are not religious principles at all, and could easily
be adopted not only by Jews, Christians and Muslims,
but also by materialists and atheists. It is indeed
remarkable how successful Abdu'l-Baha has been in this
statement of his Cause to the people in the West, in
shaking off every vestige of the old Babi order, and
clothing his movement in more modern garments suited
to the new age. Regarding these changes Professor
Browne wrote in 1918:(56) "The political ideals of
the Baha'is have undergone considerable evolution since
their propaganda achieved such success in America,
where they have come into more or less connection with
various international, pacifist and feminist movements.
These tendencies were, however, implicit in Baha'u'-
llah's teachings at a much earlier date, as shown in
the recommendation of a universal language and script
in the *Kitab-i-Aqdas*, the exaltation of humanitarian-
ism over patriotism, the insistence on the brotherhood
of all believers, irrespective of race or colour, and
the ever-present idea of 'the Most Great Peace'."

A brief consideration of these Principles will
suffice here. The independent investigation of truth
was not a new idea, for the Shi'ite theologians had
long ago maintained that in matters which concern the
fundamentals of religion, personal investigation
(*tahqiq*) is obligatory.(57) The question arises, what
possibility remains for independent investigation when
Abdu'l-Baha is the only authorized interpreter of the
Baha'i Scriptures, and when he tells us,(58) "Whatever
emanates from the Center of the Covenant is right.....
while everything else is error?" Nor is the doctrine
of the oneness of humanity new, either to readers of
the Bible, or to Iranians who memorized in childhood
the beautiful verse of the thirteenth century poet
Sa'adi, who wrote, "The children of Adam are members
of one another, created from one essence," created from
one source. Baha'u'llah had early issued pronouncements about reducing armaments because of their great
expense, and had forbidden religious war (*Jihad*). When
Old Testament prophecies were interpreted as predictions of the coming of Baha'u'llah, it was easy to
take the words in Micah(59) about the time when men

would beat their swords into plowshares as a promise
of his "Most Great Peace." It is indeed distressing
that during the century following this promise of
peace the most terrible wars of history have been
waged, and there is no peace on earth.

The "conformity of religion to science and reason"
is something that was entirely new, no trace of which
can be found in the teachings of Baha'u'llah. Whence
came this new element? It seems to have come from
France. The Baha'i faith was introduced into France
by Hippolyte Dreyfus a Jewish convert, who in his
effort to make it acceptable to the rationalistic
people of France presented it as a scientific religion.(60) Previously the Muslim ancestors of the
Baha'is had gloried in miracles, but now the miraculous becomes taboo, and all miracles in the Scriptures
are interpreted spiritually. Abdu'l-Baha welcomed
this French flavoring for his Faith.

All sorts of "prejudice must be banished." This
would follow from the unity of mankind. Abdu'l-Baha
well knew the evil of the prejudice and hatred from
which the Bab and Baha'u'llah had suffered. He also
must have recognized the bitterness in the attitude
of the Baha'is toward the Azalis, and of him and his
followers to the Unitarians. Hence, from personal
experience he could insist on the need for the elimination of all prejudice.

As for the "equality of men and women," Baha'u'llah
knew nothing of this principle, which would have seemed to him quite heretical. In the *Kitab-i-Aqdas* a man
is permitted to marry two women, and both the divorce
and inheritance laws allow privileges to men which are
denied to women.(61) This new teaching emanated not
from Akka but from the West. The "working together of
all classes of society in love and harmony" is a beautiful ideal, expressed long ago in the divine command
to love one's neighbor as oneself. But how are men
to be changed so that they will have both the desire
and the power to so act?

The idea of the "parliament of man" is no doubt
derived from the House of Justice proposed by

Baha'u'llah, which would have full authority after the death of his two Branches, Abbas Efendi and Mirza Muhammad Ali. It was of course to be composed of Baha'is, and chosen by Baha'is, to rule over a Baha'i State. It would, therefore, be some time before this principle could be realized in practice. Meanwhile, the United Nations composed mostly of "unbelievers" is trying to assist the peoples of the world at least to talk to each other.

Baha'u'llah commanded(62) that Baha'is educate their children, and this many of them have faithfully done. The thought of "universal education" was introduced by Abdu'l-Baha after seeing what was done in this field in the West. And, finally, the command that "one language be chosen and taught to everybody" so that people would not disagree was from Baha'u'llah, (63) but it was never determined which language it was to be. Esperanto was tried for a time, but was a failure.

From the point of view of Baha'i organization the most important of the writings of Abdu'l-Baha is his Last Will and Testament, a lengthy document in Persian and Arabic, which was published in 1924 in Cairo by the Baha'i Spiritual Assembly. It appears that the different portions of the Will were written at different times, some being quite early. The Will, in addition to other matters, contains (a) allegations against Subh-i-Azal, (b) allegations against Mirza Muhammad Ali, (c) allegations against Mirza Badi'u'llah, (d) provisions for the Guardianship, and (e) provisions for the national and international Houses of Justice. Excerpts from the Will have been translated and published in English.(64) Also, excerpts in the original languages, with a full discussion of the contents of the Will, are found in *Azal's Notes*.(65) According to Azal, this Will was never probated.(66)

The portions of this document which are of principal interest to us at this point are those which make provision for the leadership of the Baha'i Cause after the death of the Center of the Covenant. We have already explained at the beginning of Chapter IX that Baha'u'llah had made it quite clear in the *Kitab-i-Aqdas* and

in his Will that on the death of his eldest son Abbas
Efendi the leadership was to go to a younger son, Mirza
Muhammad Ali. He did not appoint a successor to
Muhammad Ali, but commanded that thereafter matters
should be referred to the House of Justice, and determined by members of that House in accordance with his
inspired writings.(67)

One would have assumed that the man who called himself the "Slave of Baha" would have scrupulously obeyed
his father's command, and in his Last Will and Testament would have turned over the leadership to his
brother Mirza Muhammad Ali. This, however, he did not
do. After having for years stigmatized his brother as
a "Covenant-breaker," Abdu'l-Baha in his Last Will
and Testament completely ignored his father's Covenant,
and appointed as his successor not his brother but his
grandson Shoghi Efendi,(68) with the title "Guardian
of the Cause" (*Waliu'l-Amr*). We will quote some of
the provisions of the Will as translated in the *Baha'i
World*.(69)

"O my loving friends! After the passing away of
this wronged one, it is incumbent upon the *Aghsan*
(Branches), the *Afnan* (Twigs)(70)....the Hands of the
Cause of God,(71) and the loved ones of the Abha
Beauty [Baha'u'llah] to turn unto Shoghi Effendi.....
as he is the sign of God, the guardian of the Cause
of God.....He is the expounder of the words of God,
and after him will succeed the first-born of his
lineal descendants.

"The sacred and youthful branch, the guardian of
the Cause of God, as well as the Universal House of
Justice, to be universally elected and established,
are both under the care and protection of the Abha
Beauty.....Whatsoever they decide is of God. Whoso
obeyeth him not, neither obeyeth them, hath not obeyed
God; whoso rebelleth against him and against them hath
rebelled against God; whoso opposeth him hath opposed
God.....whoso disputeth with him hath disputed with
God; whoso denieth him hath denied God; whoso disbe-
lieveth in him hath disbelieved in God.....May the
wrath, the fierce indignation, the vengeance of God

rest upon him!.....It is incumbent upon the members
of the House of Justice, upon all the *Aghsan*, the
Afnan, the Hands of the Cause of God to show their
obedience, submissiveness and subordination unto the
guardian of the Cause of God, to turn unto him and
be lowly before him.....The Hands of the Cause of God
must be ever watchful and so soon as they find anyone
beginning to oppose and protest against the guardian
of the Cause of God, cast him out from the congregation of the people of Baha and in no wise accept any
excuse from him.

"It is incumbent upon the guardian of the Cause of
God to appoint in his own lifetime him that shall become his successor, that differences may not arise
after his passing. He that is appointed must manifest
in himself detachment from all worldly things, must be
the essence of purity, must show in himself the fear
of God, knowledge, wisdom and learning. Thus, should
the first-born of the guardian of the Cause of God not
manifest in himself the truth.....and his glorious
lineage not be matched with a goodly character, then
must he (the guardian) choose another branch to succeed
him.

"The Hands of the Cause of God must elect from their
own number nine persons that shall at all times be
occupied in the important services in the work of the
guardian of the Cause of God.....and these.....must
give their assent to the choice of the one whom the
guardian of the Cause of God hath chosen as his successor.....The Hands of the Cause of God must be nominated and appointed by the guardian of the Cause of
God. All must be under his shadow and obey his command. Should any....disobey and seek division, the
wrath of God and his vengeance will be upon him.....
The obligations of the Hands of the Cause of God are
to diffuse the Divine Fragrances, to edify the souls
of men, to promote learning.....They must manifest the
fear of God by their conduct, their manners, their
deeds and their words.....

"Wherefore, O my loving friends! Consort with all
the peoples, kindreds and religions of the world with

the utmost truthfulness....kindliness, good-will and
friendliness....Should other peoples and nations be
unfaithful to you show your fidelity to them....should
they show their enmity be friendly toward them, should
they poison your lives sweeten their souls....

"And now concerning the House of Justice which God
hath ordained as the source of all good and freed from
all error, it must be elected by universal suffrage,
that is, by the believers. Its members must be manifestations of the fear of God....By this House is meant
the Universal House of Justice; that is, in all countries a secondary House of Justice must be instituted,
and these secondary Houses of Justice must elect the
members of the Universal one. Unto this body all
things must be referred. It enacteth all ordinances
and regulations that are not to be found in the explicit Holy Text. By this body all the difficult problems are to be resolved, and the guardian of the Cause
of God is its sacred head and the distinguished member
for life of that body....Should any of the members
commit a sin, injurious to the common weal, the guardian of the Cause of God hath at his own discretion
the right to expel him, whereupon the people must
elect another one in his stead.....Unto the Most Holy
Book (*Kitab-i-Aqdas*) every one must turn and all that
is not expressly recorded therein must be referred to
the Universal House of Justice. That which this body,
whether unanimously or by a majority doth carry, that
is verily the Truth and the Purpose of God Himself."

In closing his Will Abdu'l-Baha makes another
appeal to all Baha'is to be loyal to the Guardian.
He writes: "O ye faithful loved ones of Abdu'l-Baha!
It is incumbent upon you to take the greatest care of
Shoghi Effendi....that no dust of despondency and
sorrow may stain his radiant nature....For he is,
after Abdu'l-Baha, the Guardian of the Cause of God
....He that obeyeth him not hath not obeyed God; he
that turneth away from him hath turned away from God
.....To none is given the right to put forth his own
opinion or express his particular convictions. All
must seek guidance and turn to the Center of the Cause
and the House of Justice. And he that turneth unto
whatsoever else is indeed in grievous error."

From these provisions for the future of the Cause
it is evident that as Abdu'l-Baha, without ever calling himself a Manifestation, had assumed for himself
the same authority that had been claimed by Baha'u'-
llah, so by bestowing absolute authority on Shoghi
Efendi as the infallible Guardian of the Cause of God,
and by authorizing him to appoint his son or one of
his lineal descendants as his successor, Abdu'l-Baha
intended to extend indefinitely the Baha Manifestation,
making it hereditary in his family, similar to the
Shi'ite Imamate. He commanded that the members of
the Universal House of Justice and the Hands of the
Cause and all believers must be completely obedient
and subservient to the Guardian, and no one is to have
the right to question anything he says or does. It is
not clear how the doctrine of the infallible and omni-
potent Guardianship is to be reconciled with the Principle of the Independent Investigation of Truth. Nor
is it clear how the command for all believers to turn
to the Most Holy Book (*Kitab-i-Aqdas*) could have been
obeyed, since no authorized translation of this rare
Arabic book had been published.

As for the establishment of Houses of Justice, the
reader will recall(72) that Baha'u'llah in his provisions in the Aqdas for the Houses of Justice anticipated
the time when some nation or nations would accept his
religion and would be ruled by a Baha'i government and
Baha'i laws. The legislative body would then be what
he termed the House of Justice, to which all matters
not provided for in the *Kitab-i-Aqdas* would be referred
for decision, and the laws enacted by this body would
be enforced by the Baha'i government. It seems that
Abdu'l-Baha's plan for the House of Justice was similar
to that of his father, for in his Will, in a section
omitted from the "Excerpts From the Will And Testament
Of Abdu'l-Baha" in *The Baha'i World 1926-1928*, he
states:(73) "The House of Justice is the legislative
authority and the government the executive power. The
legislative body must reinforce the executive; and the
executive must aid and assist the legislative body, so
that, through the connection and consolidation of these
two forces, the foundation of fairness and justice may
become firm and strong, that regions (of earth) may
become....Paradise." Thus, though Abdu'l-Baha knew

that no nation in the near future would adopt the
Baha'i faith as its established religion, he nevertheless commanded that national Houses of Justice and
an international House of Justice be established, and
that Shoghi Efendi as Guardian of the Cause of God be
the head of the Universal House of Justice. It is
evident that so long as there is no government to
enforce the decisions of the House of Justice, this
body would function more like a church court than a
political parliament, and many of the laws of the
Kitab-i-Aqdas would be ineffectual. In the following
chapter we will see how the commands of the Center of
the Covenant were carried out by his grandson.

NOTES

1. *Aqdas*, p. 56, *Bahai Scriptures*, p. 261.

2. *Aqdas*, p. 34.

3. Ibid., pp. 39, 56, 70. In his reply to "Warqa"
    (quoted in the Will of Mirza Muhammad Ali, pp.
    18-19, refer to *Azal's Notes*, p. 1099), Baha'u'-
    llah stated that by "Book" he intended only the
    Kitab-i-Aqdas. Since he did not name the "Branch"
    from whom interpretation of the Aqdas should be
    sought, it would seem that both of his sons had
    the right of interpretation of the Book.

4. *Scriptures*, p. 282. The Will of Baha'u'llah,
    which he called "the Book of My Covenant," is
    found in the official history of the Baha'i move-
    ment written by Ayati (Avareh) under the title
    Al-Kawakib Al-Durriyya, published in Cairo in
    1924, in vol. II, pp. 20-22. From this document
    it is clear that Abdu'l-Baha was authorized only
    to maintain the law of the Aqdas, and to explain
    the Aqdas to any who could not understand it.
    Since it was written in Arabic it was a closed
    book to most Baha'is. There seems to be nothing
    in Baha'u'llah's Will to substantiate Abdu'l-Baha's
    statement here quoted.

5. Ibid., p. 547.

6. *Aqdas*, p. 57.

7. Ibid., p. 29, see Chapter VIII.

8. *The Religion of the Baha'is*, J. R. Richards, London 1932, p. 98, quoting *Mokatib-i-Abdu'l-Baha*, Vol. III, p. 372.

9. *Aqdas*, p. 53.

10. Ibid., pp. 40, 53.

11. *Richards*, p. 98, quoting *Mok.*, Vol. III, p. 370.

12. *Materials*, pp. 102, 103.

13. *The Outlook*, H. H. Jessup, June 22, 1901, p. 456.

14. Psalm 2:12.

15. Isaish 4:2.

16. Zechariah 6:12,13.

17. *Richards*, pp. 161, 162.

18. Matthew 16:27.

19. Revelation 11:15.

20. *Richards*, pp. 163, 164.

21. *Aqdas*, p. 34.

22. *Scriptures*, pp. 284, 285.

23. *Richards*, p. 94, quoting *Mok*, Vol. III, p. 189.

24. See *Baha'i Scriptures*, 1923.

25. *Baha'i World 1926-1928*, published by Baha'i Publishing Committee 1928, p. 81.

26. *Baha'i World Faith*, Baha'i Publishing Trust, Wilmette, Illinois, 1943.

27. *Scriptures*, p. 266.

28. Ibid., p. 461.

29. Ibid., p. 466.

30. Ibid., p. 554.

31. Ibid., p. 482.

32. Ibid., p. 459.

33. 1 John 3:1,2.

34. *Scriptures*, p. 330.

35. Ibid., p. 331.

36. Ibid., p. 382.

37. Ibid., pp. 382, 461.

38. Ibid., pp. 457, 458.

39. Ibid., pp. 356-359.

40. Ibid., p. 454.

41. Ibid., p. 450.

42. Ibid., p. 553.

43. Ibid., p. 448.

44. Ibid., p. 275.

45. Ibid., p. 286.

46. Ibid., p. 289.

47. Ibid., p. 361.

48. Ibidl, p. 309.

49. Ibid., pp. 316, 317.

50. *A Traveller's Narrative*, pp. 156-160. Baha'u'llah stated to the Shah that his followers have made no disturbance or rebellion.

51. *Scriptures*, p. 393.

52. Ibid., p. 394.

53. Ibid., pp. 335, 336.

54. *Scriptures*, p. 351.

55. Ibid., pp. 275-279.

56. *Materials*, p. XIX.

57. *al-Babu'l-Hadi Ashar*, William McElwee Miller, Luzac, London, 1928, p. 7.

58. *Scriptures*, p. 547.

59. Micah 4:1-5.

60. *Richards*, pp. 101, 112.

61. *Aqdas*, pp. 29, 40-43.

62. Ibid., pp. 37, 38.

63. Ibid., p. 74.

64. *Baha'i World 1926-1928*, pp. 81-89.

65. *Azal's Notes*, pp. 150 ff., and facsimile of the printed copy of the Will in the original text. See Appendix II, Nos. 12, 14, 15, 18, 19, and 46.

66. Ibid., p. 150.

67. *Aqdas*, pp. 31, 38, 39.

68. Abdu'l-Baha had no son. Shoghi Efendi was the son of his eldest daughter Ziyaiyya and Mirza Hadi of Shiraz. It is said that Munira the wife of Abdu'l-Baha set her heart on having her grandson as the successor, and incited her husband to appoint him (*Azal's Notes*, pp. 296, 659).

69. *Baha'i World 1926-1928*, pp. 84-89.

70. The *Aghsan* were the sons of Baha'u'llah, and the *Afnan* were relatives of the Bab (*Materials*, p. 49, n. 2).

71. The "Hands of the Cause" were formerly the leaders. Later in 1951 Shoghi Efendi made the "Hands" an office, and appointed certain people to it.

72. See Chapter VIII.

73. *Azal's Notes*, pp. 823, 824, *Will and Testament of Abdu'l-Baha*, issued by the Baha'is of Lancaster, Pennsylvania, U.S.A., pp. 14, 15.

12

The Guardianship of Shoghi Efendi: Organization of the Cause

The death of Abdu'l-Baha in 1921 marked the end of an era of Baha'i history, and the beginning of a new and different day. As Shoghi Efendi, the Guardian of the Cause of God, writes:(1) "The Heroic, the Apostolic Age of the Dispensation of Baha'u'llah.....had now terminated.....The Formative Period, the Iron Age, of that Dispensation was now beginning..." The story of this "formative period," which is no doubt of importance to devoted Baha'is who are concerned about the development and growth of their Faith, is of much less general interest than the stirring events of the "heroic age." Baha'u'llah and his son Abdu'l-Baha were, as we have seen in the preceding chapters, very strong and impressive personalities. Whatever one may think of their claims and their conduct, they undoubtedly possessed great personal magnetism, and were able to win and hold the complete allegiance of numbers of people in the West as well as in the East. They also made many enemies who bitterly opposed them. In the new age there were no leaders of equal stature, and both the devotion and the animosity shown to the successor of Abdu'l-Baha were proportionately less.

In designating his grandson Shoghi as his successor, Abdu'l-Baha in his Will says of him:(2) "Behold, he

is the blest and sacred bough that hath branched out
from the Twin Holy Trees.....that primal branch of
the Divine and Sacred Lote-Tree.....the most wondrous,
unique and priceless pearl that doth gleam from out
the twin surging seas.....he is the sign of God, the
chosen branch, the guardian of the Cause of God.....
He is the expounder of the words of God, and after him
will succeed the first-born of his lineal descendants
.....whoso opposeth him hath opposed God."

The reference in the term "Twin Holy Trees" is to
Shoghi's parents. His mother was Ziyaiyya Khanum,
eldest daughter of Abdu'l-Baha. His father was Mirza
Hadi Afnan of Shiraz, a distant relative of the Bab.
Shoghi was, therefore, a "branch" from the two holy
families. He was born in Akka on March 3, 1896, and
was designated by Abdu'l-Baha as his successor when
he was about ten years of age.(3) Persian was his
mother tongue, and Arabic, the language of the people
of Akka and Haifa, was known to him and his family.
He received an English and Arabic education in the
American University of Beirut, but was not an outstanding student. One of his professors told the author
that Shoghi was more interested in novels than in his
studies. Later he was sent to Oxford University in
England, and remained there till his grandfather died,
when he returned to Haifa to assume the responsibili-
ties of the Guardianship.

In March, 1923 the author was passing through Beirut
on his way from Iran to America, and was given a note
of introduction to Shoghi Efendi by one of his former
teachers. Having met a number of Baha'is during my
residence in Iran, I was eager to see the new leader
of the movement, and arranged to stop off in Haifa on
my way to Jerusalem. On my arrival I walked to his
residence, presented the note of introduction, and
received a warm welcome. Shoghi Efendi himself led
me into his handsome and well-furnished home. He was
a young man, short of stature and unimpressive in
appearance, but courteous and friendly. I was at
once introduced to his father Mirza Hadi, who knew
no English. I, therefore, suggested that we converse
in Persian, but Shoghi Efendi said that he could
express himself more easily in English, so most of

our conversation was in that language. Had the command of Baha'u'llah that everybody learn one of the
languages of the world(4) been obeyed, we would not
have encountered this difficulty!

My host was most humble, making no claims for himself, and insisting that he was entirely unworthy of
the great responsibility which had been laid upon him.
He urged me, with the courtesy of an Iranian gentle-
man, to sit in the seat of honor (the chair farthest
from the door), and when I refused and urged him to
take it, he acquiesced. A bright little Japanese
believer with a long beard brought me a cup of tea,
and Shoghi Efendi himself gave me an orange. When I
requested that he kindly give me a picture of himself,
he replied that he would prefer to give me one of his
grandfather. This he did, writing an inscription on
it in both Persian and English, the latter being:
"A Precious souvenir presented to my dear friend Mr.
Miller, Haifa, Palestine, March 23, 1923. Shoghi
Rabbani."(5)

In answer to my questions Shoghi Efendi said that
Baha'u'llah was not an Incarnation, for God is (in His
Essence) beyond all reach, and cannot dwell in flesh
and blood. He was rather a Manifestation of God, and
in him all the attributes of God were found and could
be known. The Bab who prepared the way for him, and
Abdu'l-Baha who carried on his work after him, were
quite different in rank from the Manifestation, for
they were only divinely prepared men. He said that
Abdu'l-Baha had not considered himself sinless, but
used constantly to confess his sins and ask God for
pardon. His grandfather had appointed him "to carry
on the Movement," and he was busy organizing the World
Council which was to be associated with him in this
task.(6) He stated that his principal effort would be
to unite the "friends" of the East with those of the
West.

When asked what the Baha'i religion had to offer
which Christianity did not have, Shoghi Efendi replied
that the principles of both were the same, and only
the outward forms differed, and Baha'is thought the

teachings of Baha'u'llah were best for today (he did
not specify why, or in what respects). He said that
many people wanted to limit the Baha'i Cause, and
narrow it, but it must be broad and include *all* religions, even Buddhism and other faiths, for all were
from God. It was evident that the Guardian was more
interested in the organization and the ethical teachings of the Cause than in its philosophical and theological foundations. How very different was this
friendly informal visit of mine to the Guardian of the
Cause of God from the audience granted to Professor
Browne by Shoghi Efendi's great-grandfather Baha'u'-
llah! (7)

   Early next morning I climbed to the top of Mt.
Carmel, and while descending I chanced upon the Guest
House where pilgrims from Iran were entertained. When
I addressed in Persian an Iranian who was standing
outside, he invited me in, and I was cordially received
and given a breakfast of tea and bread and cheese, in
the style of Iran. I soon found that these Baha'is
knew of my visit to their Master on the previous afternoon, and when I rose to go they kindly offered to take
me to see the Mausoleum of the Bab and Abdu'l-Baha
which was nearby. On entering we took off our shoes,
and walked over the gorgeous Persian carpet to the
threshold of the shrine itself. There my conductor
prostrated himself and repeated the Arabic formulas
appointed for the "visitation." Since it was necessary
for me to go on to Jerusalem that morning, I was unable
to accept the gracious invitation of Shoghi Efendi to
accompany him to the shrine of Baha'u'llah in Akka.

   We have seen in the earlier chapters of this book
how, after the deaths of the Bab and Baha'u'llah,
bitter quarrels regarding the succession arose among
the believers. Fortunately on the death of Abdu'l-Baha
no one disputed the succession. This, however, did not
indicate that all the followers of Baha'u'llah welcomed
the accession of the Guardian, and were ready to obey
him. We recall that in the early years of the rule of
Abdu'l-Baha, most of the members of the family of
Baha'u'llah vigorously protested against what they
considered unlawful assumption of authority on the

part of one who called himself the "Slave of Baha,"
and as a result were rejected by Abdu'l-Baha.(8)   At
the time of his death, the only members of Baha'u'llah's
family who had not been rejected by Abdu'l-Baha were
his sister, his wife, his four daughters and their husbands.(9)   He showed great bitterness towards his
brothers Mirza Muhammad Ali and Mirza Badi'u'llah, and
devoted large sections of his Will to a denunciation
of Mirza Muhammad Ali, charging his own followers to
avoid him altogether.   Naturally Mirza Muhammad Ali
and all other members of the family who sympathized
with him were not ready to yield unquestioning obedience to Abdu'l-Baha's grandson, especially since Baha'-
u'llah in his Will ("My Covenant") had made it clear
that after his eldest son Abbas Efendi, the leader of
the Baha'i Cause was to be his second son Mirza
Muhammad Ali.

During the life of Abdu'l-Baha, his brother Mirza
Muhammad Ali did not advance any claim to the leadership of the movement, though he did protest the pronouncements and acts of Abdu'l-Baha, on the grounds
that they resembled those of a new Manifestation. When
Abdu'l-Baha died, why did not Mirza Muhammad Ali,
knowing that his father had specificly named him as
the successor to his brother,(10) put forward his
claim and declare himself the leader of the Cause and
the infallible interpreter of the words of God?   Why
did he not dispute the appointment of Shoghi Efendi
as Guardian as being contrary to the *Kitab-i-Aqdas*
and the Covenant of Baha'u'llah?   The reason was twofold.

In the first place, Mirza Muhammad Ali was unwilling to refer the matter to a Muslim court, where the
Will and other writings of Baha would most certainly
be investigated, and his claim to be a Divine Manifestation and the founder of a new religion superior to
Islam, which he and his followers had carefully concealed all the years they were in Akka, would be
brought to light.   This would be dangerous for all
members of the family, including Mirza Muhammad Ali
and his followers.   For the same reason Shoghi Efendi
never had his grandfather's Will probated in a court.
(11)

Abdu'l-Baha and his Grandson,
Shoghi Efendi the Guardian

The second reason why Mirza Muhammad Ali did not press his claims was that Abdu'l-Baha had been success-ful in winning to his side the great majority of Baha'is, both in Iran and in the West, and had convinced them that Mirza Muhammad Ali was indeed a wicked Covenant-breaker and an enemy of God. Mirza Muhammad Ali, there-fore, knew in advance that any effort on his part to claim the heritage and position assigned to him by his father was sure to meet with defeat from those who revered Abdu'l-Baha as the Center of the Covenant and the infallible Expounder of the Baha'i teaching. Had he not decreed that the successor should be Shoghi Efendi, the first Guardian of the Cause of God, and that he should in turn be succeeded by his eldest son? Whatever he decreed was the decree of God, and must be accepted. So Shoghi Efendi assumed the Guardianship unopposed.(12)

The honor of being Guardian was not an empty one, for in his Will Abdu'l-Baha arranged that his grandson should be well provided for financially. In the *Kitab-i-Aqdas* Baha'u'llah had commanded(13) that believers pay to God a 19% "Purification Tax" on capital funds (gold). This money was to be expended only as Baha'u'llah permitted. The payment of this tax lapsed at the death of Baha'u'llah, for in his Will he stipulated that "God has not decreed for the Branches [Baha's sons] a right in one's property."(14) However, in this matter as well as in others, Abdu'l-Baha disregarded his father's Will, claimed this tax for himself (in addition to the voluntary offerings of believers),(15) and in his own Will commanded(16) that "a fixed money offering (*huququllah*, 'the rights of God') be paid to the guardian of the Cause of God, that it may be expended for the diffusion of the Fragrances of God and the exaltation of His Word, for benevolent pursuits and for the common weal." This provision was omitted from the Excerpts from the Will printed in the *Baha'i World 1926-1928*. It is reported on good authority that Shoghi Efendi kept all the income for his plans and purposes, and failed to share it with other members of the family of Abdu'l-Baha, who kept quiet lest they "make a breach in the Cause of God."(17)

It seems that Shoghi Efendi, pleading inability to enter upon the duties of his office forthwith, retired into solitude for several years after his return to Haifa, leaving the management of Baha'i affairs in the hands of the older members of the family of Abdu'l-Baha. Bahiyya Khanum, the "Supreme Leaf," the daughter of Baha'u'llah, who had remained loyal to her brother, became the "titular head" of the movement, while Munira Khanum, the grandmother of Shoghi Efendi, who had induced her husband to make him the Guardian and successor, was the power behind the throne.(18)

After a time, however, Shoghi Efendi began to realize the extent of the authority vested in him by the Will of Abdu'l-Baha,(19) came forth from his seclusion, and proceeded to exercise his power as Guardian of the Cause. Acting in accordance with the provisions of the Will, he "took over the reins of the Baha'i Administration, and demanded ready and implicit obedience from the servants of God, in default of which any servant of God was liable to excommunication or summary expulsion from the faith under some pretence or pretext....His decisions were absolute and final and his words authorative."(20)

It is not surprising that this policy brought the Guardian into conflict not only with numerous believers but also with the members of his own family, and resulted in their excommunication. The first person to be purged by Shoghi Efendi was his grandmother Munira Khanum, wife of Abdu'l-Baha, the first lady of the Baha'i realm, to whom the Guardian, to a considerable extent, was indebted for his position.(21) Later all the members of Abdu'l-Baha's family, his daughters, his descendants, his sons-in-law, the brothers and sisters of Shoghi Efendi, and last of all his own parents were excommunicated.(22) Riyadh Rabbani, a younger brother of the Guardian, has stated (23) that he for years had assisted Shoghi Efendi in his work. Then when Shoghi excommunicated his parents he called upon Riyadh to make a choice between him and his parents. Riyadh decided to side with his parents, whereupon he was rejected by his brother. It seems that Shoghi Efendi's family accepted this severe

discipline without resistance, for to whom could they
appeal for redress?

Several quarrels, however, took place at the center
of the Cause, one of which was over the custodianship
of the shrine of Baha'u'llah in Akka. While Abdu'l-
Baha lived, he in accordance with Muslim law as eldest
son had the responsibility for his father's grave. When
he died the custodianship should have gone according to
law to Baha'u'llah's eldest surviving son Mirza
Muhammad Ali. Not long after his accession to the
Guardianship, Shoghi Efendi ordered the caretaker of
the shrine to refuse entrance to certain people. Then
the keys were taken from the caretaker by someone, and
handed to the legal custodian Mirza Muhammad Ali, and
neither the American Baha'is who intervened nor the
British High Commissioner were able to dispossess
Mirza Muhammad Ali of his rights. Shoghi Efendi could
not go to court over this, for the Will of his grandfather which appointed him Guardian had not been probated. Finally, Shoghi Efendi approached the British
District Commissioner, and he sent his Arab assistant
who was on friendly terms with both parties to arrange
a settlement out of court. This was done, the keys
were turned over to Shoghi Efendi, and Muhammad Ali
and his partisans were allowed free access to the tomb
of Baha'u'llah, without let or hindrance.(24)

Many years later in 1952 the daughter of Mirza
Badi'u'llah, Mrs. Qamar Bahai, went to Akka accompanied
by a friend, and attempted to visit the tomb of her
grandfather Baha'u'llah. The caretaker employed by
Shoghi Efendi was rude to them, and denied them
entrance to the shrine. Whereupon Mrs. Bahai brought
an action in the Israeli District Court in Haifa
against Shoghi Efendi, to show cause why she was
denied access to the tomb of her grandfather. She
appeared in court in person accompanied by her counsel.
Shoghi Efendi did not appear, but was represented by
his counsel and two American Baha'is. The President
of the Court, in an effort to settle the matter out
of court, took Mrs. Bahai into his office and asked
her if she would meet Shoghi Efendi for an amicable
settlement, and she agreed. But to the great surprise

of the President of the Court, the two American Baha'is
rejected the proposal. Finally, the matter was referred to the Minister for Religious Affairs in the
Israeli Government, who called in the parties separately, and worked out a settlement, whereby free access
to the shrine, without let or hindrance, was granted
to all members of the family of Baha'u'llah, and to
this both parties subscribed.(25)

During the lifetime of Baha'u'llah, Abdu'l-Baha
and his family had resided in the town of Akka, while
his brothers and their families had lived in the Bahji
Palace several miles from Akka near their father.
After the death of Baha'u'llah they continued to live
there, owning undivided shares in the property, but
without the income which Abdu'l-Baha received they
were unable to keep this large property in good repair.
When Shoghi Efendi became the head of the Baha'i Cause,
he naturally felt it was important for him to control
all the sacred sites. He, therefore, proposed to
Mirza Muhammad Ali that he and the others move out of
the Palace to nearby buildings, that Shoghi might
repair the Palace, and this was done. When they moved
out they took with them the household equipment that
they had been using, and this was replaced by Shoghi
Efendi.(26) Thus the Palace also became a place of
pilgrimage for Baha'is.

No doubt the Guardian was happy to turn away from
these family problems and direct his attention and
energies to the task of establishing the Administrative Order in which he was especially interested. In
the *Kitab-i-Aqdas* Baha'u'llah had commanded(27) that
a "House of Justice" be established in every city,
consisting of nine or more members. Accordingly,
Shoghi Efendi wrote to Baha'is in America and elsewhere instructing them to form, in every place where
there were nine or more believers, Baha'i groups
which would be called "Spiritual Assemblies," "an
appellation that must in the course of time be replaced
by their permanent and more descriptive title of
'Houses of Justice,' bestowed upon them by the Author
of the Baha'i Revelation."(28) This was done, and in
the *Baha'i World 1926-1928*(29) the addresses of

eighty-five Assemblies are given, most of them being
in America.(30)   It was the function of these
Assemblies to advance the Baha'i Cause in every way
possible.   These local Assemblies were "the base of
the edifice which the Architect of the Administrative
Order [Abdu'l-Baha]....had directed them to erect."
(31)

The next step was to form, in countries where the
local groups had sufficiently advanced in numbers and
influence, "National Assemblies," which had been
designated in the Will of Abdu'l-Baha as "Secondary
Houses of Justice," the members of which were to be
elected by the local Assemblies.   The National Assemblies, in turn, were to elect the members of the
"Universal House of Justice" provided for in the Will.
In the *Baha'i World 1926-1928*(32) nine National
Assemblies are listed.   The National Assemblies
appointed National Committees to be responsible for
the numerous aspects of the program of the Cause, and
a list of sixty-one of these committees has been
supplied by Shoghi Efendi.(33)   How quickly the Cause
of God became Americanized!

In his booklet on "The Administrative Order of the
Dispensation of Baha'u'llah,"(34) Shoghi Efendi
explains the unique excellence of this Order, which
has no parallel, he says, in any other religion or
political system in the world.   Then he continues:
"An attempt, I feel, should at the present juncture
be made to explain the character and function of the
twin pillars that support this mighty Administrative
Structure - the Institution of the Guardianship and
the Universal House of Justice.....two fundamental
organs of the Will of Abdu'l-Baha.....These twin
institutions should be regarded as divine in origin,
essential in their functions and complementary in
their aim and purpose.   Their common, their fundamental object is to insure the continuity of that
divinely-appointed authority which flows from the
Source of our Faith....Acting in conjunction with
each other these two inseparable institutions administer its affairs.....and are permanently and fundamentally united in their aims."

He then proceeds to explain the essential nature
of both Guardianship and House of Justice. "Divorced
from the institution of the Guardianship, he says,
"the World Order of Baha'u'llah would be mutilated
and permanently deprived of that hereditary principle
.....which has been invariably upheld by the Law of
God.....Without such an institution the integrity of
the Faith would be imperilled."(35) All that Shoghi
Efendi says in this connection is in full accord with
the provisions in the Will of Abdu'l-Baha which
insure that the Guardianship shall be continued in
his family to future generations, and he quotes the
Will to substantiate his statements.

Next he shows the importance of the House of Justice. "Severed from the no less essential Universal
House of Justice," he says, "this same System of the
Will of Abdu'l-Baha would be paralyzed in its action
and would be powerless to fill in those gaps which
the Author of the *Kitab-i-Aqdas* has deliberately left
in the body of his legislative and administrative
ordinance." And he quotes the command of Abdu'l-Baha
that everyone must turn to the *Kitab-i-Aqdas*, and
matters not provided for in it must be referred to
the Universal House of Justice,(36) of which the
Guardian is to be the permanent head and distinguished
member for life.(37)

"From these statements," continues Shoghi Efendi,
"it is made indubitably clear and evident that the
Guardian of the Faith has been made the Interpreter
of the Word, and that the Universal House of Justice
has been invested with the function of legislating on
matters not expressly revealed in the teachings."(38)
Then the Guardian modestly disclaims equality with his
famous grandfather, the Center of the Covenant. Though
he insists that the Guardianship and the Universal
House of Justice are "twin" institutions, both essential in the Baha'i Cause, it is noteworthy that the
Guardian for thirty-six years guided the Cause without
the cooperation of the Universal House of Justice, since
no such House was established during his lifetime. However Shoghi Efenti appointed a number of persons from
different countries to be "Pillars of the Cause of God,"

and "Heralds of the Covenant," to assist him in his
work. In the *Baha'i World 1928-1930* he states that
of these, 19 were in Iran and 19 in Europe and
America.(39)

In 1926 the American Baha'i community adopted a
National Constitution, which became the model for the
other National Assemblies. A "Trust" was adopted and
legally incorporated under the name, "The National
Spiritual Assembly of the United States and Canada."
By-Laws also were adopted, with regulations for membership, officers, elections, etc., which were later
translated into other languages and used by Baha'is
in other countries. After this incorporation of both
National and Local Assemblies, it became possible for
the Baha'i Cause to hold properties and receive gifts
and endowments. The "Declaration of Trust," the "By-
Laws of the National Spiritual Assembly," as well as
letters from the Guardian regarding this formal organization of the Cause may be read in the *Baha'i World
1926-1928*.(40)

Having now acquired a legal status, it became
necessary to define membership in the Baha'i Cause.
Who is a Baha'i? Abdu'l-Baha in one of his addresses
in the United States was quoted as saying that "when
Christians act in accordance with the teachings of
Christ, they are called Baha'is."(41) Clearly this
definition would be inadequate for determining who
might vote and hold office in the new organization.
Concerning this important matter Shoghi Efendi wrote
as follows on October 24, 1925:(42) "Regarding the
very delicate and complex question of ascertaining
the qualifications of a true believer, I cannot in
this connection emphasize too strongly the supreme
necessity for the exercise of the utmost discretion,
caution and tact.....I would only venture to state
very briefly.....the principal factors that must be
taken into consideration before deciding whether a
person may be regarded a true believer or not. Full
recognition of the station of the Forerunner [Bab],
the Author [Baha'u'llah], and the True Exemplar of the
Baha'i Cause as set forth in Abdu'l-Baha's *Testament*
[Will]; unreserved acceptance of, and submission to

whatsoever has been revealed by their Pen; loyal and
steadfast adherance to every clause of our Beloved's
sacred *Will*; and close association with the spirit as
well as the form of the present-day Baha'i Administration throughout the world - these, I conceive, to be
the fundamental and primary considerations that must
be fairly, discreetly and thoughtfully ascertained
before reaching such a vital decision."

It might have been helpful to the American Baha'is
who did not know Arabic and Persian if the Guardian
had explained how they could honestly promise "unreserved acceptance of and submission to whatsoever has
been revealed" by the pens of the Bab and Baha'u'llah
and Abdu'l-Baha, when according to his own statement
(43) most of the writings of the Bab have been lost,
and those that remain are not accessible, and even the
Arabic *Kitab-i-Aqdas* of Baha'u'llah, to which so much
importance was attached, had not at that time been
translated and published by Baha'is in other languages.
However, the American believers, without question or
comment, incorporated this statement from the infallible Guardian in their By-Laws.(44)   Undeterred, it
seems, by this question of honesty, 2584 persons in
the United States Census of 1936 declared themselves
as Baha'is.

While busy with affairs in other lands, the Guardian was also interested in establishing adequate
facilities for the Cause in Haifa. Near the Mausoleum
of the Bab and Abdu'l-Baha two "International Archives"
were provided in which "priceless treasures" were
deposited and displayed to visiting pilgrims. "These
included portraits of both the Bab and Baha'u'llah;
personal relics such as the hair, the dust and garments of the Bab; the locks and blood of Baha'u'llah
...His watch and His Qur'an; manuscripts and Tablets
of inestimable value....the Persian Bayan...." There
on Mt. Carmel, says Shoghi Efendi, will eventually be
established "that permanent world Administrative
Center of the future Baha'i Commonwealth."(45)

Early in the Guardianship of Shoghi Efendi in the
year 1925 an event occurred in Egypt which doubtless

to the Baha'is concerned seemed a tragedy, but which
in the eyes of the Guardian was a great blessing to
the Cause. For a half-century Baha'is had been residing in Egypt, but they had apparently been so successful in concealing their faith that the Muslims of
Egypt had not realized that they followed a faith
different from Islam. At last, however, in a village
where some Muslims had become Baha'is, the Muslim
clergy pronounced them apostates, and in accordance
with Islamic law, decreed that their Muslim wives must
be taken from them. The case was finally referred to
the highest religious authorities in Cairo, where the
decision of the lower court was upheld, the marriages
were annulled, and the converts to Baha'ism were condemned as heretics. The verdict was as follows:(46)
"The Baha'i Faith is a new religion, entirely independent, with beliefs, principles and laws of its own,
which differ from, and are therefore in conflict with,
the beliefs, principles and laws of Islam. No Baha'i,
therefore, can be regarded a Muslim or vice-versa."
It seems that the death penalty for the crime of
apostacy was not pronounced against them, and it was
decreed that if they repented and returned to Islam
their wives would be restored to them. It is not
known whether or not they did so.

The result of this event was that in Egypt and in
some other lands, Baha'is attempted to gain recognition from their respective governments as members of
an independent religion. In Egypt, then under British
rule, they achieved considerable though not complete
independence. In Palestine, also under the British,
they were even more successful. In Western countries
it was not difficult to gain official recognition.
But in Iran, where most of the Baha'is resided, no
recognition was granted them, and they were officially
considered to be Muslims, though a limited amount of
tolerance was shown to them. It seems that Shoghi
Efendi had become strongly opposed to his followers
having a dual religious affiliation, and he began to
urge all of them in all lands to avoid all dissembling
of their faith, and as far as possible live according
to the laws of the *Kitab-i-Aqdas*, to sever their connections with their former religions, and openly
profess their Baha'i faith.

In *Baha'i News* of July 1935 the Guardian wrote as
follows: "Concerning membership in non-Baha'i religious associations, the Guardian wishes to re-emphasize
the general principle already laid down.....that no
Baha'i who wishes to be a whole-hearted, sincere up-
holder of the distinguishing principles of the Cause
can accept full membership in any non-Baha'i ecclesiastical organization....During the days of the Master
[Abdu'l-Baha] the Cause was still in a stage that made
such an open and sharp dissociation between it and
other religious organizations, and particularly the
Muslim Faith, not only inadvisable but practically
impossible to establish. But since his passing events
throughout the Baha'i world....have developed to a
point that has made such an assertion of the independence of the Cause not only highly desirable but
absolutely essential."

This command undoubtedly disturbed the believers in
Muslim lands where such open profession would result
in persecution, and also surprised some friends in the
West who thought they could adopt Baha'i principles
while maintaining membership in their churches. For
instance, Mr. Mountfort Mills, an outstanding leader,
who drafted the Baha'i Declaration of Trust and By-
Laws, was Senior Warden of the Protestant Episcopal
Church of St. Mark in New York, and, according to a
report in the *New York Times*, in 1925 arranged a presentation of Baha'ism in his church, and himself stated
that one could become a Baha'i and still remain a Christian, Muslim or Jew. It is not known what Mr. Mills
did in regard to his dual affiliation after receiving
orders from Haifa.(47) However, according to Shoghi
Efendi,(48) the loyal believers in East and West responded and "through the severance of all ties of
affiliation with, and membership in, ecclesiastical
institutions of whatever denomination....have arisen
to proclaim with one voice the independent character
of the religion of Baha'u'llah."

To the eyes of Shoghi Efendi the black cloud of
Muslim opposition which had darkened the sky for the
Baha'is in Egypt had a silver lining, but in some
other lands opposition to the Cause arose which

brought little blessing to the believers. In Iraq the
Baha'is had kept possession of the house in which
Baha'u'llah had lived during most of the time he was
in Baghdad, and this holy site had become a place of
pilgrimage. However, the Muslims of Iraq, acting no
doubt on the assumption that the Baha'is were apostates, and that according to Muslim law their property
could be taken from them, seized and refused to give
up the house. Fortunately for the Baha'is, Iraq had
become a British Mandate, and they were able to appeal
their case from one court to another, till it was
finally brought in 1928 to the League of Nations. The
decision was favorable to the Baha'is, and the case
received considerable publicity, for which the Baha'is
were grateful. But before the house was returned to
them, the British Mandate terminated, and Iraq became
a member of the League of Nations, and the Baha'is
never got possession of their holy place.(49)

Likewise, the first *Mashriqu'l-Adhkar* to be built
by Baha'is, which was located in Russian Turkistan,
was taken from them by the Soviet government in 1938,
and converted into an art gallery. The community of
believers was scattered, some having been imprisoned
or exiled, and the majority were deported to Iran,
their native land.(50) In Germany during the Nazi
regime "the public teaching of the Faith, with its
unconcealed emphasis on peace and universality, and
its repudiation of racism," writes Shoghi Efendi,(51)
"was officially forbidden; Baha'i Assemblies and their
committees were dissolved....and the publication of
all Baha'i literature was suspended."

In addition to these attacks from without, the Baha'i
Cause continued to suffer from internal dissension and
defection of some of its influential members. An American by the name of Mrs. Ruth White, who had met Abdu'l-
Baha in Boston in 1912, and who twice visited him
shortly before his death in Haifa, became an enthusiastic admirer and disciple of the Master. When he
died in November, 1921, a cable signed by the sister
of Abdu'l-Baha was received in America in January, 1922,
stating that Shoghi Efendi had been appointed in the
Will as "Guardian of the Cause and Head of the House

of Justice." This news came to Mrs. White and others
in America "like a thunder bolt out of a blue sky,"
for they had never heard Abdu'l-Baha say anything
about appointing a successor. After four weeks a
typed copy of the Will was received in America, undated and unsigned. As Mrs. White studied this document she eventually came to realize that it contained
laws which, in her opinion, would change completely
the Baha'i teaching. Of these she mentions the
following:(52)

"First, the appointment of a continual line of
successors or popes for a thousand years who are to
control man's conscience....Second, these successors
are to be supreme dictators over the House of Justice
....Thirdly, the taxes....which were to be paid to
the House of Justice are to be paid to Shoghi Efendi.
Fourthly, there was to be no organization of the
religion itself, and no paid officials or priestcraft, yet despite this the Baha'is, at the dictation
of Shoghi Efendi, have incorporated the Baha'i Religion and are trying to control it through a more
bigoted priestcraft than almost any other in existence."

As time passed Mrs. White became convinced that
this alleged Will could not be authentic. She therefore requested Mr. Holley and Mr. Mills, the chief
men in the American Baha'i Administration, to submit
a photographic copy of the Persian original to an
expert and get his opinion. They did not do this.
So Mrs. White herself, at great personal expense and
trouble, went to England in 1928 and succeeded in
acquiring a photographic copy of the Will, and gave
it to a recognized expert to examine. While in
England she discovered that there "the administration
of Shoghi Efendi has brought chaos to the Baha'i
Cause. Lady Bloomfield(53).....said there was practically no longer a Baha'i Cause in England."(54) The
handwriting expert for the British Museum, Dr. C.
Ainsworth Mitchell, after long and careful study, on
June 3, 1930 wrote a detailed report to Mrs. White,
in which he stated: "A minute comparison of the
authenticated writing [of Abdu'l-Baha] with the writing on every page of the alleged will....has failed

to detect in any part of the will the characteristics
of the writing of Abdul Baha."(55)   In four of her
books and pamphlets(56) Mrs. White professed complete
devotion to Abdu'l-Baha, but brought a most scathing
indictment against his grandson and the Baha'i Administration.   Later, however, it seems that Mrs. White
transferred her devotion from Abdu'l-Baha to a man in
India named Mehr Baba, who had a considerable following as a result of maintaining unbroken silence since
the year 1925, and in 1957 she wrote enthusiastically
about visiting her new hero.   It is reported that in
1969 Mrs. White, at the age of 100 went to India "to
take Mehr Baba's Daushan."(57)

Regarding Mrs. White's efforts to prove that the
Will was a forgery, Shoghi Efendi wrote as follows:
(58) "The agitation provoked by a deluded woman who
strove diligently both in the United States and in
England to demonstrate the unauthenticity of the
Charter....and even to induce the civil authorities
of Palestine to take legal action in the matter - a
request which to her great chagrin was curtly refused
- as well as the defection of one of the earliest
pioneers and founders of the Faith in Germany whom
that same woman had so tragically misled,(59) produced no effect whatsoever."   It is evident that whatever the merits of the case were, the civil authorities of Palestine would be unable to take any action
on a Will which had not been probated.   Accordingly,
the Baha'i Administration, unwilling to submit the
Will for a probate, and unhappy that anyone should
undertake an "independent investigation of truth" as
to the authenticity of the Will, did nothing but
denounce the investigator and ignore her charges.

While some like Mrs. White had their doubts as to
the authenticity of the Will, there were others who
accepted the Will as authentic, but were unhappy about
the way in which the Guardian used the authority which
the Will had bestowed upon him.   Among these were two
devoted Baha'is, one an American and the other an
Iranian.   As their story is instructive it will be
told in some detail.

When Abdu'l-Baha in 1919 sent to America the Tablets containing the "Divine Plan," the man to whom he
entrusted them was Mirza Ahmad Sohrab, who had himself
written the Tablets at the Master's dictation.(60)
Sohrab was born of a Baha'i family in Isfahan, Iran,
was educated in Teheran and Egypt, was intimate with
Abdu'l-Baha and his friends in Haifa, and was instructed in the Baha'i Faith by Mirza Abu'l-Fazl, foremost
among the Baha'i teachers and writers.(61) When the
latter went to America for missionary work Sohrab
accompanied him, being sent on this mission by Abdu'l-
Baha as the interpreter. Some years prior to this
mission, when Mirza Abu'l-Fazl was in Iran, he was
arrested and imprisoned in Teheran on the charge of
being a "Babi." When he was interrogated by the
officials he denied that he was a Babi, and called
down God's curse on them and their chief.(62) In
spite of this he was trusted by Abdu'l-Baha and held
in high honor by the Baha'is, and the American tour
was a great success.

In 1912 when Abdu'l-Baha himself made a tour of
America, Sohrab was one of those who accompanied him
everywhere he went. His picture may be seen in the
Baha'i World 1926-1928, p. 150, as he was engaged in
writing down the words of his Master. He returned
with Abdu'l-Baha to Haifa, and was with him there till
1919, when he returned to America to travel with
Fazel, another Iranian Baha'i missionary. Thus
Sohrab met many people and became widely known as a
Baha'i leader.(63) When Abdu'l-Baha died in 1921
Sohrab's financial support ceased, and he supported
himself by lecturing and writing in California.

When in New York on a visit in 1927, Mirza Ahmad
Sohrab was introduced to Mrs. Lewis Stuyvesant
Chanler, a gifted and enthusiastic Baha'i, who insisted that Sohrab should come to New York and serve
the Cause there. He did so, and delivered a series
of educational lectures on Persian literature in the
home of Mr. and Mrs. Chanler. Later he gave twelve
lectures at the Baha'i Center in New York which were
largely attended. When he was not invited to deliver
more lectures at the Center, Mrs. Chanler arranged

another series which was given in a hotel salon. Later
she urged him to give the people "more spiritual food
than you are giving them." So he rather reluctantly
began speaking on the Baha'i faith on Sunday evenings.
Many Baha'is and others attended, but some of the
Baha'i leaders became unhappy because this successful
effort did not have official approval from the Spiritual Assembly.(64)

The meetings were then moved to the Chanler home,
where on April 5, 1929 a group of those present decided
to form what they called "The New History Society," for
the purpose of furthering the Baha'i Cause, which they
felt was making no progress whatever. This decision
brought down on them the wrath of the Baha'i Administration, which accused them of causing division, and
soon the Guardian began writing frequent letters to
Mrs. Chanler about this effort. Shoghi Efendi knew
Sohrab well, as they had been close friends in Haifa
before he became Guardian. But now the situation had
changed. Shoghi Efendi had given his hearty approval
to the organization set up in America by the able and
tireless leaders Horace Holley, who acted as Secretary
of the National Spiritual Assembly for many years, and
his devoted coworker Mountfort Mills. Exercising his
unlimited authority as Guardian, he had bestowed great
authority under him to the National Spiritual Assembly
of the U.S.A. and Canada.(65) Any insubordination to
this body, therefore, must be interpreted as opposition to him, and had not Abdu'l-Baha said in his Will,
"Whoso opposeth him [Shoghi Efendi] hath opposed God?"
The Guardian, therefore, was not at all happy that
another man from Iran, older than he, who had been
with Abdu'l-Baha more than he, and who probably knew
more than he about the Baha'i Faith, and who had many
more personal acquaintances among the Baha'is of
America and their friends than he had, should carry
on an independent and successful missionary campaign
in New York.

To protect Sohrab, Mrs. Chanler took full responsibility for all that was being done. She gave the
Guardian frequent reports of their activities, and he
at first expressed "keen appreciation." "Your manifold

services," he wrote,(66) "are truly worthy of praise
and admiration." Mrs. Chanler begged him to support
her in the independent efforts she and Sohrab were
making to advance the Baha'i Cause. But when the
National Spiritual Assembly informed all Baha'is that
"the activities conducted by Ahmad Sohrab through the
New History Society are to be considered as entirely
independent of the Cause....and hence in no wise
entitled to the cooperation of Baha'is....," the
Guardian approved their action.(67) In this way in
the year 1930 Mirza Ahmad Sohrab and Mrs. Julie Chanler
were excommunicated. In all the correspondence Mrs.
Chanler demonstrated remarkable restraint and a spirit
of love toward those who opposed her. She did not
allow these disappointments to dampen her ardor, for
under her direction and that of Sohrab the work of the
New History Society was expanded. Meetings were
arranged at which outstanding speakers discussed
world problems, Prize Competitions were conducted for
young people on such topics as world peace, world
religion, etc., books and pamphlets were published in
a number of languages, a monthly magazine was published in English, and an organization named "The Caravan"
was established to unite young people in different
countries, and various other methods were used to get
the Bahai Message to the peoples of the world.

In November, 1939 they opened the "Bahai Bookshop"
in New York. A month later they were informed by a
law firm representing the Spiritual Assembly of the
Baha'is of New York that it was illegal for them to
use the term "Bahai,"(68) which had been registered
by the National Spiritual Assembly of Baha'is in the
U.S. Patent Office, No. 245,271, as a trade mark, and
therefore their use of the name for the Bahai Bookshop
"constitutes trade mark infringement."(69) Mrs.
Chanler employed a lawyer, who attempted to explain
that she was a Baha'i and was working for the Baha'i
Cause, and therefore was entitled to use this name for
the Bookshop. However, the Spiritual Assembly brought
suit against her, and on January 23 Shoghi Efendi gave
the Assembly his encouragement and blessing by sending
a cable: "Praying victory....be achieved over the
insidious adversaries...."(70)

Fifteen months passed. Then on April 1, 1941 a
message was delivered to Mrs. Chanler and Mirza Ahmad
Sohrab which caused them to weep for joy. They had
won their case! And they considered this a victory
not alone for themselves but also for the cause of
religious liberty in America. The opinion of the
Supreme Court of New York was that "the complaint
failed to state a good cause of action. The plaintiffs
have no right to a monopoly of the name of a religion.
The defendants, who purport to be members of the same
religion, have an equal right to use the name of the
religion in connection with their own meetings,
lectures, classes and other activities." The Spiritual Assembly appealed the case, but lost again.
Naturally they were unhappy over the outcome of the
suit, and the Guardian was more than unhappy when he
wrote thus about his old friend Mirza Ahmad Sohrab:(71)
"He is no doubt the most subtle, resourceful and inde-
fatigable enemy the faith has had in America...Obscure
in his origin, ambitious of leadership....odious in
the hopes he nurses, contemptable in the methods he
pursues, shameless in his deliberate distortions of
truth he has long since ceased to believe in, he....
cannot but in the end be subjected, as remorselessly
as his infamous predecessors, to the fate which they
invariably have suffered."

Sohrab stated that after his excommunication he had
for eleven years kept silence, but that this law suit
had finally impelled him to speak out. So he wrote
and published the book *Broken Silence*, from which we
have been quoting. The book is a denunciation of what
Sohrab considered to be the totalitarian spirit and
methods of the Baha'i Administration. He maintains
that he is a true Bahai, believing in Baha'u'llah and
Abdu'l-Baha, and he insists that the Will of Abdu'l-
Baha is valid, but says it has been overemphasized
while other important pronouncements of Abdu'l-Baha
have been neglected.(72) He accepts the appointment
of Shoghi Efendi as Guardian, but insists that Shoghi
has been despotic in the use of his authority. He
feels strongly that the American Baha'i leaders, in
forcing the Baha'i Cause into the strait jacket of
Trust and By-Laws, have killed its spirit. To Sohrab

the Baha'i Cause means freedom, love, joy, service.
"What is a Bahai?" he asks.(73)   "A Bahai is a torch
in the darkness, a joy for grief, a sea for the thirsty,
a refuge for the unfortunate, an arm for the oppressed."

In his denunciation of the Administration, Sohrab
quotes the saying of Abdu'l-Baha:(73) "You cannot
organize the Bahai Movement. The Bahai Movement is the
spirit of the age. It is the essence of all the highest ideals of the century. The Bahai Cause is an
inclusive Movement. The teachings of all religions
and societies are found here." It is Sohrab's belief
that the Cause should be open to *all*, no matter what
their creed may be. It includes, he contends, and
brings together people of all religions, and is not
itself a new religion. It is "a golden thread on
which the spiritual jewels of all religions were to
be strung."(74) He, therefore, strongly opposes the
requirements for membership as stated in the By-Laws
of the National Spiritual Assembly, and the provision
that a Baha'i must sever his connection with his
former religion.(75) He is likewise opposed to the
order of the National Spiritial Assembly that Baha'is
should not vote in political elections in which two
or more candidates were competing for office, and
should not hold any political office, which if obeyed
would completely isolate believers, and prevent them
from performing their duties as citizens.(76) Also he
sternly rejects the right of Shoghi Efendi to excom-
municate believers.(77) And he protests the censor-
ship which was established by Shoghi Efendi in 1922,
when he wrote:(78) "Not only with regard to publication, but all other matters without any exception
whatsoever, regarding the interest of the Cause in
that locality, individually or collectively, should
be referred exclusively to the Spiritual Assembly....
which shall decide upon it." This edict, says Sohrab,
brought to an end for Bahais all freedom of speech and
of the press, and made impossible the "Independent
Investigation of Truth," one of the most important of
the Principles of the Faith.

In 1954 a friend called to the attention of Mirza
Ahmad Sohrab the fact that "in the presence of Baha's

Will and Testament, Abbas Efendi's Will and Testament
appointing Shoghi Efendi as guardian was null and
void." Sohrab in reply admitted that the Will of
Abdu'l-Baha was in fact invalid, but added that he
could not bring himself to denounce it in public, as
such a move on his part was bound to ruin the business
of the Caravan (New History Society).(79) So it
appears that even after his declaration of independence
from the Baha'i Administration, Sohrab was unwilling to
profess and follow the truth which he through independent investigation had discovered. Had he been willing
to proceed further in pursuit of truth, he would have
also admitted that it was indeed the purpose of both
the Bab and Baha'u'llah to establish new religions,
which would take the place of all former religions,
(80) and that Shoghi Efendi was following their lead
when he insisted that Baha'is sever their connections
with synagogues, churches and mosques.(81)

The opposition of Sohrab to the Administration was
in part the rebellion of a poetic Iranian against the
organization of his Faith by Americans, but it was
chiefly a power struggle between two ambitious men.
Shoghi Efendi could not tolerate the presence in the
leadership of the Cause in America, from which much
of his support came, of an able and popular missionary
like Sohrab, and so he used the National Spiritual
Assembly as a facade to eliminate him. It is not
known how many devoted believers like the Chanlers
were lost to the Guardian by this unfortunate conflict.
The majority, however, were loyal to him, and believed
that his rule at the head of the Administrative Order
was essential to the Baha'i Cause.

Thus Shoghi Efendi, supported by the Will of his
grandfather, with the able and zealous assistance of
the American believers, in spite of many difficulties,
succeeded in establishing the Baha'i Administrative
Order, of which he was the Head.

Stanwood Cobb writing in *World Order* (82) takes the
reader to the year 2001 A.D. and shows him the world
as it will have been reconstructed by that time according to the Baha'i plan, a wonderful Utopia, in which

there is no war, no poverty, no illiteracy, and no religious division. "The apex and keystone of this world structure," he writes, "is the institution of the Guardianship established by Baha'u'llah as the focal point around which the world's thought and action revolve, creating a functional unity unassailable by the disruptive quality.....Permeating universally the ordering and functioning of this new [Baha'i] government is the practice of collective turning to the Divine Ruler of the Universe [the Guardian] for guidance in the solution of all the difficult legislative and administrative problems."

NOTES

1. *God Passes By*, Shoghi Effendi, Baha'i Publishing Company 1965, p. 324.

2. *Baha'i World 1926-1928*, Vol. II, pp. 81, 82, 84.

3. *Azal's Notes*, p. 312.

4. *Aqdas*, p. 74.

5. The surname of the father of Shoghi Effendi was Afnan. To distinguish his offspring from those of another son-in-law with the same surname, it is said that Abdu'l-Baha gave to them the surname Rabbani (Divine), and hence Shoghi and his brothers used this as their family name. However, after becoming Guardian Shoghi largely gave up the use of Rabbani, and signed his name "Shoghi Effendi," which was equivalent to "Mr. Shoghi." His followers always addressed him by this name. See *Azal's Notes*, pp. 730, 731.

6. This is presumably the body provided for in the Will of Abdu'l-Baha, where he commanded: "The Hands of the Cause of God must elect from their own number nine persons that shall at all times be occupied in the important services in the work of the guardian of the Cause of God" (*Baha'i World*, Vol. II, p. 85).

7. See Chapter VIII.

8. See Chapter IX.

9. *Azal's Notes*, p. 45.

10. See Chapter IX.

11. *Azal's Notes*, p. 45.

12. Mirza Muhammad Ali died in Haifa in 1930 (*Azal's Notes*, p. 40).

13. *Aqdas*, pp. 50, 51.

14. *Azal's Notes*, p. 316.

15. Ibid., pp. 50, 51.

16. *Will and Testament of Abdu'l-Baha*, Lancaster, Penna., p. 15.

17. *Azal's Notes*, p. 52.

18. Ibid., p. 46.

19. *Baha'i World 1926-1928*, Vol. II, p. 85.

20. *Azal's Notes*, p. 47.

21. Ibid., pp. 440-442.

22. Ibid., pp. 53, 98, 340, 441-443, 680. One well acquainted with the situation has stated that the chief cause of these unhappy family divisions was "the love of money."

23. Ibid., p. 680.

24. Ibid., pp. 91, 92, *God Passes By*, p. 356.

25. *Azal's Notes*, pp. 92, 93.

26. Ibid., pp. 341, 342, *God Passes By*, p. 356.

27. *Aqdas*, p. 31.

28. *God Passes By*, p. 331.

29. *Baha'i World 1926-1928*, Vol. II, pp. 182-185.

30. The U.S. Census of 1926 gives the number of Baha'i Assemblies in the U.S.A. as 44, and the number of Baha'is as 1247.

31. *God Passes By*, p. 332.

32. *Baha'i World 1926-1928*, Vol. II, p. 181.

33. *God Passes By*, p. 334.

34. Written in 1934, published by Baha'i Publishing Trust, sixth printing 1960, pp. 5-6.

35. *Administrative Order*, p. 6.

36. *Baha'i World 1926-1928*, Vol. II, p. 87.

37. Ibid., p. 87.

38. *Administrative Order*, p. 8.

39. *Baha'i World*, Vol. III, pp. 80, 81, 84, 85.

40. *Baha'i World*, Vol. II, pp. 89-107, *God Passes By*, pp. 335-337.

41. *Scriptures*, p. 382.

42. *Baha'i World 1926-1928*, Vol. II, p. 106.

43. *Dawn-Breakers*, Shoghi Effendi, American edition, p. 655, *Azal's Notes*, pp. 329, 330.

44. *Baha'i World 1926-1928*, Vol. II, p. 93.

45. *God Passes By*, pp. 347, 348.

46. Ibid., p. 365.

47. Later, for some unknown reason, Shoghi Effendi excommunicated Mr. Mills. When word reached Haifa of the death of Mills in April 1949, the Guardian cabled Wilmette to forbid all American Baha'is from attending his funeral and from honoring his memory in any way (Letter to author from Mr. Will Orick, May 21, 1969).

48. *God Passes By*, p. 374.

49. Ibid., pp. 356-360.

50. Ibid., p. 361.

51. Ibid., p. 362.

52. *The Bahai Religion and its Enemy the Bahai Organization*, by Ruth White, The Tuttle Company, Rutland, Vermont 1929.

53. Author of *The Chosen Highway*, Baha'i Publishing Trust.

54. *Abdul Baha and the Promised Age*, by Ruth White, 1927, Appendix, p. 17.

55. *Abdul Baha's Alleged Will is Fraudulent*, by Ruth White, 1930, p. 16.

56. Some years later Mrs. White wrote yet another book, *Bahai Leads Out of the Labyrinth*, 1944, which is similar to *Abdul Baha and the Promised Age*.

57. Letter from Mollie Lux, Mehr Spiritual Center, Myrtle Beach, S.C., to J. Anthony Sistrom. It is reported that Mehr Baba died in 1969.

58. *God Passes By*, p. 362.

59. Mr. Hermann Zinner, one of the pioneers of the Baha'i Faith in Germany, proved his devotion to the Cause by going at his own expense, and at the risk of his life, to Berlin during World War II, in an attempt to have the ban on Baha'is removed, but he did not succeed. He has stated that his friend Mr. Wilhelm Herrigel, also one of the Baha'i pioneers in Germany, was *not* "misled" by Mrs. White, as Shoghi Effendi stated, but came to the same conclusion by independent study of the evidence, and as a result, formed the "Free Baha'is" with a number of members who rebelled against the Guardian and the Baha'i Organization. Mr. Zimmer also is opposed to what he calls "Baha'i totalitarianism," and has written extensively against it. (Letters from Mr. Zimmer to J. Anthony Sistrom).

60. *Broken Silence*, Mirza Ahmad Sohrab, Universal Publishing Co., New York 1942 (608 pages), pp. 298, 299.

61. Ibid., pp. 37, 320, *Baha'u'llah and the New Era*, Esselmont, first edition, p. 229, *Payam-i-Padar*, Subhi, p. 188, *Baha'i World 1926-1928*, Vol. II, p. 48.

62. *Broken Silence*, p. 302, *Azal's Notes*, p. 440, *Payam-i-Padar*, pp. 50-52 (where the interrogation is reproduced).

63. *Broken Silence*, pp. 41, 55, 56.

64. Ibid., pp. 63-67.

65. Ibid., p. 322.

66. Ibid., p. 81.

67. Ibid., pp. 104, 107, 113.

68. Sohrab spelt the name of his faith *Bahai*.

69. *Broken Silence*, pp. 126, 127.

70. Ibid., p. 135.

71. Ibid., pp. 424, 253 (*Baha'i News*, July and October, 1941).

72. Ibid., pp. 26, 47, 49, 422.

73. Ibid., p. 141.

74. Ibid., pp. 150, 275, 277.

75. Ibid., pp. 324, 325.

76. Ibid., pp. 325, 485-512.

77. Ibid., p. 448.

78. Ibid., pp. 388, 391, *Baha'i Administration*, pp. 23, 24.

79. *Azal's Notes*, p. 56.

80. It seems that Sohrab believed there were two Manifestations at the same time, the Bab, a Manifestation of God for Islam, and Baha'u'llah, a Manifestation of God for the whole world. This belief was totally at variance with the teachings of both the Bab and Baha'u'llah, as has been explained in previous chapters. See *The Caravan*, Vol. XXVI, No. 4, October 1960.

81. Mirza Ahmad Sohrab died on April 20, 1958 in New York, and is buried in the churchyard of St. Paul's at Glen Cove, Long Island. The New York *Herald Tribune* of March 12, 1961 reports the death of Mrs. Chanler on March 11, 1961.

82. *World Order*, April 1937.

13

The Guardianship of Shoghi Efendi: Losses and Gains

While in America Sohrab and Mrs. Chanler and their
companions in the Caravan went their own way, devoted
to the Bahai Cause, but rejected by the Baha'i
Administration.   There were in Iran several former
leaders in the Cause who not only repudiated the
Administration,   there were in Iran several former
whole Babi-Baha'i Movement, and who wrote and published books in Iran, telling in detail why they had
defected.   One of these defectors was a man named
H. Niku, who was for fourteen years a Baha'i, and
became one of the leading missionaries of the Cause.
His picture is to be seen in the *Baha'i World 1926-
1928*,(1) seated in the midst of a group of Burman
Baha'is.   He said that even after he had given up the
Baha'i faith, the Baha'is of Teheran continued to
claim him as one of themselves, and he was forced to
write several volumes in Persian entitled "The
Philosophy of Niku," to prove that he had left the
movement.   In an able and interesting manner Niku
described the things which he had seen and heard
which disillusioned him, such as the worldly ambition
of Abdu'l-Baha, his greed for money, and his flattering epistles to great and wealthy people whom he
hoped to win as disciples.   He gave a list of all

the places in the world where there were Baha'is, and estimated that the number of men was 5207.(2)

Another man who deserted the Cause was Ayati, to whom Abdu'l-Baha had given the name Avareh (Wanderer). For twenty-one years he was a Baha'i; he was appointed one of the Hands of the Cause, and was chosen by Abdu'l-Baha for a certain very important mission.(3) He became one of the outstanding writers and missionaries of the Movement, and was greatly revered by the Baha'is. Abdu'l-Baha commissioned him to write the official history of the Babi-Baha'i Movement, which he did in Persian.(4) He is referred to by the famous Baha'i writer Dr. Esselmont as "the learned Persian historian of the Baha'i Movement," to whom he is "greatly indebted," and whom he quotes as an authority.(5) Avareh served Shoghi Efendi for a number of years, and was sent by him to Europe to make converts, but on his return he left the Movement.(6) After coming back to Iran he was excommunicated by the Guardian. He then wrote a book in Persian in three volumes entitled *Kashfu'l-Hiyal* (The Exposure of Deception), in which he related how he had become a Baha'i, and why he had defected. He said that before he left Iran he had been told that there were millions of Baha'is in Europe and America, and he believed it.(7) Later when he went to Akka he began to discover the fraud and corruption which existed there at the center of the Cause, and his faith began to waver. He said that when he wrote the history of the Movement, Abdu'l-Baha forced him to misrepresent the facts, insisting that there should be no discrepancy between this new history and *A Traveller's Narrative* (written by Abdu'l-Baha), and that it should not conform to the *Nuqtatu'l-Kaf* of Mirza Jani. After he had defected Avareh wrote:(8) "I hereby declare that *al-Kawakib-al-Durriya* [the title of the history], of two volumes, has totally lost its character of authority." When Avareh went to Europe and failed to find the "millions of believers" of whom he had so often heard he realized how greatly they had all been deceived. It was probably to Avareh that Shoghi Efendi referred when he wrote:(9) "The volumes which a shameless apostate composed and disseminated.....in

his brazen efforts, not only to disrupt that Order but
to undermine the very Faith which had conceived it,
proved....abortive."

   A third Iranian Baha'i leader to desert the Cause
was Mirza Subhi, a member of a Baha'i family, and a
relative of the third wife of Baha'u'llah. He was for
a number of years the Persian amanuensis of Abdu'l-Baha,
and was intimately acquainted with all members of his
family, including Shoghi Efendi before he became Guardian. Later he was sent to Iran for missionary work,
but there he began to show a lack of zeal in the service of the Cause, and was excommunicated by Shoghi
Efendi.(9) As a result, Subhi was unable to find
employment in Teheran, for Muslims rejected him as a
Baha'i agent, and Baha'is rejected him as an apostate
from their faith. It was then that a friend found a
position for him in a Christian mission school, saving
him from dire need. Later he became a famous teller
of stories for children on the Teheran Radio.

   Subhi wrote two books in Persian explaining why he
had given up the Baha'i religion. In the second
volume entitled *Payam-i-Padar* (A Father's Message),
"acts and deeds of Shoghi Efendi....are brought into
bold relief in a manner far from flattering to Shoghi
Efendi."(10) When a friend once invited Subhi to
become a Christian, he replied: "We who have left
Baha'ism are like people who had been invited to a
great feast, and had been promised all sorts of deli-
cious foods, and had been seated at a table loaded
with many big dishes and platters, all covered - but
when the lids were taken off, the dishes were found
to be empty. We were promised the finest of spiritual
foods in the Baha'i Faith, but we came away hungry.
It is now hard for us to believe that there is any
truth anywhere." It is probably to Subhi that Shoghi
Efendi refers when he mentions "the infamous and insidious machinations of a former secretary of Abdu'l-Baha."
(11) If these men who left the Movement were as evil
as Shoghi said they were, it is indeed strange that
they were permitted to serve the Baha'i Cause for so
long in such important positions.

The publication of the books of Niku and Avareh and Subhi one after another produced quite a stir in Iran, for they were eagerly read by Muslims and Baha'is. Soon, however, all available copies were bought up, presumably by Baha'is, to be destroyed. Numerous Baha'is as a result of reading these damaging disclosures followed the example of the defectors and gave up their Baha'i connections. It seems, however, that the majority of the Baha'is in Iran, like their Guardian, ignored the charges brought against their beloved Cause as untrue or unimportant, and failing to practice their Principle of Independent Investigation of Truth, continued for one reason or another to follow their Guide.

Like his grandfather and great-grandfather, Shoghi Efendi was a prolific writer. He wrote reams of letters to the believers in America and other lands. These letters have been published in several volumes entitled *Messages to America, Messages to the Baha'i World, Baha'i Administration*, etc.(12) An important service to the Baha'i Cause which Shoghi Efendi rendered in the field of literature was his translation into English of several books, such as the *Iqan* and the *Epistle to the Son of the Wolf* and *Hidden Words*, all by Baha'u'llah. He also translated the first part of *Nabil's Narrative*, an account of the early days of the Movement, under the title, *The Dawn Breakers*.(13) For some reason he did not translate the *Kitab-i-Aqdas*, which he called "the Mother-Book of the Baha'i Revelation," nor did he undertake the codification of the laws and ordinances contained in this basic document of Baha'i faith and government. (14)

Perhaps the most pretentious work by the pen of the Guardian was *God Passes By*, a book of more than 400 pages, which purports to be a history of the Babi-Baha'i Movement during the first century of its existance (1844-1944). This volume is a mine of information, not all of which, however, is correct. It is the fourth official Baha'i history, the first three being the *New History*, and *Traveller's Narrative*

by Abdu'l-Baha, and *Nabil's Narrative*. Nabil was one
of those Babis who in the Baghdad period claimed to
be He-Whom-God-Will-Manifest, but later withdrew his
claim and became a disciple of Baha'u'llah.(15) In
his history, Shoghi Efendi has failed to give any
documentary support whatever for his statements, perhaps on the assumption that statements of the infallible expositor of the Words of God needed no such
confirmation. The book would have been far more
valuable had the author made use of the *Nuqtatu'l-Kaf*
of Mirza Jani, and depended less on the inaccurate
accounts given by Nabil and Abdu'l-Baha. Regarding
the historical value of these various accounts, one
who knows the history well has written:(16) "By the
passage of time Baha'i accounts have assumed a cham-
eleonic character, totally divorced from truth. Simple
events and incidents are distorted and misrepresented
in the furtherance of private ends and personal ambi-
tions. The cases treated in these pages [of *God Passes
By*] are glaring examples of misrepresentations of
historical facts." It was said that Shoghi Efendi
when a student in Beirut was very fond of reading
novels, and *God Passes By* should be considered an
historical novel rather than authentic history.

In reading this book one is disappointed to find
that the Guardian of a Cause which has professed
allegiance to peace and love and world-brotherhood
and absence of any sort of prejudice should have
expressed such bitterness toward many of the members
of his own family. He refers(17) to Baha'u'llah's
second son Mirza Muhammad Ali as "the Prime Mover of
sedition," he speaks of the third and fourth sons as
"the vacillating Mirza Diya'u'llah and the treacherous
Mirza Badi'u'llah,"(18) and he calls the sons-in-law
of Baha'u'llah "infamous" and "crafty." In his
Messages also the Guardian sometimes condemned with
great severity those who differed with him. The cable
from Shoghi Efendi addressed to the Baha'is of the
United States, which was printed in *Baha'i News*, No.
256, and dated April 15, 1952, a part of which will
be quoted below, is a sample of his style. In this
Message the Guardian announced the death in Haifa of
Sayyid Ali Nayyir Afnan, a grandson of Baha'u'llah,

and husband of Shoghi's eldest sister Ruhangez. It
is said that Sayyid Ali "had a charming personality,
and associated with, and befriended, men of all walks
of life." He expressed himself strongly as being
opposed to the Guardian's policy of rejecting anyone
who did not fully agree with him, and as a result he
was himself excommunicated (*Azal's Notes*, p. 1107).
The 300-word cable begins thus:(19)

"God's Avenging Wrath

          "Inform National Assemblies (that) God's
avenging wrath....(has) now struck down....Siyyid Ali
Nayer Afnan, pivot (of) Machinations, connecting link
(between) old (and) new Covenant-breakers. This
alone (will) reveal extent (of) havoc wreaked (by)
this virus (of) violation injected, fostered over two
decades (in) Abdul Baha's family....(who) was repeatedly denounced by Center (of the) Covenant (as) his
chief enemy........."

Thus did the Guardian announce to the friends in
America the decease of his brother-in-law. Of course
in speaking thus he was only following the example of
Baha'u'llah in his denunciations of his brother Sub-i-
Azal, and of Abdu'l-Baha in his recriminatory charges
in his Will against his brother Mirza Muhammad Ali.
If these characterizations of members of the family
of Baha'u'llah were true, it would seem that the Manifestation was not particularly successful in his
training of his own children. And if they were false,
it does not speak well for the infallibility of the
Guardian.

From his writings it is evident that though Shoghi
Efendi had been appointed in Abdu'l-Baha's Will to be
the "expounder of the words of God,"(20) he had little
interest in theology. He seems to have accepted all
the doctrines handed down to him by Baha'u'llah and
Abdu'l-Baha, and to have added nothing to them. There
was one problem, however, which had faced the former
leaders of the Movement, and which the Guardian of the
Cause also, because of differences of opinion among
believers, was forced to face. This was the definition

of the Station of the Bab, and the authority of the
Bayan. Baha'u'llah, as was seen in Chapter VI, had
for the purpose of magnifying himself as a major
Manifestation, minimized the status of the Bab by
speaking of him as his forerunner,(21) in the way that
John the Baptist was the forerunner of Christ. Abdu'l-
Baha in his book *A Traveller's Narrative*, written in
1886, adopted the same attitude toward the Bab.(22)
It appears that twenty-five years later Abdu'l-Baha
had changed his mind, for in his Will he spoke of the
Bab as "the Manifestation of the Unity and Oneness of
God, and the Forerunner of the Ancient Beauty [Baha]."
(23)   What, then, was Shoghi Efendi to say about the
Bab?   In his Introduction to the *Dawn-Breakers* Shoghi
Efendi writes:(24) "As John the Baptist had been the
Herald or Gate of the Christ, so was the Bab the
Herald or Gate of Baha'u'llah." Later, however, he
was quoted as saying:(25)   "The Bab has been compared
to John the Baptist, but the station of the Bab is
not merely that of the herald or forerunner. In himself the Bab was a Manifestation of God, the founder
of an independent religion, even though that religion
was limited in time to a brief period of years. The
Baha'is believe that the Bab and Baha'u'llah were
Co-Founders of their Faith."(26)

And what did Shoghi Efendi say about the binding
character of the doctrines and laws of the Bab's
book the Bayan? Baha'u'llah had said(27) that the
Bayan had not been abrogated, that is, it was incumbent on Baha'is to accept its teachings and obey its
precepts. However, in the *Kitab-i-Aqdas* Baha'u'llah
changed a number of the laws of the Bayan.(28) Later
Abdu'l-Baha said the Bayan had been abrogated, and
asked Nicholas why he had translated this abrogated
book into French.(29)   Shoghi Efendi in this matter
disagreed with his grandfather, for in his requirements for membership in the Baha'i Faith he stipulated
that a Baha'i must profess "unreserved acceptance of,
and submission to, whatsoever has been revealed by
their Pen" (that is, the writings of the Bab, Baha'u'-
llah and Abdu'l-Baha).(30)   Hence, according to Shoghi
Efendi, the Bayan of the Bab had not been abrogated,
and believers must submit to its doctrines and laws,

even though they have never seen or been taught the
book. In these difficult matters it seems that the
Expositor of the Words of God did not greatly clarify
the Baha'i teaching.

In addition to Shoghi Efendi, the Baha'i Cause
boasted a number of gifted writers in English, among
whom were J. E. Esselmont, Horace Holley, Marzieh
Gail, Stanwood Cobb, Lady Bloomfield and George
Townshend. It is most unfortunate that these authors,
most of whom had little or no knowledge of Persian and
Arabic, were either unable or unwilling to study the
basic documents of the Babi-Baha'i Movement, and by
following blindly the accounts given by the Baha'i
leaders have misled their many readers. The result
of this is that the legendary story of the Cause has
been generally accepted as history, and anyone who
tries to relate the true history is charged with
ignorance or intentional falsification of the facts.

The key figure in the development of the Baha'i
Movement in America during the Guardianship of Shoghi
Efendi was Horace Holley, whose executive and literary
efforts were outstanding. It was he who drafted the
official "Administrative Order" of the National Spiritual Assembly of America, which became the model for
other Assemblies round the world, it was he who edited
the large volume entitled *Baha'i Scriptures*,(31) and
as Secretary of the National Spiritual Assembly from
1924 to 1955 he edited the large and informative year-
book of the Cause entitled the *Baha'i World*, and wrote
a number of the leading articles in each volume. Over
a period of thirty years, twelve volumes of the *Baha'i
World* were published by Holley, the one for 1940-1944
having 1003 pages. These volumes contain detailed
information of the progress of the Baha'i Cause throughout the world, with many pictures of groups of converts
in various countries, reprints of the Baha'i Constitution and By-Laws in a number of languages, commendations
of the Cause by the pen of numerous notables, lists of
the places where there are Assemblies or Groups of
believers, and of books and periodicals favorable to
the Cause (critical accounts are usually not listed).
Holley also wrote several books about the Faith. He
died on July 12, 1960.

One of the great achievements which brought joy to
many Baha'i hearts was the completion of the *Mashriqu'l-
Adhkar* in Wilmette, Illinois. As was related in
Chapter X, the ground for this Temple was dedicated by
Abdu'l-Baha in 1912, but the plans were large, and the
friends were few, so the task they had undertaken was
truly tremendous. Plans for a unique and beautiful
structure, pictures of which may be seen in many Baha'i
publications, were drawn by the Canadian architect
Louis J. Bourgeois. Construction began in 1920. In
1925 a three-year drive to collect $400,000 for this
building was undertaken by the National Spiritual Assembly, the plan being that each of the 1,247 Baha'is in
America(32) should contribute $9.00 a month for the
three years.(33) The superstructure was completed in
1931, and a devotional service was conducted in the
Temple on May 1, 1931, just 19 years after the dedication of the land. The beautification of the structure continued for twelve more years, and was completed
in December 1942, shortly before the celebration of the
Centenary in 1944. It had taken twenty-two and a half
years to build the Temple, the first to be erected in
the West, and the total cost was $1,342,813.09. (was
the .09 accidental?). The full story of this undertaking, with pictures of the Temple, is told in the *Baha'i
World 1940-1944* and the *Baha'i Centenary 1844-1944*,
both by the pen of Horace Holley.

Abdu'l-Baha had attached great importance to the
building of this first *Mashriqu'l-Adhkar* in the Western
World. He was quoted as saying:(34) "When that Divine
Edifice is completed, a most wonderful and thrilling
motion will appear in the world of existence.....It
marks the inception of the Kingdom of God on earth."
Realizing the urgency of the erection of this Temple,
it seems that the believers devoted most of their
gifts, apart from what they sent to the Guardian in
Haifa,(35) to its completion. According to the architect who designed this remarkable building,(34) "Into
this new design is woven, in symbolic form, the great
Baha'i teaching of unity - the unity of all religions
and of all mankind." Since its completion, untold
thousands of tourists have visited the nine-sided Temple, so different from anything else in Wilmette, and

no doubt some have been attracted by it to the Baha'i
Faith.

In preparation for the observance of the 1944
Centenary of the Movement, a "Seven Year Plan" in
true American style was adopted in 1937 by the National Spiritual Assembly, the aim of which was to make
new converts to the Cause, and to establish a Spiritual Assembly in every state and province in North
America where there had been none. This determination
was in accord with and in obedience to the command
found in the Will of Abdu'l-Baha:(36) "O ye that
stand fast in the Covenant!....It is incumbent upon....
all the friends and loved ones, one and all to bestir
themselves....to diffuse the sweet savors of God, to
teach His Cause and to promote His Faith....They must
disperse themselves in every land, pass by every clime
and travel throughout all regions....The disciples of
Christ forgot themselves and all earthly things....
scattered far and wide and engaged in calling the
peoples of the world to the divine Guidance, till at
last they made the world another world....Finally in
various lands they suffered glorious martyrdom. Let
them [Baha'is] that are men of action follow in their
footsteps!" Accordingly, there was a burst of missionary zeal in the ranks of the believers, and in seven
years the number of Assemblies in North America rose
from 70 to 124, the number of new areas being 34.
Since it was the policy of the Administration not to
report the number of members, it is not known how many
new converts were made in this period.

Not only in North America but also in other lands
an aggressive campaign for extending the Faith was
carried on under the guidance of the Guardian. The
order went out from Haifa that Baha'is should become
"pioneers," leave their homes, and go to the unoccupied
places and establish Groups (less than 9 members) which
would grow into Assemblies (more than 9). Shoghi
Efendi was for some reason especially concerned that
the pioneers go to many of the isolated islands of the
world to tell the Good News.(37) Missionaries from
North America went south, and established centers in
a number of cities in South America, and they went also

to European countries and to other lands. It seems
that growth in Great Britain was slow. In writing of
the missionary service of these pioneers of the Faith,
Shoghi Efendi says(38) that most of the activities
"have been carried out through the resourcefulness
of the members of the American Baha'i Community, who
have assumed direct responsibility for the spiritual
conquest of the vast majority of these countries....
Through such efforts as these the breezes of God's
vitalizing Revelation have been blown upon the uttermost corners of the earth."

From Iran also missionaries went forth to other
lands. It was reported(39) that a hundred new centers
had been opened by them in East Africa. In 1959 when
the author was in Asmara, Ethiopia, he met there a
Baha'i dentist from Iran who was practicing his profession and propagating his Faith, and had converted
a German doctor residing there. The doctor said that
he had gone to the dentist for treatment of a tooth,
and while he was in the chair, with his mouth open,
the dentist suddenly said to him, "Do you know that
Jesus Christ has come again?" The patient was
startled, and thought the dentist must have gone out
of his mind. But after work on his teeth had been
finished, the dentist kept him for two hours, and
told him the Good News of the coming of Baha'u'llah,
and as a result the doctor believed. "I had been a
Roman Catholic," he said, "but in medical school in
Germany I lost my faith. Now I am a believer." And
he quoted several verses from the New Testament to
demonstrate his faith. A few Ethiopians also had
gathered about the zealous missionary. Glowing reports of the labors and successes of the pioneers are
found in every volume of the *Baha'i World*.

Among the outstanding missionaries of the Cause
was Martha Root, whom Shoghi Efendi describes(40) as
"that archetype of Baha'i itinerant teachers," to
whom, he says, "must be awarded....the title of
Leading Ambassadress of His Faith and Pride of Baha'i
teachers, whether men or women, in both the East and
the West." For twenty years she travelled, circling
the earth four times, visiting China, Japan and India,

and all important cities in South America. She pro-
moted the translation and distribution of Baha'i
literature, she interviewed important people in many
lands, and is said to have converted Queen Marie of
Rumania.(41) She died while on a journey to Honolulu
in 1939. And there were others, such as Mrs. May
Maxwell, who had visited Abdu'l-Baha in Akka in 1898,
and who died when working in Argentina, and Dr. Susan
Moody (d.1934) and Miss Keith Ransom-Kehler (d.1936)
who died in Iran.(42) Whatever one may think of the
Cause for which these missionaries labored, one cannot
but admire their devotion and zeal in propagating
their Faith. However, there were some Baha'is who
felt that, since it was the boast of their Faith that
it should be spread by the voluntary efforts of believers and not by a paid "clergy," it was not in accordance with the teachings of Baha'u'llah to send out
these paid pioneers, effective though their efforts
in winning converts had proved to be, especially in
Africa.(43)

In 1948 the political situation in Palestine radically changed, and Akka and Haifa became a part of
Israel. Though the Baha'is in the past had been
closely linked to the Muslim Arabs, it seems that the
new Government accepted their presence and afforded
them the same liberty which they had enjoyed under
the British Mandate. The President visited the shrine
of the Bab and called on Shoghi Efendi.(44) No doubt
Israel was the more ready to tolerate the presence of
this non-Jewish institution in Haifa because of its
value as a tourist attraction, and because the Baha'is
there seem to have given up the Muslim customs which
were always followed prior to the death of Abdu'l-Baha,
and also because no effort was made in Israel to convert others to the Baha'i Faith. It is said that most
of the Iranian Baha'is left Israel voluntarily, or
were sent away by Shoghi Efendi.

During this period how was the Baha'i Cause faring
in Iran, the land of its birth? Because of the
necessity for avoiding publicity, there is not a
great deal to be found in the volumes of the *Baha'i
World* regarding the progress of the Faith in Iran,

where the majority of the Baha'is of the world resided.
The first National Convention of Baha'is was held in
Teheran in 1934, the picture of which is shown in the
Baha'i World, and about the same time the first National
Spiritual Assembly was organized.(45) In 1940 the large
and impressive *Haziratu'l-Quds* (Headquarters) was completed in Teheran.(46) Here many believers and their
friends used frequently to assemble for various activities. But Baha'i activity often resulted in increased
opposition from fanatical Muslims. In the *Baha'i World*
1944-1946 (pp. 35-46) there is a long and detailed
report of persecution in various parts of Iran, during
which property was destroyed, Baha'is were beaten, and
several were killed. In 1955, when anti-Baha'i feeling
was strong in the country, the large dome of the
Haziratu'l-Quds was destroyed, and the property was
taken over by the Government. Later it was restored
to the Baha'is. It is impossible to estimate the number of Baha'is in Iran at this time. An interesting
and informative article written in 1955 by Mr. E. A.
Bayne, an American economist who was sent to Iran by
the United States Government, presents the favorable
impression he received of the character of the Baha'is
he met in Iran, and from this we will quote extracts
at some length:(47)

"Depending upon the ferocity of opposition, Baha'is
have been forced in Iran to operate more or less
secretly. Mail is often carried by hand from center
to center, and printed matter is smuggled in from
America or United Kingdom sources. The whole makes
for a national network, if you choose to look at it
as such, even though it might be used solely for religious purposes. Baha'i centers throughout the country
(there are about 100 of them) took on some of the
aspects of an underground railway. The district
governor of Kazvin (Qazvin), for example, told me the
other day that although the records of the Kazvin
center indicated that there were only fifteen members
of the sect locally (there are about 200,000 in the
country), the records showed an annual budgetary
expenditure of more than $20,000, which financed
among other things, a ten-bed dormitory.....

"While Baha'is maintain that the sect requires implicit obedience to its national and international hierarchy and theoretically exacts from all its members 19 percent of their income, its methods of recruitment seem somewhat lax and virtually anyone who professes to peace, world union, honesty, and the reliability of a faith that accepts the history of other faiths can be accounted a member. Judging from its propaganda, its membership claims seem somewhat grandiose, and often involve mere association or even simple proof that the 'member' has received Baha'i literature. Periodically, according to some members, there are purges of the centers, and backsliders are asked to resign.

"Two years ago (1953) there were a number of such disciplinary actions in Iran ordered by the central authorities, preparatory to the undertaking of a ten-year expansion program that has encouraged members to leave Iran and establish centers in Africa and India. More than a hundred new centers are claimed to have been established since then in East Africa alone. Another objective was the constitutional recognition of the faith in Iran, an objective that would appear to be hopeless.

"Baha'is in Iran have established a reputation for honesty (A banker in the Teheran bazaar: 'As a Muslim banker, I tell you that the Baha'is are the most reliable element in the bazaar. Being a Baha'i is a good credit rating in itself. They are honest clever people!'), and have often been placed in positions of trust in business and in government (something like finding Chinese cashiers in Japanese banks and vice versa). In the Iranian government they hold many positions of some importance, despite the fact that they can never hope, under the constitution, to attain ministerial or even truly senior civil status. The army, for example, has several hundred Baha'i officers, at least one of whom is a major general. The National Bank employs several scores of Baha'is, as do most governmental agencies. Payrolls of Point IV(48) activities include several hundred Baha'is. The American Embassy and other embassies use Baha'is. It is

safe to assume that there are more Baha'is in official
agencies than there are members of any other minority
group; and certainly there are more Baha'is than
Christians, who are equally barred from ministerial
posts, although they, with the Jewish minority, are
permitted delegates to the Parliament(49).....Teheran
has the largest concentration of the sect, with an
estimated 40,000 adherents, who constitute an important segment of the middle-class and much of its administrative strength."

Mr. Bayne then gives an account of the 1955 persecution of the Baha'is in Iran. "The Shah's physician, a
Baha'i who had served him for twelve years, was dismissed. A dozen Baha'i employees of the government
propaganda office were fired. Three hundred army officers are being quietly retired. The Baha'is have been
liquidating their businesses, and in so doing have been
drawing substantial funds from the operating capital of
the bazaar. The result has been a series of major bank-
ruptcies, carrying with them a score of minor crashes,
because the bazaar is a sensitive center of Iranian
commerce, in a country always short of operating capital. The fundamental clash between the mullas and the
Baha'is is a clash between the traditional authority
and social prestige of the mullas, and the development
of an educated middle-class which the Baha'is partly
represent.....Like all minority sects that are subject
to persecution, the Baha'is appear to have developed
clannish characteristics, and despite their alleged
admirable qualities they are now the target for the
suspicions of ignorant and insecure people.....

"It [Baha'ism] offers a faith that detracts little
from the history of other faiths, offers an ethical
code, and.....presents an interesting syncretism that
could be appealing to a casual believer.....It appears
to serve in Persia (Iran) as a standard around which
persons of responsibility can rally and have rallied,
persons who as a group represent progress and modern
thought in regard to social and economic problems."

Those who have resided in Iran longer than Mr.
Bayne would agree with him that many Baha'is are able

businessmen, and by assisting their fellow-believers
to get jobs have not only increased the membership of
the Faith, but have also raised the economic level of
the whole community. Usually by concealing their
faith they have been able to hold positions in many
government agencies. During the twentieth century
there has been but little real persecution of Baha'is
in Iran. That of 1955 was short-lived, and soon the
Baha'is in the bazaar and elsewhere carried on as
usual. They are hated by confirmed Muslims because
they hold that Baha'u'llah has taken the place of
Muhammad, whom they consider the last and the "Seal"
of the Prophets. It is true that on the whole they
are more progressive than many Muslims, and, since
"honesty is the best policy," they may in business
be more honest than some other groups.

However, after listening to this **favorable** account
written by a foreigner who had but a brief acquaintance with the people of Iran, it would be well to
hear the opinion of Dr. Sa'eed Khan, a highly-respected
physician and a man of absolute integrity, who had as
a doctor treated the second widow of the Bab, and had
for a lifetime known intimately both Babis and Baha'is
in Hamadan and Teheran. His verdict was that if the
morals of Baha'is were not worse than those of Muslims,
they were not better. Writing in 1926 he said:(50)
"There is no conscience with them, they keep to no
principle, they tell you what is untrue, ignoring or
denying undoubted historical facts, and this is the
character of both the leader and the led.....As to
morality and honesty, the whole system has proved
sadly disappointing.....I have been in contact with
many Baha'is, and have had dealings with many and have
tested many, and unfortunately I have met not a single
one who could be called honest or faithful in the full
sense of these words."

And Avareh, after being an effective and honored
missionary of the Faith for twenty years, and after
writing the history of the Movement, stated after his
defection from the Cause, "We have seen little of it
[honesty] among the Baha'is, indeed we have not seen
it at all."(51) He then related with some glee how

he had himself once deceived Dr. Esselmont in giving
him false information about the history of the Movement. He says of Esselmont, "He is absolutely uninformed as to the principles of Baha'ism. He thanked
me for correcting the errors in his book (*Baha'u'llah
and the New Era*), whereas the book is so faulty that
it is beyond correction." It is indeed unfortunate
that this book is still recommended as "a standard
introductory text-book, outlining the history and
teachings of the Faith."(52) Was Avareh lying when
he said this about Esselmont's book, or when he wrote
his two-volume history of the Movement?

To understand the antagonism to the Baha'i Cause
in Iran, one must remember that from the first there
were political as well as religious aspects of the
Movement which were obnoxious to many people. It was
widely believed by Muslims that the zealous Babis at
Shaykh Tabarsi planned to march to Teheran and overthrow the government and set up a Babi regime in its
place. Likewise, Baha'u'llah in the *Kitab-i-Aqdas*
promulgated the laws by which the Baha'i religious-
political state would be governed for a thousand
years. And Shoghi Efendi, though realizing how remote
such a day might be, continued to hold before his
flock the hope of world dominion. Thus in the *Baha'i
World 1934-1936* (p. 199) he is quoted as saying:
"Former faiths inspired hearts and illumined souls....
The Faith of Baha'u'llah, likewise renewing man's
spiritual life, will gradually produce the institutions of an ordered society fulfilling not merely the
functions of the churches of the past, but also the
functions of the civil state. By this Manifestation
of the Divine Will in a higher degree than in former
ages, humanity will emerge from that immature civilization in which church and state are separate, and
partake of a true civilization in which spiritual and
social principles are at last reconciled as two aspects of one and the same Truth."

Again in the *Baha'i World 1936-1938* (p. 247) the
Guardian of the Cause says: "The Spiritual Assemblies
....in future....will be enabled to add to their present functions those powers....necessitated by the

recognition of the Faith of Baha'u'llah, not merely
as one of the recognized religious systems of the
world, but as the State Religion of an independent
and Sovereign Power. And as the Baha'i Faith permeates
the masses of the peoples of East and West, and its
truth is embraced by the majority of the peoples of a
number of the Sovereign States of the world, will the
Universal House of Justice attain the plenitude of its
power, and exercise, as the supreme organ of the Baha'i
commonwealth, all the rights, the duties, and responsi-
bilities incumbent upon the world's future super-state."

Such a prediction of a Baha'i "super-state," in
which church and state would be one, would evoke only
a smile from most Westerners. But in Iran where Baha'is
claimed that they were two million strong, and where
their Movement had usually remained "underground," it
is not surprising that they were often suspected of
plotting to take over the control of the country and
make Iran a Baha'i state, or else of being the secret
agents of some foreign government. Hence recognition
of the Baha'i Faith by the government of Iran is un-
likely.

In his Will Abdu'l-Baha had commanded:(53) "It is
incumbent upon the guardian of the Cause of God to
appoint in his own lifetime him that shall become his
successor, that differences may not arise after his
passing......The Hands of the Cause of God must be
nominated and appointed by the guardian of the Cause
of God. All must be under his shadow and obey his
command......The obligations of the Hands of the Cause
of God are to diffuse the Divine Fragrances, to edity
the souls of men, to promote learning......The Hands
of the Cause of God must elect from their own number
nine persons that shall at all times be occupied in the
important services in the work of the guardian of the
Cause of God, and these....must give their assent to
the choice of the one whom the guardian of the Cause
hath chosen as his successor." In December, 1951,
just thirty years after becoming Guardian, Shoghi
Efendi made his first appointment of "Living Hands."
At first 12 were named, and later the number was
increased to 19, and then in 1957 to 27. There is

no record that these Hands ever chose the body of nine
to assist the Guardian, and to give assent to the one
appointed as his successor. In 1954 the Guardian
ordered the Hands outside Haifa to appoint five "Auxiliary Boards," one for each continent.(54) When any
of the Hands died, the Guardian appointed others to
take their place, so that at his death there were still
27 "Living Hands." No more were appointed. According
to Abdu'l-Baha's Will, the Hands were to obey the
Guardian. When he died, whom were they to obey?

Also, the Will of Abdu'l-Baha provided for the establishment of the Universal House of Justice, of
which the Guardian was to be "the sacred head and the
distinguished member for life."(55) However, during
the lifetime of Shoghi Efendi the House of Justice
never came into being. But, according to the *Baha'i
World 1950-1954* (p. 40), "In January, 1951 the
Guardian made known to the National Spiritual Assemblies of East and West his 'weighty epoch-making
decision' to form the first International Baha'i
Council, as a forerunner of the Universal House of
Justice 'destined to emerge in the fulness of time.'"
The President of the Council was Charles Mason Remey,
and all the members were in Haifa. Remey later
stated(56) that the members of the Council took
orders directly from the Guardian, but "as a Council
or functioning body, we never undertook any services
of any nature whatsoever." Thus from his delay in
appointing Hands, and his failure to establish the
Universal House of Justice, and even to allow the
Council to function effectively, it is evident that
Shoghi Efendi preferred to govern the Cause alone. In
the following chapter we will describe the confusion
caused by the appointment of Mason Remey to this
position. Long letters written to Holley and others
by Mason Remey as President of the Council are published in *Baha'i World 1950-1954* (pp. 378-390).

The leaders of the Baha'i Cause have learned how
to make good use of their anniversaries to inspire
their followers to action. As the 100th anniversary
of the Declaration of the Bab approached, elaborate
plans were made for the celebration of the Centenary

in 1944, and goals were set for the extension of the Cause. In the *Baha'i World*(57) enthusiastic reports were published of the victories won during this campaign by the zealous missionaries of the Faith. It was reported that Baha'is had established residence in 78 countries, and their literature had been translated and published in 41 languages. The Baha'i endowments in Palestine were worth 500,000 pounds sterling, and those in America were valued at $1,700,000. Impressive celebrations of the Centenary were held in Wilmette and other places in the West, and at Haifa at the Shrine of the Bab, and in Shiraz where his Declaration was made. A large Centenary volume was prepared by the indefatigable Horace Holley which contained many pictures of historic sites and personages and articles about the progress of the Faith during its first century.

In 1950 the 100th anniversary of the martyrdom of the Bab was observed, and the Shrine of the Bab on Mt. Carmel was greatly enlarged and beautified and a golden dome was placed on it, at a cost of $750,000. (58) In 1952 the Centenary of the alleged "intimation of mission," which Baha'is say came to Baha'u'llah in the prison in Teheran, was duly celebrated. And in 1953, in preparation for the alleged announcement of Baha'u'llah's mission in the Rizwan Garden near Baghdad in 1863, a "Ten-Year International Teaching Plan" was adopted, with 27 (9x3) objectives - "the most challenging task ever set for the followers of a prophet to achieve."(59) Among the objectives were the establishment of the Faith in 131 new lands, the translation of Baha'i texts into 91 new tongues, and the organization of 48 new National Spiritual Assemblies. Four "Intercontinental Teaching Conferences" were held in 1953 to launch the campaign, one in Uganda, the second in Chicago at which 2300 people were present, a third in Sweden, and the fourth in New Delhi, India. Mason Remey the President of the International Council and other Hands of the Cause were the leaders of these gatherings, and in Chicago portraits of the Bab and Baha'u'llah the "Twin Manifestations of God" were presented. Several regional conferences also were held to inspire the believers to advance the Cause.

BAHA'I HEADQUARTERS

On the slopes of Mt. Carmel above Haifa, showing
the domed Shrine of the Bab and Abdu'l-Baha,
and the Archives Building in the lower center.

It is surprising to one who turns the thousands of pages of the twelve large volumes of the *Baha'i World* covering the years 1921-1954, which contain so many interesting pictures and so much biographical material concerning the Baha'i leaders, to find no pictures of the Guardian of the Cause, and very little information about his life and labors for the Faith. It seems that for some reason Shoghi Efendi did not desire this kind of publicity, though he was not at all reluctant to make known in his voluminous correspondence and his messages to the believers his convictions and commands concerning the Faith. His residence was always in Haifa, and he seldom visited other lands, and never followed in the steps of his grandfather in making grand tours in Europe and America. Having excommunicated most of the members of his family, his life must have been a somewhat lonely one.

Shoghi Efendi was to have married his cousin Maryam, daughter of Mirza Jalal Shahid, but decided not to do so.(60) Finally, in 1937 when he was forty-one years of age, he married Mary Maxwell, to whom he gave the name Ruhiyyih Khanum (Lady Spiritual). In this marriage East and West were united.

Mary Maxwell was the daughter of May Bolles, who had been a member of the first party of Americans to visit Akka in 1898, and who from that time till her death devoted herself to the propagation of the Baha'i Faith. She in 1902 married a Canadian architect William Sutherland Maxwell, who in 1903 became a Baha'i, the first in Canada. The Maxwells resided in Montreal, and their home became the center for Baha'i activities in that city, and in 1912 had the honor of welcoming Abdu'l-Baha as a guest. In 1910 Mary, their first and only child, was born, and was from childhood like her mother a devoted believer. In 1923 mother and daughter spent seven months in Haifa, and again in 1937 they visited the Guardian and assisted him in his work. It was then that Shoghi Efendi chose Mary to be his wife. A revealing account of this marriage, which must have come as a great surprise to the believers, especially those in Iran and the East, was given in London in 1963 in a large meeting of Baha'is by

Ruhiyyih Khanum herself, and was quoted by the Baha'i
writer Jessyca Gaver as follows:(61)

"When the day of our marriage came," said the bride,
"I was dressed entirely in black, because in those days
they wore black whenever the ladies went out on the
street in the East. I had a black turban on my head
and black shoes and a black bag and a black suit and
black gloves. I had on a white blouse, I admit, but
that was my wedding outfit.

"I came over to the Master's House (where Abdu'l-
Baha had lived) - I'd been frightfully cross to my
parents all morning, because I was so terribly, terribly nervous. Most people only get married once, but
not everybody gets married to a Guardian. So, I
would alternately get cross with my parents, then
throw my arms around their necks and weep and beg
forgiveness all morning.

"By the time the afternoon came, I went over and
the beloved Guardian came out and got into his car.
I got in beside him, and the heavens fell in Haifa,
because no one had wind of this. They were all simply
astonished at the Guardian, since going off in an auto-
mobile with a Western Baha'i woman was simply unheard
of.....We went over to the Shrine of Baha'u'llah [at
Akka] and prayed, and this ring that I wear was Shoghi
Effendi's Baha'i ring.....We just had prayers in the
Shrine, and he put the ring on my finger. That was
all. Silently. It was no place for conversation.....
And we went back and in the room of the Greatest Holy
Leaf [sister of Abdu'l-Baha] we had this simple ceremony of Baha'u'llah - putting hand in hand, and I
recited a verse which I had learned with great difficulty in Arabic and he recited it and that was all!
Then I think he went over and sat with his family for
a few moments, and I finally went back to the pilgrim
house and waited for him to come over for dinner just
as he always did - we sat with my mother and father,
and I was there with his brother, just like we did
every other night.....and then after dinner my luggage
was carried across the street upstairs.

"We went and sat and visited for some time in a room with his parents and brothers and sisters, and that was our marriage. Just as simple as that. No wedding veil, no special flowers, no long Tablets chanted.....It seemed to me very wonderful and very precious.....I had a room next to his bedroom which was also his working room. He had his bed and his desk side by side, because he used to work until he was *so* exhausted that he just *fell* into bed, and then he would go on working in his bed. And *nothing* I did could get Shoghi Effendi to separate his bedroom from his office." For sixteen of the twenty years that they were together Ruhiyyih Khanum acted as the secretary for her husband. They were not blessed with offspring.

If ever a wife adored her husband Mary adored Shoghi. Her adoration is vividly expressed in the address she gave at the meeting of Baha'is in London six years after his death, as reported by Jessyca Gaver.(62) A few sentences quoted from her address will clearly reveal her feelings. "I don't know how anybody could convey the sweetness and the loveableness of the Guardian.....I have never seen such expressive eyes in my whole life, never seen eyes that could change so much.....I always thought that these beautiful, beautiful eyes looking at you with such enthusiasm were like two suns rising over the horizon ....He had exceedingly beautiful hands....They were sensitive and highly developed....He was the humblest person that I have ever met in my whole life....But when it came to the Cause of God he was just like a lion....When he was angry, which he was sometimes, justifiably, his voice was just like the crack of a whip. Nobody could withstand his anger. It was the Wrath of God.....He loved mountaineering and used to go for these long, long walks....in the mountains. He climbed some high mountains in Switzerland....He seemed to find a great comfort from the mountains, even up to the end of his life....One of the strongest characteristics of the Guardian was his absolutely iron principle that *nothing* could interfere with what he considered right. Nothing swayed him at all. Neither love nor hate nor danger - absolutely nothing..."

And she told of his tireless and unremitting labors,
his love of order in everything, even in the arrangement of the papers on his deak, his desire to do everything himself, even when it came to arranging the
flower plots in the garden or building a staircase.
It seems that he did not know how to delegate tasks to
others, and so save his own time and strength. Perhaps
this tendency was accentuated by the conviction that
the Guardian of the Cause of God is infallible, and
others are not.

For the sad story of the last illness and death of
the Guardian we are again indebted to Jessyca Garver
(63) and to Ruhiyyih Khanum.(64) Shoghi Efendi and
his wife went to London in October, 1957 for the purpose of ordering furniture and fixings for the Archives
Building on Mt. Carmel in which both were deeply
interested. It is also said that he went to seek
medical advice, since his health was not good.(65)
On October 27 he felt quite unwell, and his wife also
became ill, and the physician who visited them said
they both had Asiatic influenza, and ordered rest.
Ruhiyyih Khanum recovered after a few days, but Shoghi
Efendi did not. He was restless, and insisted on reading his mail and carrying on his work. He was trying
to complete the map he was preparing to show the progress of the Ten-Year Crusade at its halfway point,
and would not listen to his wife when she begged him
to desist. However, he seemed better, and the doctor
agreed to his leaving for Haifa soon. But on the
morning of November 4 when Ruhiyyih Khanum went to his
room she found him dead. The doctor said he had suffered a heart attack, and had died peacefully in sleep.

Fortunately for his bereaved widow, "half-mad with
grief," kind friends rushed to her assistance. Hands
of the Cause soon arrived from near and far, and
helped her inform the Baha'i World Community of what
had happened, and also make plans for the burial.
Unwilling to "deal the naked blow to the hearts of
other Baha'is which she herself had received," she
sent the following cable to Haifa hoping it would
prepare the believers for the news: "Beloved Guardian desperately ill Asiatic flu tell Leroy (Ioas)

inform all National Assemblies inform believers suppli-
cate prayers divine protection Faith." This method of
breaking bad news gently is one that is widely practiced in Iran.

Ruhíyyih Khánum and the other Hands of the Cause
were greatly concerned that the body of the Guardian
be buried exactly in accordance with the laws laid
down by Bahá'u'lláh in the *Kitab-i-Aqdas*.(66)   "God
has commanded," wrote Bahá'u'lláh, "that the dead be
buried in (coffins of) crystal or rare stones or beautiful hard woods, and that engraved rings be placed on
their fingers. Indeed, He is the Knower, the Predeterminer." On the rings are to be inscribed in Arabic
the words: "I had my origin in God and I returned to
Him; I am separated from all but Him, and I hold fast
to His Name, the Merciful, the Compassionate." And
Bahá'u'lláh continued: "And (God commanded that) you
wrap (the dead body) in five garments of silk or
cotton. Whoever is unable to do this, one of them
will be sufficient for him.......It is unlawful for
you to carry the dead body farther than the distance
of an hour from the city. Bury him with joy and
sweetness in a nearby place."

Before burial the body must be washed. Who should
render this last service to the Guardian? Ruhíyyih
Khánum decided to ask the Hand of the Cause Adelbert
Muhlschlegel, a physician, to come from Germany to
do this, since he was "a man known for his spirituality, (and) would not only be able to endure the sorrow
of performing the last service for the beloved Guardian
of washing his blessed body, but would do it in the
spirit of consecration and prayer called for on such
a sacred occasion. He accepted immediately, with
deepest gratitude for this inestimable privilege."
The widow then purchased "nine yards of the heaviest
and finest white silk available and nine yards of
slightly lighter weight for the first shroud, as well
as towels and cloths and soap to wash the body....She
waited in an anteroom while he (the doctor) washed
the precious remains and wrapped them in the first
shroud, anointing the body with attar-of-rose."

Later Dr. Muhlschlegel wrote thus to Ruhiyyih about this experience: "Something new happened to me in that hour that I cannot, even after a few days, speak of, but I can mention the wisdom and love that I felt pour over me. In that room.....there was a tremendous spiritual force such as I have only felt in my life in the holy Shrines.....As I washed each member of his body and anointed it, I thanked those beloved hands which had worked and written to establish the Covenant, those feet that had walked for us, that mouth that had spoken to us, that head that had thought for us, and I prayed and meditated and supplicated that in the short time left to me, the members of my body might hasten to follow in his path of service..."

The problem which caused Ruhiyyih Khanum, and the other Hands who had hastened to London to assist her, much concern was that of finding a suitable place of burial not more than an hour's journey from London. After considerable search an ideal spot was discovered in the Great Northern Cemetery at New Southgate, a plot was immediately purchased, and four small cypress trees were planted at the four corners, "in memory of the hundreds of cypress trees that the beloved Guardian had planted...around the Holy Places in Bahji and Haifa," and all was made ready for the burial in "a strong, deep vault."

"After much deliberation it was decided that for the present, as well as the future, the wisest course would be to have a lead coffin which could be hermetically sealed, and that this should be placed in a beautiful bronze casket, the most dignified, costly and enduring that could be found. By doing this the Hands were assured that in the future when the means of transport become so rapid that the journey from London to Haifa can be accomplished in an hour, it would be possible to convey the sacred remains of the Guardian to the Holy Land." Since the casket weighed nearly half-a-ton, special bearers were chosen to carry it. In view of the great difficulty of carrying out the provisions of the *Kitab-i-Aqdas* in a non-Baha'i city, the devoted Hands of the Cause will surely be forgiven for their failure to provide a crystal coffin and the properly-inscribed ring for the deceased Guardian, especially since they may never have read this passage in their Most Holy Book.

On Saturday, November 9 "more than sixty automobiles, accommodating over three hundred and sixty people, moved off in solemn file.....It was probably the largest column of vehicles seen in London for many years in attendance on a funeral.....Already a great crowd of believers was waiting at the door of the Chapel (in the cemetery) when the funeral cortege drove up; on every face was written its own measure of heart-break and many sobs were heard.....The Great Guardian was carried in and laid on the soft green covering of the catafalque. The Chapel was crowded to the doors, and many had to remain outside. All stood while the wonderful prayer, ordained by Baha'u'llah for the dead, was chanted in Arabic. Six other prayers and excerpts from the Teachings were then read by friends with beautiful voices, some in English, some in Persian, and representative Baha'is from Europe, Africa, America, Asia - Negro, Jew, and Aryan." The casket was then taken to the grave, and "as all stood, silently waiting for the coffin to be lowered into the grave, Ruhiyyih Khanum felt the agony of the hearts around her penetrate into her own great grief. He was their Guardian. He was going forever from their eyes, suddenly snatched from them by the immutable decree of God.....She decided to ask for it to be announced that before the coffin was placed in the grave, the friends who wished might pass by it and pay their respects. For over two hours the believers, eastern and western, filed by. For the most part they knelt and kissed the edge or the handle of the casket. Rarely indeed in history can such a demonstration of love and grief have been seen."

"When the last believers in this grief-stricken procession had filed by, Ruhiyyih Khanum approached the casket, kissed it and knelt in prayer for a moment. She then had the green pall spread over it.....Then the mortal remains of him whom Abdu'l-Baha designated 'the most wondrous, unique and priceless pearl that doth gleam from out the Twin Surging Seas'(67) were slowly lowered into the vault.....All this time - a service that had lasted almost four hours - the representative of the Israeli Government, obviously deeply moved, had been in attendance, himself stepping beside the coffin, and, with bowed head, paying his solemn respects." When the majority of mourners had left, the

Hands of the Cause and other leaders remained to see the vault sealed. Then more prayers were said in many foreign languages, and flowers were heaped about the tomb, "symbols of the love, the suffering, of so many hearts, and no doubt the silent bearers of vows to make the Spirit of the Guardian happy now, to fulfil his plans, carry on his work, be worthy at last of the love and inspired self-sacrificing leadership he gave them for thirty-six years of his life."

Shoghi Efendi, great-grandson of Baha'u'llah, had been gathered to his fathers, and buried far from his fathers' native land. Speedily the Hands of the Cause of God made their way to Haifa to read the Will of the Guardian, and learn what provision he had made for a successor.

NOTES

1. *Baha'i World 1926-1928*, Vol. II, p. 149.

2. *Filsafa-i-Niku*, Vol. II, p. 210, 213.

3. *Azal's Notes*, pp. 240, 241.

4. *Al-Kawakib Al-Durriyya*, by Ayati, 2 Vol., Cairo 1924. See *Azal's Notes*, pp. 1099-1100.

5. *Baha'u'llah and the New Era*, J. E. Esselmont, first edition, Brentano's, New York, p. 8, 22, 215.

6. *Azal's Notes*, p. 27.

7. Avareh quoted by *Esselmont*, pp. 215, 216.

8. *Azal's Notes*, p. 231, Avareh in *Kashfu'l-Hiyal*, Vol. I, sixth impression, pp. 139, 140.

9. *Azal's Notes*, p. 35, *God Passes By*, p. 327.

10. *Azal's Notes*, p. 36.

11. *God Passes By*, p. 327.

12. In *Baha'i Books*, the Literature Catalogue of the Baha'i Publishing Trust, Wilmette 1967, these books by Shoghi Efendi, along with books by Baha'u'llah and Abdu'l-Baha, are listed under the title, "Baha'i Sacred Writings and Texts." The word "Scripture" is not used in designating any of them.

13. It is to be regretted that these translations are not always accurate. It is evident that in some instances Shoghi Efendi intentionally mistranslated the Persian original. See Chapter V, note 70, and *Azal's Notes*, pp. 590, 591, 653.

14. *God Passes By*, p. 411. There is a report that Shoghi Efendi did translate the *Aqdas*, in whole or in part, into English, but if he did this translation was not published.

15. *Azal's Notes*, p. 500. *Nabil's Narrative* is no more reliable than are the first two "official" Baha'i histories.

16. *Azal's Notes*, p. 500.

17. *God Passes By*, p. 247.

18. Mirza Badi'u'llah died in Haifa on November 12, 1950, aged 82.

19. See Appendix II, #71.

20. *Baha'i World*, Vol. II, p. 85.

21. *Azal's Notes*, pp. 254, 255, *Aqdas*, pp. 26, 29, 54, 55, 58, 59. It is noteworthy that while Baha'u'-llah called the Bab his "forerunner," he also in the Aqdas referred to him as "God," "The Point of the Bayan," and "The Master of the Worlds."

22. *A Traveller's Narrative*, pp. xv, xvi, 230.

23. *Baha'i World 1926-1928*, p. 87. See Appendix II, #46.

24. *The Dawn-Breakers*, American Edition, 1932, p. xxx.

25. *Baha'u'llah and the New Era*, Esselmont, Revised Edition, First Printing, 1937, p. 26.

26. *Azal's Notes*, pp. 123, 125, 260, 261.

27. Ibid., pp. 165, 599 (Letter No. 1 of Baha). See Appendix II, #4.

28. See Chapter VIII.

29. The reply of Nicholas to Abdu'l-Baha is quoted in *Azal's Notes*, p. 1116.

30. *Baha'i World 1926-1928*, p. 93.

31. *Bahai Scriptures*, Brentano's, New York, 1923.

32. U. S. Census 1926.

33. *Abdul Baha's Alleged Will is Fraudelent*, Ruth White, 1930.

34. *God Passes By*, p. 351.

35. In ten weeks in 1925, $9,806 was sent by the National Spiritual Assembly in America to Shoghi Efendi in Haifa (*Abdul Baha and the Promised Age*, Ruth White, 1927, Appendix, 1929).

36. *Baha'i World 1926-1928*, p. 84.

37. Letter from Mr. Will Orick, October 28, 1964.

38. *God Passes By*, p. 379.

39. Mr. E. A. Bayne, see note 47.

40. *God Passes By*, p. 386.

41. The conversion of Queen Marie to the Baha'i Faith was widely and joyfully acclaimed by Baha'is as the fulfillment of Baha'u'llah's prophecy in the Aqdas (pp. 46-47) that kings would support his Cause (*Baha'i World*, Vol. II, pp. 173-176, *God Passes By*, pp. 387-395). However, regarding this alleged conversion Mother Alexandra, now Mother Superior of the Orthodox Monastery of the Transfiguration, wrote to Mr. J. Anthony Sistrom on August 7, 1970 as follows: "It is perfectly true that my mother, Queen Marie, did receive Miss Martha Root several times.....She came at the moment when we were undergoing very great family and national stress. At such a moment it was natural that we were receptive to any kind of

spiritual message, but it is quite incorrect to
say that my mother or any of us at any time contemplated becoming a member of the Baha'i faith."

42. *God Passes By*, pp. 398, 400.

43. Mason Remey's *Statement* of January 1967.   It
seems that some of the "pioneers" supported
themselves in various ways.

44. *Baha'i World 1950-1954*.

45. *Baha'i World 1934-1935*, pp. 268, 335.

46. *Baha'i World 1940-1944*.

47. *Bahais Again: The Larger Question of the Contin-
uing Persecution of the Bahai Religious Sect in
Iran*, letter from E. A. Bayne, June 2, 1955,
American Universities Field Staff Reports.

48. "Point IV" was a U. S. government agency which
provided assistance in various fields to Iran.

49. The Iranian Constitution recognizes three
religious minorities, Zoroastrians, Jews, and
Christians, and grants them representation in
Parliament, but does not recognize Baha'is as
belonging to a separate religion. Baha'is vote
as Muslims.

50. *Mission Problems in New Persia*, Beirut, 1936,
pp. 83, 87, 88.

51. *Kashfu'l-Hiyal*, Vol. I, First Edition, Avareh,
pp. 16, 64.

52. *Baha'i Books*, Baha'i Publishing Trust, October
1967, p. 13.

53. *Baha'i World 1926-1928*, pp. 85, 86.

54. *Baha'i World 1950-1954*, pp. 38, 108-114, *1954-
1963*, p. 333.

55. *Baha'i World 1926-1928*, p. 87.

56. *Proclamation of Mason Remey*, April 1960.

57. *Baha'i World 1944-1946*, pp. 77, 142-145.

58. *Baha'i World 1950-1954*, pp. 21-30.

59. Ibid., p. 26.

60. *Azal's Notes*, p. 724.

61. *The Baha'i Faith*, by Jessyca Russell Gaver, Award Books, New York, 1967, pp. 122-124.

62. Ibid., pp. 116-121.

63. Ibid., pp. 129-140.

64. *The Passing of Shoghi Effendi*, Baha'i Publishing Trust 1958. The quotations which follow are all taken from this valuable document.

65. *Azal's Notes*, p. 725.

66. *Aqdas*, pp. 57-58.

67. *Baha'i World 1926-1928*, p. 81.

14

The Rule of the People

The Bab several months before his execution in July
1850 appointed Subh-i-Azal as his successor. Baha'u'-
llah sixteen years after the death of the Bab
repudiated Subh-i-Azal's appointment, and declared
that he himself was a new Manifestation. He in his
Will appointed his two eldest sons to succeed him in
turn, first Abbas Efendi, and after him Mirza
Muhammad Ali. But Abbas, better known as Abdu'l-
Baha, ignored his father's Will, and in his own Will
appointed his grandson Shoghi Efendi as his successor
and Guardian of the Cause of God, stipulating that he
should be succeeded by his eldest son. But when
Shoghi Efendi died in 1957 he left no Will and
appointed no successor, thereby violating both the
command of Baha'u'llah that "the writing of a Will
has been made incumbent on everyone,"(1) and also
the provision in the Will of Abdu'l-Baha that he
should "appoint in his own lifetime him that shall
become his successor, that differences may not arise
after his passing." "After him will succeed the
first-born of his lineal descendants." And, in case
the first-born is not worthy, he must "choose another
branch to succeed him."(2) Since the Guardian died
childless, and therefore no "branch" existed, he may

be forgiven for his failure to carry out this provision in the Will of his grandfather on which he had
leaned so heavily for his authority.

But why did Shoghi Efendi not write a Will? Had
he not read the *Kitab-i-Aqdas*, which, he had said,(3)
"may well be regarded as the brightest emanation of
the mind of Baha'u'llah, as the Mother Book of His
Dispensation, and the Charter of His New World Order?"
Or had death overtaken him unprepared? Or was he,
infallible as he was supposed to be, unable to solve
the problem of the succession, or unwilling to continue any longer the game of playing Divinity, and
by failing to leave a Will intentionally ended the
Guardianship? Perhaps his wife and his close friends
knew what was in the mind of Shoghi Efendi, but if
they knew they have not divulged his secret to others.
(4)

It seems clear that the "Hands of the Cause,"
appointed by the Guardian to assist him in everything, were not expecting this eventuality. According
to *Time Magazine*,(5) twenty-six of the twenty-seven
"Hands" hastened to Haifa shortly after the death of
the Guardian, and "ransacked the headquarters at No.
7 Persian Street; they searched Shoghi Efendi's safe-
box without success, all week long they met in secret
session, were tight-lipped about rumors of stormy
rivalry between two candidates for the Guardian - one
of them said to be an American. At last they announced
the solution: there would be no new Guardian at all,
but a nine-man Council of Hands at Haifa, titled
'Hands of the Cause of God on Holy Land.' The new
body will have no powers to interpret scripture.
'Everything would certainly have been much simpler
if Shoghi had made a Will,' said a Hand from Paris
when the meeting was over." The interim Council was
called the "Custodian Hands of the Faith."

On November 25, 1957, about three weeks after the
death of Shoghi Efendi, the Hands issued a long statement, explaining to the Baha'is of the world what
they had done. In this they said: "In our capacity
as Chief Stewards of the embryonic World Commonwealth

of Baha'u'llah, we Hands of the Cause have constituted
a body of nine Hands to serve at the Baha'i World
Centre." The document ended with the words, "In service to the Faith of Baha'u'llah," and was signed by
all 26 of the Hands who were in Haifa. The full statement is published in *Baha'i World*, vol. XIII, p. 251ff.

Truly the Hands inherited a very difficult problem.
Since Shoghi Efendi had no offspring he could not
appoint a successor in accordance with Abdu'l-Baha's
Will, and Abdu'l-Baha had made no provision for the
succession in case Shoghi Efendi should be childless.
Hence, as the Hands realized, there was no way in
which a successor could be appointed that would be in
conformity to the Will. Abdu'l-Baha was mistaken in
the supposition that there would be Guardians in his
family generation after generation.

The plan which the Hands adopted was that the Universal House of Justice, in accordance with the provision in the Will of Abdu'l-Baha, should at last be
established, and should head up the Baha'i Faith. But
had they forgotten that it was stipulated in the same
Will that the head of the House of Justice must be the
Guardian, or someone appointed by him?(6) Therefore,
without a Guardian or someone appointed by him to
preside over the Universal House of Justice, this
body, when elected, would have no head - and headless
bodies do not function helpfully. Moreover, according
to the Will, the Hands of the Cause are to be appointed
by the Guardian, and are required to turn to him, and
guard him, and "be occupied in the important services
in the work of the Guardian," "be under his shadow and
obey his command."(7) But if there is no Guardian,
whom will the Hands obey, and whom will they serve?
Hands without a head to direct them are at best
ineffective. Accordingly, if the Will of Abdu'l-Baha
is taken as authoritative, with the death of Shoghi
Efendi the whole Baha'i Structure collapsed, Guardianship, Hands of the Cause of God, and Universal House
of Justice. It must have seemed to some that God had
failed them, or, as others explained the situation,
that He had changed His mind about the future of His
Cause.

What, then, could the devoted Hands who gathered
in Haifa do to rescue the Cause of God from extinc-
tion? Apparently, they did the only thing possible
under the circumstances, they ignored the provisions
of the Will of Abdu'l-Baha regarding the Guardianship,
while retaining the institutions of the Hands of the
Cause and the National and Universal Assemblies prescribed by him, and went back to the provisions in the
Kitab-i-Aqdas and the Will of Baha'u'llah according
to which the affairs of the Cause, after the deaths
of the two Branches Abbas Efendi and Mirza Muhammad
Ali, were to be ordered by the House of Justice. (8)

Were there no loyal believers in the infallibility
of Abdu'l-Baha present at Haifa to protest this treatment of the Center of the Covenant, the Exponent of
the Word of God? Only the Hands know what was said in
the secret sessions, and having been sworn to secrecy
they, with one exception, have revealed nothing. It
is indeed amazing how easily the great majority of
Baha'is seem to have forgotten immediately all they
had said and written about the absolute indispensa-
bility of the Institution of the Guardianship, and to
have accepted cheerfully and without question the more
democratic system of rule through the Universal House
of Justice.

There was one, however, who had a better memory
than the rest, and greater reverence for the Will of
the Master. He was Charles Mason Remey, a member of
the Custodian Hands in Haifa. Mr. Remey, born in
1874, a member of an eminent American family, was
reared as a Christian, was educated as an architect,
and had an outstanding career. His achievements and
honors are recorded in *Who's Who in America*. He
became a Baha'i when he was a young man in 1899, and
served the Cause zealously for many years. In 1909-
1910 he made a round-the-world tour on behalf of his
faith. He wrote many books and pamphlets about the
Baha'i Cause, which are deposited in the Library of
Congress and fifty other libraries in the U.S.A. and
abroad. (9) His name appeared frequently for many
years in the Baha'i records. He was appointed to
draw the plans for the Archives Building on Mt. Carmel

and the Baha'i temples in Africa and Australia. Shoghi
Efendi called Mason Remey to Haifa, where he remained
for ten years, made him a Hand of the Cause, and when
he established the first "International Baha'i Council"
in 1951 he appointed Remey as the President of this
body, which, according to Shoghi Efendi, would eventually become the Universal House of Justice, and
always gave him the place of honor next to himself.(10)
At the death of Shoghi Efendi the Government of Israel
in their official year book for 1957 gave the name of
Mason Remey as "the New Head of the Baha'i Faith."

Mr. Remey has stated in his various writings that
since both Abdu'l-Baha and the First Guardian had made
it clear that there must always be a Guardian, he had
after the death of Shoghi Efendi earnestly tried to
persuade the other Hands that the Guardisnship must be
continued, but they all refused to listen to him. Gradually he came to realize that since Shoghi Efendi had
made him the President of the International Council, he
himself was the one appointed by the First Guardian to
succeed him. He says he waited more than two years
for the Hands in Haifa to realize this fact, and on
their own initiative concur in his assuming the leadership as the Second Guardian. However, it became evident they did not want to have a Second Guardian, and
were gradually preparing the believers to accept a new
type of organization. So at the end of 1959 he left
the Hands in Haifa, returned to America, and issued in
April, 1960 a statement proclaiming himself as Guardian,
and calling on all Baha'is to accept him. His printed
"Proclamation to the Baha'is of the World" was sent to
the Annual Convention of Baha'is of the U.S.A., meeting
in Wilmette, Illinois. After giving in detail his
reasons for claiming the Guardianship and the grounds
on which he based his claim, Remey says, "I am now
declaring my position of command in the Cause to
believers here in America....and through this Convention to all the Baha'i World." He then ordered the
Hands in Haifa to desist at once from the plans they
were making for 1963, presumably plans for electing
the Universal House of Justice, and says, "I alone in
all the world have been given the authority and the
power to accomplish this....It is from and through the

Guardianship that infallibility is vested and that the
Hands of the Faith receive their orders." He says he
bases his authority on his appointment by Shoghi
Efendi to the Presidency of the International Council.
It seems that this plea for fidelity to the Guardianship and to him as "Second Guardian" fell largely on
deaf ears, for the Hands went ahead with their plans
for 1963, and only a small minority of Baha'is rallied
about the "Second Guardian." The majority wearied,
perhaps, by the demands of a Divine Dictator, had discovered that the Guardian had not been infallible, and
desired to change to a more democratic form of government of the Cause.

Mr. Remey published in 1960 a small book of 52 pages
entitled A LAST APPEAL TO THE HANDS OF THE FAITH - "A
Private and Secret Document to be Read Only by the
Hands of the Faith," in which he with a conciliatory
spirit and at great length exhorts them "to abandon
their program for 1963, and that they seek to find the
Second Guardian of the Baha'i Faith, and that they
uphold the Will and testament of the Master Abdu'l-Baha
and the Administration of the Faith as established by
the Beloved Guardian Shoghi Effendi, that at present
is under a cloud of violation that threatens the fulfillment of its mission to mankind."

Since no minutes were kept in the meetings of the
Hands, and none was permitted to reveal what was said
and done in these sessions, Remey's account of the
proceedings, now available to the public after his
formal break with the Hands of the Faith, is of considerable historical importance. We will, therefore,
quote a number of passages that tell the story and
reveal the attitude of the Baha'i leaders' at this
critical time.

"Now at this date the guidance of the Cause is off
the track, as it were; for it is not the province of
the Hands of the Faith to guide the Faith. They are
to serve the Guardian of the Faith and are to carry
on and carry out his commands. It is therefore upon
these grounds that I, President of the Baha'i International Council, command them to desist from their

attempts and cease their program of tampering with
the International Council and give up their Program
for 1963, that is a violation of the Will and Testament of the Master Abdu'l-Baha, as well as a violation of the Administration of the Beloved Guardian
built up in accordance with the command of Abdu'l-Baha.
Whether the Beloved Guardian realized or knew of his
approaching death, he left his Cause fully protected
when he appointed me President of the Baha'i International Council; for by so doing he vested in me, Mason
Remey, the authority to guard the Faith against this
violation of the Administration..." (p. 6).

"HANDS OF THE FAITH!   Abandon your program! Awake!
Desire that the Guardianship continue and diligently
seek your Guardian....The Guardian of the Faith who
will ere long appear is calling to you to make you
ready for his coming. Awake, Hands of the Faith,
and make yourselves ready to meet him, the Second
Guardian of the Baha'i Faith" (p. 7).

"An influential group of individuals within the
body of the twenty-seven Hands of the Faith consulted
together in private from the others (and) made a
covenant between themselves and then proceeded to
put this over the others....This is indeed a violation of the Will and Testament, a violation clear and
distinct! There is but one Baha'i method of meeting
violation and that is to cut it out completely and
cast it out of the Cause without any compromising
whatsoever!" (p. 8).

"All the Hands of the Faith know of the defection
of Ahmad Sohrab....Now why is it that the Hands of
the Faith cannot see that the stand that they are now
united upon is one of violation? ....Their's is the
same stand as that taken by Ahmad Sohrab! Ahmad
Sohrab announced in print that he accepted the teachings of Baha'u'llah and Abdu'l-Baha, but without the
Guardianship. Why is it that the Hands of the Faith
cannot see this point in my argument?" (p. 9).

"When the first conclave of the Hands of the Faith
assembled at Behje [palace of Baha'u'llah near Akka]

to learn that no Will or Testament of Shoghi Effendi
could be found amongst his papers, prayers were
chanted and read and the conclave closed to convene
on the following morning.

"For the most part, if not all the American Hands
returned to Haifa for the night, while for the most
part, if not all, the ten Hands who were Persians
were quartered for the night at Behje. When the conclave went into session the following morning one of
the Persian Hands arose making the statement that
since Shoghi Effendi left no son to inherit the Guardianship and since no Will or Testament of his could
be found among his papers, that the Guardianship of
the Faith must be considered to be ended....thereupon
all of the other Persian Hands quickly arose in
support of this move, with the result that this move
had the immediate support of the majority of the Hands.

"Circumstantial evidence of the situation shows
beyond a doubt that the Persian friends had consulted
amongst themselves between these two meetings....and
that they had come to an agreement between themselves
that the Guardianship be abandoned. Thus in the confusion and heat of the moment the Guardianship was
definitely abandoned by the majority of the conclave.
Thus was violated the Will and Testament of the Master
Abdu'l-Baha.

"Since that first conclave all of the proceedings
of the Hands of the Faith in conclave, and the objects
and support by the Custodian Hands of the Faith in the
Holy Land, have been based upon the assumption that
the Guardianship is now closed forever, although this
has not been said definitely to the Baha'i world.....
That this was all a preplanned move on the part of
these Persian Hands was most obvious" (pp. 10, 11).

"Without the institution of the Guardianship there
can be no Administration, the two are one and co-
existent. The two divine verities....form the message
that the Baha'is had for the world in the days of the
Guardianship....During the present interregnum of the
past two years and more, the teachers of the Faith,

the pioneers, have had no message for the world, for
as things are now in the Faith, with no assurance of
Guardianship, they are no longer able to teach the
Will and Testament. In other words, the Faith is at
a standstill, the dangers of which are so increasing
daily that this is indeed a time of peril such as
this Cause has never before faced in its entire
history" (pp. 11, 12).

"For the past year and more I've tried to use
gentle and pacific reasons for arguments in defence
of the Guardianship against the united intention of
the body of the Hands that there shall never be
another Guardian. Now seeing that this violation
of the Master's Will and Testament is daily becoming
stronger until it threatens to become the accepted
way of life of the Cause, as a last resort I am
obliged single handedly to come out into the open
and use my prerogatives as President of the International Baha'i Council as appointed by our late
Beloved Guardian, to force the Hands of the Faith
to relinquish their united stand against the Guardianship....My way of forcing this issue is simply by
announcing to the Hands that in no way shall I countenance their right to do anything at all about or
with the Baha'i International Council.....I take the
stand that there can be no functioning of the Council
until there be a recognized and accepted Guardian of
the Faith to institute it. The Hands of the Faith
have no right to command the election of an International Council....In other words, I block their
actions in this...." (p. 13).

"The Holy Spirit in this dispensation only functions through the channel of the Guardianship....The
present promises being made by the Hands of the Faith
of the election....of an International Baha'i Council
and the Universal House of Justice to follow are not
for the Hands of the Faith to institute but for the
Guardian of the Faith himself to create and inaugurate
.....The Second Guardian mercifully delays his advent
into the active Baha'i world in order to give these
Hands a little more time that they may awake and be

prepared to accept him when he proclaims himself, but the time is short" (pp. 14, 16).

Those Hands who wanted the Guardianship abolished "offered to form a substitute infallibility to the infallibility of the Guardianship; (11) namely the fallacious infallibility that they claimed the House of Justice would have that they proposed to establish in 1963" (p. 26).

"Why is it thus that the resident Hands in the Holy Land don't want a Second Guardian? Why is it so? It looks to me as if they personally don't want their easy way of life disturbed by the presence amongst them of a Guardian who would command the Cause and very probably curtail their luxuries and perquisites that they are enjoying during this inter-regnum and that they never had in the days of the Beloved Guardian" (p. 27).

"When I made my stand in the last conclave (1959) for the continuation of the Guardianship and I refused to sign my name endorsing the fallacies of the present program of the Hands of the Faith, the Hands as a body, took the ground that I would cause a split in the Cause the world around; and again subsequently after the conclave, several of the Hands came to me individually urging and entreating me not to continue with my refusal to sign my name to the edicts issued by the body of the Hands, telling me of the evils of disunion and inharmony among the Baha'is, and that all should uphold and with all sincerity relinquish their own personal opinions.... and support the ideas of the majority. In each of these cases I replied to them that this present pro- blem in our Faith which I had precipitated was not a matter of inharmony and disunity but one of violation that had to be treated not by coming together in union but by separating and casting out the violation and to isolate it so that it could no longer harm the Cause.....This matter of violation no one of the friends could understand. They had become so condi- tioned to the thought that the Guardianship be ended that they just couldn't see that the Will and Testament

was being violated.....No one of the Hands but I saw
this, therefore, I had to arise alone and make this
stand in order to save the Baha'i Cause" (p. 29).

"These Hands of the Faith propose that the mass of
the Baha'is form an International Assembly which they
claim will have the infallibility necessary to guide
the Faith without regard to the divinely inspired
element necessary that only the Guardian can provide.
It just doesn't make any sense at all, for it is the
antithesis of the philosophy and teaching of the Will
and Testament, namely these Hands plan the destruction
of Abdu'l-Baha's plan of the Administration of the
Kingdom, to be replaced by a purely republican or
democratic form that has none of the elements of the
Kingdom of God necessary to make it a Kingdom, a King
and his nobility and his people" (p. 37).

The Hands decided that "in sending out their
letters of information and instructions.....all nine
of us were to sign these letters under the words
'In the Service of the Beloved Guardian of the Faith.'
To me this....was one of those fallacies invented to
support and reinforce the fallacy previously made,
that of no more Guardianship.....When one violation
starts there is no stopping it. It is a devastating
disease in the body Baha'i....Therefore I refused to
sign my name as still being in the service of Shoghi
Effendi, (who is) dead and in the Abha Realms of
existence, whereas we of the Faith in this world
according to the Administration should be now signing
ourselves 'In the Service of the Second Guardian
of the Baha'i Faith'" (p. 38).

"The Guardianship on one side, and the International
Assembly upon the other side, are the two supports of
the Universal House of Justice as explained by the
Beloved Guardian and accepted by all of the believers.
The Universal House of Justice can only function in
its infallibility when it has these two supports....
The International Assembly that is the voice of the
mass of the people of the Faith and is chosen by them
is alone and by itself not endowed with infallibility!
This I have explained many times in the conferences of

the Custodian hands in Haifa as well as to the body
of the Hands in both the second and third conclaves,
but apparently all to no effect." For the Hands hold
that the International Assembly is itself infallible
without the Guardianship, which they think is non-
existent. "How any one of normal mental capacity can
reason thus is a mystery to me....This lack of logic
and reasoning not only makes no sense but is positively
pernicious. .....It is like a disease that the body of
the Hands brought upon themselves when they forsook
the Guardianship at their first conclave" (p. 44, 45).

Mason Remey says that he had kept his promise and
had discussed these secret matters only with the Hands
of the Faith. But having after two years of earnest
effort failed to convince the other Hands that they
were violating the Will and Testament, he was forced
to break with them, to announce that he as President
of the International Council was the one appointed by
the First Guardian to succeed him, and he therefore
felt no longer bound by the promise to keep all these
matters secret.

Did it ever occur to Mr. Remey that in claiming
to be the Guardian he was himself violating the Will,
which required that the successor to the Guardian be
"the first-born of his lineal descendants," or
"another branch," another of his children? And had
he never read the provision that Baha'u'llah made in
his Will for the succession, and realized that in
appointing Shoghi Efendi as Guardian, Abdu'l-Baha
violated his father's Will? And it is probably too
much to expect that he should have delved deep enough
into the early history of the Movement to discover
that Baha'u'llah in claiming to be a Manifestation
had flagrantly violated the Bab's provision for his
successor. Had he known more of Baha'i history Mr.
Remey would not have been so amazed at the conduct
of the Hands of the Faith in this crisis of the
Cause.

Later, in a long statement addressed to Dr. S. R. Levy, Librarian of the State Archives in Jerusalem, Mason Remey in September, 1962, wrote as follows: "This most recent [Baha'i] Dispensation differs from those of the past in that past prophetic dispensations experienced periods of occultation between the missions of the Prophets or Manifestations.....With the death of the Prophet, periods as long as a thousand years passed before the advent of another Manifestation.....In this Day of God's Kingdom Triumphant Upon Earth, however, a continuous uninterrupted shower of Blessings has been assured mankind. By virtue of the Institution of the 'Guardianship' of the Baha'i Faith, a living point of Divine Guidance for the people of the world is accomplished. This means that the world will never again witness periods of abject Spiritual Darkness..."

In this same statement to Dr. Levy, Mason Remey explains his belief that, according to predictions of the ancient prophets and apostles, a terrible catastrophe is to occur on the earth in the near future, in which two-thirds of the population of the world will perish. This, he thinks, will be the result of a slip of the crust of the earth, which some scientists have predicted as a possibility, with the result that the position of the poles will change, the climate of large sections of the earth will be radically altered, and most of the lowlying lands will be inundated by the oceans. Mt. Carmel, according to Mr. Remey, will not be submerged, but Jerusalem will become a seaport. After this deluge God's Kingdom through Baha'u'llah will be established on earth.

In a pamphlet entitled "The Impending World Catastrophe" dated March, 1962, Mr. Remey writes that in 1909 Abdu'l-Baha, in reply to his questions about the prophecies in the Book of Daniel, replied, "After the year 1917 there is coming a very great catastrophe in the world." When asked about the exact time he said, "Not soon after or distant."(12) Then the author continues: "Having been endowed with infallible guidance as Guardian of the Baha'i Faith, Mason Remey not only warns the people again

of this destruction, but states that it will happen
very soon. It may come any time after April, 1963."
So sure is Mr. Remey that this calamity will soon be
upon us that he had all his personal records removed
in 1961 from Chicago to Santa Fe, New Mexico, U.S.A.,
which is 7000 feet above sea level and would not be
flooded. He himself, unable now to reside in Jerusalem
as he hopes one day to do, is living in Florence, Italy,
"on one of the high surrounding hills that will be....
above the inundations of the seas in which the Great
Cities of both Europe and America will go down under
the rising waters." He very thoughtfully wrote to the
author of this book on September 17, 1964, "Since Iran
according to my calculations will not be inundated....
I trust you may at that time of Tribulation find your-
self in Teheran." As the Iranians say, "We will see!"

On August 9, 1964 Mason Remey issued a statement
"on the Infallibility of the Guardianship," in which
he says: "The 'infallible Guidance' flowing from the
Holy Spirit to the Living Guardian of the Faith guides
him in his decisions....The seat of infallibility can
only be vested in one living person - The Guardian(11)
- in order that dissension, discord and differences
of opinion may be avoided....The Unity of the Faithful
as a Body is maintained throughout this epoch of the
Triumph of the Baha'i Faith under the Living Guardianship."

Then in his letter to "friends" of January, 1967,
Mason Remey made a statement which must have come as
a great surprise to devout believers in the infallibility of their former leader, but not to others. He
wrote: "As the friends read this letter let them be
prepared for another shock - namely that Shoghi
Efendi was all wrong in teaching that the future
world government would be installed on Mt. Carmel....
In other words, Shoghi Efendi was a sick and dis-
organized soul....It is very unpleasant for Mason
Remey to have to tell the Baha'i World these viola-
tions of the Faith that were made unwittingly by
Shoghi Efendi." About the same time he wrote to a
Spiritual brother in Iran: "We may consider the
Manifestation of God - Baha'u'llah - to be Infallible;

the Master, Abdu'l-Baha, is infallible at times and
at times may not be clear in his statements and may
make mistakes; while the Guardians of the Faith are
under the protection of God they are not Infallible."
It is refreshing to find in a man 93 years of age
such willingness to face the facts and repudiate the
convictions of a lifetime, and should Mason Remey be
able and willing to delve yet more deeply into Baha'i
history he might include yet others in his list of
non-infallibles.

Mr. Remey is distressed by some modern Baha'i
teachings, which he considers a distortion of the
true Baha'i Faith. In a letter of March, 1968 to a
believer he writes: "For the past seven years I have
been begging the Believers to study the Book of Some
Answered Questions [by Abdu'l-Baha], and they *will
not do it*....Some of these old Baha'is know nothing
about the Laws of God....The Green Acre Summer School
has become an enemy of the Baha'i Faith. Baha'is go
there and are exhorted to study and to practice all
the ancient religions of the past....So with all this
mess of contradictory truths of the present and super-
stitions of the past it has become the center of
spiritual disturbance and spiritual illness, contam-
inating the Baha'i Faith the world around. When a
Baha'i is confirmed in his faith he stops there, and
ceases to search for truth in any of the older religions." This appears to be a protest against syncretism in the Baha'i Faith. In another letter written
about the same time Remey says, "One of the greatest
sins that a Believer can commit is to change the Holy
Baha'i Texts. I am now finding how confused the most
sincere Believers are becoming by these alterations
and changes and additions to the Holy Teachings." He
had been shocked to read in the introduction to a
certain Baha'i book the statement: "Briefly it [The
Baha'i Faith] is not so much a New Religion but
Religion Renewed." "This is most misleading," says
Mr. Remey. "The Baha'i Faith is not a renewal of
Christianity. It is an entirely New Religion that
is going to supersede Christianity." In this important matter, therefore, Mason Remey "agreed with the
First Guardian, and disagreed with Mirza Ahmad Sohrab.

In 1968 the "Second Guardian" announced the appointment of "the first five Elders of the Baha'i Epoch,"
from four countries, with Donald Harvey as first, and
the probable appointee as Remey's successor. He also
urged the believers to pay the tax prescribed in the
Kitab-i-Aqdas,(13) to cover the expenses of the office
in Florence. And he has chosen for those loyal to him
the name, "The Orthodox Abha World Faith." The minority of Baha'is loyal to the "Hereditary Guardianship"
of Mason Remey, carried on various activities in
America and Pakistan and some other lands. From
their headquarters in Santa Fe they published for
several years "The Glad Tidings - A Bulletin of the
Baha'is Under the Hereditary Guardianship," in which
messages from the Second Guardian and news of the
progress of the "true" Baha'i Faith were published
monthly. A National Spiritual Assembly was organized,
and was registered by the U. S. Government as an
organization separate from that of the Baha'is with
headquarters at Wilmette who rejected Remey. On November 6, 1964 the Santa Fe Baha'is brought suit
against the Wilmette Baha'is for the ownership of
all the Baha'i properties worth several million dollars, but the Wilmette party previously had changed
their Declaration of Trust, omitting from it all
mention of the place of the Guardian in the Baha'i
organization. So with no legal ground to stand on,
the Santa Fe party lost the suit. Then the Wilmette
Baha'is sued the Santa Fe party for misuse of the
Baha'i names and symbols, and in June, 1966 a Federal
Court in Chicago gave a decision in their favor. It
seems that Mason Remey has not been involved in these
suits, and has told his followers to desist, and to
dissolve their National Spiritual Assembly which they
did. However, he has been disturbed by dissension
among his followers, and has written a strong letter
to them about the evil of backbiting and quarreling,
and the danger of becoming so involved in problems of
administration that they would neglect their primary
duty of giving spiritual teaching to needy people.

Though Mason Remey stood loyally in support of the
thirty-six year old tenet of the Baha'i Administration
that it was God's will and absolutely essential to the

Cause that there always be an Infallible Guardian, he
was rejected by the great majority of the Baha'is of
the world, and every effort was made by them to min-
imize the importance of the schism which had occurred
in the Faith. The only reference to it in *The Baha'i
World*, vol. XIII, is on page 353, where "yet another
severe test" is mentioned. This veiled statement is
explained by the following footnote: "The defection
of Mason Remey, who after signing the Proclamation of
November 25, 1957, claimed in April, 1960 to be the
'heredity Guardian' of the Cause of God. This attempt
to create schism in the Faith resulted in his expulsion by the Hands of the Cause. (Conclave of October
1960)."

The decision to dispense with the Guardianship was
as radical a step for the Baha'is to take as a vote
by the Cardinals to abolish the Papacy would be for
the Roman Catholics, yet that was what they did. It
seems that there were many besides Mrs. White and Mrs.
Chanler and Sohrab who had resented the dictatorship
of Shoghi Efendi, but had of necessity submitted to
his absolute control of the Movement. The death of
the Guardian gave them an opportunity to free themselves, and they promptly did so. Hence, for the
first time in more than a century the majority of
members of the Movement found themselves without a
living head whom they held to be divinely-appointed
and infallible.

As has been noted more than once in the preceding
pages, one of the matters which has for many years
surprised students of the Baha'i Cause is the failure
of Abdu'l-Baha and Shoghi Efendi to publish an
authorized translation of the *Kitab-i-Aqdas*, to which
both referred as the most important of the writings
of Baha'u'llah. This failure made it impossible for
most of the Baha'is to obey Abdu'l-Baha's command in
his Will(14) that "Unto the Most Holy Book (*Kitab-i-
Aqdas*) everyone must turn, and all that is not
expressly recorded therein must be referred to the
Universal House of Justice." For years Mr. Will Orick,
an American lawyer who had many contacts with Baha'is,
and was a careful and informed observer of the Movement,

but was not himself a Baha'i, had sought for an
English translation of the Aqdas, but without success.
Finally, in 1954 he wrote to the Baha'i Publishing
Committee in Wilmette to ask if they could supply him
with a copy, and was told by the Manager that they
had never had a complete copy of the Aqdas. He then
wrote to Mr. Horace Holley, the Secretary of the
National Spiritual Assembly of the Baha'is of the
United States, saying that he was "baffled by the
fact that, while I read in the Will of Baha'u'llah
'Reflect upon that which is revealed in my book, The
Aqdas,' and in the Will of Abdu'l-Baha 'Unto the Most
Holy Book (the Aqdas) every one must turn,' your
believers, after all these years, can neither reflect
upon nor turn to the Aqdas: because it is not available to them....There must be a reason for having
withheld the Most Holy Book, the very basis of Baha'i
teaching, judging from the words of both Baha'u'llah
and Abdu'l-Baha, from American believers." And the
reason was asked for by Mr. Orick.(15)

    Mr. Holley replied at some length, saying that the
Laws of Baha'u'llah are found in many of his writings
which are available to Baha'is, and that the Aqdas
is a document which cannot be administered till the
supreme legislative body of the Baha'i Faith comes
into being. And he pointed to the Guardianship which
provides guidance for the community.(16) Mr. Orick
replied that even if it were inadvisable at this time
to put the Aqdas into the hands of all Baha'is, he
would be grateful if Mr. Holley would send him a copy
from his own files, which he would return after
perusal.(17) To this request Mr. Holley replied
that he did not have a copy of the Aqdas on file.(18)
Undiscouraged, Mr. Orick then wrote to the Guardian
Shoghi Efendi in Haifa, telling him of Mr. Holley's
inability to supply him with a copy of the Aqdas, and
calling his attention "to the unfavorable impression
all of this cannot fail to make on intelligent American readers." "They," he continues, "when brought
face to face with the evident non-compliance by the
successors to Baha'u'llah and Abdu'l-Baha of the
plainly worded directions of these founders of the
Baha'i faith, will inevitably suspect an abrogation

of the original teachings, even though this may not
exist. I, for one, view the withholding of *The Aqdas*
from an unbiased student of Baha'i teachings as a
serious handicap to their understanding. And I feel
that by your sending me a copy from your files at the
earliest possible date, preferably an English translation, much could be accomplished in enabling me to
present a clearer picture of the Baha'i aims (in my
book."(19) To this request a brief reply came signed
by "R. Rabbani," presumably the wife of the Guardian,
saying that the Aqdas was going to be translated in
full, but this was a difficult task, and would
require both time and able scholarship. And nothing
was said about supplying the request for a copy of
the Aqdas.(20)

In 1960 Mr. Orick once more wrote to Mr. Holley at
Wilmette to ask whether it was possible for him yet
to supply him with an English translation of the
Aqdas. He was informed that at the Wilmette headquarters they still did not have an English translation of the Aqdas, and they did not know when it would
be translated. Also, Mr. Orick was informed that Mr.
Holley had died.(21)

Unable to get any assistance from the Baha'i leaders,
Mr. Orick turned to others for help. He persuaded Dr.
E. E. Elder, an acknowledged Arabic scholar,(22) to
undertake this task, with the assistance of the author
of this book. The translation was checked and approved
by scholars intimately acquainted with the Arabic language as well as with Baha'i terminology and practice,
and was accepted for publication as a scholarly work
by the Royal Asiatic Society in London.(23) The Arabic
text from which the translation was made was published
at the command of Baha'u'llah in Bombay about 1890, and
the copy which was used had been autographed by Abdu'l-
Baha on March 25, 1899, and presented to Mrs. Lua
Moore Getsinger when she visited him in Akka. Photographic copies of the 65 pages of the Arabic text are
preserved in the Public Library of New York, and are
available to scholars. The autographed copy was from
the Bahai Caravan Library, 132 East 65th Street, New
York City.

Mr. Orick has stated that Mrs. Julie Chanler, the
owner of the rare copy of the Aqdas which she had
kindly though reluctantly loaned to him for translation, earnestly requested that the translator should
not put into English certain passages of the original.
She was especially anxious that the command, (25)
"Whoever burns a house intentionally, burn him," be
omitted, for she said, "What would converts from
Christianity say to that!" Neither Mr. Orick nor Dr.
Elder was willing to tamper with the text of the Most
Holy Book. (47)

The reception given this translation by Baha'is
was interesting. Mason Remey at once welcomed it,
wrote letters of appreciation to the authors, and
urged his followers to read it and so become acquainted with the laws of Baha'u'llah. However, the authorities in Wilmette rejected it, and forbade their
members to read it. The News Bulletin of September
1962 issued by Baha'is in California says that the
National Spiritual Assembly [Wilmette] has informed
them of the translation of the *Kitab-i-Aqdas* by Dr.
Elder, and states that "not only is the translation
poorly done, but in many instances it gives the wrong
impression of the provisions of the *Aqdas*.....The
believers.....should completely ignore this poor and
prejudicial translation." Mr. Orick wrote to Wilmette
to inquire on what grounds they had condemned Dr.
Elder's translation as inadequate. In their reply
they failed to give any reasons, and said that they
did not wish to enter into any controversy with anyone whomsoever regarding the translation of the *Kitab-
i-Aqdas* or any other work of Baha'u'llah by any non-
Baha'i.....and did not wish to endorse or circulate
Dr. Elder's translation for reasons of their own. (26).
And so Mr. Orick's question remained unanswered.

However, Mr. Jelal Azal, a scholar whose competence
to translate Baha'u'llah's Arabic into English cannot
be questioned, after reading the Elder translation
wrote: (27) "The translators of the *Aqdas* are to be
congratulated on their excellent work. The work itself
is worthy of being warmly recommended to all students
of Comparative Religion and the history of Religious

Evolution.....The hostile reception accorded by the
Baha'is to the excellent rendering into English of
the *Aqdas* is not a matter of surprise to me. Professor
Browne received a similar condemnation when he traced,
printed and published the text of Haji Mirza Jani of
Kashan's *Nuqtatu'l-Kaf*." The appearance of an authorized Baha'i translation of the Most Holy Book, which
will be no less accurate and scholarly than that of
Dr. Elder, is still being awaited.(24)

Unabashed by their failure to make it possible for
"every one" to obey the command of Abdu'l-Baha and
"turn unto the Most Holy Book," and undeterred by the
appeals of Hand of the Cause and President of the
First International Baha'i Council, Mason Remey, to
continue the Guardianship, the remaining Hands of the
Cause proceeded with their plans for the future government of the Cause without a Guardian. The International Baha'i Council was reorganized in Haifa in
1961, presumably by the Custodian Hands, with some
new members, and with Mr. Charles Wolcott, former
Secretary of the National Spiritual Assembly of the
U.S.A. as Secretary-General. The Council would cease
to exist when the Universal House of Justice was
formed. Arrangements were made for a World Congress
of Baha'is to be held in London in 1963, to celebrate
the Centenary of the alleged Declaration of Baha'u'llah
in the Garden of Rizwan near Baghdad in April, 1863
(Chapter V, end), and also to elect the nine-member
Universal House of Justice. For membership in this
supreme tribunal, which was supposed to possess the
infallibility formerly residing in the Guardian, four
Iranians, three Englishmen and three Americans were
chosen. No woman was elected to the House of Justice.
The President was *not* the Second Guardian, a son of
Shoghi Efendi, as was stipulated in the Will of
Abdu'l-Baha. The election was by the delegates from
the 81 National Spiritual Assemblies in as many
different countries. It is said that 7000 Baha'is
attended the Congress, only a fraction of whom were
voting delegates.

Of this historic event, Hand of the Cause Mr. Paul
Haney spoke as follows in June, 1967 in Honolulu: (28)

"The living Guardianship came to an end.....why, we
do not know. But the promise of Baha'u'llah that
'This is the day that shall not be followed by night'
was fulfilled through the establishment of the Universal House of Justice, in the right way in the right
time. For the first time in human history there has
been Divine guidance flowing into the world not through
a divinely-guided and infallible individual such as
Abdu'l-Baha and the Guardian, but through an Institution, a group of Baha'is such as you and I.....but only
when they meet together as an Institution are they
infallibly guided, in the sphere of their responsibility.....The world has never had an Institution such as
the House of Justice.....Only to the deliberations and
decisions of the Universal House of Justice is infallibility vouchsafed.(11) Therefore, it is our refuge and
the future salvation of the Baha'is and of the world
.....The institutions must be channeled for the flow of
the spirit, for it is this spirit which will furnish
the basis for the establihhment of Baha'u'llah's World
Order, and when we realize this, and understand our
true objectives, we will hasten their accomplishment,
under the infallible guidance of the Universal House
of Justice." It is not evident who "vouchsafed" this
unique infallibility to the Universal House of Justice,
or in which of the pronouncements of Baha'u'llah or
Abdu'l-Baha is it stated that this kind of Universal
House of Justice, without the Guardian as its head,
will possess infallibility.

However important in the eyes of the Baha'is the
Universal House of Justice may seem to be, it is
quite evident that the real rulers in the Cause of
God after the death of Shoghi Efendi were the nobles
of the realm, the Hands of the Cause, of whom the
most influential was probably Amatu'l-Baha Ruhiyyih
Khanum, the widow of the Guardian, one of the two
Living Hands who were women. Since the Hands were
aging, and some had died, and no others were to be
appointed in their place, they chose to assist them
in their task of propagating the Faith numerous
members of "Auxiliary Boards" in different lands, and
the Universal House of Justice, in consultation with
the Hands, established for the same purpose a dozen

"Continental Boards of Counsellors." Ruhiyyih Khanum
and three other Hands resided in Haifa, and other
Hands were assigned to twelve different parts of the
world in which the Continental Boards had been established. The following cable from the Universal House
of Justice informed the world community how this
ecclesiastical machinery was to function:(29)

"CONTINENTAL BOARDS ENTRUSTED IN CLOSE COLLABORATION
HANDS CAUSE WITH RESPONSIBILITY DIRECTION AUXILIARY
BOARDS AND CONSULTATION NATIONAL SPIRITUAL ASSEMBLIES.
HANDS CAUSE GOD WILL HENCEFORTH INCREASE INTERCONTIN-
ENTAL SERVICES ASSUMING WORLDWIDE ROLE PROTECTION
PROPAGATION FAITH. MEMBERS AUXILIARY BOARDS WILL
REPORT BE RESPONSIBLE TO CONTINENTAL BOARDS OF COUN-
SELLORS. HANDS CAUSE RESIDING HOLY LAND IN ADDITION
SERVING LIAISON BETWEEN UNIVERSAL HOUSE OF JUSTICE
AND CONTINENTAL BOARDS COUNSELLORS WILL ASSIST FUTURE
ESTABLISHMENT INTERNATIONAL TEACHING CENTER HOLY LAND
FORESHADOWED WRITINGS BELOVED GUARDIAN."

From this it is evident that the Cause was now being
administered in accordance with efficient American
business practices.

The leaders of the Cause knew well from past
experience the value of frequent conferences and
assemblies in celebration of the important events in
the history of the movement, both to increase the
zeal of the believers and also to impress the outside
world. Hence, following close on the 1963 Congress
in London, more great meetings were planned for 1967.
These were to celebrate "the centenary of Baha'u'llah's
proclamation of his Message in September/October 1867
to the kings and rulers of the world.....," and also
to celebrate the 150th anniversary of his birth.

The *Baha'i News* of December, 1967 contains reports
of the six Intercontinental Conferences which were
held simultaneously in Panama City, Wilmette, Sydney,
Kampala, Frankfurt and New Delhi. In Panama Ruhiyyih
Khanum laid the cornerstone of the temple to be
erected there and addressed the assembly. At Wilmette
where 3000 Baha'is gathered, three Hands of the Cause

made addresses, the oldest of whom was Mr. Samandari
of Iran who had seen Baha'u'llah with his own eyes.
(30)   There was a telephone hook-up with the five
other Conferences, and "what a thrill it was to hear
Dr. Daniel Jordan speak words of greeting, and then
to hear similar greetings from each of the five other
continents." When an appeal was made for pioneers to
serve the Cause, 216 persons came forward as volunteers.

"Only when it [the Conference] was over," wrote one
of those present,(31) "did one realize that all the
events of this North American Conference had been
arranged to bring him closer to Baha'u'llah. He had
looked upon His face as recorded by an actual photograph, had seen and heard one who had looked upon His
living face and heard His voice, and had been shown
the places where He had walked. The Universal House
of Justice, that supreme, infallible vehicle of divine
guidance today, had focused the light on Baha'u'llah
alone. Seeking no glory for themselves, they had
taken loving care to enable each one to 'gaze on' His
'beauty, and observe whatsoever is in' His 'book'."

The Conferences in Frankfurt, Kampala, New Delhi
and Sydney were not as large as that in Wilmette, but
were no less enthusiastic in their welcome to the
Hands who visited them and in their devotion to the
memory of Baha'u'llah. It seems that by this time all
had become used to the idea that the infallible House
of Justice had taken the place of the infallible Guardian, and no explanation or defence of this transfer
of authority is found in the reports of the Conferences.
Truly a new day had dawned in the history of the Cause.

Fortunately another important event had occurred in
1868, and accordingly plans were made for a centenary
celebration in August, 1968 of Baha'u'llah's journey
from Edirne to Akka. In November, 1967 the Universal
House of Justice sent forth the following message by
cable:(32)

".....ANNOUNCE CONVOCATION TWENTY-THIRD TO TWENTY-
FIFTH AUGUST 1968 FIRST OCEANIC CONFERENCE BAHA'I WORLD
PALERMO SICILY HEART SEA TRAVERSED GOD'S MANIFESTATION

CENTURY AGO PROCEEDING INCARCERATION MOST GREAT PRISON.
TWOFOLD PURPOSE CONFERENCE CONSIDER MOMENTOUS FULFILL-
MENT AGE-OLD PROPHECIES TRIUMPH GOD'S MESSENGER OVER
EVERY GRIEVOUS CALAMITY AND CONSULT PLANS PROPAGATION
CAUSE ISLANDS LANDS BORDERING MEDITERRANEAN SEA. PAR-
TICIPANTS INVITED HOLY LAND IMMEDIATELY FOLLOWING
CONFERENCE ATTEND COMMEMORATION ARRIVAL LORD HOSTS THESE
SACRED SHORES RECONSECRATE THEMSELVES THRESHOLD HIS
SHRINE PROSECUTION GLORIOUS TASKS AHEAD."

The Universal House of Justice has not explained
why it continues to couch its pronouncements in such
uncouth language. In any case, the friends understood
the message, and some 2300 of them assembled in Sicily
in August, 1968 to remember the sad journey of Baha'u'-
llah and his little group of relatives and friends,
political prisoners being sent to the penal colony of
Akka. From Sicily 1800 of the pilgrims went on to
Haifa, and it was reported that on September 7, Baha'is
from 70 countries gathered at the Bahji Mansion near
Akka where Baha'u'llah had lived, and commenorated
there the arrival of the prisoners a century before.
(33)

In connection with this celebration, Hand of the
Cause Ugo R. Giachery writes enthusiastically of the
amazing growth of the Baha'i movement since Baha'u'-
llah was exiled to Akka.(34) He states that the Cause
has now been established in 135 independent nations,
has published its literature in more than 400 languages,
135 Auxiliary Board members are aiding the Hands in
advancing the Cause. And at the top of the structure
is "that supreme organ of the Baha'i Commonwealth, the
Universal House of Justice.....The bejeweled crown
resplendent in its genuine beauty, infallible, created
of equity, justice and universal love now leads the
Faith of Baha'u'llah to its ultimate destiny.....The
stupendous dome of an indestructible structure, the
Universal House of Justice, the splendor and glory of
the Baha'i world."

Mason Remey and other Baha'is were convinced that
without a living infallible Guardian the Cause of God
would suffer irreparable loss. The fact is, however,

that after 1957, and even before the "infallible"
House of Justice came into being, the Cause took on
new life. A "Nine Year Plan" was adopted in 1964 by
the Universal House of Justice for the purpose of
achieving certain goals by 1973, one of which was
to improve greatly the property of the "World Center"
on Mt. Carmel at Haifa. To make this possible large
budgets were adopted, the 1967-1968 budget in the
U.S.A. being $1,060,000, of which 21% was to go to
the World Center. More than half of the budget was
to come from endowments and publications, and the
balance (about $45,000) was to be supplied by contri-
butions from the 17,000 Baha'is in the U.S.A., which
would be an average gift of $27 a member for the year.

However, the chief goal of the Nine Year Plan was
to get new members. To this end most aggressive
efforts were put forth to inform and interest people
in the Cause, and to convert them to it. At the
Convention in Wilmette in 1967 it was reported(35)
that in Canada there is a "plan for six annual phases
of proclamation, each directed towards a particular
segment of the population. Delegations are being
sent to thirty-four religious organizations to present *The Proclamation of Baha'u'llah* and on October
15 a copy of this book is being presented to the
Prime Minister. Ten thousand clergymen are receiving
a series of four letters from the Canadian Baha'i
community, these letters to be dispatched at eight
week intervals. Proclamation material will be sent
to Indian Chiefs of Councils and Reservations and
there will be a special emphasis on Baha'i teachings
on social justice in the hope that eventually the
majority of the Canadian Baha'i membership will be
Indians."

In the U.S.A. the campaign for new members was
headed up by a retired Air Force officer who was
chairman of the National Teaching Committee. It was
reported that he was assisted by 900 public information representatives located throughout the country.
Proclamation of the Baha'i Cause concentrated on major
media(36) promotion and public meetings for seven
special events: World Peace Day (September 15), United

Nations Day (October 24), Birthday of Baha'u'llah (November 12), Human Rights Day (December 10), World Religion Day (January 19), No Ruz (Iranian New Year, March 21), and Race Unity Day (June 8). By taking an active part in these events Baha'is hoped that numerous contacts would be made with interested people, who could then be brought into "firesides," i.e., meetings in private homes.(37) Also films were shown describing "the progress of the Baha'i Faith in over 56,000 localities throughout the world."

Those who are persuaded to become members "declare" themselves to be Baha'is by signing a card which is then forwarded to Wilmette. The card reads as follows: "I..........(Signature) accept the qualifications of the faith as defined on reverse side of this card, and apply for enrollment as member of the Baha'i community." On the reverse side is the statement by Shoghi Efendi: "The principal factors that must be taken into consideration before deciding whether a person may be regarded as a true believer or not.....Full recognition of the station of the Forerunner [the Bab], the Author [Baha'u'llah], and the True Exemplar [Abdu'l-Baha] of the Baha'i Cause, as set forth in Abdu'l-Baha's Testament; unreserved acceptance of, and submission to, whatsoever has been revealed by their Pen; loyal and steadfast adherance to every clause of our Beloved's sacred Will; and close association with the spirit as well as the form of the present day Baha'i administration throughout the world."

It would seem that for one to be able to sign this statement with understanding and honesty he would have to spend many months in study, and would need to know both the Persian and Arabic languages to be able to read all that is extant and available of the voluminous writings "revealed by their Pen." And if the applicant for membership were able to do all this, which probably no living Baha'i has done, could he today give "steadfast adherance" to the clauses of Abdu'l-Baha's Will requiring that there always be a Guardian in the line of Shoghi Efendi when now the Cause is without a Guardian? It seems, however, that these considerations have not deterred eager applicants from becoming

devoted converts to the Cause. When the card, signed
by the new believer, has been sent to headquarters,
the convert is entitled to attend the "feast," that
is, the meeting for worship which is held every 19
days. He is also expected to contribute to the Baha'i
"fund," and to hold his own "firesides" for the purpose of converting others. He will receive each month
a copy of *Baha'i News*, which is "for circulation among
Baha'is only."

According to Baha'i reports, the "Nine Year Plan"
adopted in 1964 was most successful. In the U.S.A. the
number of registered members increased from 17,000 in
1967 to 22,000 in 1969, a third of whom were said to
be in California.(38) *The American Baha'i* of April,
1973 announces that the number of Baha'is in the U.S.A.
has tripled in the past ten years, and there are now
members of the Faith in 6000 localities. Most of the
members are young people and people from minority
groups. In a few weeks in the winter of 1970-1971
thousands of black people in the southern part of the
U.S.A. were converted.

A reporter from Dillon, S. C. in February, 1971
wrote as follows: "Like a hungry flame news of the
new Faith of God spread itself from town to town and
village to village.....Inspired by the cry of 'Win
Increasing Numbers,' a meager handful of Baha'is.....
spread out .....seeking souls who would respond to
their message: 'Have you heard the good news?.....
God has sent a new Prophet to the world.....His name
is Baha'u'llah.....His laws will eliminate poverty,
prejudice, injustice......'" (*The American Baha'i*,
April, 1973). Multitudes of souls responded.

In the *New York Times* of April 8, 1972 there
appeared an announcement of the showing of a Baha'i
film, which tells the story of "more than 20,000
Americans in South Carolina (who) have enrolled in
the Baha'i Faith since 1970." One who was interested
to learn who these new converts are and how they were
converted made a journey to South Carolina, and reported
as follows in a letter to the editor of *The Christian
Century*:(39) "I am currently writing a book about

Baha'i in America and recently visited several of the 'mass conversion' regions in South Carolina and Maryland. The method of conversion: roving groups of visiting Baha'is went from house to house up and down the roads asking the rural blacks if they believed in peace, brotherhood and equality. When the response was Yes the blacks were told that in that case they were Baha'is and should sign the declaration cards to affirm their belief. They were not told about many of the restrictions which the Baha'i faith would place on them.....In some instances rural blacks were led to believe that educational, scholarship and welfare programs would result from this membership in Baha'i."

In April and May of 1973 there was a general celebration of the successful conclusion of the "Nine Year International Teaching Plan," which had been "a period of unprecedented growth of the worldwide Baha'i community." Some of the results as stated in *The American Baha'i* (April 1973) were:

113 National Spiritual Assemblies elected;

A House of Worship, the first in Latin America, dedicated in Panama City in 1972;

Baha'i literature translated into 501 languages;

15 Intercontinental Conferences conducted by the Universal House of Justice;

Youth Conferences held in Pakistan, India, Costa Rica, as well as in the U.S.A.

In the *National Baha'i Review* ("for Baha'is only") of February, 1973 it was stated that 505 of the Local Assemblies in the U.S.A. have this year contributed toward the Budget of $1,716,000, and Baha'is are encouraged to contribute regularly. In this issue of the *Review* there was no statement of how this large sum of money is to be disbursed. A list was published of nearly seventy localities in different parts of the U.S.A. in which the Local Assemblies were "in jeopardy," because the number of members in each had fallen below nine, and it was stated that "homefront settlers are needed in these localities" to bring the number up to nine.

Though the reports indicate that the increase of
members has been great, there are indications that
there is also a considerable cooling off or even falling away of members who were formerly quite active. It
is said that one reason for this is the authoritarian
rule of the present Administration. If some Baha'is
thought that by the elimination of a Guardianship that
was dictatorial they would get more freedom, they have
been sadly disappointed. It is reported that members
of the Faith spy on one another, and live in fear of
what might happen to them if they are suspected of being disloyal to their rulers. It seems that the
"Infallible Universal House of Justice" of nine members has inherited both the position and the spirit
of the Infallible Guardian, and no one dares to question its authority. For example, all Baha'is were
ordered to have no dealings with Mason Remey, who had
been expelled, and not even to open letters from him.
One old friend received a personal invitation from
Mr. Remey to visit him in Florence, and was so unwise
that he not only read the letter but also sent a polite
note in reply saying that he could not accept. For
this offense he was punished by the Baha'i rulers. Of
course some believers like a dictatorship, whether it
be by the rule of one or of nine. But if this sort
of rule continues, it is probable that there will be
yet more Assemblies "in jeopardy."

What is the total number of Baha'is in the world?
A leader of the Cause speaking in a public meeting in
New York in 1964 stated that the number is two million,
but he did not indicate where all these believers are
to be found. When asked how many Baha'is are now in
Iran, one of their leaders in that land replied, "It
is very difficult to give the number of adult Baha'is
in Iran, because any figure we give you in Iran or
any part of the world today is obsolete tomorrow with
the Faith growing so rapidly." Likewise, in all Baha'i
publications and pronouncements the impression is given
that the growth of the movement is phenomenal, and that
it is exercising a great influence in all parts of the
world. However, when the author sought information
from non-Baha'is in a dozen different countries in
Asia and Africa as to the progress of the Faith, the

impression he received was quite different. A correspondent who has been intimately acquainted with, and
has travelled widely in, all the North African countries for a number of years wrote:(40) "I wish I could
give you some information regarding this sect in North
Africa, but up to the present it has been so restricted
that I have not come across a single Baha'i, foreign or
native." When inquiries were made from an authority on
the religious situation in Burma regarding the alleged
conversion of a whole village to the Baha'i Faith(41),
the reply was as follows:(42) "I do not recall having
any contact with Baha'is in Burma, unless it had been
an occasional American traveler going through.....In
the twelve years I was in Burma I was not conscious of
any group of Baha'i people.....I do not know of any
educational, medical or social work carried on [in
Burma] under Baha'i auspicies." The reply from the
Philippines was:(43) "I have not seen any evidence of
this religion until recently I came across a little ad
in the Manila Times."

A long-time resident in Korea states(44) that the
Baha'i Cause was established in that land in 1950 at
the time of the Korean War by several American service-
men in the Medical Corps, and most of the Korean converts have been people "from service-connected civilian
or military groups," or from universities. The Baha'is
are now beginning to try to make converts from the
Christians in the churches. They claim a membership
of 11,000, but probably have no more than 4000 members,
and do not seem to be increasing in numbers. Their
movement is small, compared to the Protestant church
membership in Korea of some 1,800,000. The Baha'i
organization is loose, and people drift into their
meetings and out again without severing their connection with the church. As far as is known they have
no medical or educational or charitable work in Korea.
"They are introspective, meditative, academic, not
aggressively outreaching.....They claim to give their
converts all that is good in Christianity, but *more*."
Three of the nine members of the National Spiritual
Assembly have American names.

In West Pakistan, according to an American Baha'i
who was resident there, there were in 1969 "more than

1,000, but not over 3,000" Baha'is, the majority of
whom are of Iranian Muslim extraction, though some
were formerly Hindus or Christians. Some of the leaders of the Cause are well educated. Converts are
drawn to this faith by its teachings of love and world-
brotherhood and the other Baha'i "Principles." The
Cause is not growing rapidly, though recently in
Karachi fifteen Muslims were converted. A person well
acquainted with East Pakistan has stated that apart
from one couple who were from another country, he had
not in that land come across any Baha'is, nor had he
seen any evidence of their literature or their propaganda. When he made inquiry of this couple they told
him that they had no knowledge of any indigenous
Baha'i work in East Pakistan.(45)

Letters sent to long-time residents in Japan, India,
Yucatan, Indonesia, Lebanon and other lands brought no
reply, presumably because of lack of information regarding the presence of Baha'is in those lands. It seems
that they are not yet in most countries like "a city
set on a hill which cannot be hid."

From Iran, however, two reliable informants who
have for many years been in close touch with the Baha'i
Cause, and whose near relatives are among the Baha'i
leaders of that land, wrote full replies to the ques-
tionnaire sent them. They among other things(46) said:
"The Baha'is do not have educational institutions.
They have big firms and factories.....and employ large
numbers perhaps many thousands. They mostly employ
Baha'is. There are also many well-known doctors and
specialists [who are Baha'is]. There are also many
in high places in Government service."

"There are two to three hundred local groups of
not more than a hundred each in Teheran, making a
total of around 20,000." No estimate was given as to
the number in the provinces of Iran, but it is probably not greater than in the Capital. While Baha'is are
ready to conceal their faith when the situation
requires it, many are proud to profess their faith
openly. No Jews are now becoming Baha'is, "unless
for personal benefits." In reply to the question,

"What factors induce people in Iran to become Baha'is?"
the reply was: "Finding jobs; Honor among Baha'is;
Marriage; Thinking Baha'ism agrees with Modernism and
free life, and satisfaction of being religious and
pleasing God."

The Baha'i religion is not recognized by the government of Iran, but Baha'is are not persecuted by the
government if they are good citizens, and the people
of Iran do not generally oppose them.   It is probable
that some of the Baha'is in high positions have taken
an important part in the recent reforms in Iran, but
they did not do so as Baha'is.   To the question, "How
do average Baha'is compare with Muslims in Iran in
moral character?" the reply was that since they consider Baha'ism to be a "modern religion," they are
less honest and moral than religious Muslims.   "They
think they are only required to believe in Baha'u'llah."
To the question, "Will Iran ever become a Baha'i country?" the reply was: "NEVER.   It may become anything
but Baha'i.....Baha'i laws are not practical for
managing the Government."   The Baha'is in Iran who
were questioned by my correspondents professed ignorance of the claims of Mason Remey, or else brushed
them aside as of no consequence.

One of the recent achievements of the Baha'i
leaders is the publication in 1970 of Volume XIII of
The Baha'i World, a large book of nearly 1300 pages,
which provides much valuable material from the years
1954 to 1963 A.D.   This volume, issued by The Universal House of Justice, Haifa, Israel, is appropriately
dedicated "To Shoghi Effendi, 1897-1957, Guardian of
the Baha'i Faith.....in love and homage, in pride and
sorrow."   It contains a long account (168 pages) of
the life and labors and achievements of the Guardian
written by his widow, with many pictures of him, and
of the sacred places in Haifa and Akka which he had
developed and beautified.   It also contains selections
from the writings of the Bab, Baha'u'llah, Abdu'l-Baha
and Shoghi Efendi - but none from the *Kitab-i-Aqdas*.
There is also an account of the important events which
followed the death of the Guardian and the rule of the
Hands of the Cause.   There are pictures of the Hands,

of believers who have died in recent years, and of
the many nine-member National Assemblies in countries
round the world. There are pictures of groups of
believers and of large Baha'i gatherings. And there
are exhaustive lists of countries and towns in all
lands in which Baha'is reside, but without addresses.
There are valuable lists of books in many languages
about the Baha'i Faith, written by Baha'is and non-
Baha'is. And there are several Baha'i hymns with
notes. It was no doubt difficult to produce such a
book without the aid of Horace Holley, who had prepared most of the preceding volumes of *The Baha'i
World*.

It is said that most of the Baha'is cannot afford
to attend at their own expense the numerous conferences and conventions which are held to inspire the
friends to greater activity, with the result that the
same people go year after year to the state and national meetings. If the report is correct, only one-third
of the elected delegates were able to attend the international convention at Haifa in 1968. America and
Europe were solidly represented, but only a few Baha'is
from Africa, Asia and Latin America were present. From
this it would seem that the Western influence in the
Cause is now predominant. Though there are more Baha'is
in Iran than in all the other countries put together,
only two men from Iran were elected in 1968 to the
nine-member Universal House of Justice.

One of the achievements of the Cause, for which
Baha'is are rightly proud, and into which they have
poured their contributions for many years, is the
establishment of the Headquarters at Haifa and Akka
(Acre) in Israel. The very beautiful buildings and
grounds in which the sacred shrines are located are
visited annually by tens of thousands of tourists,
both from Israel and from foreign lands, and doubtless
the impression made on many of them is most favorable.
The Baha'i leaders, shortly after the establishment
of the State of Israel, declared that they would make
no effort to convert the Jews to their religion, and
it is said that they have faithfully kept their word.
As a result, they have enjoyed the favor of the Israeli

Government, and have recently received official recognition as being one of Israel's religions. No doubt the tourists bring considerable income to the country. It is said that at the shrines Baha'i literature is given only when it is asked for by visitors.

In the time of Baha'u'llah and Abdu'l-Baha, the Baha'is in Akka and Haifa, who were mostly Iranians, lived and worshipped like the Sunni Muslims about them, and the local population as well as the officials considered them a sect of Islam. But since the increase of Western control in the Baha'i Faith, and especially since the establishment of Jewish rule in Palestine, it seems that little evidence of Islamic influence remains at the Baha'i Headquarters. If the Muslims, Christians and Jews residing in that region of Israel knew what the Baha'is really believe, they might not be on as friendly terms with them as they are said to be. But care is taken that they remain in ignorance. It seems rather strange that the Baha'i missionaries are attempting to convert all the people of the world, except those nearest to them in Israel.

NOTES

1. *Aqdas*, p. 53.

2. *Baha'i World 1926-1928*, p. 85.

3. *God Passes By*, p. 213.

4. It is quite evident from Shoghi Efendi's voluminous writings that he had read not only the Aqdas and the Bayan, but also all the available literature on the Babi-Baha'i movement, both oriental and occidental (*Azal's Notes*, p. 1125). He was aware that the institution of Guardianship, created in the Will of Abdu'l-Baha, was a violation of the Will of Baha'u'llah. He knew that he had no right to appoint anyone as his successor, and so he did the only thing he could do. It seems that by failure to leave a Will he attempted to terminate the

whole Baha'i Administrative Order which he had
spent his life in building up.

5. *Time*, December 9, 1957.

6. *Baha'i World 1926-1928*, p. 87.

7. Ibid., pp. 85, 86.

8. Baha'u'llah's House of Justice was intended to be
a legislative body, and the executive body was to
be a Baha'i government. But as no Baha'i government exists, the provision for the House of Justice
cannot in accordance with Baha'u'llah's Will be
carried out, and the "Universal House of Justice"
which Baha'is have set up is not the sort of institution which Baha'u'llah intended.

9. In the Library of Congress 23 writings of Mason
Remey are listed.

10. *Baha'i World 1950-1954*, p. 41, and *Open Letter*
of Remey to the Custodian Hands at Haifa.

11. In the Aqdas (p. 37) Baha'u'llah says that infallibility belongs only to the Manifestation. "The
Rising-Place of Command [Baha'u'llah] has no partner in the Very Great Preservation from Error.....
A partner in this Great and Unapproachable Dignity
has not been destined for anyone else." It is
therefore clear that the claims of Abdu'l-Baha and
Shoghi Efendi and others to infallibility, partial
or total, were contrary to the decree of Baha'u'-
llah (*Azal's Notes*, pp. 1123, 1124).

12. See also *Abdul Baha and the Promised Age*, pp. 174,
175.

13. *Aqdas*, p. 50.

14. *Baha'i World 1926-1928*, p. 87.

15. Braun to Orick, January 25, 1954, Orick to Holley,
February 18, 1954.

16. Holley to Orick, March 8, 1954.

17. Orick to Holley, March 15, 1954.

18. Holley to Orick, March 24, 1954.

19. Orick to Shoghi Efendi, October 27, 1954.

20. R. Rabbani to Orick, November 24, 1954.

21. Wolcott to Orick, July 7, 1960, and March 2, 1961.

22. Among Dr. Elder's writings are: *Arabic Grammar*, by E. E. Elder, American University at Cairo, 1937, 348 pages, and *A Commentary on the Creed of Islam* (Taftazani on the Creed of Nasafi). Translated and with Introduction and Notes, Earl Edgar Elder, Columbia University Press, New York, 1950, 187 pages.

23. *al-Kitab al-Aqdas*, or The Most Holy Book, by Mirza Husayn Ali Baha'u'llah, Translated from the Original Arabic and Edited by Earl E. Elder, Ph.D., D.D. and William McE. Miller, M.A., D.D. Published by the Royal Asiatic Society, London, 1961. Dr. Elder died on April 11, 1973.

24. In the February 1973 issue of *National Baha'i Review* ("for Baha'is only"), the following notice occupies the whole front page:

KITAB-I-AQDAS:

Synopsis and Codification to be Published at Ridvan Joyfully Announce Completion Synopsis Codification *Kitab-i-Aqdas* for Publication Ridvan Synchronizing Celebration 100th Anniversary Revelation Most Holy Book Fulfilling World Centre Goal Nine Year Plan. Confident Release this Publication Envisaged by Beloved Guardian and whose Main Features He Outlined will Constitute Another Significant Step Path Leading Baha'i Community Full Maturity Establishment World Order Baha'u'llah

- The Universal House of Justice

Haifa, Israel,
January 19, 1973

The author was happy to purchase a copy of this book from the Baha'i Publishing Trust in Wilmette, Illinois, U.S.A. The title is *A Synopsis and Codification of THE KITAB-I-AQDAS the Most Holy Book of BAHA'U'LLAH*, Baha'i World Centre, Haifa, 1973. It is an attractive little book of 66 pages, printed in England.

In the Introduction, the great importance of the
Kitab-i-Aqdas is duly emphasized, and reasons are
given for the long delay in translating and
publishing it. "Shoghi Effendi, towards the end
of his life, adopted as one of the goals of the
Ten Year Crusade the codification of the laws and
ordinances of the *Kitab-i-Aqdas*, and he himself
worked upon it, leaving an outline of a synopsis
and codification in English, and notes in Persian.
This constituted a great part of the task which
the Universal House of Justice included as a goal
of the Nine Year Plan and which it then completed
according to the pattern he had set" (*Synopsis*,
p. 7).

All who have wished to know more about the contents of the Aqdas, which because of its Arabic
language and its unavailability has been to most
people a sealed book, will be grateful to the
Universal House of Justice for this first attempt
by Baha'is to make known in English all of its
laws and teachings.

After the Introduction, 18 pages of the *Synopsis*
contain "passages from the *Kitab-i-Aqdas* translated by Shoghi Effendi, which had been previously
published. These include a few of the laws, but
are chiefly exhortations and statements of the
high claims of Baha'u'llah.

Then follow 19 pages of "Synopsis and Codification"
of the laws of the Aqdas, divided into six main
sections. The numerous topics mentioned in the
Aqdas are listed, and in a number of instances the
content of the laws is briefly stated.

Unfortunately, neither the Arabic text nor an
English translation is provided, so the reader is
unable to consult the original ordinance as written
by Baha'u'llah. Anyone who is well acquainted with
the Aqdas will recognize that some of the ordinances listed are not found in the Aqdas, but are
taken from other writings of Baha'u'llah, or else
are interpretations of Abdu'l-Baha and Shoghi
Effendi. For example, we read in the *Synopsis*
(p. 35): "I.   The Appointment of Abdu'l-Baha as

the Successor of Baha'u'llah...." It is correct
that Abdu'l-Baha was appointed by his father to
succeed him, but this provision is found not in
the Aqdas but in the Will of Baha'u'llah. Also,
one might inquire where in the Aqdas is it stated
that, "should the weather be too cold the use of
warm water is recommended" (in making the ablutions before prayers - *Synopsis*, p. 37). A number
of such interpretations have found their way into
the laws which are said to be from the Aqdas.

While some of the Aqdas laws are accurately stated
and explained in the *Synopsis*, others are not. For
example, under the heading (y) *Prohibitions* on
p. 47, 32 actions are listed, such as "Interpretation of the Holy Writ," "Slave trading," "Use of
pulpits," "Arson," "Murder," etc. The *Synopsis*
does not state that Baha'u'llah in the Aqdas (p.
40) decreed that: "Whoever burns a house intentionally, burn him. Whoever kills a person with
intent, kill him" (or else sentence them to life
inprisonment).

One of the things listed as "prohibited" is
"plurality of wives." This is indeed surprising.
For Baha'u'llah himself had three wives who were
alive at the same time. Also, in the Aqdas (p.
40) it is written: "God has ordained marriage.
Beware lest you go beyond two (wives), and whoever
is satisfied with one of the handmaidens, his soul
is at rest, and so is hers." This law encourages
monogamy, but most certainly does not prohibit
"plurality of wives." In his explanation in
Synopsis (p. 59, Note 17), Shoghi Effendi definitely contradicts the law of Baha'u'llah.

Similarly, Baha'u'llah's detailed laws for the
division of Inheritance (Aqdas, pp. 29-31) are
practically annulled by the interpretation in the
Synopsis (p. 46), which is not found in the Aqdas,
which states: "Any person is at liberty to will
his possessions as he sees fit." Baha'u'llah
decreed that every one must write a Will (Aqdas,
p. 53). If each person writes his Will as he sees
fit, what becomes of Baha'u'llah's elaborate scheme

for the division of Inheritance, and his concern
that children get a large share? It was Baha'u'-
llah himself who said: "He who speaks other than
that sent down in My Tablets is not one of mine"
(Aqdas, p. 55).

The publication of this little book, inadequate
as it is, is welcome, and it is hoped that an
accurate translation of the whole of the *Kitab-
i-Aqdas* by the "infallible" Universal House of
Justice will soon follow.

25. *Aqdas*, p. 40.

26. Linfoot to Orick, February 25, 1963.

27. *Azal's Notes*, pp. 1-5. Mr. Azal kindly pointed
    out several errors in the Introduction to Elder's
    Translation of the Aqdas, in statements concern-
    ing the Bab's relation to the Letters of the
    Living, the abrogation of the Bayan, etc. Correc-
    tions for these errors have been incorporated in
    Chapters II, III and IV of this volume.

28. *Hawaii Baha'i News*, July 1967.

29. *Baha'i News*, August 1968.

30. Mr. Samandari died in 1968 at the age of 93.

31. *Baha'i News*, August 1968, p. 20.

32. Ibid., December 1967.

33. *Jerusalem Post Weekly*, September 9, 1969. This
    full-page report of the event, with a resume of
    Babi-Baha'i history, is marred by as many inaccur-
    acies as are usually found in articles the infor-
    mation for which has been supplied by Baha'is.

34. *Baha'i News*, December 1968, p. 5.

35. Ibid., December 1967, p. 14.

36. Here is a sample of Baha'i newspaper advertising
    taken from the Thursday, November 12, 1970 copy
    of the *Gazette* of Scotia, New York:

    The world has entered a new stage of history, the
    age of the maturity of man and the beginning of a
    world civilization. The source of this new

development was a Man who was exiled, tortured, banished and imprisoned for more than 40 years. He lived during the last century. His name -

B A H A ' U ' L L A H

THE GLORY OF GOD

Baha'u'llah is the latest in the succession of Divine Messengers sent by God since the beginning of man's existence. He is the Promised Age of Fulfillment mentioned in all the prophecies of the past. Baha'u'llah brings God's Plan for world peace, world justice and world unity.

FOR INFORMATION:

> BAHA'I FAITH
> Box 2581, Schenectady, N.Y. 12309

37. In the *Daily News Post* of Monrovia, California of Friday, September 19, 1969 is an article under the heading BAHA'I COMMUNITY OF MONROVIA WILL ATTEND WORLD PEACE DAY IN PASADENA. It states that the theme of this year's World Peace Day will be "Youth - Builders of a New World," and the Day will be observed on Sunday by members of the Baha'i communities located in over 2,500 American cities. Also, the article states that "there are weekly firesides (talks and discussions) held in Monrovia every Friday evening." A phone number is given for further information.

38. Baha'i sources report that as of April 21, 1970 there are 23,879 members of the Faith in the U.S.A., excluding Alaska and Hawaii, of whom 5,000 are missing. There was a net increase of 3,219 members in the preceding year.

39. Letter of C. L. Seeberger, *The Christian Century*, May 5, 1971.

40. Mr. H. W. Stalley to Miller, January 24, 1969.

41. *Baha'i World 1926-1928*, pp. 141-150.

42. Dr. Paul Clasper to Miller, January 30, 1969.

43. Dr. F. Dale Bruner to Miller, May 6, 1969.

44. Dr. Samuel Moffett to Miller, July 12, 1969.

45. Mr. Warren Webster to Miller, November 3, 1969.

46. Mr. Jollynoos Hakim and Mr. Azizollah Mebesser to Miller, March 10 and 31 and April 8, 1969.

47. Mason Remey died in his residence in Florence, Italy, on February 4, 1974, just 99 days before his 100th birthday. It is probable that his body will be buried in the Pompey Hill Cemetery in the state of New York in his family plot. The decision regarding his successor has as yet not been made known.

15

Conclusions

Any system that makes a claim to be a universal religion thereby invites the earnest consideration and careful appraisal of all who are seeking for God and for true life in this world and the next. The "Baha'i World Faith" is not just a crusade for world peace and unity and equity, important as these goals are. Rather, as has become clear in the preceding chapters, it claims to be the one true faith for the whole world for a thousand years, uniting in itself and taking the place of all previous religions. As is stated in the Introduction to vol. XIII of *The Baha'i World*, "It is the avowed faith of Baha'is that this Revelation has established upon earth the spiritual impulse and the definite principles necessary for social regeneration and the attainment of one true religion and social order throughout the world." It is, therefore, our privilege and responsibility to weigh the validity of this high claim with all due care.

Whoever peruses the thousands of pages of the thirteen large volumes of *The Baha'i World* will be impressed by the fact that the Baha'i Faith is indeed a world faith. For Baha'is, as well as for Christians

and Muslims, "the field is the world," and it is their
aim to bring to all peoples the Good News of Baha'u'-
llah, and to unite all the conflicting religions in
one. In a world that is today sorely divided, any
effort to unite mankind in the bonds of true brotherhood is to be commended. It order to convert the
people of the world to this Faith, Baha'is have been
most zealous in their missionary work. Believing that
they have the latest and best religion in the world,
they use every means in their power to propagate it,
not only in their home communities, but also in foreign lands where, in obedience to the command of their
leaders, they have gone to reside. One cannot but
admire the zeal of those who with heart and mind and
hands work for a cause in which they believe.

Of course zeal, and even the readiness to die for
a cause, do not necessarily prove the validity and
value of the cause, for history reminds us there have
been many martyrs who have died for error as well as
for truth. Whether the devoted missionaries are
Mormons or Muslims, Baptists or Baha'is, their message
must be examined and evaluated on its merits. What
then shall we say of the teachings of the Baha'i
Faith as set forth in the writings of Baha'u'llah and
those who followed him? It would seem that in the
official literature of the Faith special emphasis is
placed on the "Principles" which were listed and discussed in Chapter XI. Though the tabulation of these
Principles should be attributed to Abdu'l-Baha rather
than to his father, and though they are not original
with him, certainly most persons of good will would
readily assent to the importance of "Independent
investigation of truth," "Unity of mankind," "International peace," "Conformity of religion to science
and reason" (provided it is true science and sound
reason), "Banishment of all prejudice," "Equality of
men and women," "A world parliament," "Universal
education" and "A universal language." These are
social and ethical teachings which people of most
religions, or of no religion, might adopt. They are
not strictly religious principles, and there is no
mention of God in connection with them.

To evaluate the Baha'i system as a religion, it is necessary to go back of the Principles to the Laws of Baha'u'llah which are contained in his *Kitab-i-Aqdas*, a summary of which has been given in Chapter VIII. As the unprejudiced reader peruses the regulations which Baha'u'llah gave for worship in the Arabic language, for the 19-day fast, for the division of inheritance, for the establishment of a 19-month calendar of 19 days in each month, for severe punishment for an arsonist and light punishment for an adulterer, for polygamous marriages, etc., is he convinced that this is the code of laws by which the lives of all the people of the world should be regulated for the next one thousand years? It has been said by some Baha'is that the world is not yet ready to receive the laws of the *Kitab-i-Aqdas*. This is no doubt true. But will it ever be ready to adopt this code of laws?

Moreover, it is clear from the *Aqdas* and from the writings of later leaders that the Baha'i Faith is political as well as social and religious in its purpose and program. Baha'is look forward eagerly to the day when the rulers of the nations will become believers and will use their political power to support the Baha'i Faith and enforce its laws, when the Universal House of Justice will become the Supreme Court of the World, and when not only the personal lives of believers but also the political affairs of the world will be ordered according to the laws of Baha'u'llah. In the Baha'i system there is to be no separation of Church and State. Prior to the death of Shoghi Efendi in 1957, one of the chief merits of the Faith, according to Baha'i writers, was the abiding presence in the world at all times of a living infallible leader and guide, who would be the supreme head of the world "Church-State." Since the First Guardian died without appointing a successor, most of the Baha'is agree that the rule now resides in the 9-member Universal House of Justice, and for this body also infallibility is claimed. It would indeed be a welcome and wonderful change to live in a world the rulers of which were infallible, but such a hope has been shattered by Baha'u'llah himself when he stated(1)

that infallibility belongs to the Manifestation (Baha'-
u'llah) alone.

Since "the tree is known by its fruit," we may ask
how effective Baha'is have been in practicing their
Principles and obeying their Laws. It seems that
their greatest success has been in demonstrating the
absence of racial prejudice and promoting good race
relations. From the early days in America when
"Amity" meetings were held to bring together members
of different races, to the present time when it is
said that one-third of the believers in America are
blacks, the efforts of the Baha'is here and in other
lands are most commendable, and it is not surprising
that members of minority groups are attracted to a
movement that cordially accepts them. It would seem
that in America and probably also in other lands the
strongest appeal of the Faith is not so much its
teachings as the fellowship which it offers, the
feeling of belonging to a community, something which
had not been found elsewhere. Since the local Baha'i
units are usually not large, the members are drawn
close together in the service of the Cause.

A young man in California who was urged by an
acquaintance to attend Baha'i meetings wrote of his
experience as follows: "The bond of community was
very strong. I noticed that strangers from out of
town would appear at a meeting, declare themselves
Baha'is, and the following week Baha'is had found
them a job and a place to stay. I thought the practice of embracing every Negro and Oriental that came
to the meetings terribly patronizing.....Out of a
history of deception and intrigue has come the para-
dox of a community of earnest and generous souls.
But an intense community life can be a hideous thing
when it turns a deaf ear to the suffering of human
beings outside the cozy club."(2)

As for "International Peace," Baha'is like many
other groups religious and secular have talked much
about peace and have no doubt done what they could
to achieve the goal predicted by the ancient prophets
of Israel and announced by Baha'u'llah as the "Most

Great Peace." In addition to what individuals may have done in their writings and addresses, *The Baha'i World*, vol. XIII, contains a proposal submitted by the "Baha'i International Community" to the United Nations for a revision of its Charter. Here is a portion of the long statement: "The Baha'i concept of world order is defined in these terms: A World Super-State in whose favor all the nations of the world will have ceded every claim to make war, certain rights to impose taxation, and all rights to maintain armaments, except for purposes of maintaining internal order within their respective dominions. This State will have to include an International Executive adequate to enforce supreme and unchallenged authority on every recalcitrant member of the Commonwealth, a World Parliament whose members are elected by the peoples in their respective countries and whose election is confirmed by their respective governments, a Supreme Tribunal whose judgment has a binding effect even in cases where the parties concerned have not voluntarily agreed to submit their case to its consideration." It seems that the United Nations did not view this proposal for revision of its Charter with favor.

In their understandable desire to show that the Baha'i Faith has had an influence for good on the history of the world, Baha'is have sometimes made the mistake that others have made of claiming credit for something that was not theirs. An example is the statement made by Guy Murchie(3) that "Woodrow Wilson's daughter was an ardent student of the Baha'i teachings; it is said that she was instrumental in influencing her father to include the Baha'i principles in his 'Fourteen Points' at Versailles." When questioned as to the accuracy of this statement, which has been frequently repeated by Baha'is, the Rev. Francis Sayre, grandson of President Wilson and Dean of the Cathredal in Washington, D.C., replied(4) that his aunt had no interest in the Baha'i movement, and there was no foundation for the claim that the "Fourteen Points" were in any way influenced by her or by the Baha'i Principles.

In education and medicine and other fields Baha'is
in Iran and in other lands have rendered valuable
service, usually in a private capacity and not in
the name of their Faith. In vol. XIII. of *The Baha'i
World* which reports fully the activities of believers
in all lands for the years 1954-1963 the reader found
only one mention of a Baha'i service institution,
which was a home for the aged in Wilmette.

As has been pointed out in the previous chapters,
Baha'is have not been outstanding in their practice
of the fine Principle designated "Independent investigation of truth." One wonders how it would be possible for an openminded Baha'i to investigate the history
and doctrine of his religion while under the rule of an
infallible Center of the Covenant or Guardian or House
of Justice who claim the sole authority to interpret
the sacred writings. Such investigation becomes yet
more difficult when the *Kitab-i-Aqdas*, ranked by
Shoghi Efendi(5) as "the brightest emanation of the
mind of Baha'u'llah," has not yet been made available
to Baha'is, who have been strictly forbidden to read
a translation of the *Aqdas* by non-Baha'i scholars. We
have told the story of the fate of Ahmad Sohrab and
Mrs. White and Niku and Avareh and others who were
rash enough to make known the results of their inves-
tigations. Anyone who questions the accuracy of the
authorized version of Babi-Baha'i history is denounced
as an enemy of the Cause of God.

Important as are the laws and ethical and social
teachings of a religion, its basic beliefs about God
and man on which all else depends are of yet greater
importance. What answer does it give to the questions
which men in all ages have been asking - Who or What
is God? What is man? How can man know God? What
must man do to be accepted by God? How can he get
rid of the sin and evil which darkens his life and
separates him from both God and man? What does God
want man to be and to do? Is there life after death?
The value of any religion depends to a considerable
degree on its ability to provide adequate answers to
these and similar questions.

What does the Baha'i Faith tell us about God?
Baha'u'llah taught that God is unknowable, except
through his Manifestations, who are Adam, Noah, Abraham, Moses, Jesus, Muhammad and Baha'u'llah, each
Manifestation being more perfect than the one which
preceded it. He held that all the Manifestations are
one, as the sun of today is the same as the sun of
yesterday. However, anyone who takes a close and
careful look at these "Suns" will realize that they
differ greatly from one another, and it would seem
that on each appearance God has changed his character
as well as his laws, and not always for the better.
When later Zoroaster, Buddha and finally Krishna were
included in the Manifestations, the confusion became
compounded. The Bab had taught that there could be
only one Sun in the heavens at a time to reveal the
One God. But if Zoroaster, Buddha and Krishna also
are Manifestations, then there would have been two or
more Suns in the sky at once, and it would seem that
God had become twins or triplets. Hence the message
of the modern Baha'i Faith about God is far from
clear and is by no means adequate. Probably each
believer brings into his Baha'i faith the conception
of God which he had gotten from his previous faith,
or no-faith. The Jews, Christians and Muslims would
think of God as One, and the Hindus might continue to
believe in a multitude of gods. The reply of the
Baha'is would no doubt be that in this age God is
revealed more perfectly than ever before in Baha'u'-
llah. Is it improper to inquire which of the divine
attributes are revealed more perfectly in Baha'u'llah
than in the great prophets of the Old Testament and
in Jesus Christ? And whether God's love is more perfectly manifested in Baha'u'llah's service to the
world than in the service of any other messenger of
God?

One of the phrases frequently found in Baha'i
literature is "progressive revelation." It is said
that people usually think of prophets as men who
lived and revealed God in the distant past, and do
not imagine it possible for God to reveal himself
now. "Yet Baha'u'llah not only lived in our time,

but was contemporary in the fullest sense of the word.
His teachings are....extremely advanced," says one
Baha'i writer.(6) We are compelled to ask, "Is
Baha'u'llah really contemporary? He died in 1892,
eleven years before the Wright brothers made their
first flight, before automobiles were seen on our
roads, before TV pictures were shown to incredulous
eyes, and before anyone dreamed that bombs would be
made that could blow up the world. If it is God's
plan in "progressive revelation" to send new Manifestations to guide the people of the world in new
situations, surely something more relevant than the
Kitab-i-Aqdas is needed for today, and a person
closer to us than Baha'u'llah. But, according to
Baha'u'llah, no new Manifestation will come before
2866 A.D. If many of Baha'u'llah's pronouncements
seem to fit our modern situation, so do the Ten
Commandments of Moses and the Sermon on the Mount
of Jesus. A study of the Aqdas will make it clear
that Baha'u'llah is closer to the Middle Ages than
to the world of 1973.

What is the Baha'i doctrine of man? Since in
Baha'i teaching God is not usually called "Father,"
except when Christians are being addressed, man is
considered not a child of God but a servant or slave
of God. However, the Baha'i view of man is quite
optimistic, for it is thought that all man needs is
laws and precepts and an Educator. The evil that
resides in man's heart, be he savage or civilized,
evil that causes the horrible crimes that have
blotted the pages of the histories of the most
"advanced" nations, is largely ignored. Neither in
the writings of the Bab nor in those of Baha'u'llah
and the later leaders, except when they are denouncing their enemies, is there any adequate consideration of man's deadly disease which is sin. Few are
the appeals to men to repent of their sins as the
prophets of old appealed,(7) few the assurances of
God's love for sinners and his promises to them of
forgiveness and a new life of holiness.

Since the diagnosis of man's disease is faulty,
the provision which the Baha'i faith makes for his

cure is inadequate. In all Baha'i literature can
there be found a promise of a Savior from sin, or a
picture of welcome by God to a penitent as appealing
as the parable of the Prodigal Son? What would
Abdu'l-Baha have said to give hope to a drug addict
on skid row, or to guide and comfort a convict in a
death cell? Sinners need salvation, and the Baha'i
Faith fails to provide a Savior.

"If a man die shall he live again?" asked Job. To
this vital question the reply of Baha'u'llah is vague
and unsatisfying. "Resurrection" in the Baha'i system
means the coming of a new Manifestation. Such terms
as "entering the Abha Kingdom," "drinking the wine of
immortality," "hastening to the Supreme Concourse,"
"Paradise of Abha, the everlasing abode of glorious,
sacred souls," are found in the *Aqdas* and other writings. But it is not clear whether personal immortality
is promised, or merely the merging of man with the
Infinite, like the return of a raindrop to the sea
from which it came.

For many students of the Baha'i history, one of its
most disappointing aspects is the failure of its
founders and leaders to reveal in their personal
lives, and in their dealings with members of their
families and others who differed with them, the spirit
of love of which they so often spoke and which they
enjoined on others. In the preceding chapters it has
become abundantly clear that Baha'u'llah in his relations with his brother Subh-i-Azal, Abdu'l-Baha in his
relations with his brother Mirza Muhammad Ali, and
Shoghi Efendi in his relations with numerous relatives
and former friends revealed an attitude of bitterness
that was hardly a worthy example for their followers.
We are reminded of the question asked by an apostle
of old,(9) "He that loveth not his brother whom he
hath seen, how can he love God whom he hath not seen?"
And how can he adequately and effectively manifest
God's love to others?

With its lack of clarity in its doctrine of God;
with its legalism which characterizes its Most Holy
Book; with its prescription in this Book of practices

long since outdated; with the inadequacy of its treatment of sin and of its provision for the cure of evil
in man; with the vagueness of its teaching about life
after death; with the gross failure of its founders
to exemplify among their own families the love they
so strongly advocated - with these and other defects
which are manifest in its history, can the Baha'i
World Faith be an adequate religion for the world for
today, and for the millennium to come? Only one
answer is possible, and that is decidedly negative.

NOTES

1. *Aqdas*, p. 37.

2. A. J. Sistrom to Miller.

3. *Chicago Sunday Tribune*, article by Guy Murchie:
   "I am a Baha'i," July 3, 1958, p. 4.

4. Sayre to Sistrom, April 25, 1969.

5. *God Passes By*, Shoghi Efendi, p. 213.

6. *Manifestation - Not Incarnation*, by Albert
   Entzminger, Baha'i Publishing Trust 1968, p. 8.

7. Baha'u'llah commanded his brother Subh-i-Azal,
   who had refused to submit to him, to repent and
   believe, and he promised to forgive him if he did
   so (*Aqdas*, p. 73). Also in "The Ninth Glad
   Tidings" of Baha'u'llah sinners are commanded
   to confess to God and ask his forgiveness (*Bahai
   Scriptures*, p. 142).

8. *Job* 14:13.

9. *1 John* 4:20.

Appendix 1

Translation
of Al-Kitab Al-Aqdas

ORIENTAL TRANSLATION FUND

NEW SERIES VOLUME XXXVIII

AL-KITĀB AL-AQDAS

or

THE MOST HOLY BOOK

by

MĪRZĀ ḤUSAYN 'ALĪ BAHĀ'U'LLĀH

Translated from the Original Arabic and Edited

by

EARL E. ELDER, PH.D., D.D.

and

WILLIAM McE. MILLER, M.A., D.D.

Published by

THE ROYAL ASIATIC SOCIETY

and sold by its Agents

LUZAC & COMPANY, LTD.

46 GREAT RUSSELL STREET, LONDON, W.C. 1

1961

PRINTED IN GREAT BRITAIN BY
STEPHEN AUSTIN AND SONS, LTD., HERTFORD, HERTS

PREFACE

Anyone who studies Baha'ism learns very soon of the volume sacred to those who profess this religion and known as "The Most Holy Book". Of this book Bahā' in his Will said, "... reflect upon that which is revealed in my book the Aqdas." And his son and successor 'Abdul Bahā' said in his Will, "unto the Aqdas everyone must turn."

Yet, strange to say, although the teachings of Bahā' have been widely proclaimed in Great Britain and America, only fragments of *al-Kitāb al-Aqdas* have been translated previously into English. Another interesting point is that it is written in Arabic, although the founder of the religion was Persian and the first promulgation of this doctrine was in Persia (now known as Iran), where Arabic is not generally known.

When a translation was contemplated reliance was placed on an edition published in Arabic at Baghdad, Iraq, in 1931. However, the attention of those interested was turned to a copy of the work, a gift of 'Abdul Bahā' to one of the first American Bahā'īs to visit him in Palestine. This copy had been autographed by 'Abdul Bahā' on 25th March, 1899. By the permission of the present owner, this version has been used in the translation.

It was this text which was first distributed by Bahā' among his followers—in handwriting. About 1880 he sent one of his sons and a disciple to India to prepare the manuscript for publication. Photographic copies of the sixty-five pages of this text are in the collections preserved in the Public Library of New York City. It is available there to any who wish to pursue the investigation of the text in the original Arabic.

Since the Bahā'ī Administration at Wilmette, Illinois, admittedly does not possess a copy of the book, nor has it been circulated in America, this translation will afford many the opportunity of gaining at first hand knowledge of the principles of the faith.

In comparing this rather authentic copy with the Baghdad edition one discovers a great many differences of minor importance. The omission of three lines appearing in the Baghdad copy from the text on page 57 and again of four lines on page 60 of this edition constitute the most conspicuous differences. However, no important doctrine is introduced in these lines that has not already been stressed. In fact in both cases the words are exhortations to the recognition of God's power and might. These have often been stressed previously.

In translating the Bahá'í holy book one faces the problem of giving a critical study of the manifold differences in the text, or of ignoring the elaborate apparatus for collating readings and presenting a readable translation with explanatory notes. The latter method was chosen with the idea of making the book interesting to a wider circle of readers. The Arabic, like that of the Qur'án, is often lofty and sometimes difficult to express in language easy to be understood by Westerners.

The reader must remember that Bahá' was of Persian origin and the Arabic words and terminology sometimes have a Persian flavour. Some references to the shades of difference in meaning in the two languages are to be found in the notes.

When A. H. Tumansky translated *al-Kitáb al-Aqdas* into Russian more than sixty years ago, he felt an introduction was imperative. That it reached to three times the length of the original work translated is not surprising when one remembers that the background is crammed with a long history. An introduction and full notes on many points unfamiliar to a Western reader were absolutely essential. Much of the interpretive explanation in the Notes has been secured from one thoroughly familiar with Baha'ism through years of close connection with the movement.

In conclusion, lest readers imagine the translation was not sufficiently checked, it is only right to mention that it has been reviewed not only by those who know Arabic and Persian well, but by three persons who have an intimate acquaintance with the teachings of Bahá'u'lláh.

The transliteration of the Arabic words has often been given to enable Arabists to know the original. At times words which rhyme give some suggestion of the style of the composition, resembling the rhyming prose of the Qur'án. Further discussion of style and subject matter is unnecessary since the book speaks for itself.

Among those who have reviewed the translation and introduction, mention should be made of Mr. Will Orick and Rev. Cady H. Allen. Mr. Orick, among many services in connection with this work, arranged for the typing of the entire manuscript for the printers. Rev. Cady H. Allen has given invaluable assistance in many suggestions regarding punctuation and phrasing.

The figures given in parenthesis in the text are the pages of the copy from which the translation has been made.

EARL E. ELDER.

AL-KITĀB AL-AQDAS

In the name of Him who is the Ruler (al-ḥākim) over what was and what will be.

The first thing which God ordained (kataba) concerning His creatures (al-'ibād) is the knowledge of the Sunrise-place (mashriq) of His revelation and the Rising-place (maṭla') of His Cause (amrihi), who was the Station (maqām) of Himself in the world of command and creation.[1]

Whoever attains unto Him (fāza bihi) attains unto all good, and whoever is deprived of Him is of the people of error (al-ḍalāl), even though he performs all (good) works (al-a'māl).

Whenever you attain unto this most noble Station and most high Horizon (ufuq), every soul must follow what has been commanded by the Desired One (al-maqsūd), because these two [2] are (to be taken) together; and one is not accepted without the other. This is what the Rising-place of Illumination (al-ilhām) has ruled (ḥakama).

Those who have been given sight by God see the stipulations (al-ḥudūd, bounds) of God, (which are) the greatest cause for the setting of the world in order and the preserving of the nations.

Whoever is careless is of the rabble (hamaj) and the ruffians (ra'ā').

We have commanded you to break the bounds of the self and passion (al-hawā); not that which was written (ruqima) by the Most High Pen (al-qalam al-a'la).

It is the spirit of Life (rūḥ al-ḥayawān) for whoever is in the (realm of the) possible (al-imkān).[3] (3) The seas of wisdom and explanation have raged (mājat) with that whereby the breeze of the Merciful (al-raḥmān) was violent (hājat).

Seize the opportunity, O possessors of minds (ūlā'l-albāb)! Those who broke the covenant of God (manifest) in His commands and turned back from the path of justice are of the people of error (al-ḍalāl) before the Exalted Self-Sufficient One (al-ghanī al-muta'āl).

---

[1] The " world of command " is the unseen world of reality; the " world of creation " is the material world. E. G. Browne adds the following note (Journal of Royal Asiatic Society, 1889, p. 972): " The first thing necessary to men is that they should know Beha', the present ' Manifestation ' of God in the world, without which knowledge good actions are of no avail."

[2] " These two," that is, knowing and obeying.

[3] Al-imkān (the possible) is a term for all creation which occurs often in al-Kitab al-Aqdas.

O multitudes (*mala'*) of the earth, know that My commands are the lamps of My providence among My creatures and the keys of My Mercy to My people (*barriyatī*). Thus was the command sent down (*nuzzila*) from the heaven of the will of your Lord, the Possessor (*mālik*) of religions.

Were one to find the sweetness of the explanation which appeared from the mouth of the will of the Merciful, he would spend what he has, even though it were the treasures of the whole earth, in order to establish one of His commands which arise from the horizon of providence and benefits (*al-alṭāf*).

Say : From My stipulations there passes the sweet smell (*'arf*) of My gown and by them the standards of victory are erected on hillocks and hills.

The tongue of My power (*qudratī*) has spoken in the might (*jabarūt*) of My greatness, addressing My people, (saying), " Perform My stipulations out of love for My beauty (*jamālī*)."

Blessed is the lover who found the sweet smell of the beloved (coming) out of this word from which aromas of grace were diffused, that they be not described (only) by remembrances !

I swear by My life (*la 'amrī*), whoever drinks of the pure wine (*rahīq*) of equity from the hands of the benefits will make the circuit of My commands which arise from the horizon of new things (*al-abdā'*).

Do not reckon that We have sent down the commandments to you, but rather We have opened the seal of the sealed pure wine by the fingers of power and might. What was sent down from the Pen of Revelation (*al-wahy*) bears witness to that. Think thereon, (4) O possessors of thoughts.

Worship (*al-ṣalāt*) has been ordained for you—nine prostrations (*raka'āt*) to God Who has sent down the verses ; when noon is past (*al-zawāl*), in the morning (*al-bukūr*) and in the late afternoon (*al-aṣāl*).[1] We have exempted (*'afawna*) (you) from the other number on account of a command in the Book of God.[2] Indeed He is the Powerful, the Choosing, the Commanding One.

---

[1] The prayers may be said from sunset until two hours after sunset, from sunrise until noon, and from noon until late afternoon.

[2] According to Islamic law prayers are to be said five times a day (cf. *Encyclopedia of Islam*, iv, 98 ff.), but Bahā'u'llāh reduced the number to three. By " the Book of God " is meant *al-Kitāb al-Aqdas*.

Whenever you desire to worship, turn your face towards My most holy direction (*shaṭrī*), the Holy Station which God made the place of circumambulation for the angels (*al-mala' al-a'lā*), and the direction for worship of the people of the cities of continuing eternity, and the source of command to all who are on the earths and in the heavens, and at the setting of the Sun of Reality and clear Explanation, the Resting-place (*al-maqarr*) which we have decreed for you.[1] He is the Knower, the Strong One.

Everything is realized by His confirmed command whenever the Sun of commandments rises from the horizon of Explanation (*al-bayān*) that all may follow them even if by a command by which are cleft asunder the heavens of the hearts of religions.[2]

He does what He wills and He is not questioned about what He willed and what the Beloved One rules.

He is, indeed, Beloved and the Possessor of Invention.

Whoever finds the sweet smell (*'arf*) of the Merciful and of the Rising-place of this Explanation will meet with his eyes the arrows for establishing the commandments among mankind. Blessed is the one who came and attained unto the message of the discourse !

We have analysed worship at length in another paper.

Blessed is the one who did as commanded by the Possessor of persons (*al-riqāb*) !

In worship for the dead the saying of six *takbīras* has been sent down (as a commandment)[3] from God who sends down the verses.

(5) Whoever knows how to read must read what has been sent down beforehand, and if he does not God has forgiven him. He is indeed the Forgiving, the Mighty One.

Hair does not make void your worship, nor does that which has been deprived of spirit, such, for example, as bones and other things.[4]

Wear sable (*sammūr*) just as you wear silk and squirrel-skin and

---

[1] Browne (*JRAS.*, 1889, p. 973) takes this as a reference to Acre, the place where Bahā'u'llāh was at the time. ~~But it may also mean that in worship Bahā'īs should face Bahā'u'llāh himself, wherever he may be. When he dies they are to face the person who will be appointed to succeed him.~~ Muslims in prayer face Mecca.

[2] This means that this command may even oppose the laws of other religions.

[3] In Islam the saying of the words " *Allāhu akbar* " (God is most great) is called the takbīr. Cf. *Enc. of Islam*, iv, 627. Instead of saying " *Allāhu akbar* " as Muslims do, Bahā'īs say " *Allāhu abha* " (God is most splendid).

[4] Touching hair or bones (or buttons made of bones) renders worship void in Islam (cf. A. J. Wensinck, *A Handbook of Early Muhammadan Traditions*, p. 191). Bahā'u'llāh here abrogates this law.

other things. Indeed, this was not forbidden in the Furqān (i.e. the
Qur'ān), but the learned ones were uncertain about it. Indeed He is
the Knower, the Mighty One.

Worship and Fasting are obligatory to you on your coming to
maturity [1] a command from God, your Lord and the Lord of your
early fathers.

Whoever is weak from illness or advanced age, God exempts him
because of a Grace on His part.

He is the Generous One, the Forgiver.

God permits you to prostrate yourselves on everything pure, and
we have taken away the ruling stipulated in the Book.[2]

God knows and you do not.

Whoever does not find water, let him repeat five times, " bi-sm-
illāh, al-aṭhar, al-aṭhar " (In the name of God, the Purest, the Purest,)
and then begin worship.

This is what the Master of the worlds commanded.

In those lands where nights and days are long they may perform
worship by (using) clocks and objects which determine the times.

He is the Wise One, the Explainer.

We have exempted you from worship (on the occasion) of wonders.[3]
Whenever they appear, make mention of God with greatness and
power. He is the Hearing One, the Seeing One. Say : " al-'aẓama
lillāh, rabb mā yurā wa mā lā yurā, rabb al-'ālamīn " (Greatness
belongs to God, the Lord of what is seen and what is unseen, the Lord
of the worlds).

(6) Worship as individuals has been ordained for you ; the
commandment regarding group worship is remitted (rufi'a), except
in worship for the dead.[4]

He is the Wise One, the Commanding One.

God has exempted women from worship and fasting ; whenever
they find blood (in menstruating). They have to perform ablutions
and praise God ninety-five times from afternoon to afternoon, saying

---

[1] Both boys and girls come to maturity according to the Bahā'ī law at the age of
fifteen.

[2] In Islam it is forbidden to perform prostrations on certain things even though
they are ceremonially pure. " The Book " in this case is presumably the Qur'ān.

[3] Islam requires special prayers to be said at the time of wonders like earthquakes
and eclipses (cf. Wensinck, op. cit., p. 65 f.). This is not necessary for Bahā'īs.

[4] Under certain conditions in Islam group worship, as in the mosque on Friday,
is favoured (cf. Qur'ān, 62 : 9 and Wensinck, op. cit., 192 f.), but Bahā'u'llāh
abrogated this with the exception of prayer over the dead.

كتب عليكم الصلوة وادى قد نفع حكم الجماعة الا فى صلوة الميت

انه لهو الامر الحكيم قد عفا الله عن النساء حين ما يجدن القمر

الصوم والصلوة ولمن ان يتوضان ويبتمر خمسا ويبيز

مرة من زوال الى زوال سبحان الله ذى الطاعة والجاه هذا

ما قد ذكر الكتاب ان انتم من العالمين ولكم ولمن فى الاسفار

اذا انزلتم واسترحتم المقام الامن مكان كل صلوة سجدة واحدة

واذكروا ايها سبحان الله ذى العظمة والاجلال والموهبة

والافضال والذكر عز يقول سبحان الله انه يكفيه بالحق انه

لهو الكافى الباقى الغفور الرحيم وبعد اتمام السجود لكم و

لمن ان يقعدوا على هيكل التوحيد وتقولوا ثمان عشرة مرة

سبحان الله ذى الملك والملكوت كذلك يبين الله سبل

الحق والهدى واتها انتقت الى سبيل واحد وهو هذا الصراط

المستقيم اشكروا والله هذا الفضل العظيم احمدوا الله

هذه الموهبة التى احاطت السموات والارضين اذكروا الله

هذه الرحمة التى سبقت للعالمين قل قد جعل الله مفتاحا

الكنز حق المكنون لو انتم تعرفون لولا المفتاح لكان مكنونا
فى ازل الآزال لو انتم توقنون قل هذا المطلع الوحى و مشرق الآثار
الذى به اشرقت الآفاق لو انتم تعلمون ان هذا هو القضاء
المثبت و به ثبت كل قضاء محتوم يا قلم الاعلى قل
يا ملأ الانشاء قد كتبنا عليكم الصيام اياما معدودت
و جعلنا النيروز عيدا لكم بعد اكمالها كذلك اضاءت شمس
البيان من افق الكتاب من لدن مالك المبدء و المآب و جعلوا
الايام الزائدة عن الشهور قبل شهر الصيام انا جعلناها مظاهر
الهاء بين الليالى و الايام لذا ما تحددت بحدود السنة
و الشهور ينبغى لاهل البهاء ان يطعموا فيها انفسهم و ذوى
القربى ثم الفقراء و المساكين و يهللن و يكبرن و يسبحن
و يمجدن ربهم بالفرح و الانبساط و اذا تمت ايام الاعطاء
قبل الامساك فليدخلن فى الصيام كذلك حكم مولى الانام
ليس على المسافر و المريض و الحامل و المرضع من حرج عفا الله عنهم
فضلا من عنده انه لهو العزيز الوهاب هذه حدود الله التى

" *subḥān Allāh dhī al-ṭalʿa wa l-jamāl* " (Praise be to God, the Possessor of Countenance and Beauty). This is what we decreed in the Book,[1] if you be of the knowing ones.

And for you men and women, if, on journeys you stop and rest in a safe location, (there is required) in place of the whole ritual of worship (only) one prostration and the saying of the words, " *subḥān Allāh dhī al-ʿaẓama waʾl-ijlāl waʾl-mawhiba waʾl-afḍāl* " (Praise be to God, the Possessor of Greatness and Majesty, the Free Gift and the Graces).

Whoever is unable (to do this) will say, " *subḥān Allāh* " (Praise be to God). Thus is the duty sufficiently performed. He is the Satisfying, the Continuing, the Forgiving, the Merciful One.

After completing the prostration, you and the women are to sit at the temple of Unity (*haykal al-tawḥīd*) [2] and say eighteen times, " *subḥān Allāh dhī al-mulk waʾl-malakūt* " (Praise be to God, the Possessor of the kingdoms of this world and the next).

Thus God explains the ways of Reality and Guidance. They end, indeed, in one way which is the Straight Path (*al-ṣirāṭ al-mustaqīm*).

Give thanks to God for this great Grace. Praise God for this free gift which encompassed the heavens and the earths.

Remember God for this mercy which preceded the worlds.

Say : God has made my hidden love the key (7) of the treasure, if you would only perceive.

Were it not for the key, it would be hidden for the eternity of past eternities, if you were only certain.

Say : This is the Rising-place of Revelation and the Sunrise-place of the Brilliance by which the horizons became light, if you only knew.

This is the established decision (*al-qaḍāʾ*). By it every settled decision is established.

O Pen of the Most High, say : O multitudes of creation (*al-inshāʾ*), we have ordained the Fast for you, certain limited days. After the completion of them we have made *al-Nayrūz* (*Nawrūz*) a feast for you.[3] Thus has the Sun of Explanation shone from the horizon of the

---

[1] It seems that by " Book " the Aqdas is intended.

[2] This expression is said to mean sitting on the floor with one's feet crossed under him and his hands resting on his knees.

[3] This passage is translated by E. G. Browne in *A Traveller's Narrative*, p. 423. " From all this it would seem that the restoration of the old Persian solar year in place of the Arabian lunar year ; the solemn sanctioning of the great national

Book from before the presence of the Possessor of the Place of Beginning and Return.

And place prior to the month of fasting the (intercalary) days which are in excess of the months.[1] We have, indeed, made them manifestations of al-hā' [2] among the nights and days.

Therefore these five days are not included in the year and the months. It is fitting, then, that in them the People of Bahā' (Splendour) feed themselves and their relatives, then the poor and poverty-stricken. They must exalt, magnify, praise, and glorify their Lord with joy and gladness.

And whenever the days of giving [3] are completed, before the refraining (from food) let them enter upon the fast. So has the Master of Mankind (mawlā al-anām) commanded.

This does not cause difficulty for the one who is on a journey, for the ill, for the pregnant woman, or the one who is nursing. God has exempted them as a Grace on His part.

He is the Mighty One, the Free Giver.

These are the stipulations of God which (8) were written by the Most High Pen in the books and tablets.

Hold fast to the orders and commandments of God. Be not of those who have held to their own principles (uṣūl) and have cast behind them the principles of God in following their opinions and illusions.

Restrain yourselves from eating and drinking from the rising (of

---

festival of the Nawruz, which corresponds with the beginning of this solar year, the quickening of the earth after its winter torpor, and the entry of the Sun into the sign of Aries ; the division of the year into nineteen months of nineteen days each ; and the nomenclature certainly of some and probably of all of these months were integral portions of the system devised by the Bab ; while the provision of the five intercalary days . . . and the enactments relating to their observance were supplementary details introduced by Beha." Ibid. p. 424.

[1] The arrangement is that, beginning with the Iranian New Year (Nawruz, which usually falls on 21st March), there will be eighteen months of nineteen days each. Then will come the five intercalary days. After them will begin the nineteenth month, the month of fasting. Immediately after it will come the next Nawruz, the feast of the New Year, according to ancient Iranian custom. The Arabic Nayruz is from the Persian Nawruz (cf. E. W. Lane, Lexicon, p. 2783).

[2] The Arabic letter al-hā', which means " him " or " his ", also has the numerical value of five. It may here refer to Him (God) or to " hospitality ". The five days are to be a time of rest and kindness to others before the fast begins.

[3] " Days of giving," that is, the five intercalary days.

رقت من اقلام الاعلى في الزبر والالواح تمسكوا بها واوامراته
واحكامه ولا تكونوا امن الذين اخذوا اصول انفسهم ونبذوا
اصول الله وراءهم بما اتبعوا الظنون والاوهام كونوا انفسكم
عن اكل والشرب من الطلوع الى الافول بانكم يمنعكم الهوى
عن هذا الفضل الذي قدر في الكتاب قد كتب لمن دان بالله الذي
ان يغسل في كل يوم يديه ثم وجهه ويقعد مقبلا الى الله ويذكر
خمسا وتسعين مرة الله ابهى كذلك حكم من لدن الامر اذ استوى
على اعراش الاسماء بالعظمة والاقتدار كذلك توضأوا
للصلوة امن امر الله الواحد المختار قد حرم عليكم القتل
والزنا ثم الغيبة والافترا اجتنبوا عما نهيتم عنه في الصحائف
والالواح قد قسمنا المواريث على عدد الراء منها قدر
لذرياتكم من كتاب الطاء على عدد المقت وللازواج من كتاب
الحاء على عدد التاء والنساء وللاباء وللابا من كتاب الراء على عدد
التاء والكاف وللامهات من كتاب الواو على عدد الزبيع
وللاخوان من كتاب الهاء عدد الشين وللاخوات من كتاب

the sun) until its setting. Beware lest passion hinder you from obtaining this grace which has been decreed to you in the Book.

It has been ordained that whoever professes the religion of God, the Rewarder (*al-dayyān*), should wash his hands every day, then his face, and sit facing toward God [1] and say ninety-five times, " *Allāhu abhā* " (God is most Splendid). So did the Former (*fāṭir*) of the heavens command as He sits on the Thrones of the Names (*al-asmā'*) with Greatness and Power.

In like manner, perform ablutions before Worship because of a command from God, the Only One, the Choosing One.

Murder and adultery are unlawful for you, also back-biting (*al-ghayba*) and calumniation (*al-iftirā'*). Avoid what you have been forbidden in the Books and the Tablets.

Inheritances We have divided according to the number *al-zā'* (seven). Of them we have apportioned to your seed from the book *al-ṭā'* (nine), according to the number *al-maqt* (540) ; to husbands or wives from the book *al-ḥā'* (eight), according to the number of *al-tā'* and *al-fā'* (480) ; to fathers from the book *al-zā'* (seven), according to the number of *al-tā'* and *al-kāf* (420) ; and to mothers from the book *al-wāw* (six), according to the number of *al-rafī'* (360) ; and to brothers from the book *al-hā'* (five), the number of *al-shīn* (300) ; and to sisters from the book (9) *al-dāl* (four), the number of *al-rā'* and *al-mim* (240) ; and to teachers from the book *al-jīm* (three), the number of *al-qāf* and *al-fā'* (180). Thus commanded He who gave Good News of Me and who made mention of Me at nights and at daybreaks (*al-aṣhār*).[2]

---

[1] Presumably the place where Bahā'u'llāh is.

[2] Bahā'u'llāh here quotes the law of inheritance given by the Bāb. Instead of using numerals he uses the letters of the Arabic alphabet and words from which the numerical value can be derived. The arrangement was for the property of the deceased to be divided into nine unequal parts. Two parts were used for funeral expenses and the balance divided as follows among the heirs :—

(1) To Children	9/42 or 540/2520	
(2) To Husbands or Wives	8/42 or 480/2520	
(3) To Fathers	7/42 or 420/2520	
(4) To Mothers	6/42 or 360/2520	
(5) To Brothers	5/42 or 300/2520	
(6) To Sisters	4/42 or 240/2520	
(7) To Teachers	3/42 or 180/2520.	

" He who gave good news " of the coming of Bahā'u'llāh was the Bāb.

Indeed when We heard the clamour of the offspring in the loins (*al-aṣlāb*), We doubled their wealth and took away from others.[1]

He is the Powerful One over what He wills and He acts with His authority as He desires.

Whoever dies having no offspring, his rights return to the House of Justice (*bayt al-'adl*) in order that the Stewards of the Merciful (*umanā' al-raḥmān*) may spend it on orphans and widows, and on what benefits the multitude of people. This, that they may thank their Lord, the Forgiving, the Mighty One.

Whoever has offspring but does not have anyone else of those stipulated in the Book—two-thirds of what he leaves goes to his offspring and one-third to the House of Justice.

Thus ruled the Self-Sufficient One, who is exalted with Greatness and Majesty.

Whoever has no children [2] but has relatives, sons and daughters of a brother or sister, they are to have two-thirds. Otherwise the inheritance goes to paternal and maternal uncles and paternal and maternal aunts ; after them to their sons and daughters. The third goes to the Resting-place (House) of Justice (*maqarr al-'adl*). This is because of a command in the Book from God, the Possessor of Persons.

Whoever dies without having any offspring of those whose names have been sent down by the Most High Pen, the whole of his wealth goes to the above-mentioned Resting-place, (10) to be spent as God commanded.[3]

He is the Powerful, the Commanding One.

We appointed the dwelling house and the special garments (of the deceased) for the males of the offspring, not for the females and (other) heirs.

He is the Bountiful Giver.

Whenever a man who has offspring dies, while his father is still living, his offspring inherit what was their father's according to the Book of God. Divide among them with pure justice. Thus the sea

---

[1] Bahā'u'llāh says that when he heard the protests of unborn children that they would not get enough of the inheritance, he doubled the amount for children and decreased the amounts for others. He does not state here what the proportion will be, but it is given in a Persian book called *Question and Answer*.

[2] Lit. : " has no heirs."

[3] Evidently when there are no heirs of the classes mentioned, all the property goes to the House of Justice (see Note 3, p. 31).

الدال عدد الرآء والميم وللمعلّمين من كتاب الجميع عدد القاف والفاء

كذلك حكم مبتشر الذي يذكرون في الليالي والاسحار انّا آما سمعنا

ضجيج الذرّيّات في الاصلاب بذناضعفا عنهم ونقصنا عن الأخرى

انّه لهو المقتدر على ما يشآء يفعل بسلطانه كيف ارا د

من مات ولم يكن له ذرّيّة ترجع حقوقهم الى بيت العدل الجير فوّها

امناء الرحمن في الايتام والارامل وما ينتفع به جمهور الناس الشكروا

رحمتم العزيز الغفّار والذي له ذرّيّة ولم يكن ما دون فها عما أحد

في الكتاب يرجع الثلثان مما تركه الى الذرّيّة والثلث الى

بيت العدل كذلك حكم الغني المتعال بالعظمة والاجلال ومن

والذي لم يكن له من يرثنه وكان له ذوالقربى من ابناء الاخ و

الاخت وبناتهما فلهم الثلثان والا للاعمام والا للاخوال والاعمّا

والخالات ومن بعدهم ومن بعد هن لابنائهم وابناء هنّ وبناتهم

وبناتهنّ والثلث يرجع الى مقرّ العدل امرا ًمن الكتاب من لدى

مالك الرقاب من مات ولم يكن له احد ممّن الذين نزّلت

اسمائهم من القلم الأعلى ترجع الاموال كلّها الى المقرّ المذكور

of God raged, and the pearls of commandments were cast by the Possessor of People.

If weak (minor) offspring are left behind, their wealth is to be given to a guardian to trade with until they reach maturity, or to a company. Appoint to the guardian a proper amount from what he has made by trading and gain. All this is to be paid after God receives His rights and the debts are paid, if there are any, as well as providing the things necessary for the shroud, the burial, and the carrying (of the body) with honour and glory.

So ruled the Possessor of the Beginning and the Return.

Say : This is the hidden knowledge which never changes because it begins with al-ṭā' (nine),[1] which indicates the treasured, manifest, well-fortified and unapproachable Name.

The inheritance which We have assigned especially for the offspring is of the favour (faḍl) of God that they may thank their Lord, the Merciful, the Compassionate.

These are the stipulations of God. Do not transgress them because of your own passions.

Follow what you are commanded to do (11) by the Rising-place of Explanation (al-Bayān).[2]

The sincere ones will see the stipulations of God, the Water of Life to the people of (all) religions, and the Lamp of Wisdom and Prosperity to those who are in the earths and heavens.

God has ordained that in every city they make a House of Justice,[3] and the souls according to the number of al-Bahā' will assemble in it. There is no harm if the number increases. They shall see as though they are entering the presence of God, the High, the Most High. And they shall see Him who is not seen. They must be stewards of the Merciful among (those in the realm of) the possible and agents of God for the whole earth.

And God has ordained that they shall consult about the welfare of

---

[1] Nine is the numerical equivalent of bahā' (b—2, h—5, ā—1, '—1, which add up to nine).

[2] " The Rising-place of Explanation " is evidently Bahā'u'llāh. ~~Perhaps he intends to suggest by this expression that he is the source of the Bāb's book, The Bayān.~~

[3] In every city there is to be a House of Justice consisting of nine (the numerical value of bahā') or more persons, " the members of which must regard themselves as the trustees and representatives of God in the world, and strive to fulfill for the public good the trust placed in them." E. G. Browne, JRAS., 1889, p. 974.

creatures (al-'ibād) for the sake of God, just as they consult about
their own affairs, and that they choose what is the choice.

Thus commanded your Lord, the Mighty One, the Forgiver.

Beware lest you neglect what is inscribed in the Tablet.[1] Fear God,
O you who see.

O multitude of Creation, furnish houses (of worship) in the most
complete way possible in the name of the Possessor of Religions in
the lands. Decorate them with what is fitting, not with pictures and
statues. Then make mention in them of your Lord, the Merciful,
with joy and sweetness (bi l-rawḥ wa l-rayḥān). Is it not by
mentioning him that breasts are enlightened and eyes are consoled ?

God has ruled that those of you who are able—except the women—
make the Pilgrimage (ḥajj) to the House.[2] God has exempted the
women as a mercy on His part.

He is the Munificent One, the Generous One.

(12) O People of al-Bahā', it has been made incumbent on everyone
of you to work at something, in artisan crafts, in gain or something
like that. We have made your working at them your very worship
('ibāda) of God, the Real One.

O people (yā qawm), think upon the mercy and benefits of God.
Then thank Him at eventide and sunrise. Do not waste your time in
idleness and laziness. Work at something that will benefit you and
others. Thus decided the Command in this Tablet, which has shone
from the horizon of the Sun of Wisdom and Clear Explanation
(al-tibyān). God hates most those who sit and beg.

Catch hold of the Rope of Causes, trusting in God, the Causer of
Causes.

The kissing of hands is forbidden in the Book.[3] This (kind of
reverence for religious leaders) is what you were forbidden by your
Lord, the Mighty, the Wise.

No one need beg forgiveness of another.[4] Repent to God for
yourselves. He is the Mighty and Relenting Giver and Forgiver.

O creatures of the Merciful One, rise to the service (khidma) of the

---

[1] By " Tablet " is probably meant the Aqdas.

[2] Presumably this refers to the house Bahā'u'llāh occupied while in Baghdad.

[3] In the East reverence for those who are considered great may be shown by
kissing their hands, and religious leaders sometimes encourage this practice.
Bahā'u'llāh in his book (al-Aqdas) forbids it.

[4] As in confession to priests.

Cause that griefs caused by those who disbelieved in the Rising-place of the Verses (al-ayāt) may not overtake you.[1]

When the Promise came and the Promised One appeared, the people disagreed and each faction held to its own opinions and illusions. Some people sit in a Row of Sandals (saff al-niʿāl),[2] seeking the seat of honour (ṣadr al-jalāl). (13) Say : Who art thou, O careless, conceited man (al-gharrār) ?[3] Of them there is he who claims the Hidden (al-bāṭin) and the Hidden of the Hidden.[4]

Say : O liar, by God, what thou hast is husks. We have left it for you as bones are left for the dogs. By God, the Truth, if one were to wash the feet of everybody in the world and worship God in thickets and in green valleys, on mountains, hill-tops, and summits, and at every stone, and tree, and clod, and yet the fragrance of My good pleasure be not diffused from him, he would never be accepted.

This is what the Master of Mankind has ruled.

How many a creature in the isles of India has withdrawn from the world and deprived himself of what God has made lawful for him and endured retreats and hardships ; yet these things will not be remembered by God who sends down the Verses.

Do not make deeds (al-aʿmāl) a snare of hopes (sharak al-āmāl). Do not deprive yourselves of this end which was the hope of those who drew nigh (to God) in the eternity of past eternities.

Say : The spirit of the deeds is my good pleasure ; everything depends on my acceptance.

Read the Tablets in order to know what is the purpose of the books of God, the Mighty One, the Munificent.

Whoever attains unto My love has a right to sit on a throne of native gold in the chief seat in (the realm of) possibility. Whoever is

---

[1] Presumably the meaning is that Bahā'īs are to serve the Cause in such manner that they will not be made sad by the opposition of unbelievers. Perhaps " signs " instead of " verses " ; and so often.

[2] On entering a room, people leave their shoes near the door, hence the lowest place near this is called the " row of sandals ". Some sitting here hope that the host will say, " Come up higher ! " and they will thus get more honour.

[3] The Arabic dictionaries translate this word " deceiver, seducer ". But the Persian word ghurūr is " pride " and maghrūr is " a proud man ". Perhaps he has deceived himself into thinking he is something when he is nothing. Bahā'u'llāh, being a Persian, seems to have used the word in the Persian sense.

[4] Presumably this refers to one of the mystics who claimed to have esoteric knowledge.

c

deprived of My love, were he to sit on the ground, it would take refuge in God,[1] the Possessor of Religions.

Whoever claims Command (amr) before the completion of a thousand years is (14) a false liar.[2] We ask God to help him to return. If he repents, He is the Relenting One. If he persists in what he has said, one who will have no mercy on him will be sent against him. He is the Strong in punishment. Whoever explains this verse or interprets it in any other way than that plainly sent down, he will be deprived of the Spirit and Mercy of God, which preceded the worlds.

Fear God and follow not your illusions. Follow what your Lord, the Mighty and Wise One, commands.

The sound of bleating [3] shall arise from most of the lands. O people, avoid every vile sinner and do not follow him. This is what we informed you when we were in Iraq, in the land of the Secret (fī arḍ al-sirr),[4] and in this illuminating Spectacle (al-manẓar al-munīr).

O people of the earth, when the sun of My beauty goes down [5] and the heaven of My temple is hidden, do not be troubled. Arise to the help of My Cause and the exaltation of My Word among the worlds. We are with you in all circumstances. We shall help you with Truth. We have been able. Whoever knows Me let him arise to My service with an arising at which the hosts of heavens and earths do not cause him to sit down. People are asleep. Were they to wake they would

[1] In Islamic lands it is customary to say, "I take refuge in God!" when one expresses horror at the thought of something. The earth would be horrified that a person who did not love Bahā'u'llāh should pollute it by sitting on it.

[2] The word amr means "a command, a thing" and is also used by Bahā'īs to designate their religion or cause. The meaning here seems to be that anyone who claims command before the end of a thousand years is a false prophet. To prevent someone from appearing after a few years with the claim that he is a new Manifestation, and the interpretation of a "thousand years" as meaning a thousand days or something else, Bahā'u'llāh insists that the plain meaning of the words is the correct meaning.

[3] "Bleating," i.e., the clamour raised by opponents of the Truth.

[4] Bahā'u'llāh was in Baghdad, Iraq, with his brother Subh-i-Azal from 1853 to 1863, when they were deported to Adrianople, here referred to as the "Land of the Secret", because it was there that the secret of his being a new Manifestation was divulged. Then in 1868 he and his followers were sent to Acre, which he calls "This Illumined Spectacle".

[5] That is, when Bahā'u'llāh will die.

hasten with all their hearts to God, the Knower, the Wise One. They would throw away what they have, even were it all the treasures of the present world, that their Master may remember them (15) with a word from Him.

Thus He who has knowledge of the Unseen announces to you in a Tablet what appeared in the realm of possibility and what only His Self, the Overseer of the Worlds, has examined.

The drunkenness of passion has seized upon them because they do not see the Master of mankind (al-warā), whose cry is raised from all directions : " There is no God besides Me, the Mighty, the Wise."

Say : Do not rejoice in what you possess at nightfall, when at sunrise another will possess it. Thus does the Knower, the Omniscient One, inform you.

Say : Have you seen that your possessions remain or are loyal to you ? No ! By My soul, the Merciful. If only you were of the just ! The days of your life pass as pass the winds. The carpet of your glory shall fold up as did that of the ancients. Think, O people ! Where are your past days ? Where are the eras that have elapsed ? Blessed are the days that have passed in the remembrance of God and the times spent in the remembrance of Him, the Wise One.

By My life, the might of the Mighty shall not abide, nor the vanities of the rich, nor the pomp of the wicked.[1] All shall pass away by a word from Him. He, indeed, is the Powerful, the Mighty, the Strong One.

Their household goods will not benefit people. They have been careless of what benefits them. They shall be aroused and yet not find what has passed them by in the days of their Lord, the Mighty, the Praiseworthy. If they only knew (16), they would spend what they have, so that their names might be remembered before the Throne, are they not of the dead ?

A certain man has been puffed up by learning and has been deprived thereby of My Self-Subsistent Name, and whenever he hears the sound of footsteps behind him, he thinks himself bigger than Nimrod.[2] Say : Where is he (Nimrod), O rejected one (al-

---

[1] Lit. : " wretched ".

[2] Nimrod, according to Islamic tradition, disputed with Abraham and claimed to have the power of life and death (cf. Qur'ān 2 : 260 and Enc. of Islam, iii, 842 ff.). Bahā'u'llāh says that there is a man who, when he hears the sound of the footsteps of his disciples following him, is so puffed up with pride that he is prouder than Nimrod.

mardūd) ? By God, he is certainly in the lowest hell-fire ! Say :
O assembly of the learned,[1] do you not hear the scratching of My Most
High Pen ? Do you not see the Sun rising from the most splendid
(*al-abhā*—from the same root as *Bahā'*) Horizon ? How long will you
pray in seclusion to the idols of your passions ? Leave the illusions
and face towards God, your Eternal Master.

The religious endowments (*al-awqāf*)[2] given especially for charity
have been returned to God, the Appearing-place of Verses (*maẓhar
al-āyāt*). No one may spend them except after permission of the
Rising-place of Revelation. After him the command goes back to the
Branches,[3] and after them to the House of Justice. If His Cause is
established throughout the lands, let them spend the endowments in
the high places of this Cause and for what they were commanded
by the Powerful, the Mighty One. Otherwise let them (the endowments) return to the people of *al-Bahā'* who only speak after
permission is given by Him, and only command that which God has
commanded in this Tablet. Those are the Guardians of Victory
between the heavens and the earths. (17) Let them spend them in the
way defined in the Book by a Generous, Mighty One.

Neither show grief nor joy in times of calamity. Seek that which
is between two extremes, which means the remembering (of God)
when in that state and the being aware of what the outcome may be.
So does the Omniscient Knower announce to you.

Do not shave your heads. God has adorned them with hair. In
that there are certainly signs to him who considers the requirements
of nature (*al-ṭabī'a*) from the standpoint of the Possessor of Mankind.
Indeed, He is the Mighty, the Wise. It is not fitting to go beyond
the limits of the ears.[4] This is what the Master of the worlds
commanded.

Banishment and prison have been commanded (as punishment)

---

[1] By *al-'ulama'*, the theologians of Islam are intended.

[2] In Islam there are properties of great value which have been bequeathed by
pious people to shrines, mosques, or schools and are administered by religious
leaders or the state. Bahā'u'llāh here rules that all such endowments should
" return to God ", that is, to his own control.

[3] The religious endowments are to be controlled by Bahā'u'llāh as long as he lives.
At his death the " command " or control of them goes to the " Branches ", that is,
the sons of Bahā'u'llāh. When they die the House of Justice will assume control.

[4] Men are not to wear their hair lower than their ears.

for the thief. For the third offence put a sign on his forehead.[1] Thus he will be known, so that the cities and the provinces of God do not receive him.

Beware lest pity (al-ra'fa) take hold on you in (following) the religion of God. Do what you have been commanded to do by the Tender-hearted (al-mushfiq), Merciful One. We have disciplined you with the rods of Wisdom and commandments that you may keep yourselves and exalt your positions, just as fathers discipline their sons.

By My life, if you only knew what We desire for you by Our holy commands, you would have devoted your souls to this Holy, Mighty, and Impregnable Cause.

There is no harm in using vessels of gold and silver [2] if one desires to do so. Beware of dipping your hands in large plates (al-ṣiḥāf) and basins (al-ṣuḥūn).[3] (18) Hold to what is closer to cleanliness.[4] He desires to show you the customs of the people of Paradise (ahl al-riḍwān) in His Impregnable, Unapproachable Kingdom. Hold fast to cleanliness in all circumstances, lest the eyes fall on that which you and the people of Paradise abhor. Whoever transgresses (the rule of cleanliness), his work at once becomes futile. If he has an excuse, God exempts him for He is the Generous, the Powerful.

The Rising-place of Command has no partner in the Very Great Preservation from Error (al-'iṣma al kubra). He is, indeed, an Appearing-place. He does what He wishes in the Kingdom of Creation. God has reserved this Station exclusively for Himself. And a portion in this Great and Unapproachable Dignity has not been destined (quddira) for anyone else. This is the command of God. It was concealed in the veils of the Unknown. We manifested it in this Manifestation. By it We pierced the veil of those who knew not the command of the book and were among the careless.

It has been ordained for every father to educate his son and daughter in learning, handwriting and other things defined in the Tablet. Whoever neglects what he has been commanded, the

---

[1] This command abrogates the law of al-Bayān that force was not to be used in punishment of the Babīs.

[2] The use of such vessels was forbidden by Islamic law (cf. Muslim, al-Imām Abū 'l-Ḥusayn, al-Ṣaḥīḥ, 2 vols. Cairo, A.H. 1327, Vol. ii, 203 ff.).

[3] Bahā'u'llāh forbids the Eastern custom of eating with the fingers, probably intending that forks and spoons be used.

[4] Lit. : " Delicacy," passim.

Stewards must take from him whatever is necessary for their education : that is, if he is rich. Otherwise, their education is referred to the House of Justice. We have made it the shelter (*ma'wā*) of the poor and the needy.

Whoever educates (19) his son or any one's sons, it is as though he had educated one of My sons. On him be My Splendour (*bahā'ī*), My Providence and My Mercy, which preceded the worlds.

God has commanded that every adulterer and adultress pay a fine (*diya*—blood money) to the House of Justice. The sum is nine *mithqāls* of gold.[1] For the second offence double the punishment. This is what the Possessor of Names commanded for this world, and for the world to come a degrading punishment has been destined for them. Whoever is overcome by a sin, let him repent and turn back to God. He, indeed, forgives whom He wills and He is not to be questioned about what He wills. He is the Relenting, the Powerful, the Praised.

Beware lest praises of glory (*subuḥāt al-jalāl*) hinder you from the purity of this sweet water (*zulāl hādhā l-silsāl*). Take the bowls of prosperity on this morning in the name of the Breaker of the Morning Dawn (*fāliq al-ṣabāḥ*). Then drink in remembrance of Him, the Mighty Inventor (*al-badī'*).

We have made it lawful to you to listen to (singing) voices and to songs. Beware lest listening take you beyond the bounds of good breeding and dignity. Rejoice in the joy of My Greatest Name with which hearts are entranced and the minds of those brought near (to God) are attracted. We have made (music) a ladder for the ascent of spirits to the highest Horizon. Do not make it a wing (*janāḥ*) of the self and passion. I dislike that you be (20) among the ignorant.

We have returned a third of all the fines to the Resting-place of Justice. We admonish its men to do absolute justice, that they spend all that has been collected by them in the way commanded by a Wise Knower.

O men of (the House) of Justice, be shepherds of the sheep of God in His kingdom and keep them from the wolves who appear in garments (of sheep), just as you keep your sons. Thus does the faithful Adviser advise you.

---

[1] A *mithqāl* is approximately five grammes or one-seventh of an ounce (cf. *Enc. of Islam*, iii, 528 ; E. W. Lane, *Lexicon*, p. 345). It is possible that the Bābī *mithqāl* is intended, in which case the amount of the fine would be about $21.

If you differ on a matter, bring it back to God while the sun shines from the horizon of this heaven. Whenever it sets, go back to that which was sent down from Him.[1] It is sufficient for the worlds.

Say : O People, be not troubled when the kingdom of My Manifestation has disappeared and the waves of the sea of My Explanation are calm. Indeed, in My Manifestation there is wisdom and in My Disappearance there is another wisdom. No one knows this except God, the Omniscient, the Solitary.

We see you from the most splendid (abha) horizon and We assist him who rises up to aid My Cause with the hosts of My most exalted (heavenly) beings and a tribe of angels who are brought near (to God).

O multitudes of the earth, by God, the Truth, there have burst forth sweet palatable rivers from rocks which took of the sweetness of the explanation of your Lord, the Chooser, while you have been careless.

Leave (21) what you have ! Then fly with the minions of Separation beyond Innovation.[2] Thus commands the Possessor of Invention, who by the moving of His Pen turns worlds upside down.

Do you know from what horizon your Most Splendid (abha) Lord calls you ? Did you know by what Pen your Lord, Possessor of the Names, commands you ? No ! And by My Life, if you had known, you would have forsaken the present world, coming with your hearts to the side of the Beloved. The shaking of the Word has taken hold on you because the great world has been shaken by it, and how (not) this small world ?

Likewise rains of My generosity have fallen from the heaven of My providence as a favour from Me that you may be thankful.

As for the commandments about wounds and blows, they differ just as there is a difference in the intensity (of wounds and blows). The Rewarder has ruled that for every degree there is a fixed fine. Indeed, He is the Mighty, Powerful Ruler. If We wished We might truly go into detail as a promise on Our part. He is the Learned One who fulfills (His promises).

Hospitality has been prescribed (as an obligation), once every month, even though it be with water only. God desired to bring

[1] As long as Bahá'u'lláh lives, disputed points are to be referred to him. When he dies they are to refer to his Book, which will be all-sufficient.

[2] Evidently this means to soar above the world of change to the changeless world of Reality.

hearts together even, if necessary, it be by the causes of heavens and earths. Beware lest affairs of self and passion divide you. Be like the fingers of the hand and the limbs of the body. Thus does the Pen of Revelation warn you, if you are of the believers. Look to the Mercy of God and His benefits.

He commands you (22) what yet benefits you, since He has no need of the worlds.

Your evil deeds will not harm Us, just as your good deeds do not benefit Us. We invite you only for the sake of God. Every knowing person who sees bears witness to that.

When in hunting you use birds of prey, make mention of God.[1] Then whatever they catch for you is lawful, even though you find it dead. Indeed, He is the Omniscient, the Knower. Take care not to be wasteful in that (hunting) ; hold to the Path of Justice and Equity in all matters. Thus does the Rising-place of Manifestation command you, if you are of those who know.

Indeed, God has commanded you to love your relatives, but He has not decreed for them a right in one's property.[2] He has no need of the worlds.

Whoever burns a house intentionally, burn him.

Whoever kills a person with intent, kill him.

Take the ordinances (sunan) of God with hands of power and might. Then desert the ordinances of the ignorant. If you condemn them (the incendiary and the murderer) to perpetual prison, you have done no harm according to the Book. Indeed, He is the Ruler over what He desires.

God has ordained marriage (al-nikāḥ) for you. Beware lest you go beyond two (wives), and whoever is satisfied with one of the hand-maidens, his soul is at rest and so is hers, and one does no harm in taking a virgin into his service.[3] So is the matter prescribed in truth by the Pen (23) of Revelation.

[1] This may also mean that when you discharge missiles, you are to make mention of God.

[2] After one's death his relatives, beyond those already mentioned, have no right to claim a part of the inheritance.

[3] In his book, Materials for the Study of the Bābī Religion, pp. 320 f., E. G. Browne gives the names of Bahā'u'llāh's wives and children. He says, " Bahā'u'llāh had two wives, each of whom bore him six children." In 1835 he married Nawwab, and 'Abdul-Bahā' was the oldest son who survived from this wife. In 1849 he married his cousin Mahd-i-'Ulya, whose eldest son Muhmamad 'Ali disputed the succession

Marry, O people, that there may come from you (be born of you) those who will make mention of Me among My creatures. This is My command to you ; take it as a help for your souls.

O multitudes of Creation, do not follow your own selves ; they command passions of excess and immorality. Follow the Possessor of things Who commands righteousness and piety to you. He is the All-Sufficient without the worlds.

Beware lest you corrupt the earth after it has been made good. Whoever corrupts is not one of us and we have nothing to do with him. So was the matter testified to, in truth, from the heaven of Revelation.

Indeed, in *al-Bayān* He made the consent of the two parties the condition (for marriage). Since We desired love and affection and the union of the creatures, We made (marriage) dependent on the consent of the parents in addition to the two of them (the bride and groom),[1] lest there occur rancour and hatred. And We have other aims and so is the matter decided.

Relationship by marriage is not realized except by (payment of) dowries [2] (*al-amhār*, plural of *mahr*). The amount estimated for towns is nineteen *mithqāls* of pure gold, and for villages it is (the same amount of) silver. Whoever desires more is forbidden to go beyond ninety-five *mithqāls*. So is the matter recorded by Might. Whoever is content with the first amount (i.e., nineteen *mithqāls*), it is better for him according to the Book. He enriches (24) whomsoever

opposed the claims and conduct of
~~with~~ 'Abdul-Bahā' after the death of their father. It has been stated by other authorities who were in a position to know the facts that Bahā'u'llāh also married a wife named Gohar in 1867, who bore him a daughter named Farūqiyya, and that in his old age he married Jamāliyya, the niece of his faithful follower, Khādim Allah. It is said that all his wives survived him, except the first.

[1] Bahā'u'llāh here changes the marriage law given by the Bāb, which made only the consent of the bride and groom the condition for marriage. Bahā'u'llāh says that in order that there may be love and harmony, the parents also must give their consent.

[2] The dowry is the money which the husband gives to the wife (cf. *Enc. of Islam,* iii, 137). Often in Islam the parents of the bride require the groom to promise a large sum and write it in the marriage contract, but they do not ask him to pay it at once. In case he should wish to divorce the woman, she would demand that the *mahr* be first given to her, in this way protecting herself from divorce—since in Islamic law the right to divorce belongs entirely to the man, who can divorce at will for any cause. Bahā'u'llāh follows the Islamic custom of requiring the *mahr*, fixing the amount between nineteen and ninety-five *mithqāls* of gold for city dwellers, and the same amount of silver for villagers. (See Note 1, p. 38, for value of the *mithqāl*).

He wills by the causes of heavens and earth. God is powerful over everything.

God has ordained for every man who desires to leave his country that he appoint a time to *his spouse for his return. If he returns and keeps his promise, he has followed the command of his Master. He is one of the doers of good. By the Pen of Command it is ordained.

If he had a true excuse (for not keeping his promise), he must inform his spouse and do his utmost to return to her. If these two conditions are not fulfilled, she must yet delay nine full months. After she has completed them, there is no harm in her choosing (another) husband. If she is patient, (it is well, for) He loves patient women and patient men. Perform My commands and follow not every polytheist, who according to the Tablet is a sinner. If news comes during the time of her waiting, she must take this as a favour. Indeed, He desires reconciliation between his servants and handmaidens.

Beware lest you commit what causes dissension among you. So is the matter decided and the promise was at hand. If news of the death or murder reaches her and it is confirmed by common knowledge or by two upright persons, she is to remain at home. When the appointed months have passed, she may choose to do as she wishes.[1] He who is Strong has commanded thus in this matter.

If trouble (25) or displeasure occurs between the two of them, he must not divorce her,[2] but be patient for a whole year. Perhaps a fragrance of love may be perceived between them. After a year is completed and love's perfume is not diffused, then there is no harm in divorce. He is wise in everything. God has forbidden you, as a favour from Him, what you have done following a triple divorce, in order that you be of the thankful.[3] In a Tablet it was inscribed by the Pen of Command, whoever divorces (his wife) has the choice of returning to her at the completion of each month in (a spirit of) love and consent so long as she does not desire to marry (another). Whenever she has become the wife of another, separation has been

---

[1] The appointed time in Islam is reckoned as three months and ten days.

[2] As in Islam, Bahā'u'llāh confines the right to give the divorce to the husband. The wife cannot divorce her husband.

[3] According to Islamic law, if a man gives his wife " the triple divorce ", he cannot remarry her until after she has been married to another man and has been divorced by him. See Qur'ān 2 : 230.

realized in another way and so is the matter decided. This happens unless there is an evident command.

Thus was the command of the Rising-place of Beauty recorded in the Tablet of Majesty with honour.

If a difference occurs when a man travels with his wife, he must pay the expenses for a full year and return her to the abiding-place from which she came or entrust her to some faithful person and (provide) what she needs for the journey to get to her place. The Lord, indeed, commands as He wills by an authority which encompasses the worlds. She who is divorced because of something unworthy proved against her gets no expenses for the days of her waiting.[1] Thus the brilliance of the matter is seen from the horizon of Justice.

God loves union and agreement and hates division (26) and divorce.

Have friendly relations, O People, with joy and sweetness. By My life, everyone in (the realm of) the possible shall perish. That which continues is the good deed. God is a witness of what I say.

O My creatures, make peace among yourselves ; then listen to the counsel of the Most Exalted Pen. Do not follow a wretched tyrant.

Beware lest the world make you conceited [2] as it did a people before you. Follow the stipulations and ordinances of God. Then walk in the Path which was laid out by the True One. Those who cast off iniquity and error and take hold on piety are the choice of Creation in the sight of the True One. They are remembered by the most exalted Beings and the people of this Station which was raised up by the name of God.[3]

It is unlawful for you to buy or sell maid-servants and youths. One creature must not purchase another, since this is prohibited in the Tablet of God. Thus was the matter inscribed by the Pen of Justice through Grace.

No one should glory over another. All are slaves to Him and guides to the truth that " there is no god but He ". He is the One who is wise about everything.

Adorn (*zayyinū*) yourselves with the beautiful garments of (good) works. Whoever attains unto a good work in pleasing Him is of the people of *al-Bahā'* (Splendour). He has been remembered before the

---

[1] " Her waiting," i.e., for the year mentioned above.

[2] " Deceive you."

[3] That is, the Angels and those who are of the same rank as Bahā'u'llāh.

Throne. Assist the Possessor of Mankind by good works, then by Wisdom and Explanation. Thus have you been commanded in most of the Tablets by the Merciful One. He (27) has knowledge of what I say.

Let no one oppose another ; nor one person kill another. This is what you were forbidden in a Book which was veiled in the tent of Might.[1] Do you kill him whom God brought to life through a Spirit from Him ? This is an error, which was great before the Throne. Fear God, and do not raze by hands of oppression and tyranny what God has built. Then take a way to Truth.

When the hosts of spiritual knowledge (al-'irfān) appeared with the standards of al-Bayān (the Explanation), the hordes of religions retreated, with the exception of the one who desired to drink the river of Life (kawthar al-ḥayawān)[2] in Paradise, which came into being from the breath of the Praised One.

God has commanded that liquid semen is ceremonially pure.[3] This is one of His mercies to mankind. Thank Him with joy and sweetness and do not follow one who was far from the Rising-place of Nearness.

Arise to the service of the Cause in all circumstances. He aids you with an authority which encircles the worlds. Catch hold of the rope of Purity so that no traces of filth are seen on your clothes. This is what He has commanded, He who is purer than all the pure. There is no harm, however, in one who has an excuse (for not being clean). Indeed, He is the Merciful, Forgiving One.

Cleanse every unseemly thing (makrūh)[4] with water which has not changed in three respects. Beware of using (28) water which is changed by the air or something else. Be the very element of purity among mankind. This is what your Master, the Mighty, the Wise One desired of you. Thus God has removed the commandment regarding

---

[1] Evidently, as kings secluded themselves in magnificent tents and furnishings to show their might, so al-Kitāb al-Aqdas is said to be veiled in a tent of Might.

[2] Al-kawthar is, according to Islamic belief, the name of a river in Paradise (See commentaries on Qur'ān 108 : 1 and books of Islamic eschatology). The meaning of the passage here is that when the Bāb appeared with al-Bayān, the followers of other religions were turned back, except those who thirsted for the Water of Life.

[3] According to Islamic law semen is unclean.

[4] Makrūh in Islamic law is something disapproved (like donkey flesh) although it is not unlawful (like pork). The changes in water referred to here are changes in colour, smell, and taste.

uncleanness from everything,[1] and from other religious groups (*milal*), a free gift from God. Indeed, He is the Generous Forgiver.

All things were dipped in the Sea of Cleansing on the First of *al-Riḍwān* [2] when we appeared in glory to him who is in (the realm of) the possible with our Most Beautiful Names and our most high attributes. This is of My Favour which encompassed the worlds.

Associate with (people of) other religions and propagate the Cause of your Lord, the Merciful. This is certainly the crown of (good) deeds, if you only knew it.

He gave a command regarding the Most Great Cleansing, and the washing of things that were soiled by dirt, how solidified filth (is removed), and other matters.

Fear God and be of the purified. The prayers of the one who is seen with filth on his clothes do not ascend to God and the exalted Beings avoid him.

Use rose water, then pure perfume. This is what God, who has no beginning, loved from the beginning. This is in order that there might be diffused from you the odour that your Lord, the Mighty and the Wise, desired.

God has excused you from what was sent down in *al-Bayān* regarding the destruction of books.[3] And we have permitted you to read of the learning (of the Islamic doctors) what is useful to you, but not that which results in controversy in speech. (29) This is better for you, if you only knew it.

O assembly of kings (*al-mulūk*), the Possessor (*al-mālik*) has come

---

[1] Many things in Islamic law were considered ceremonially impure, such as swine, dogs and dead bodies. One who touches such objects has to perform certain purifying rites. Also according to the law of Shi‘ite Islam, people of other religions, such as Jews and Christians, are unclean. Bahā'u'llāh abrogates these laws and returns to the teachings of Jesus Christ (Mark 7 : 18 f.).

[2] Just before Bahā'u'llāh and other Bābīs were deported from Baghdad in 1863, they spent twelve days in a garden near the city, which they named *al-Riḍwān* (a name for Paradise). It seems that on the first day in the garden Bahā'u'llāh informed some of the people closest to him that he was a new Manifestation. Later in Adrianople he made the claim publicly. These twelve days were later commemorated by the Feast of *al-Riḍwān*, which is observed each year from 21st April, to 2nd May, the first, ninth and twelfth days being kept as feast days. Bahā'u'llāh says that at that time everything was made clean by his appearing. " To him in the possible " means " to all men ".

[3] All non-Bābī books were to be burned according to the Bāb's command. The sciences and philosophy were not to be studied (Persian, *Bayān*, iv, 10 ; vi, 6) Bahā'u'llāh abrogates these laws.

and the sovereignty (al-mulk) belongs to God, the Self-Subsistent
Overseer.

Do not worship anyone but God.

Turn with your hearts full of light to the face of your Lord, the
Possessor of Names. This is something unequalled by anything you
have, if you only knew. We see you rejoicing in what you have
gathered for others and depriving yourselves of the worlds which
only My Preserved Tablet has enumerated.

Wealth has distracted you from the End (ma'āl). This should not
be, if you only knew. Cleanse your hearts of the odour (i.e. treasures)
of the world (dhafar al-dunya) and hasten to the kingdom of your
Lord, Maker of earth and heaven. He it is by whom the earthquakes
appeared and the tribes lamented, except the one that turned away
from men and held on to what was ordered in the Hidden Tablet.

This is a day in which the Interlocutor (al-kalīm) [1] attained unto
the lights of the Eternal and drank the pure water of Union (zalāl
al-wiṣāl) from this vessel in which the seas overflowed.

Say : By God, the True One, al-Ṭūr [2] circumambulates the Rising-
place of Manifestation, and the Spirit [3] calls from the Kingdom, " Up
and come, O sons of Conceit ! "

This is a day in which the host (kūm) of God hastened because of a
longing to meet Him. Zion cried, " The Promise has come ; that
which was ordained in the Tablets of God, the Exalted, the Mighty,
the Beloved, has appeared " (30).

O assembly of kings, He has sent down the great Law in the most
illumined Spectacle. Everything concealed with the Possessor of
Destiny has appeared. He is the one by whom the Hour has come,
the moon was split, [4] and everything appointed was given in detail.

O assembly of kings, you are the slaves (al-mamālīk). The
Possessor has appeared in the best garment and He calls you to
Himself, the Self-Subsistent Overseer. Take care that conceit does

---

[1] Moses is often referred to as the kalīm of Allah, that is, the one who talks with
God. See Enc. of Islam, ii, 699 ; iii, 738 f. The " Interlocutor " is Moses.

[2] Ṭūr—meaning mountain, is the name which Muslims often use for Mount Sinai,
Qur'ān 20 : 82. See also Enc. of Islam, iv, 703 f.

[3] Jesus is referred to in the Qur'ān 4 : 169, as the Spirit of God (rūḥ Allāh). Here
Bahā'u'llāh calls him " the Spirit ".

[4] There is an allusion here to the Qur'ānic verse (54 : 1), " The hour hath
approached and the moon hath been cleft " (Rodwell's Translation, p. 76).
Bahā'u'llāh says that this prophecy has been fulfilled in and by him.

not keep you from the Sunrise-place of the Manifestation and that the present world does not hide you from the Maker of heaven.

Arise to the service of the Object of Desire (God), who created you by a word of His and made you manifestations of the Power to do what was and will be. By God, We do not desire to take possession of your kingdoms, but we have come to possess your hearts. Indeed, they are the spectacle of *al-Bahā'* (Splendour). The Kingdom of Names bears witness to that, if you only understood.

Whoever follows the Master, indeed, turns away from the world entirely. What an honoured Station is this ! Leave the houses ; come to the Kingdom. This is what benefits you in the next world and this. The Possessor of Might (*al-jabarūt*) bears witness to this, if you only knew.

Blessed is the king who arises to help My cause in My Kingdom and cuts himself off from all but Me ! He is of the companions of the Red Ship [1] which God made for the people (31) of *al-Bahā'*. Everyone must honour, esteem, and assist him to conquer the cities with the keys of My Name. He is the Overseer of all who are in the kingdoms of the Unseen and the Seen.

He is in the place of sight for mankind, the bright gleam of dawn to the Forehead of Creation and the Head of Generosity to the Body of the World. Help him, O people of *al-Bahā'*, with your wealth and your persons.

O king of Austria (*al-namsa*), the Rising-place of the Light of Unity was in prison at Acre when thou wentest to the furthest Mosque (*al-masjid al-aqṣa*).[2] Thou didst pass by and afterwards did not ask about Him, He for Whom every house was raised up and every towering door was opened. We made it the meeting-place (prayer-direction) [3] for the world for My remembrance, and thou

---

[1] The ship is the Cause of Bahā' and it is red with the blood of martyrs.

[2] The Emperor Franz Joseph visited Jerusalem in 1869. He was the first German sovereign to visit the area since his ancestor, the Emperor Frederick IV, in 1436. *Al-masjid al-aqṣa* is used in the Qur'ān 17 : 1 to denote Jerusalem. It is also referred to as *al-quds* or *al-bayt al muqaddas* or *bayt al-maqdis* (The Holy House) (See *Enc. of Islam*, ii, 1094 ff., Lane, *Lexicon*, p. 2497). If this is the visit here referred to, the *Aqdas* could have been written not long after 1869.

[3] The Jews faced Jerusalem in prayer, and at first Muhammad in imitation of them led his followers in their worship facing Jerusalem. Later he made Mecca the prayer-direction (cf. *Enc. of Islam*, ii, 985 ff., Wensinck, op. cit., p. 125). Bahā'u'llāh says that God made Jerusalem the centre in order that men might there remember him (Bahā'u'llāh).

didst neglect the One mentioned when He appeared with the Kingdom of God, thy Lord and the Lord of the Worlds. We were with thee in all circumstances. We found thee clinging to the branch (al-farʿ) and careless about the root (al-aṣl). Thy Lord is a witness of what I say. Sorrows overtook us because We saw thee going about Our Name, not knowing that we are before thy face. Open thine eyes to see this noble spectacle, to know upon Whom thou callest night and day, and to see the light shining from this flashing horizon.

Say : O king of Berlin,[1] hear the call from this conspicuous Temple, " There is no god besides Me, the Continuing, the Unique, the Eternal One." Beware lest conceit keep thee from the Rising-place (32) of Manifestation and passion screen thee from the Possessor of the Throne and the Earth. In like manner the Most High Pen counsels thee. Indeed, He is the Generous, the Gracious Giver. Remember [2] the one who was greater than thee in dignity and more exalted in position ! Where is he and his possessions ? Awake ! Be not of those who sleep. He flung the Tablet of God behind him when We informed him of what the hosts of evil-doers had brought on Us. Therefore humiliation took hold on him from every side until he returned with great loss to the dust.

O king, think of him and others like thee who subdued the lands (al-bilād) and ruled over creatures (al-ʿibād). The Merciful brought them down from palaces to graves. Consider and be one of those who remember. We desire nothing from you, O assembly of Sultans. We counsel you only for the sake of God and we are patient as we were patient about that which came to us from you.

O kings of America and chiefs of the multitude in it, hear what the Dove on the branches of Continuing Eternity warbles, saying, " There is no god besides Me, the Continuing, the Forgiving, the Generous."
Adorn the temple (body) of the Kingdom with the garment of

---

[1] " King of Berlin," probably Wilhelm I who was king of Prussia, 1861–1888.

[2] Probably this is a reference to Napoleon III of France, who was defeated by Germany in 1870, was deposed, and died in 1873. The Tablet or letter which Bahāʾuʾllāh sent to Napoleon III is described by E. G. Browne in JRAS., 1889, p. 967 f. It seems that Bahāʾuʾllāh had informed Napoleon III of the way that the Turkish government had treated him, perhaps hoping that help would be given him. Napoleon III as head of the French government claimed to be the protector of the Christians in Turkey, but apparently did nothing to help Bahāʾuʾllāh.

Justice and Piety and its head with the crown of the Remembrance of your Lord, the Maker of Heaven. Thus does the Rising-place of Names command you by a Wise Knower. The Promised One has been manifested in the noble Station at which (33) smiled the lips of Existence at the Unseen and Seen.

Lay hold on the Day of God. Indeed, meeting Him is better for you than all that the sun rises on, if you only knew.

O assembly of princes, hear the sound that arose from the Rising-place of Grandeur : " There is no god besides Me, the Knower, the Speaker." That which is broken restore with hands of Justice and that which is sound and evil break with whips of the commands of your Lord, the Wise, the Commanding One.

O assembly of Byzantium (al-rūm),[1] We hear among you the voice of the owl (al-būm). Has drunkenness of passion overtaken you or are you of the careless ones ? O Point situated on the shore of the two seas, the throne of wickedness has settled on thee and the fire of hatred has been lighted in thee. Because of this, the exalted Beings (angels) lament, and so do those who go about an Exalted Throne. In thee we see the ignorant ruling the intelligent and darkness boasting over light. Thou art (filled) with evident conceit ; has thy outward adornment made thee conceited ? It will soon perish ! By the Lord of mankind, the daughters and widows and the hordes within thee shall lament. Thus does the Omniscient, the Knower announce to thee.

O banks of the river Rhine, we have seen thee covered with blood because the swords of retribution have been drawn against thee. Thou hast another chance. We hear the moaning of Berlin even though to-day it is in evident might.

O land of al-Ṭā' (Teheran), do not be sorrowful for anything. God has made thee (34) the Rising-place of the Joy of the worlds. If He Wills, He will bless thy throne through him who rules with justice and gathers the sheep of God which have been scattered by wolves. He looks upon the people of al-Bahā' with joy and gladness. He is of the substance of Creation in the presence of the True One ! On him

---

[1] This is addressed to the Turks, by whom Bahā'u'llāh had been twice banished, first to Adrianople, and then to Acre. Rūm is the old name for Istanbul.

D

is the Splendour of God (*Bahā' Allāh*) and the Splendour (*bahā'*) of Him who is in the Kingdom of the Cause continually.

Rejoice thou in that God has made thee the Horizon of Light since the Rising-place of Manifestation was born in thee [1] and thou art called by this Name, by which the Lighting of Favour shone and the heavens and earths are illumined. Things shall be overturned in thee· and the multitude (*jumhūr*) [2] of people shall rule thee. Indeed, thy Lord is the Encompassing One, the Knower.

Be tranquil through the grace of thy Lord. The moments of benefits shall not be cut off from thee. After trouble tranquillity shall take hold of thee. Thus is the matter decided in a new book.

O land of *al-Khā'* (Khurasan), We hear in thee the voice of men remembering their Lord, the Exalted, the Self-Sufficient. Blessed be the day in which the standards of Names shall be set up in the Kingdom of Creation in My Most Splendid Name ! On that day the sincere shall rejoice in the triumph of God and the polytheists shall lament. No one shall turn his back on those who bear rule over creatures. Leave to them what they have and look to your own hearts.

(35) O most great Sea, sprinkle on the nations that which thou wast commanded by the Possessor of Eternity, and adorn the temples (bodies) of mankind with the garment of commandments by which hearts rejoice and eyes are refreshed.

If anyone possesses a hundred *mithqāls* [3] of gold, nineteen *mithqāls* of them are for God, the Maker of earth and heaven. Beware, O people, lest you deny yourselves this great favour. We have commanded you to do this although We can do without you and without all who are in the heavens and the earths. In that, there are wise and useful things of which no one has acquired knowledge except God, the Omniscient, the Knower.

Say : By that command God desired the purification of your wealth and your drawing near to those stations which are only attained by those whom God wills. Indeed, He is the Generous, Almighty Giver of Grace.

[1] Bahā'u'llāh was born in Teheran, although his family came from Mazanderan near the Caspian Sea.

[2] *Jumhūr* is the term used in Iran for a republic and some think that Bahā'u'llāh here predicts that Iran will become a republic.

[3] See Note 1, p. 38.

O People, do not be dishonest in the duties owed to God ; do not spend (God's money) except by His permission.[1] Thus is the matter decided in the Tablets and in this Powerful Tablet. Whoever cheats God is cheated by Justice, but when one does what he is commanded there descends upon him a blessing from the heaven of giving, from his Lord, the Bountiful, the Giver, the Eternal Bestower.

He desires for you that which you do not know to-day. The People shall know it whenever spirits soar and the rich carpets of joy are folded up. Thus does he who has a Preserved Tablet [2] remind you.

(36) Various petitions have been presented before the Throne by those who believe, who asked questions in them of God, the Lord of the Seen and the Unseen, the Lord of the Worlds. Therefore we sent down the Tablet and adorned it with the garment of Command.[3] Perhaps the people will act in accordance with the commandments of their Lord. In like manner We have been questioned previously for many successive years and We restrained the Pen through Wisdom on our part. Finally, letters came from numerous persons in these days. So We are answering them in truth with that which revives the hearts.

Say : O assembly of learned men,[4] do not weigh the Book of God according to the (grammatical) rules and learning which you have. It is the Balance of Truth for (all) Creation.[5] That which the nations have may be weighed by this Great Balance ; it is of Itself, if you only knew. The eye of My providential care weeps over you because you know not Him upon whom you call at night and dawn and at every evening and morning.

O People, direct your steps with white faces and hearts full of light towards the Blessed Red Spot where the Lote Tree of the Extremity (*sidratu l-muntahā*) calls;[6] " There is no god besides Me, the Self-Subsistent Overseer."

---

[1] That is, the 19/100 of capital funds which belong to God are to be spent only as Bahā'u'llāh permits.

[2] See Note 1, p. 52.

[3] From this it appears that *al-Kitāb al-Aqdas* was written at the request of Bahā'īs who wanted information and instructions as to their duties.

[4] By *'ulamā'* only those learned in Islamic lore are intended.

[5] *Al-Kitāb al-Aqdas* cannot be measured by human standards, for it is itself the Measure of all things.

[6] It is said that this is a reference to a hill near Acre which was covered with red

O assembly of learned men (*al-'ulamā'*), is anyone of you able to compete with Me in the field of Revelation and Spiritual Knowledge and go about with Me in the arena of Wisdom and Explanation ? No ! By My Merciful Lord, everyone on the earth (37) is mortal and this is the face of your Lord, the Mighty One, the Beloved.

O People, We, indeed, have appointed the (branches of) learning for the spiritual knowledge of the Known (God). But you have remained veiled by them from their source, Him by whom every hidden thing appears. If you only knew the Horizon from which the Sun of Speech arose, you would cast away people and what they have and would come to the Praised Station.

Say : This is certainly a heaven in which is treasured the Original Book (*ummu l'kitāb*).[1] If you only understood ! Indeed, this is He by whom the Rock cried out and the Lote Tree proclaimed on the lofty Mountain (*al-Ṭūr*)[2] on the blessed land : " The sovereignty belongs to God, the Mighty One, the Beloved King."

We have not entered schools. We have not perused the arguments. Hear that by which this Illiterate One (*al-ummī*)[3] calls you to God, the Everlasting. It is better for you than what has been treasured in the earth. If you only understood ! Whoever interprets what has been sent from the heaven of Revelation by taking it away from the evident meaning is one of those who have tampered with the highest Word of God and have suffered loss according to the Perspicuous Book.

There are ordained for you the paring of nails, the getting into water that covers your whole body every week, and the cleansing of your bodies with what you have used previously.[4] Beware lest your

tulips. The Lote Tree is said to be at the loftiest place in Paradise. It is called the Tree of Extremity because neither men nor angels are allowed to pass it. See *Commentaries on the Qur'ān*, 53 : 14, also *Enc. of Islam*, i, 1015.

[1] The original of the books " sent down " by God is kept in heaven. It is sometimes called " the Preserved Tablet ". It seems that Bahā'u'llāh claims to be himself that heaven from which the books emanate. For a discussion of *ummu l-kitāb*, see *Commentaries on Qur'ān*, 13 : 39, and *Enc. of Islam*, iv, 1012.

[2] This may be an allusion to the Burning Bush as a tree from which a voice came.

[3] Muhammad is referred to in the Qur'ān 7 : 156, 158, as *al-nabī al-ummī*. See *Enc. of Islam*, iv, 1016, for the explanation of the term. It is generally interpreted to mean " the illiterate prophet ", that is, unable to read or write. Bahā'u'llāh uses the term for himself although we know he had considerable education.

[4] The reference is said to be to the powder Muslims used in the bath to remove hair from the body.

carelessness prevent you from doing what you have been commanded to do by a Great and Mighty One. Enter into water that has not been used, (38) and it is not permissible to get into what has already been used. Take care not to approach the bath-houses of the Iranians (al-'ajam). Whoever goes towards them discovers their stinking odour even before entering them. O People, avoid them and be not of the ignominious. It is like pus and purulent matter, if you are among those who know. Also their stinking water-tanks, leave them alone and be of the pure ones.

We desired to see you as manifestations of Paradise on earth, that there might diffuse from you that by which the hearts of those brought near (to God) are rejoiced. It is better for one who washes his body to pour water over him instead of his getting into it.[1] Indeed, He desired to make matters easy for you because of His favour, in order that you might be of the thankful.

The wives of your fathers are unlawful to you. We are ashamed to mention the commandments regarding boys (pederasty). Fear the Merciful One, O Multitudes of the (realm of the) possible, and do not commit what is forbidden in the Tablet. Be not of those who are bewildered in the desert of lusts.

One should not be moving his tongue before people as he walks on the streets and in the markets. Whoever desires to make mention of God should do so in the places built for remembrance of God or in his own house. This is much nearer to sincerity and piety. (39) Thus has the Sun of Wisdom risen from the horizon of the Explanation (al-Bayán). Blessed are those who do (these things).

The writing of a will has been made incumbent on everyone. (In writing his will) one must adorn the top of the page with the Most Great Name and confess his faith in the Unity of God, in the Appearance of His Manifestation,[2] and mention whatever of good he wants (to remember) in order that he may bear witness to Him in the worlds of Command and Creation. Thus he will have a treasure with his Lord, the Faithful Keeper.

---

[1] According to Muslim practice, after certain acts, ablution requires that the whole body go under water. Bahá'u'lláh here abrogates this regulation. In some places in Iran at the time of Bahá'u'lláh water was scarce and the heating of it was expensive. Hence many people used the water in the tanks before it was changed. This practice was of course unsanitary, though the water was ceremonially " clean ".

[2] The Bahá'í in his will must confess his faith in Bahá'u'lláh and approve his laws and teachings, thus giving a witness to others on his death-bed.

The festivals are limited to two great feasts. The first [1] is the days in which the Merciful was revealed to those (in the realm) of the Possible by His most beautiful Names and His highest Attributes. The other [2] (feast) is the day on which We sent Him who should tell the people the Good News of this Name by which the dead are raised and those who are in the heavens and earths are assembled.[3] The other two (feasts) are observed for two days.[4] Thus was the matter decided by a Wise Commander.

Blessed is the one who attained unto the first day of the month of al-Bahā' [5] on which God put this Most Great Name! Blessed is the one who on that day manifested the favour of God to him! By his action he manifests thanks to God, an indication of His favour which encompasses the worlds.[6] Say : It is the source and beginning of the months,[7] and in it moves the breath of life among the possible (things). Blessed is the one who apprehends it with joy and sweetness. We bear witness that he is among those who attained. Say : (40) The greatest feast is the King (Sultan) of the Feasts.

O People, remember the favour of God to you when you were asleep. He aroused you with the breezes of Revelation and made known to you His clear and straight Way. If you become ill, consult the skilful ones of the physicians. Indeed, we have not set aside the means (of healing) but have rather established them by this Pen,

---

[1] This is the feast of the Manifestation of Bahā' Allāh. See Note 2, p. 45.

[2] This is the day when the Bāb in Shiraz made his claim to be the Gate (al-Bāb) to the knowledge of ~~the Hidden Imam (see Introduction)~~. The date was the fifth of Jamādi Awwal A.H. 1260, or 23rd May, 1844. Notice that Bahā'u'llāh refers to al-Bāb not as a major manifestation (ẓuhūr) as the Bābīs had considered him to be, but as a Teller-of-Good-News about the coming of Bahā'u'llāh. " We sent him," says Bahā'u'llāh.

[3] The word translated " assembled " is often used in Muslim teaching for the gathering at the last day, when after the Resurrection men are gathered before God for judgment. The Bahā'ī teaching is that by his coming to earth and by his teaching, Bahā'u'llāh has brought the long-expected resurrection of the dead.

[4] Supposedly the two feasts mentioned here are the birthdays of the Bāb and Bahā'u'llāh on the first and second days of the Muslim month Muḥarram, which are kept as one feast.

[5] The first of the nineteen Bābī months was called Bahā'. The first day of Bahā' is, therefore, the Iranian New Year (Nawrūz).

[6] By putting on new clothes, enjoying food prepared for the feast, and entertaining friends one expresses in action gratitude to God for His gifts.

[7] 21st March (Nawrūz) is the beginning of Spring.

GOD

which God has made the Rising-place of His Shining, Illuminating Cause.

God has ordained that every person appear before the Throne bringing his most priceless possessions,[1] but We have exempted you from this as a favour from Him. He, indeed, is the Generous Giver.

Blessed is the one who faces the Sunrise-place of Remembrance [2] (*mashriq al-adhkār*) in the early mornings, mentioning (the name of God), remembering, and asking forgiveness ! Whenever he enters, he sits quietly in order to listen to the verses of God, the Mighty One, the Praiseworthy King.

Say : The Sunrise-place of Remembrance is every house built for My remembrance in cities and villages. Thus has it been named before the Throne, if you are of those who know. Those who recite the verses of the Merciful in the best tones comprehend from them that which the Kingdom of the Sovereignty of the heavens and the earths does not equal. By them they find the odour of My worlds which is only known to-day by the one who has been given sight of the Noble Spectacle. Say : They (41) attract the pure hearts to the spiritual worlds which are beyond definition either by overt expression or even by gesture. Blessed are those who hear !

Help, O People, My pure ones who persevered in remembering Me in the midst of My Creation and in exalting My Word in My Kingdom. Those are the stars of the heaven of My providence and the lamps of My guidance to all creatures.

He who speaks other than that sent down in My Tablets is not one of Mine. Beware lest you follow every evil claimant. The Tablets have been adorned with the garment of the Seal of the Breaker of Dawns Who speaks between the heavens and the earths. Hold fast to the Indissoluble Bond (*bil-'urwa al-wuthqā*) and the rope of My firm and strong Command.

God has permitted those who so desire to learn different languages that they may propagate the Cause of God and tell of it in the east and west of the earth, and make mention of it among the states and

---

[1] The Báb commanded that, when his followers came to him, they should bring him as a gift their most precious possessions, but Bahá'u'lláh does not require presents from visitors.

[2] *Mashriq al-adhkár* is the name for the place of worship to be built by Bahá'ís in every place they go. It is the custom to sit in a circle about the room.

religious groups.[1] This is done in a way that hearts may be drawn thereby and every decayed bone revived.

The rational person does not drink that which takes away his reason. He should do what is incumbent on man and not that which every careless doubtful person commits.

Adorn your heads with the crown of faithfulness and integrity, your hearts with the cloak of piety, your tongues with true veracity and your temples (bodies) with the garment of good breeding. All this is the natural disposition of man, (42) if you were only of those who have insight.

O People of al-Bahā', hold fast to the rope of servitude to God, the Truth ; by so doing your Stations are made manifest, your names are enrolled, and your ranks and remembrance in the Preserved Tablet are exalted. Beware lest someone on earth keep you from this strong, exalted station.

We have recommended this to you in most of the Tablets, and in this Tablet, from the horizon of which flashed the light of the commandments of your Lord, the Powerful, the Wise.

When the Sea of Union (with Me) is dried up and the Book of Beginning is finished in the End, then turn to the one whom God desires, the one who is a Branch from the ancient Root.[2]

Look at the people and their little-mindedness. They ask for what injures them and forsake that which benefits them. Indeed, they are bewildered ! We see some people who desired freedom boasting of it. They are in manifest ignorance. The consequences of freedom end in sedition, the fire of which is unquenchable. Thus informs you the Learned Reckoner.

Know that the place where freedom arises and makes its appearance

---

[1] The learning of foreign languages had been forbidden by the Bāb. Bahā'u'llāh abrogates this command.

[2] Bahā'u'llāh here directs his followers to look to a son of his as their leader after his death. He does not say here which son. His purpose is explained in the Book of the Covenant (Kitab-i-'ahd) which is found in Bahā'i Scriptures, Brentano, 1923, pp. 259–262. There Bahā'u'llāh refers to this passage in al-Kitāb al-Aqdas and says that he is to be succeeded by the Most Mighty Branch ('Abbas Effendi), who in turn will be succeeded by the Most Great Branch (Muḥammad 'Ali). These two sons were from different mothers. The translator of Bahā'i Scriptures mistakenly translates the two titles as the Greater and the Greatest, whereas both terms have a superlative and equally great meaning. 'Abbas Effendi, known as 'Abdul-Bahā' succeeded his father.

is life. But man must be under regulations which preserve him from ignorance of himself and the harm of the crafty ones. Freedom leads a man away from things of good breeding and sobriety and makes him one of the basest (creatures). Look at (43) mankind ; they are like sheep, they must have a shepherd to keep them. This fact is certain. We believe in freedom in some situations and not in others ; we are of those who know.

Say : Freedom is in following My commands, if you only knew it. If people were to follow what We have sent down to them from the heaven of Revelation, they would most certainly find themselves in absolute freedom.

Blessed is the one who knew the desire of God in what He sent down from the heaven of His will which supervises the worlds !

Say : The freedom which benefits you is servitude to God, the True One, and whoever has found this sweetness of freedom will not exchange it for the kingdom of sovereignty of the heavens and the earths.

In *al-Bayān* it was forbidden you to ask. God has exempted you from this commandment that you may ask what your souls need, not what men before you spake. Fear God and be among the pious. Ask for what will benefit you in the Cause and Authority of God. He has opened the door of Grace to those who are in the heavens and earths.

The number of months is nineteen according to the Book of God ; the first was adorned with this Name, the Overseer of the Worlds.[1]

God has commanded that the dead be buried in (coffins of) crystal or rare stones or beautiful hard woods, (44) and that engraved rings be placed on their fingers.[2] Indeed, He is the Knower, the Predeterminer. This (inscription) was ordained for men, " To God belongs what is in the heavens and the earth and what is between them. God knows everything." This was ordained for women,[3]

O ARABIC BAYAN XI 19 WHICH FORBIDS INQUIRING ABOUT HIM-WHOM-GOD-SHALL-MANIFEST PRIOR TO HIS APPEARANCE

[1] Here Bahā'u'llāh repeats what the Bāb commanded in the *Bayān*, that is, there are to be nineteen months. The Bāb named the first month of the year Bahā'.

[2] See Nuqtatu'l-Kaf, p. lxxxviii, " Rings." The " Point of *al-Bayān* " is the Bāb.

[3] *Waraqa*, leaf, page, is often used by Bahā'īs for " woman " ; one of Bahā's wives had the title *Waraqa-i-'Ulyā* " the supreme leaf ". His sons were called " branches ". See Browne, *A Traveller's Narrative*, p. 361.

" To God belongs the sovereignty of the heavens and the earth and what is between them. God is powerful over everything."

This is what was sent down previously, when the Point of al-Bayān cried saying, " O Beloved of the World of the Possible, speak in this situation that by which the breezes of Thy benefits are diffused among the worlds." We have informed everybody that what was brought down in al-Bayān does not equal a word from Thee.[1] Thou art the Powerful over what Thou willest. Do not deprive Thy creatures of the abundance of the Sea of Thy Mercy. Thou, indeed, art the Possessor of Great Grace.

We have answered what He desired. Indeed, He is the Answering One, the Beloved.

If what was sent down at this time from God were engraved (on the rings), it would be better for the men and the women. We are the rulers. " I had my origin in God and I returned to Him ; I am separated from all but Him, and I hold fast to His Name, the Merciful, the Compassionate." [2] Thus does God assign especial Grace from Him to whom He wills. He is the Powerful, the Mighty One.

And (God commanded that) you wrap (the dead body) in five garments of silk or cotton. Whoèver is unable to do this, one of them will be sufficient for him. Thus was the matter decided by an Omniscient, who Knows.[3]

It is unlawful (45) for you to carry the dead body farther than the distance of an hour from the city. Bury him with joy and sweetness in a nearby place.

God has withdrawn that which al-Bayān commanded about limiting journeys.[4] He is, indeed, the Chooser ; He does what He wills and commands what He desires.

O multitude of Creation, hear the call of the Possessor of Names. He calls you from the direction of His Most Great Prison, saying, " There is no god besides Me, the Powerful, the Proud, the Scoffer,

---

[1] Bahā'u'llāh quotes here the command of the Bāb in the Bayān regarding the burial of the dead and asserts his superiority to the Bāb. He quotes the Bāb as calling him " the Beloved of the World ", and claims that one word of his is worth more than the whole of the Bayān.

[2] Bahā'u'llāh here substitutes for what was in the Bayān his own new inscription for the rings of the dead, the same for both men and women. The writing in the rings is of course to be in Arabic.

[3] Again the regulations of the Bāb are relaxed.

[4] The Bāb had forbidden travel to foreign lands.

the Exalted, the Knower, the Wise." There is no god besides Him, the Powerful over the Worlds. If He so willed, He might take the world by a word from Him.

Take care not to delay in this Cause to which the Most High Beings and the peoples of the cities of the Names submitted. Fear God and be not of the veiled ones. Burn the veils with the fire of My love and the curtains with this Name by which we conquered the worlds.

Raise up the two houses in the two places,[1] and (also) in other places where the Throne of your Lord, the Merciful, was settled. Thus commands you the Lord of those who know.

Take care that the affairs of the earth hinder you not from that which you were commanded by a Faithful, Strong One

Be manifestations of uprightness in the midst of mankind so that the doubts of those who do not believe in God will not hinder you when He has appeared with Great Authority (46).

Take care that what was sent down in the Book does not keep you away from this Book which speaks in truth, saying, " There is no god besides Me, the Powerful, the Praiseworthy." Look with the eye of equity at the One [2] who came from the Heaven of Will and Might. Be not of the wicked ones.

Then remember what happened through the pen of Him who told the Good News of me in mentioning this Manifestation [3] and what the rebels (against God) committed in his day. Indeed, they are among the heaviest losers ! He said, " If you comprehend what We manifest in you, you will ask from the Grace of God that He bestow on you the favour of making His abode in your secret hearts. He is Unattainable, Unapproachable Power. For Him to drink a cup of water with you is greater than that every one drink the water of His existence, nay rather of everything. If, O creatures of Mine, you would comprehend ! "

This is what was sent down from Him as a remembrance of Myself, if you only knew.

Whoever thinks on these verses and is informed of what is concealed in them of treasured pearls, by God, he will perceive the

---

[1] Presumably the two houses which must be built up or repaired are the house in Shiraz where the Báb made his claim, and the house in Teheran in the Imamzadeh Masum where, according to the Bahá'í account, the Báb's body was buried for a time before being taken to Haifa. By " Throne " is meant the body of the Báb.

[2] " The One," i.e., Bahá'u'lláh.

[3] " Who told the good news," i.e., the Báb.

odour of the Merciful from the direction of the Prison.[1] And he will
hasten with all his heart to Him with a longing which the hosts of
the heavens and the worlds can not hold back.

Say : Proof and Demonstration encompass this Manifestation.
Thus did the Merciful send it down—if you are of the fair-minded.

(47) Say : This is the spirit of the books. With it He has breathed
in the Highest Pen and those who are of creation (i.e., all creatures)
fainted except the one on whom the odour of My Mercy and the
perfume of My benefits, which supervise the worlds, took hold.

O multitude of al-Bayān, fear the Merciful One, then see what He
sent down in another place. [2]

He said, " Indeed, the Worship-Direction (al-qibla) is He whom
God manifests and wherever He turns, it turns till He is settled." [3]

Thus was it sent down from the Possessor of Destiny, when He
desired to mention this greatest Spectacle.[4] Think, People, be not of
the bewildered ones ! If you were to deny Him by your passions to
what Prayer-Direction would you turn your faces, O assembly of the
careless ? Think on this verse, then be fair to God. Perhaps you will
find pearls of mysteries in the sea, the waves of which swell by My
Mighty, Unapproachable Name.

One needs to-day to hold only to what has been manifested in the
Manifestation. This is the commandment of God both before and
afterwards, and by it the books of the ancients were adorned. This
is the remembrance of God both before and afterwards, and by it the
preface of the Book of Existence has been embellished, if you are of
those who perceive ! This is the order of God both before and
afterwards. Take care that you are not of the contemptible. Nothing
avails you to-day and no one has a refuge other than God, the Wise,
the Knower. Whoever knows Me, knows the Desired One. (48) Whoever turns his face to Me, turns his face to Him who is Worshipped.
Thus has it been told in detail in the Book and thus decided by God,
the Lord of the Worlds.

---

[1] " The prison," i.e., Acre.

[2] That is, be ready to listen to what God is saying through Bahā'u'llāh's books.
The " Multitude of al-Bayān " are the Bābīs who have accepted Bahā'u'llāh.

[3] The Muslim faces Mecca in worship, but the Bābī and Bahā'ī are to face the
Manifestation, wherever He may be. " He said," i.e., the Bāb commanded this.

[4] Bahā'u'llāh claimed that He was predicted by the Bāb as the " One Whom God
Manifests ".   ✱ BAHA'IS FACE AKKA IN WORSHIP

It is better for a person to read one of my verses than for him to read the books of the ancients and the moderns. This is the Explanation (al-Bayān) of the Merciful, if you are of those who listen.

Say : This is the truth of what can be known, if you were of those who know. Then look at what was sent down in another place and perhaps you will leave what you have and come to God, the Lord of the Worlds.

He said : " Joining together (al-iqtirān) is not lawful unless it is in al-Bayān.¹ And if one (not of al-Bayān) enters (into marriage with a Bābī) the properties belonging to the other (the Bābī) become unlawful for him, unless he returns. This (will go into effect) after the rising up of the Cause of One whom We manifest in truth, or what has been manifested in justice. That has been accepted. So then come near, perhaps you may raise up in this way the Cause of God." ²

Thus did the dove warble on the branches, mentioning her Lord, the Merciful. Blessed are those who hear !

O Multitudes of al-Bayān, I adjure you by your Lord, the Merciful, to look with the eye of equity at what has been sent down in Truth and be not of those who see the proof of God and deny it. They are, indeed, of those who perish !

The Point (nuqṭa) ³ of al-Bayān has explained (the matter) in this verse by exalting My Cause above his Cause. Every knowing person of equity bears witness to that (49) as you see to-day. It is exalted in such a way that no one may deny it except those whose eyes were intoxicated in this world, and in the other world they will have a severe punishment.

Say : By God, I am indeed his Beloved.⁴ Now he hears what was sent down from the heaven of Revelation and he laments what you committed in his days. Fear God, be not of the transgressors.

Say : O People, even if you never believe on Him, do not find

---

¹ The Bāb commanded that the marriage of Bābīs must be with other Bābīs, that is, the People of the Bayān and according to the laws of the Bayān.

² This passage is difficult for translation. It appears that according to the teaching of the Bāb, if a Bābī contracts a marriage with a non-Bābī, the property of the Bābī becomes unlawful for him and will be taken from him, unless he repents. Bahā'u'llāh sees in the passage a prediction of His coming.

³ " Point," i.e., the Bāb. See the Introduction.

⁴ That is, Bahā'u'llāh is the beloved of the Bāb. The Bāb hears what Bahā'u'llāh has said to men.

fault with Him. By God, the hosts of evil men who gathered against Him are sufficient.[1]

He has sent down some commandments in order that the Most High Pen may not move in this Manifestation except at the remembrance of His Most High Stations and his Exalted Spectacle.[2] Indeed, when We desired grace (for you), We truly explained these things in detail, and We made easy for you what We desired. Indeed, He is the Generous, the Munificent. He informed you previously what this Wise Remembrance said.[3] He spoke and His Word is true. Indeed He speaks in every condition, saying,[4] " There is no god besides Me, the Unique, the One, the Omniscient, who knows." God has made this Special Station for this Unapproachable, Extraordinary Manifestation. This is of the Grace of God, if you were among those who know.

This is of His confirmed command and of His greatest Name, and of His most exalted Word and the Rising-place of His beautiful Names—were you (50) of those who know. Rather by Him the Rising-places and the Sunrise-places are made manifest. Think, O People, on what was sent down with Truth and reflect on the results of it, and certainly be not of the transgressors.

Associate with those of other religions with joy and sweetness, that they may find in you the odour of the Merciful. Take care that the fanaticism of the Days of Ignorance (al-jāhiliyya) [5] among mankind does not take hold on you. Everything has its beginning in God and returns to Him. He is, indeed, the Creator of Creation and the Place of Return for the Worlds.

Take care not to enter a house when its owner is absent, unless (you have) his permission. Persist in doing good on all occasions, and be not of the careless ones.

---

[1] This is an appeal from Bahā'u'llāh to the Bābīs who do not want to accept him, to refrain from opposition, since he has already suffered enough.

[2] Presumably, the Bāb gave commandments only to exalt Bahā'u'llāh.

[3] Again the reference is to the Bāb.

[4] God speaks in everything, not only in rare appearances like His speaking to Moses in the Burning Bush.

[5] Muslims refer to the times prior to Muhammad's coming as the " Days of Ignorance " when the Arabs were pagans and barbarians. See Enc. of Islam, i, 999 f. Perhaps Bahā'u'llāh is here alluding to the time when the zealous Bābīs were fighting so furiously in Mazanderan, hoping to conquer the peoples of the world for their religion. Bahā'u'llāh bids his followers have friendly relations with non-Bahā'īs, rather than fight with them, the reason being that all men are from God.

It has been ordained for you that you make pure (lawful) your food and other things by paying the poor-rate.[1] This is what He who sent down the verses commanded in this Inaccessible Parchment. We shall tell you in detail of the property on which the poor-rate is paid when God wills and desires. He willed to detail what He wishes by a knowledge which He has. He is the Wise and the Knower.

It is not permissible to beg, and when one is asked (for money), it is forbidden for him to give. It has been ordained that every one earn his living. Whoever is unable to do so, let the guardians and the rich appoint for him what is sufficient.

Perform the stipulations and ordinances of God. Then keep them as you keep your eyes, and be not among the losers.

In the Book [2] you have been forbidden (51) things like quarrelling (al-jidāl), disputing (al-nizāʿ), and striking (al-ḍarb), and such like things which cause sorrows to hearts and souls. Whoever causes someone sorrow must give nineteen mithqals of gold. This is what the Master of the Worlds commanded. He has exempted you from this in this Manifestation. He exhorts you to righteousness and piety, a command from Him in this Illumined Tablet. Do not approve for another what you do not approve for yourselves.[3] Fear God and certainly do not be among the proud.

All of you were created from water and you will return to the earth. Think upon your latter end ; be not of the wicked. Listen to what the Lote Tree [4] recites to you of the verses of God. They (the verses) are, indeed, the Balance of Guidance from God, Lord of the other World and this World. By them souls soar to the Rising-place of Revelation and the hearts of those who come are enlightened. These are the stipulations of God, which have been made obligatory for you, and these are the commands of God by which you were commanded in the Tablet. Do them with joy and sweetness. This is better for you, if you are of the knowing ones.

Recite the verses of God every morning and evening. Whoever does not recite does not fulfill the covenant and bond of God. Whoever turns back from them to-day is of those who turn back

---

[1] The paying of the Poor-rate (al-zakāt) is one of the five pillars of religion in Islam. See Enc. of Islam, iv, 1202 ff. For mithqāl, see Note 1, p. 38.

[2] Presumably the Book is al-Bayān, and the Master of the World is the Bāb.

[3] This negative form of the Golden Rule is a well-known Persian saying.

[4] See Note 6, p. 51.

from God in the eternity of past eternities. Fear God, (52) all ye My creatures, all of you together !

Let not the multitude of readings and acts of worship night and day [1] make you conceited. Were one to read one of the verses with joy and sweetness, it were better for him than if he recite lazily the volumes of God, the Overseer, the Self-Subsistent One. Recite the verses of God to such a degree that you are not overtaken by lassitude and sorrows. Do not weigh down spirits with what causes them lassitude and heaviness, but put upon them that which lightens them so that they soar with the wings of the verses to the Rising-place of the explanations. This is nearer to God, if you were only wise.

Teach your offspring that which was sent down from the heaven of greatness and power so that they read the Tablets of the Merciful with the best tones in the rooms constructed (for that purpose) in the *Mashāriq* (plu.) *al-Adhkār*.[2] Indeed, the one on whom the attraction of the love of My Name, the Merciful, takes hold reads the verses of God in such a way that the hearts of those who sleep are attracted.

Good health to him who drinks the strong Wine of Life (*raḥīq al-ḥayawān*) from the Explanation (*Bayān*) of his Lord, the Merciful, in this Name by which every lofty elevated mountain is pulled down !

It was ordained for you to renew your house-furnishings after the expiration of nineteen years. Thus was the matter decided by an Omniscient Knower.[3] He desired to cleanse you and what is yours. Fear God (53) and do not be careless. God will exempt him who is unable to do this. Indeed, He is the Generous Pardoner.

Wash your feet every day in summer, and in winter once every three days.

Whoever becomes angry with you, meet him with gentleness. Whoever does evil to you, do not do evil to him. Leave him to himself and depend on God, the Avenger, the Just, the Powerful.

You have been prohibited from mounting into pulpits. Whoever desires to recite the verses of his Lord to you, let him sit on a seat placed on a platform and mention (the name of) God, his Lord and

---

[1] Here Bahā'u'llāh shows his disdain of those who consider it meritorious to recite long readings from Scripture.

[2] See Note 2, p. 55.

[3] It was ordained by the Bāb.

the Lord of the worlds. God likes you to sit on platforms and seats [1] because of the greatness of what you have of the love of God and the Rising-place of His Shining, Brilliant Cause.

Gambling and opium are forbidden to you. O assembly of Creation, avoid them. Be not of those who transgress. Take care not to use what produces lassitude in your temples [2] and injures your bodies. We only desire for you what benefits you. All things testify to that, if you would only listen.

Whenever you are invited to feasts and banquets, respond with joy and gladness, and whoever keeps his promise is secure from threats. This is a day in which every wise command has been explained in detail.

There has been manifested the Mystery (54) of Overturning for the enigma of the Chief. Blessed is the one whom God aided to acknowledge the six who were raised up by this upright Alif.[3] They are, indeed, of the sincere.

How many a pious man has turned away (from God) and how many a forsaker has come and said, " To Thee be the praise, O Desire of the Worlds ! " The matter is in the hand of God ; He gives to whom He wills what He wills and He keeps back from whom He wills what He desires. He knows the secrets of the hearts and that by which the eyes of those who wink are moved.

How many a careless one who came with sincerity We set down on the throne of welcome ! How many an intelligent person We returned to the Fire because of justice on Our part ! We are the

---

[1] In spite of the objection to high pulpits, those who recite verses of God should have the honour of sitting higher up than others.

[2] By " temple " is meant the human body. The reference is doubtless to opium which was much used in Iran.

[3] It is said that someone who is here called " the Chief " asked a question about the coming of the Hidden Imam of the Shi'ites. He was answered by Shaykh Ahmad al-Ahsa'i, the Shaykhi leader, in an enigma. It is to this reply that Bahá'u'lláh alludes. An *alif*, the first letter of the Arabic alphabet, is placed between two *waws*, the one to the left being upside down (ﻭ ﺍ ﻭ). The Numerical value of *waw* is six.

Then the *waw* to the right of *alif* indicates the six great manifestations before Bahá'u'lláh, namely Adam, Noah, Abraham, Moses, Jesus and Muhammad. The *waw* to the left, which is inverted, indicates the six manifestations which will follow. And what is the *alif* ? The numerical value of *alif* is one, and that indicates the One, who is God. So Bahá'u'lláh as the Greatest Manifestation stands between the two groups of six, and is himself The One. And He it is who raised up the Six.

Rulers. It is the Place of the Manifestation of " God Does What He Wills ", and He who sits on the Throne commands what He desires. Blessed is the one who has found the scent of the meanings in the trace of this Pen ! Whenever it moves, the breeze of God diffuses its perfume in everything else and whenever it stops, the existence of tranquillity appears in the (realm of) possibility. Exalted is the Merciful Who is the Revealer of this Great Grace.

Say : The enduring of injustice made justice to appear in what is other than God, and the acceptance of abasement caused the Majesty of God to shine among the worlds.

It is unlawful for you to carry arms except in time of necessity. The wearing of silk is made permissible for you.[1] God has lifted from you the commandment restricting (55) clothing and beards, as a favour from Him. He is, indeed, the Knower, the Commander. Do what the upright minds do not disapprove of and do not make yourselves the plaything (laughing-stock) of the ignorant. Blessed is the one who is adorned with the garment of good breeding and conduct ! He is among those who help the Lord with clear and evident action.

Build dwellings and cities of God, then remember Him in them with songs of those who are near (to God). Hearts are built up only by the tongue, just as houses and dwellings are built by hands and other means. For everything We have decreed a means from us ; lay hold on this and depend on the Omniscient, Wise One.

Blessed is the one who acknowledges God and His wonders, and who confesses that He is not to be asked about what He does. This is a Word [2] which God has made the adornment and the basis for His articles of belief, and by this Word the deed of the doers is received. Put this Word before your eyes lest the suggestions of those who turn away (from God) cause you to stumble. If God should make lawful what was forbidden in the eternity of past eternities, or vice versa, no one should find fault with Him.

Whoever pauses less than a moment is of those who show hostility. The one who does not attain unto this lofty principle and this most high Station is moved by the winds of doubt and the statements of

---

[1] Regulations in Islam forbade the wearing of silk (cf. *Muslim*, ii, 203 ff.).

[2] To become a Muslim one must confess the brief creed, " There is no god but Allah and Muhammad is the Messenger of Allah." This is often called the Word (*al-kalima*). Bahā'u'llāh puts forward his " Word " here.

the polytheists upset him. Whoever has attained (56) unto this principle has attained unto the greatest uprightness. Very good indeed is this most splendid Station by the remembrance of which every inaccessible Tablet is adorned.

Thus God teaches you what will deliver you from doubt and perplexity and save you in this world and that which is to come. He is the Generous Forgiver. It is He who sent the Messengers and sent down the Books since, "There is no god besides Me, the Powerful, the Wise."

O land of *al-kāf* (K) and *al-rā'* (R), We see thee in a condition which God does not like, and We see in thee that of which no one is informed except God, the Omniscient, the Knower.[1] We ascertain what occurs in thee in the most secret places, for We have knowledge of everything in the Perspicuous Tablet. Do not grieve because of what happened. God will manifest in thee possessors of strong courage who will remember Me with uprightness. The allusions of the learned men (*al-'ulamā'*) [2] will not hinder them nor the suspicions of the doubters veil them. Those will see God with their eyes and help Him with their persons. Truly they are of the firmly established.

O assembly of the learned men, when the verses came down and clear proofs were manifested We saw you behind the veils. This is none other than a wonderful thing. You gloried in My Name but were careless about Myself when the Merciful came with reason and proof. We tore off the veils ; take care that you (57) do not hide people with another veil. Break in pieces the chains of illusions (*al-awhām*) in the name of the Possessor of Mankind (*al-anām*), and be not of the deceivers.

Whenever you approach God and enter into this Cause, do not act corruptly in it. Do not measure the Book of God by your vain passions. This is the counsel of God before and afterwards. God's martyrs and men of sincerity bear witness to that. We are all witnesses to Him.

Remember the Doctor (*al-shaykh*) who was called Muḥammad Qabl Ḥasan. He was one of the most learned of the learned men of his age. When the True One was manifested he turned away from

---

[1] By K–R, Kerman is meant. What God disliked in Kerman was the presence there of Ḥajī Muḥammad Karīm Khān, the head of the Shaykhīs, who had opposed the Bāb.

[2] See Note 4, p. 51.

E*

Him, he and those like him, but he who winnows the wheat and the
barley came to God. The Doctor wrote,[1] so he claimed, the commandments of God by night and day, but when the Chosen One came,
not a letter of them was of benefit to him. Had there been benefit to
him, he would not have turned away from a Face by which the faces
of those brought near (to God) were illumined.

If you have believed on God at the time of His Manifestation, the
people would not have turned away from Him, and what you see
to-day would not have befallen Us. Fear God and be not of the
careless.[2] Take care that the names do not keep you away from their
Possessor or a remembrance veil you from the Wise Remembrance.

O assembly of the learned men, take refuge in God. Do not make
yourselves a veil between Me and My Creation. Thus God warns you
and commands you (58) with justice, lest your acts (of worship) be
of no avail while you are careless. Is the one who turns away from
this Cause able to establish truth in Innovation (al-ibdā‘) ? No, by
the Possessor of Invention ! But people are behind a manifest veil.

Say : By Him the Sun of Reason shone, and the Lighting of
Proof flashed on all who were in the (realm of the) Possible.

Fear God, O possessors of sight, and do not deny (Me). Take care
that the remembrance of the Prophet does not keep you from this
great prophecy, and this guardianship from the guardianship of God
which supervises the worlds.

He has created every Name by His Word and has attached every
cause to His Confirmed, Powerful, and Extraordinary Cause.

Say : This is the Day of God, and nothing shall be remembered in
it but His person which oversees the Worlds. Whatever illusions and
idols you have were troubled by this Cause. We see among you one
who takes the Book and proves God from it just as each religion has
proved God from its own book, God the Overseer, the Self-Subsistent
One. Say : By God, the True One, the books of the world and the

---

[1] The Doctor referred to above was presumably the father of Agha Najafī, a
famous religious man of Isfahan, who refused to believe in the Bāb. The learned
men of Islam turned people away from faith in the Bāb and Bahā'u'llāh, and all
the sufferings they endured were the result of this opposition. By " Face " is meant
the Bāb.

[2] Here the Baghdad text introduces the following lines : " Surely you will take
refuge in God, avail yourselves of Him, talk with Him, ask His assistance and seek
equity from Him and shrink before Him, the Lord of the heavens and the earth,
the Lord of the seen and the unseen and Lord of the Great Throne."

volumes that are in it will not suffice you to-day except this Book, which speaks in the Axis (*quṭb*) [1] of Innovation, saying, " There is no god besides Me, the Wise, the Knower."

O assembly of the learned men, (59) take care that you are not the cause of disagreement in various places as you were the cause of turning away (from God) at the beginning. Get the people to agree together on this Word (*al-kalima*) with which the stones cry out, " Sovereignty belongs to God, the Rising-place of the Signs." Thus does God warn you because of a Grace on His part. He is, indeed, the Generous Forgiver.

Remember Karīm [2] when We called him to God. Indeed, he magnified himself in that he followed his vain passion. This was after We sent to him that by which the eye of proof is made bright in the (realm of) possibility and God's demonstration was perfected for all in the heavens and the earths.[3] We commanded him to come (to God) as a Grace from the Exalted Self-Sufficient One. " Indeed, he has turned back, fleeing—" [4] until the angels of divine torment overtook him through a justice from God. We are witnesses.

Tear off the veils that the people of the Kingdom may hear the sound of their being torn. This is the command of God from before and afterwards. Blessed is the one who did as he was commanded, and woe to those who fail to do.

We desired nothing in Sovereignty (*al-mulk*) except the manifestation of God and His authority, and for Me God suffices as a Witness. We desired nothing in the Kingdom (*al-malakūt*) except the exalting of the Cause of God and His praise, and God suffices Me as a Pleader. We desired nothing in the Dominion (*al-jabarūt*) except the

---

[1] In the language of the Ṣūfīs (the mystics of Islam) the man who reveals God, the head of the order, is often called the Axis (*quṭb*), for about Him everything revolves. (cf. *Enc. of Islam*, iv, 684 ; ii, 1465 ff.). It seems that here Bahā'u'llāh is chiding the People of the Bayān for trying to prove from their book just what Jews and Christians proved from their books, namely, that Bahā'u'llāh was not from God. His reply is that only his book will suffice them, for it is the final and complete Word of God, who in Bahā'u'llāh is doing a new thing. Bahā'u'llāh is, therefore, " the Axis of Innovation."

[2] See Note 1, p. 67.

[3] It seems that Bahā'u'llāh had sent an epistle to Ḥaji Karīm Khān in Kerman in which he tried to prove that his claim was true, but Karīm was not convinced.

[4] In this Qur'ān verse (27 : 10) Moses is said to have turned away from the rod which had been changed into a serpent. In like manner Karīm had fled from the signs of God revealed in Bahā'u'llāh till God's wrath descended on him and he died.

Remembrance of God (60) and What was sent down from Him, and for Me God suffices as a Helper.

Blessed are you, O assembly of the Learned Men in *al-Bahā'*.[1] By God, you are waves of the most great Sea and the stars of the Heaven of Grace and the banners of assistance among the heavens and the earths. You are the Rising-places of uprightness among mankind and the Sunrise-places of Explanation to him who is in the (realm of the) possible. Blessed is the one who comes to you, and woe to the ones who turn away from you.[2]

To-day it is fitting that one who drinks the strong Wine of Life (*rahīq al-hayawān*) from the hand of the kindness of his Lord, the Merciful One, should be throbbing continually like the veins in the body of Possibility, that by Him the world and every decayed bone might move.

O people of Creation, whenever the dove flies from the forest of praise and makes for the furthermost hidden goal,[3] then refer what you did not understand in the Book to the Bough which branches from the Self-Subsistent Stock.

O Pen of the Most High, move over the Tablet by the permission of Thy Lord, Maker of the Heaven. Then remember thou when the Rising-place of Unity desired the School of Detachment. Perhaps those who are free will be informed as much as an eye of a needle of what there is behind the veils of the mysteries of thy Lord, the Mighty, the Knower.

Say : We entered the School of Meanings and Explanation when those in the (realm of) Possibility were off their guard, and we witnessed what the Merciful had sent down, and We received (61)

---

[1] The learned men in *al-Bahā'* are the Muslim doctors of divinity who have believed in Bahā'u'llāh.

[2] Here the Baghdad text introduces the following lines, using as in Note 2, p. 68, the emphatic form with *nūn* in all the verbs. " Surely you will seek assistance from God, O people of *al-Bahā'*, and scoff at all else but Him in the name of the Powerful, Mighty Scoffer, and you will be superior over all possible things by the superiority of your Lord, the Overseer of the worlds, and be victorious over all existent things by the authority of your Victorious, Powerful, and Wise Lord, and find your sufficiency in God, your Lord, the Self-Sufficient, Powerful, Wise, and All-Knowing One."

[3] This is another reference to questions about interpretations being referred to Bahā'u'llāh's son after his death. He does not indicate which son is intended. See Note 2, p. 56.

what He gave to Me of the verses of God, the Self-Subsistent Overseer. We heard what He bore witness to in the Tablet ; We are witnesses. We answered Him with a command on our part ; We are commanders.

O multitude of *al-Bayān*, We entered the school of God while you were reclining, and We carefully observed the Tablet while you were asleep. By God, the True One, We read it before its descent, but you were careless. We had a thorough knowledge of the Book, while you were in the loins (of your fathers).

This is a reminder according to your measure, not according to that of God ; that which is in the knowledge of God bears witness to this fact, if you only knew, and the tongue of God bears witness to that, if you were only learned. By God, if We were to lift away the veil, you would faint !

Take care not to argue with God and (dispute) His Cause.[1] He was manifested in such a way that He knows thoroughly all that was and will be. If We were to speak in this Station with the tongue of the people of the Kingdom, We would say : " God created this School before He created the heavens and the earth. And We entered into it before *al-kāf* joined its support *al-nūn*." [2]

This is the tongue of My creatures in My Kingdom (*malakūtī*). Think on what the tongue of the people of My Dominion (*jabarūtī*) [3] might utter of what We taught them as knowledge from Us, and of what is hidden in the knowledge of God and what the tongue of Greatness and Power utters in its Praiseworthy Station (62).

This is not something to be played with by your illusions. This is not a Station into which every illusioned coward enters. By God, this is the training-place (*miḍmār*) for unveiling and separation (from the world) and the race-ground (*maydān*) of Vision and Exaltation. Only the horsemen of the Merciful, who disregard the

---

[1] In this passage Bahā'u'llāh reproves the Bābīs who have not accepted him as a new Manifestation. While they were asleep new truth had been revealed, truth which he knew before they were born. One gets the impression that there were many unbelieving Bābīs.

[2] According to Muslim belief, God created everything out of nothing by speaking the Arabic word *kun* (be !) (cf. Qur'ān 3 : 42). Bahā'u'llāh teaches here that before the " k " was joined to the " n ", that is, before creation, he was in God's " School " and knew God's knowledge.

[3] Many consider *malakūt* as a high spiritual world and *jabarūt* as a yet higher world. *Enc. of Islam*, i, 986, explains how the meanings vary with different authors using the terms.

(realm of) possibility, go about in it. Those are the helpers of God in the earth and in the Sunrise-places of power among the worlds.

Take care that what is in *al-Bayān* does not keep you away from your Lord, the Merciful. By God, it was sent down as a reminder of Me, if you only knew. The sincere find in it only the odour of My love and of My Name, which oversees every witness and thing witnessed.

Say : O People, face towards what has been sent down from My Highest Pen. If you find in it an odour of God, do not turn away from it and do not deprive yourselves of the Grace and benefits of God. Thus does God counsel you ; indeed, He is the Counsellor who knows. What you do not understand of *al-Bayān* ask God, your Lord, and the Lord of your fathers, the ancient ones. Indeed, if He wills, He will explain (from the same root as *al-Bayān*) to you what came down in it, and what pearls of knowledge and wisdom are hidden in the seas of its words. Indeed, He is the Overseer of the Names. There is no god besides Him, the Self-Subsistent Overseer.

Order (*al-naẓm*) has been disturbed by this Most Great Order, and arrangement has been made different through this innovation, (63) the like of which the eye of invention has not seen.[1] Plunge into the sea of My Explanation (*bayānī*)[2] and perhaps you will become informed as to the pearls of wisdom and mysteries to be found therein. Take care that you do not delay in this Cause, in which has been manifested the authority and power of God. Hasten to Him with white faces.

This is the religion of God before and afterwards. Whoever desires, let him come ; whoever does not desire—God indeed has no need of the Worlds.

Say : This Balance (*al-qusṭās*) is the Guidance to all who are in the heavens and the earths, and the greatest proof, if you only knew.

Say : By it every proof has been established in all ages, if you were only certain.

Say : By it every poor man became rich, every learned man was taught and whoever wished to ascend to God went up.

---

[1] Bābīs objected to Bahā'u'llāh's claim to be the new Manifestation because the *MINIMUM PERIOD OF* 1511 years had not elapsed between the time of the Bāb and his appearance. It may be in answer to this that Bahā'u'llāh says that the usual order and arrangement has been changed for a better order.

[2] Here Bahā'u'llāh either claims the *Bayān* as his, or refers to his writings by that name.

Take care that you differ not about it. Be like the steadfast mountains in the Cause of your Lord, the Mighty, the Beloved.

Say : O Rising-place of Deviation, quit concealing (the truth) ! [1] Then speak the Truth in the midst of created beings. By God, My tears have flowed down My cheeks when I saw thee following thy passion and forsaking the One who created thee and fashioned thee. Remember the Grace of thy Master when We educated thee by night and day for the service of the Cause. [2] Fear God and be of the penitent to God !

Suppose people were mistaken (64) about thy affair ; art thou mistaken about thyself ?

Fear God and remember when thou wast standing before the Throne and wast writing what We dictated to thee of the verses of God, the Overseer, the Mighty, the Powerful. Take care that zeal does not hinder thee from the Unity. Face towards Him, be not afraid because of thy (evil) works. He forgives whom He wills by Grace from Him. There is no god besides Him, the Generous Forgiver. It is only for the sake of God that we give thee this advice. If thou comest, it is for thyself ; if thou turnest away, thy Lord is sufficient without thee and those who follow thee in evident delusion.

God has taken the one who seduced thee ; [3] therefore return to Him submissive, humble, and humiliated. He will pardon thy evil doings. Thy Lord is, indeed, the Relenting, the Powerful, the Merciful.

This is the counsel of God, if thou art of those who hear.

This is the Grace of God, if thou art of those who draw near.

This is the remembrance of God, if thou art of those who perceive.

This is the treasure of God, if thou art of those who know.

This is a Book that has become a lamp for the feet of all those in the world and his straightest way for the worlds.

---

[1] Presumably the person addressed is Subh-i-Ezel, the brother of Bahá'u'lláh. See the Introduction. This passage is translated by Browne in *Traveller's Narrative*, p. 98.

[2] From the Introduction we learned that Bahá'u'lláh was older than his brother. He was also his tutor.

[3] The person who, according to Bahá'u'lláh, deceived Subh-i-Ezel was someone who had been taken from this world by God. E. G. Browne says that the one alluded to was Ḥaji Sayyid Muhammad Isfahání, who was one of the Azalís killed by the Bahá'ís at Acre. See *Traveller's Narrative*, pp. 93 f., 370.

Say : Indeed, it is the Rising-place of the knowledge of God, if you only knew. It is the Sunrise-place of God's commands, if you only knew.

Do not load an animal with what it is unable to carry. We have strictly forbidden you to do this (65) in the Book.

Be manifestations of justice and equity among the heavens and the earths.

Whoever kills a person by mistake must pay blood-money to his people, and the amount is one hundred *mithqals* of gold.[1]

Do what you were commanded to do in the Tablet. Be not of those who transgress.

O people of the councils in different countries, choose a language among the languages to be spoken by those on earth. Choose likewise the handwriting to be used. Indeed, God will show you what benefits you and what makes you independent of others. This is a means for (attaining) union, if you only knew, and the greatest reason for agreement and civilization, if you would only perceive it. We have made the two matters two signs of the world's coming to maturity. The first, and it is the greater [2] foundation, we sent down in other Tablets. The second we have sent down in this innovating Tablet.[3]

The smoking of opium has been prohibited to you. We have strictly forbidden this to you in the Book. Whoever smokes (it) is not one of us.

Fear God, O people of intelligence.

By My Most Great, Most Holy, High, and Most Splendid Name !

[1] See Note 1, p. 38.

[2] The first matter is said to be *al-kīmiyā'* (alchemy, chemistry).

[3] Presumably this is the command given above to choose a universal language and alphabet.

Appendix 2

Documents Supplied by Jelal Azal

LIST OF DOCUMENTS IN ARABIC AND PERSIAN PROVIDED BY
MR. JELAL AZAL OF CYPRUS IN SUPPORT OF STATEMENTS
MADE BY HIM IN HIS COMMUNICATIONS TO WILLIAM M. MILLER
REGARDING THE BABI AND BAHA'I HISTORY. THESE LENGTHY
COMMUNICATIONS ARE CALLED "AZAL'S NOTES." 1137 PAGES
OF THESE NOTES WERE XEROXED AND PLACED IN THE LIBRARY
OF PRINCETON UNIVERSITY. ALSO NUMBERS 1 THROUGH 25
OF THESE DOCUMENTS WERE XEROXED AND PLACED IN THE
LIBRARY. NUMBERS 26 THROUGH 75 ARE IN THE POSSESSION
OF W. M. MILLER, AS ARE THE ORIGINAL HANDWRITTEN
NOTES OF MR. AZAL. MR. AZAL DIED ON APRIL 5, 1971.

#1. Facsimile of letter from Abbas Efendi Abdu'l-
     Baha justifying the murder of Mirza Riza Quli
     of Tafrish. *Azal's Notes* pp. 8-13.

#2. Facsimile of Instrument of Grant made in Baghdad
     to Mirza Husayn Ali Baha by Mirza Musa, who gave
     all his possessions to Baha. *Azal's Notes* pp.
     38, 47.

#3. Facsimile of Table of Contents of Baha's Baghdad
     Letters. *Azal's Notes* p. 206.

423

#4.   Facsimile of Baha's Baghdad Letter No. 1. *Azal's Notes* p. 206.

#5.   Facsimile of Baha's Baghdad Letter No. 46. *Azal's Notes* p. 206.

#6.   Facsimile of Baha's Will of Baghdad Period. *Azal's Notes* p. 206.

#7.   Facsimile of Baha's Information Against Subh-i-Azal, given to the Governor General of Edirne Province. *Azal's Notes* p. 206.

#8.   Facsimile of Full Family Chart of Mirza Buzurg, father of Mirza Husayn Ali and Mirza Yahya (Baha and Subh-i-Azal). *Azal's Notes* p. 206.

#9.   Facsimile of Baha's Akka Letter No. 140. *Azal's Notes* p. 206.

#10.   Note on Mirza Abdu'l-Fadl of Gulpayagan (4 pages).

#11.   Note on Sayyid Ali Akbar (Hajji Sayyid Mahdi).

#12.   Note on Will of Abbas Efendi Abdu'l-Baha.

#13.   Copy of *Rahnamayi Kitab*, containing an article about the information given by Mirza Husayn Ali Baha to the Governor of Edirne against Mirza Yahya Subh-i-Azal.

#14.   Facsimile of cover of Will of Abbas Efendi Abdu'l-Baha, with notes in handwriting of Mirza Badiullah son of Baha. *Azal's Notes* pp. 216, 234.

#15.   Facsimile of page 8 of above Will, with marginal notes by Mirza Badiullah. *Azal's Notes* p. 216, 234.

#16.   Accusations of Abbas Efendi against his brother Mirza Muhammad Ali. *Azal's Notes* pp. 216-352.

#17.   Bahai Quarterly (English) 1935, published by Shua Ullah, son of Mirza Muhammad Ali. Picture

of him with Mirza Hadi Afnan, father of Shoghi
Efendi.

#18. Documents for *Azal's Notes* on the Will of Abbas
Efendi p. 253.

#19. Documents for *Azal's Notes* on the Will of Abbas
Efendi p. 272.

#20. Documents for *Azal's Notes* pp. 276-277. Letter
of Baha to his family, with notes on persons
mentioned in letter.

#21. Documents for *Azal's Notes* pp. 276-277:
Excerpts from Memoirs of Mirza Badiullah, son of
Baha (19 pp.), tells how Abbas Efendi overcame
his father. Translated in full in *Azal's Notes*
pp. 286-305.

#22. Document for *Azal's Notes* p. 277. After Baha's
death Tablets will cease to be written.

#23. Copy of *Yaghma* (Persian magazine), 7 Aban 1339
(November 1960), pp. 404-407. Baha's correspondence with the Comte de Gobineau requesting aid
from France. *Azal's Notes* pp. 364, 378.

#24. Facsimile of letter from Hosayn Ali Baha to Comte
de Gobineau. *Azal's Notes* pp. 360, 364, 378-386.
Letter translated pp. 380-383.

#25. Full list (English) of all members of the family
of Baha'u'llah. *Azal's Notes* pp. 102-103.

#26. Facsimile of the Bab's autograph epistle appoint-
ing Subh-i-Azal as his successor. *Azal's Notes*
p. 552.

#27. A book containing a collection of facsimilies of
some of the autograph epistles of the Bab and of
his amanuensis Aqa Sayyid Husayn, including:

a) Appointment of Subh-i-Azal as his successor
(same as #26). *Azal's Notes* p. 553.

b) Conferring on Subh-i-Azal the same rank as himself. *Azal's Notes* p. 554.

c) Other epistles confirming appointment of Subh-i-Azal. *Azal's Notes* p. 554.

#28. Facsimile of a transcript made by Subh-i-Azal of the Bab's Testamentary Dispositions to Subh-i-Azal. *Azal's Notes* p. 555.

#29. Typed copy of portion of the Bab's personal Diary, which shows that according to the Bab the Babi Era commenced on Jamad Awwal 5, 1266 A.H. (March 19, 1850).

#30. Facsimile of five pages of Bab's personal Diary, in which Mirza Husayn (Baha) is referred to not by a title, but as "brother of the Fruit" (Subh-i-Azal). *Azal's Notes* pp. 605, 607, 613.

#31. The epistle of the Bab to Mirza Husayn Ali (Baha), ordering him to take the best possible care of Subh-i-Azal. This is taken from the book *Tanbihun Naimin*, p. 32. *Azal's Notes* pp. 605-608.

#32. Facsimile of the report of Mirza Aqa Khan of Kirman of his interview with Baha in Akka, in which Baha admitted that the Baha'is had planned to kill Subh-i-Azal in Cyprus, and he had restrained them. *Azal's Notes* pp. 637, 661.

#33. Facsimile of a letter written by Subh-i-Azal to the Ottoman governor of Famagusta in Cyprus, informing him that some Baha'is had come there to kill him. *Azal's Notes* pp. 637, 662.

#34. A copy of the Bab's "Homily on the Lights," in which he explained that his "denial" in the mosque of Shiraz was only a denial of being a "Bab" in the Shi'ite conception of Babhood, that is, he was not a "gate to the Hidden Imam." *Azal's Notes* p. 729.

#35. Two identical pictures of the Bab, one from Azal's files (dim), and the other from the book of A.L.M. Nicolas, "Sayyid Ali Muhammad dit le Bab," Paris 1911. *Azal's Notes* p. 829.

#36. Two pictures of Mirza Huseyn Ali Baha (at Edirne). *Azal's Notes* pp. 829-830.

#37. A copy of a statement by Subh-i-Azal to Professor Browne regarding the disposal of the body of the Bab. *Azal's Notes* p. 855, translated in the *Notes* p. 889.

#38. Persian text of pp. 301-302 of *Hasht Bihisht*, which tells of the departure of Mirza Husayn Ali Baha in anger from Baghdad, as a result of the rebuke given him by some of the Babi leaders. *Azal's Notes* p. 959.

#39. Facsimile of *Risala-i-Badi* pp. 92-93, in which Mirza Husayn Ali Baha is quoted as an authority that the murderer of Dayyan in Baghdad was Mirza Muhammad of Mazanderan. *Azal's Notes* p. 966.

#40. Facsimile of Collection of the early writings of Mirza Husayn Ali Baha - Index of Contents, and Letter No. 60 (to Sayyid Ibrahim Khalil a follower of Dayyan). *Azal's Notes* p. 970.

#41. Facsimile of *Arabic Bayan* VI:15 - "In the year nine ye will attain to all good." *Azal's Notes* p. 977.

#42. Facsimile of copy of the Bab's communication to Mulla Shaykh Ali Azim from the Bab's "Five Grades" pp. 252-290. *Azal's Notes* p. 979.

#43. Page 59 of the Bab's *Seven Proofs*, in which occurs the words *ba'd hin* (after a while). *Azal's Notes* p. 990.

#44. Page 703 from J.R.A.S. (October 1892), taken from *Istidlaliyya* of Mirza Abul Fadl of Galpayagan, giving date of the manifestation of Baha'u'llah as 1868 in Akka. *Azal's Notes* p. 996.

#45. *Persian Bayan* VI:8 (pp. 210-213), where it is stated that He-Whom-God-Will-Manifest will be uninstructed in the learning of the world, and his knowledge will be imminent. *Azal's Notes* p. 998.

#46. Facsimile of all of the Will of Abbas Efendi Abdu'l-Baha, with marginal notes by his brother Mirza Badiullah. On pp. 20-21 he states that the Bab is the "Manifestation of the Unity and Oneness of God." *Azal's Notes*, p. 1005.

#47. Pages 192-193 from *Persian Bayan* VI:3, where the Bab states that 19 years will elapse *after* the appearance of Him-Whom-God-Will-Manifest. *Azal's Notes* pp. 1006, 1006A.

#48. Facsimile of a page from *Sahifa-i-Adliyya* which was written by the Bab in Shiraz. The phrase "ere nine" in this passage has no reference to Baha. *Azal's Notes* pp. 1018-1020.

#49. Facsimile of pp. 79-80 of Baha's Tablet "O Creator of All Creation" which referred to the Bab's statement in #47. *Azal's Notes* pp. 1006, 1021.

#50. Facsimile of pages 44, 45, 206, 207, 248 of a book by Mirza Muhammad Jawad, dated 1896, in which the claims of Abdu'l-Baha are rejected, and states that Baha'u'llah's declaration was in 1863. *Azal's Notes* pp. 1021-1023.

#51. Page 62 of *Arabic Bayan* XI:19, in which it is stated that no one is permitted to make inquiries about Him-Whom-God-Will-Manifest before he appears. *Azal's Notes* pp. 1036-1038.

#52. A copy of the complete reply of the Bab to Mulla Baqir of Tabriz, in which the Bab rebuked him for asking about Him-Whom-God-Will-Manifest. *Azal's Notes* pp. 1036, 1038-1052.

#53. Facsimile of excerpts from the reply of the Bab to Mulla Baqir of Tabriz, taken from *Kitab-i-Zuhur al-Haqq*, vol. III, pp. 19-22. *Azal's Notes* pp. 1036-1038.

#54. Facsimile of pp. 1, 8, 9, 37 of Baha'u'llah's *Risala*, date 1869. *Azal's Notes* pp. 1037, 1045.

#55. Page 86 of *Persian Bayan* III:11, in which it is stated that the Manifestation is the Creator of all the Letters, and is not himself one of the Letters of the Living. *Azal's Notes* pp. 1037, 1047.

#56. Page 208 of *Persian Bayan* VI:7. Letters of the Living will be generated by Him-Whom-God-Will-Manifest after his appearance. *Azal's Notes* pp. 1037, 1048.

#57. Pages 99 and 235 of *Persian Bayan* III:15 and VI:16, in which provision for the Covenant is made. *Azal's Notes* pp. 1037, 1052.

#58. Lithographed and autographed Will of Mirza Muhammad Ali, second son of Baha'u'llah, signed and dated by him A.H. 1344 (1925), 24 pages.

#59. Facsimile of part of the Will of Baha'u'llah, taken from Ayati's (Awara's) *Al-Kawakib Al-Durriyya*, Vol. II, pp. 20-22. Provisions for the succession, first Abbas Efendi and then Mirza Muhammad Ali. *Azal's Notes* p. 1039A.

#60. Pages from the *Persian Bayan* relating to the Bab's theory of Manifestations and Him-Whom-God-Will-Manifest, I:2-19, III:4-8, VII:10. *Azal's Notes* pp. 1037A, 1038A.

#61. Facsimile of pp. 356-357 of Baha'u'llah's *Risala-i-Badi*, in which he says that he maintains the Bayan of the Bab. *Azal's Notes* p. 1055.

#62. Facsimile of pp. 31, 32, 40 of printed copy of
     Huwa Sahifa Al-Hub va Al-Wifaq Fi Bayan etc.,
     date 1899. Mirza Muhammad Ali the son of Baha
     and Mirza Aqa Jan were given authority to revise
     some of the writings of Baha'u'llah, including
     the Aqdas. *Azal's Notes* p. 1059.

#63. Page 34 of *Arabic Bayan* VIII:7, in which the Bab
     states that the Prayer Direction is the Manifes-
     tation. *Azal's Notes* p. 1061.

#64. Page 198 of *Persian Bayan* VI:6, in which the Bab
     forbids the reading of books related to previous
     Manifestations. *Azal's Notes* p. 1076.

#65. Pages 130-132 of *Persian Bayan* IV:10, which con-
     tains further regulations about reading and
     writing books. *Azal's Notes* p. 1076.

#66. One page from *The Ninth Ishraq*, in which Baha'u'-
     llah states that the Bab had revealed laws, and
     he had implemented some of them, and revealed
     them in *Al-Kitab Al-Aqdas*. *Azal's Notes* p. 1086.

#67. Three pages of *The Eighth Ishraq*, in which Baha'u'-
     llah says he has amended the Aqdas by explaining
     the political character of the House of Justice.
     Azal's Notes p. 1089.

#68. Facsimile of Cover and page 16 of *Shamshir-i-*
     Burran (Teheran 1948), in which there is a refer-
     ence to *Tablet to the Hague* about Peace, written
     in 1919. *Azal's Notes* p. 1089.

#69. Facsimile of eleven pages of *Tablet of Good News*
     (*Bisharat*) by Baha'u'llah, containing 15 Commands
     or Principles. *Azal's Notes* pp. 1090-1098.

#70. Facsimile of pp. 188-189 of *Kashf-al-Hiyal*, Vol.
     III, third printing, by Ayati, which contains a
     sample of "Khatt-i-Badi," the script invented by
     Mirza Muhammad Ali and approved by Baha'u'llah.
     Azal's Notes pp. 1091-1092.

#71. Message of Shoghi Efendi of April 15, 1952,
   announcing the death of Sayyid Nayyir Afnan,
   great-grandson of Baha'u'llah. Also, a statement from U. S. Assembly about credentials for
   travel.

#72. Facsimile of pages 1, 12, 14-15 of *Ishraqat,
   Tarazat, Tajalliat* which contain a Tablet written
   by Baha'u'llah shortly before his death in 1892,
   in which he admits that murders committed by
   Baha'is in the early days were by orders. *Azal's
   Notes* pp. 1110-1113A.

#73. Facsimile of extracts from a Tablet of Baha'u'-
   llah, in the handwriting of Mirza Muhammad Ali,
   which indicates that Baha was in close touch
   with events in the outside world. *Azal's Notes*
   pp. 1110, 1114-1115.

#74. Facsimile of pp. 58-60 of *Tablet of Ishraqat*,
   in which Baha'u'llah states that only the Manifestation possesses the "Most Great Infallibility."
   Azal's Notes, p. 1124.

#75. Facsimile of p. 123 of *Kalimat-i-Firdausiyya*
   (Words of Paradise) by Baha'u'llah. It is taken
   from the same book as #74, and contains provisions for a Legislative Body. *Azal's Notes* p.
   1132.

Index

About the Author

William McElwee Miller, born in Middlesboro, Kentucky, received his A.B. in 1912 and M.A. in 1913 from Washington and Lee University. He acquired a Phi Beta Kappa key and in 1919 received the B.D. from Princeton Theological Seminary. From there he went to Persia (Iran) as a missionary of the Presbyterian Church and, except for receiving the D.D. from Washington and Lee University in 1932, he remained in service in Persia until retirement in 1962. He and his wife now reside in Philadelphia.

While living in Meshed, the sacred city of Shi'ite Muslims, he learned to speak Persian fluently. Miller discovered and translated an ancient Arabic creed, which was published by the Royal Asiatic Society in London. In Iran Miller soon came in touch with followers of Baha'u'llah, who was born in that country. Wishing to understand this movement and its history and doctrines more thoroughly, he began a study of the literature of the Babis and Baha'is which he has continued for fifty years. He published a book on Baha'ism in 1932, and has also written many articles on the subject. He cooperated with Dr. E.E. Elder in translating and publishing the *Kitab-i-Aqdas*, the most important writing of Baha'u'llah. From a scholar in Cyprus he received a large amount of historical material about the Babi-Baha'i Movement which has not been published previous to this volume.

". . . the first standard book on the subject."
*Dr. William N. Wysham, Author, Editor, Lecturer
on World Religions*

"No serious student of the Baha'i faith, tradition, and community can afford to overlook this
significant work." *T. Cuyler Young, Garrett
Professor of Persian Language and History, Emer-
itus, Princeton University*

". . . an authoritative and readable work compiled by one who has had intimate acquaintance
with the subject." *Rev. Cady H. Allen, Missionary of the Presbyterian Church in Iran for 44
years*

"This brings together for the first time many
of the little known events and incidents which
focus the light of history upon the beginnings
of the faith Baha'u'llah proclaimed for this
era." *Dr. Warren Webster, Author and Lecturer
on Islam*

Price $8.95

William Carey Library

533 HERMOSA STREET • SOUTH PASADENA, CALIF. 91030 • TEL. 213-682-2047

0-87808-137-2